S0-ATC-157

Bounty and Benevolence
A History of Saskatchewan Treaties

The 1999 Supreme Court of Canada decision in *Regina v. Marshall* regarding the treaty rights of the Mi'kmaq dramatically underscored our need to understand the history of treaty relationships between Canada's First Nations and the Crown. The numbered treaties covering Canada's prairie provinces represent the culmination of the country's pre-modern treaty–making era, which ended in the early twentieth century. Sizable portions of the territories covered by six of these accords are located within the boundaries of Saskatchewan. *Bounty and Benevolence* offers a unique perspective and examination of the history of treaty-making in this province.

Arthur Ray, Jim Miller, and Frank Tough draw on a wide range of documentary sources to provide a rich and complex interpretation of the process that led to these historic agreements. The authors explain how Saskatchewan treaties were shaped by long-standing First Nations–Hudson's Bay Company diplomatic and economic understandings, treaty practices developed in eastern Canada before the 1870s, and the changing economic and political realities of western Canada during the nineteenth and early twentieth centuries. Ray, Miller, and Tough also show why these same forces were responsible for creating some of the misunderstandings and disputes that subsequently arose between the First Nations and government officials regarding the interpretation and implementation of the accords.

Bounty and Benevolence offers new insights into this crucial dimension of Canadian history, making it of interest to the general reader as well as specialists in the field of First Nations history.

ARTHUR J. RAY is a professor of history at the University of British Columbia.
JIM MILLER is a professor of history at the University of Saskatchewan.
FRANK TOUGH is the director of the School of Native Studies at the University of Alberta.

MCGILL-QUEEN'S NATIVE AND NORTHERN SERIES
BRUCE G. TRIGGER, EDITOR

Bounty and Benevolence

A History
of Saskatchewan Treaties

ARTHUR J. RAY

JIM MILLER

AND FRANK J. TOUGH

McGill-Queen's University Press
Montreal & Kingston · London · Ithaca

© McGill-Queen's University Press 2000
ISBN 0-7735-2023-6 (cloth)

Legal deposit second quarter 2000
Bibliothèque nationale du Québec

Printed in Canada on acid-free paper

Publication of this book has been made possible
through the aid of the Office of the Treaty Commissioner.

McGill-Queen's University Press acknowledges the financial support of the Government of Canada through the Book
Publishing Industry Development Program (BPIDP) for our
publishing activities. We also acknowledge the support of
the Canada Council for the Arts for our publishing program.

Canadian Cataloguing in Publication Data

Ray, Arthur J., 1941-
Bounty and benevolence: a documentary history of
Saskatchewan treaties
Includes bibliographical references and index.
ISBN 0-7735-2023-6 (bnd)

1. Indians of North America – Saskatchewan – Treaties –
History. 2. Indians of North America – Canada – Treaties –
History. 3. Indians of North America – Saskatchewan –
History. 4. Northwest Territories – History – 1870-1905.
5. Saskatchewan – History.   I. Miller, J.R. (James Rodger),
1943-   II. Tough, Frank, 1952   III. Title.
KES529.R39 2000   971.24'00497   C99-901622-9

This book was typeset by Typo Litho Composition Inc.
in 10.5/13 Times.

CONTENTS

FOREWORD

It is my great pleasure, as Treaty Commissioner for Saskatchewan, to present this new and important look at the history of treaties in Saskatchewan to the public. Originally commissioned as a research report for the Office of the Treaty Commissioner in Saskatoon, the manuscript has evolved into a major publication that will be of interest to a wide audience.

In order for you, the reader, to understand the context in which this book was researched and written, it is important to provide some background on our office and its mandate. In 1989, the Federation of Saskatchewan Indian Nations (FSIN) and the Government of Canada created the Office of the Treaty Commissioner (OTC) to research and provide recommendations on the issues of treaty land entitlement and education for First Nations in Saskatchewan. The original five-year mandate (which expired in March 1996) resulted in the signing of Treaty Land Entitlement Agreements between twenty-eight First Nations and the governments of Canada and Saskatchewan.

Based on the success of the original OTC, FSIN and Canada decided to renew the office with a new five-year mandate effective 1 January 1997 to 1 January 2002. This new mandate was broadly defined and instructed the OTC to facilitate discussions between the parties of the Federation of Saskatchewan Indian Nations and the Government of Canada, and through these discussions to strive for common understandings on treaty rights and/or jurisdiction in the areas of child welfare, education, shelter, health, justice, treaty annuities, hunting, fishing, trapping, and gathering, and lands and resources.

It was my honour to be appointed as treaty commissioner through an Order of the Governor-in-Council to guide the OTC through its new term. It is an interesting historical note that my appointment as treaty commissioner was consistent with the manner of appointment of the original Indian commissioners who negotiated the western numbered treaties, including Treaties 4, 5, 6, 8, and 10 (those treaties entered into with First Nations in what is now Saskatchewan).

Although the manner of my appointment was consistent with that of the original Indian commissioners, it should be stressed that my role, and the role of the OTC, is different in many substantial ways from that of the Indian commissioners who originally negotiated the numbered treaties. First, and most importantly, we are not here to negotiate new treaties, or renegotiate the terms of the original treaties – these represent sacred undertakings between the First Nations and the Crown that cannot be altered. Instead, it is our role to discuss the meanings of the original treaties and work towards the implementation of their terms in a way that is consistent with the original spirit and intent of those treaties as it was and is understood by the parties. Second, the OTC is not intended to represent the interests of the Crown, or the Government of Canada but rather to act as an independent and neutral office to provide a forum and a process to facilitate discussions between the Federation of Saskatchewan Indian Nations and the Government of Canada.

In the beginning of our mandate in 1997, our first priority was to undertake research that would illuminate the historical context of the treaties in Saskatchewan in order to provide a platform for modern-day discussions between the parties. In other words, first we had to get some sense of what the treaties were originally intended to accomplish, the manner in which they were created, and how the different parties understood the terms of the treaties and the treaty relationship. To this end, we traveled throughout the province of Saskatchewan, holding meetings in the different treaty territories to hear from Elders as the keepers of oral tradition and history. These meetings with Elders provided great insights into the way in which First Nations understood the treaty relationship and treaty promises, as passed down through oral tradition.

This, however, showed us only part of the picture. The other part was to understand the motivations and intentions of the Government of the Dominion of Canada (representing the Crown) when it entered into treaties in what is now Saskatchewan. This required extensive research into historical records and documents and an astute analysis of those documents.

In the fall of 1997 Dr Frank Tough (then head of the Native Studies Department at the University of Saskatchewan) was approached to help bring the pieces of the puzzle together into a comprehensive and balanced picture of the history of treaties in Saskatchewan. Dr Tough subsequently invited Dr Jim Miller at the University of Saskatchewan and Dr Arthur Ray at the University of British Columbia to participate in the project. In this way, a team of researchers was assembled who could use their combined research experience and skills to produce a detailed report in a relatively short period of time.

The three authors of this publication responded admirably to the challenge and produced a manuscript draft and final report in a timely fashion. The final report was presented to the parties on 15 March 1998 and was available to inform discussions at the Treaty Table in a positive and meaningful way. The findings of this report formed an integral part of the *Statement of Treaty Issues: Treaties as a Bridge to the Future*, produced by our office in October 1998, which highlighted the common understandings reached through our Treaty Table discussions.

Originally the authors of the report were asked to incorporate both oral history (as provided through meetings with the Elders) and the written record into their report, in order to present a holistic view of the past. However, it was soon discovered that this amount of information could not be adequately contained in a single report, and a separate report was commissioned to present the oral history information. This report, authored by Harold Cardinal and Walter Hildebrandt, is titled *My Dream* and is also in preparation for publication in the near future. Taken together, these reports form two complementary halves of a whole.

In and of itself, however, the present publication uses the written record to show a balanced picture of the history of treaties in Saskatchewan and manages to bring out the concerns and perspectives of both the First Nations and the government parties with regard to the treaties. It cannot be emphasized enough that the authors of this report were given full academic license to follow their research wherever it might take them and to report their findings without censure. Thus, although this publication reflects the results of commissioned research, it should not be viewed as partisan or one-sided.

The authors of the work, in keeping with the impartial and objective role of the OTC, were not asked to emphasize any particular perspective or to follow a specific agenda. Rather, they were given the freedom to explore the documentary record according to their own judgment and areas of academic interest. This is reflected in the detailed and thoughtful attention paid to such issues as the role of the fur trade in establishing the precedents to treaty-making, the economic ramifications of treaties and treaty-making, and the nature of Native and non-Native relations at the time of treaties and beyond – the areas of expertise held respectively by Dr Ray, Dr Tough, and Dr Miller.

It is my hope, and the hope of the OTC, that this publication can help provide the historical context needed to intelligently and respectfully forge new relations between First Nations people and non-Aboriginal people in the province of Saskatchewan. It has already done so, in part, by facilitating the work of our office in bringing together the parties of FSIN and Canada to reach common understandings and to use the treaties as a bridge from the past to the future. The next step is to make this information more widely available to the people of Saskatchewan and Canada, so that we can learn from the past and work together towards a future built on cooperation and mutual respect.

Judge David M. Arnot
Treaty Commissioner for Saskatchewan
August, 1999

ACKNOWLEDGMENTS

During the preparation of this report, we have benefited from the generous cooperation and support of many individuals and institutions. The Publications Fund Committee, University of Saskatchewan, provided a publication grant, which facilitated preparation of the manuscript. We would like to acknowledge the enthusiastic cooperation and support of the Office of the Treaty Commissioner. Commissioner David Arnot, Executive Assistant Kay Lerat, and Research Officer Tracey Robinson were unfailingly cheerful and efficient as we went to them for advice, approval, and assistance. Judge Mary Ellen Turpel-Lafond, Anita Gordon Murdoch, and Lloyd Martel of the Federation of Saskatchewan Indian Nations also provided invaluable assistance. We would like particularly to express our thanks to Judge Turpel-Lafond, whose belief in and enthusiastic support for historical research were inspiring. David Hawkes of the Government of Canada also supported and facilitated the initiation of the project.

Harold Cardinal was also cooperative concerning the many complexities that arose concerning the collection and use of oral history evidence. The project has benefited greatly from his experience, wisdom, and dedicated work in this area. It is also appropriate at this point to express our appreciation to Walter Hildebrandt, who, in addition to working with Harold Cardinal and Tracey Robinson on the oral history, provided us with a draft of his report on Treaty 4 that was prepared for the Federation of Saskatchewan Indian Nations.

We have worked very closely with our research assistants, Sheldon Krasowski and Robin Smith, whose intelligence, dedication, and sheer hard work have been critical to advancing our contribution to the project to this point. Robin deserves special thanks for the fine tables of treaty data that she prepared. Our work on Treaty 10 and on the section on treaty implementation has also benefited from the contributions of Dr Anthony Gulig and Mary Miller respectively.

Finally, Jim Miller would like to acknowledge and express his gratitude to the officials of the University of Saskatchewan who provided critical support to the project. The President, Dr George Ivany, the Head of the Department of History, Dr Bill Waiser, and the Director of Libraries, Mr Frank Winter, all went the extra mile at the beginning of the project to make it possible for Miller to be part of the research team. We would like to thank Mary Miller for her help compiling the index.

Our gratitude to all these people and organizations who have facilitated, encouraged, and supported the work that is embodied in this report extends to the point of exonerating them from any responsibility for its shortcomings. Arthur J. Ray, Jim Miller, and Frank Tough accept full responsibility for the deficiencies.

INTRODUCTION

At the end of the 1990s, treaty-making and related issues were prominent in Canadian public affairs and scholarly research. On 1 April 1999 the new northern territory of Nunavut, a political creation of a claim settlement between Canada and the Tungavik Federation of Nunavut, came into being. Comprehensive claims such as this one of the Eastern Arctic Inuit are in reality modern-day treaties: they are the first resolutions of disputes over land tenure in regions in which treaties had never been made. Also in the spring of 1999, the landmark treaty between the Nisga'a of the Nass Valley, British Columbia, and Canada dominated public debate in that Pacific province and attracted nervous attention among the political and chattering classes in Ottawa. Nunavut and Nisga'a were merely the two most prominent of a range of treaties that were under negotiation in the northern territories and British Columbia. Treaty-making, in short, was a prominent public policy issue as the twentieth century drew to a close. This public policy prominence had been foreshadowed in some fifteen years of revisionist scholarship on treaty-making that earlier had influenced academic debates. Scholars such as John Tobias, who in 1983 had reexamined the strategy of Prairie First Nations to demonstrate that the Cree had sought accommodation by treaty rather than confrontation with Canada, was supported by the oral history research of Aboriginal historian Blair Stonechild, who proved a similar case in both article and coauthored book on the role of Plains First Nations in the Northwest Rebellion of 1885.[1] In parallel fashion, Manitoba historian Jean Friesen threw new light on the assumptions and objectives of Aboriginal treaty negotiators in a pair of articles.[2] As well, two different inquiries in Alberta that relied on recently collected oral history evidence of Cree and Blackfoot informants provided dramatically new interpretations of the Aboriginal roles in the making of Treaty 6 and Treaty 7.[3] Collectively, by the latter part of the 1990s these endeavours had worked a revolution in the academic understanding of the Aboriginal peoples' motives and influence in treaty-making.

Because of the prominence of treaty-making in both academic and public policy discussions, the authors of this book were intrigued when Hon. David Arnot, treaty commissioner for Saskatchewan, proposed a historical research project on treaties in the summer of 1997. The Office of the Treaty Commissioner (OTC) informed Dr Frank Tough, professor of Native Studies at the University of Saskatchewan, that it wanted a history of the five Saskatchewan treaties (Treaty 4, 1874; Treaty 5, 1875–76; Treaty 6, 1876; Treaty 8, 1899–1900; and Treaty 10, 1906–1907). In part this request was another manifestation of First Nations' growing interest in the history of their relations in Canada with European newcomers. There was, however, also a more practical reason for the request. Commissioner Arnot explained that he wanted a comprehensive historical account that he could use for two purposes. The first would be to employ it as a platform underpinning a portion of the Statement of Treaty Issues that the OTC, in cooperation with the Federation of Saskatchewan Indian Nations (FSIN) and the government of Canada were developing. The second would be to use the commissioned history in a public education program on the treaties in Saskatchewan that the OTC was beginning to develop.

Although the original idea was to embody both oral and documentary evidence in a single account, this objective proved to be impossible, given time constraints. So it was decided that the oral history component would be addressed in a separate project directed by Harold Cardinal, who was assisted by Walter Hildebrandt. To carry out the documentary-based history, Frank Tough invited Arthur J. Ray and Jim Miller to take part.

The documentary record that underpins most of the account that follows is extensive and varied. The conventionally cited archival sources that we have consulted consist mainly of selected records of various departments of the government of Canada, especially those of the Department of Indian Affairs in the National Archives of Canada (Record Group 10). Almost as important were the chronicles of the Hudson's Bay Company, which are housed in Winnipeg. The proficient staff of the Hudson's Bay Company Archives section of the Provincial Archives of Manitoba graciously made them available to us. Likewise, we have examined the personal papers of some of the government treaty negotiators (such as those of Sir Adams Archibald and Alexander Morris), politicians who had particular responsibilities for Indian Affairs (most notably Sir John A. Macdonald and Edgar Dewdney) and of bureaucrats who occupied important posts in the Department of Indian Affairs. Hayter Reed was the most important of the latter, having served as agent at Battleford (1881–83), assistant Indian commissioner (1883–88), Indian commissioner (1888–93), and deputy superintendent general of Indian affairs (1893–97). We have also used Canadian government publications such as the annual reports of the Department of Indian Affairs and other official published documents. The latter include the Royal Proclamation of 1763, statutes (e.g., the Indian Act and the Manitoba Act), orders-in-council, and so on. Finally, we have consulted published secondary works that analyze various aspects of ethnography, the fur trade, Canadian government policy, and other topics that help us understand the Saskatchewan treaties.

We are aware that our considerable reliance on governmental sources creates an imbalance in the evidence that could tilt our interpretation towards the governmental point of view. We have worked hard to avoid this problem. No doubt we have succeeded only in part. However, as we note in our conclusion, the documentary record does yield surprising insights into First Nations' views on critical issues, most notably the themes of livelihood and relationships with the Crown. Certainly, the various archival and published sources that we have examined do not support the contention that the written version of a treaty is an adequate representation of the terms and principles of a treaty relationship.

We hope that our history will advance the reexamination of Euro-Canadian understanding of the treaties that has been underway in the academic world for the past fifteen years. The reinterpretation we offer here contends that First Nations played a more active role in initiating and shaping treaties than academic scholarship has acknowledged to the present. We argue further that less praise is due the federal government and Canadians at large for the making of the treaties than older scholarship has suggested. Our title, *Bounty and Benevolence*, is intended to capture, with an ironic twist, this ambivalent rereading of the treaty story. The official government texts of the numbered treaties invariably include a clause, such as the following one from Treaty 4, which states that it is Canada's desire "to make a treaty and arrange with them [First Nations] so that there may be peace and good-will between them and Her Majesty, and between them and Her Majesty's other subjects; and that Her Indian people may know and be assured of what allowance they are to count upon and receive from Her Majesty's bounty and benevolence." Clauses such as this raise the question of which treaty party has been truly kind and generous.

The narrative that follows devotes considerable attention to topics that, at first glance, might seem to be unnecessary background material. Our research has convinced us, however, that this information is essential for understanding what transpired during treaty-making in Saskatchewan during the three decades or so after 1874. For instance, many First Nations attitudes towards Europeans and Euro-Canadians had been shaped by the relations they had established with the Hudson's Bay Company during the early phases of the western fur trade. For this reason we have devoted chapter 2 to this theme. Because Canada's approach to treaty-making in the 1870s was conditioned by earlier colonial diplomatic traditions, in chapters 3 and 4 we address the Royal Proclamation of 1763, treaty-making in Upper Canada/Canada West in general (emphasizing the Robinson Treaties of 1850), the Selkirk Treaty of 1817, the Rupert's Land Transfer Act of 1868, and the Manitoba Act of 1870. Treaty-making developments outside the present boundaries of Saskatchewan between 1870 and 1873 directly influenced First Nations and government negotiating approaches beginning in 1874. For this reason, chapter 5 discusses the precedents that were set by Treaties 1, 2, and 3. The rapid social, political, and economic change of the late 1860s and the early 1870s created problems and posed opportunities that Saskatchewan First Nations sought to address through treaties. Accordingly, chapter 6 looks at the socioeconomic circumstances of these nations on the eve of Treaty 4. Chapters 7 through 11 offer detailed examinations of the five Saskatchewan treaties in chronological order. Chapter 12 follows with a discussion of the problems that Canada and the First Nations encountered implementing the accords. This discussion explores a limited sample of incidents that in our opinion provide documentary evidence of what the First Nations' understandings of the treaties were and what they had expected from these agreements. In chapter 13 we close by recapitulating our major findings and contrasting our interpretation with what existed in the slim literature pertaining to treaties that was available in the early 1990s.

We hope that you, our readers, will find the evidence and conclusions of our work as interesting and informative as we did in the experience of uncovering them.

CHRONOLOGY

1670 The Hudson's Bay Company is founded

1763 Royal Proclamation of 7 October

1816 Battle of Seven Oaks

1817 Selkirk Treaty, signed 18 July

1850 Robinson Treaties, signed 7 and 9 September

1867 Confederation of Canada, 1 July

1870 Rupertsland Transfer (Order of Her Majesty in Council Admitting Rupertsland and the North-Western Territory into the Union), 23 June

1870 Northwestern Territory and Rupertsland transferred to the Dominion of Canada, 15 July

1871 Treaty 1 (the Stone Fort Treaty), signed 3 August

1871 Treaty 2 (Manitoba Post Treaty), signed 21 August

1873 Treaty 3 (North-West Angle Treaty), signed 15 September

1874 Treaty 4 (Qu'Appelle Treaty), signed 15 September

1875 Treaty 5 (Lake Winnipeg Treaty), signed 20 September

1876 Treaty 6 (Fort Carlton and Fort Pitt Treaties), signed 23 August

1899 Treaty 8, signed 21 June

1905 Province of Saskatchewan is formed

1906 Treaty 10, signed 28 August

ABBREVIATIONS

CO   Colonial Office

CMS   Church Missionary Society

CSP   Canada, *Sessional Papers*

DCB   *Dictionary of Canadian Biography*

DIA   Department of Indian Affairs

DIAND   Department of Indian Affairs and Northern Development

HBC   Hudson's Bay Company

HBCA   Provincial Archives of Manitoba, Hudson's Bay Company Archives

IFS   International Financial Society

MG   Manuscript Group

NA   National Archives of Canada

NWC   North West Company

OA   Archives of Ontario

OMI   Oblates of Mary Immaculate

OTC   Office of the Treaty Commissioner

PAM   Provincial Archives of Manitoba

RCAP   Royal Commission on Aboriginal Peoples

RG   Record Group

RNWMP   Royal North West Mounted Police

UK   United Kingdom

Artist's sketch of the signing of the Hudson's Bay Company's charter in 1670. Charles II granted the company title to a vast portion of First Nations' territory that the English called Rupert's Land. Courtesy of Hudson's Bay Company Archives, Provincial Archives of Manitoba

TRADING CEREMONY AT YORK FACTORY

Hudson's Bay Company.

INCORPORATED 2ND MAY 1670

A Hudson's Bay Company painting of an eighteenth-century trading ceremony at York Factory. These ceremonies combined First Nations and English diplomatic traditions and were carried over into treaty relations with Canada. Courtesy of Hudson's Bay Company Archives, Provincial Archives of Manitoba

Treaty 1 (The Stone Fort Treaty) talks. Treaty 1 was Canada's initial treaty with the First Nations of the parkland/grassland region. Treaty 2 is almost identical. Subsequently, Aboriginal negotiators sought and obtained better economic concessions from Canada than Treaties 1 and 2 provided. Courtesy of National Archives of Canada, c56481

Alexander Morris (1826–1889) served as lieutenant-governor of
Manitoba (1873–78) and as lieutenant-governor of the North-West
Territories (1872–76). He helped negotiate Treaties 3, 4, and 6 and
wrote the first published history (1880) of treaty making in western
Canada. Courtesy of Provincial Archives of Saskatchewan

W.J. Christie served as a government representative in Treaty 4 talks and as an Indian commissioner for those associated with Treaty 6. Previously he had served for several years as chief factor
for the Hudson's Bay Company in the Saskatchewan District. Courtesy of Hudson's Bay Company Archives, Provincial Archives of Manitoba

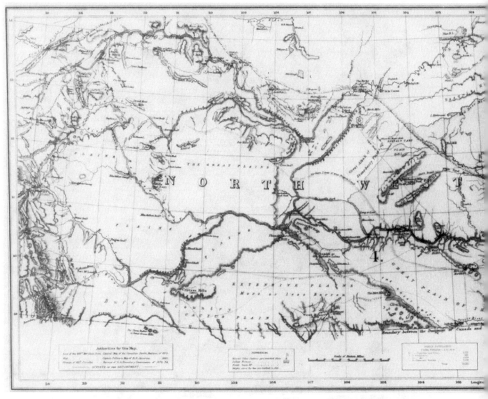

Dominion map dated January 1875 showing treaty areas 1–4 and adjacent territories that were subsequently included in Treaties 7 and 8. This map included information taken from maps of the Canadian Pacific

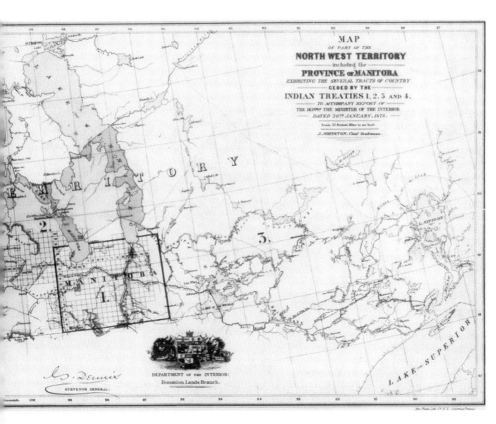

Railway, Captain John Palliser, and the boundary commission of 1872–74. It identifies environmental regions in the prairies based on their potential for agricultural colonization. Courtesy of National Archives of Canada, NMC 19685

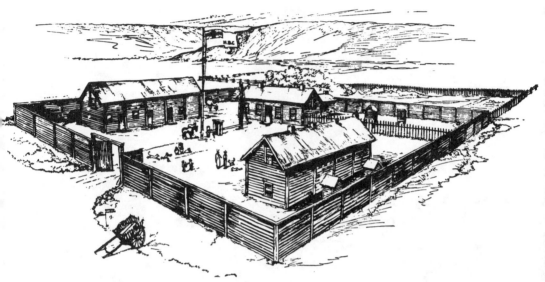

Etching of Fort Qu'Appelle, which served as one of the primary locations for Treaty 4 talks of September 1874. Courtesy of Hudson's Bay Company Archives, Provincial Archives of Manitoba

Saulteaux Chief Waywayscape. During talks for treaties 4 and 6, government negotiators regarded the Saulteaux (Ojibwa) as troublemakers because of the demands they made. Courtesy of Provincial Archives of Saskatchewan

Ometoway (The Gambler) vociferously objected to the Hudson Bay Company's sale of Rupert's Land to Canada during Teaty 4 talks, pointing out that the territory belonged to Aboriginal people. Courtesy of Provincial Archives of Saskatchewan

Painting of Fort Carlton, 1864. Prior to the 1860s and the retreat of the bison herds, this post had served as one of the HBC's most important parkland posts for the trade of buffalo robes, hides, grease, dried meat, and pemmican. It was the most important site for Treaty 6 talks. Courtesy of Hudson's Bay Company Archives, Provincial Archives of Manitoba

Etching of treaty talks at Fort Carlton, August 1876. Courtesy of National Archives of Canada, C 64741

Red Pheasant, one of the leaders of the Battle River Cree who took part in treaty talks at Fort Carlton. Courtesy of Provincial Archives of Saskatchewan

Poundmaker (Pitikwahanapiwiyin) in captivity, 1885. During Treaty 6 talks he was apparently the first chief to ask that the government provide relief in times of famine and pestilence. Courtesy of National Archives of Canada, c 1875

Etching of Fort Pitt, where talks continued after they had been completed at Fort Carlton. Here Chief Sweet Grass, who had been one of the first Plains Cree to petition Canada for a treaty, signed an agreement in the hope that it would address hardships his people faced. Courtesy of Hudson's Bay Company Archives, Provincial Archives of Manitoba

Bounty and Benevolence

CHAPTER ONE

Aboriginal–Hudson's Bay Company Relations before 1800

The First Nations of western Canada forged their relations with Europeans in the crucible of the fur trade. Successful long-term commercial intercourse required the development of institutions and practices that accommodated the sharply different diplomatic, economic, political, and social traditions of the two parties. When First Nations treaty-making with Canada began in the nineteenth century, Aboriginal people carried over into negotiating practices and strategies many long-established fur trading customs that they incorporated into the treaties.[1] Consequently, a proper understanding of the treaties today requires us to review the development of First Nations–fur trader relations, particularly those involving the Hudson's Bay Company (HBC) prior to the mid-nineteenth century.

EARLY HUDSON'S BAY COMPANY COMPACTS

It is unclear when the Aboriginal peoples of Saskatchewan first became involved in the fur trade indirectly through the medium of trading specialists or middlemen. It is likely this occurred before the middle of the seventeenth century. A little more than a decade after the founding of the HBC in 1670, some groups began direct involvement by traveling to York Factory (1684). The manner in which Aboriginal peoples and traders conducted their affairs at this post established many of the precedents for Aboriginal-White relations that followed, including treaty negotiations and relationships with the Canadian government.

Following French precedents, the HBC sought to accommodate Aboriginal customs as much as possible. Accordingly, even though Charles II had granted to the company "in free and common socage" (freehold tenure) all lands draining into Hudson's Strait, the directors (known as the governor and committee) decided it would be prudent to obtain Aboriginal consent to build posts and conduct trade in their territories. Accordingly, on 21 May 1680 they wrote to their governor in James Bay, John Nixon, and informed him:

There is another thing, if it may be done, that wee judge would be much for the interest & safety of the Company, That is, In the severall places *where you are or shall settle*, you contrive to make compact wth. the Captns. or chiefs of the respective Rivers & places, whereby it might be understood by them that you had purchased both the lands & rivers of them, and that they had transferred the absolute propriety to you, *or at least the only freedome* of trade, And that you should cause them to do some act wch. by the Religion or Custome of their Country should be thought most sacred & obliging to them for the confirmation of such Agreements.[2]

In a postscript to this letter, the governor and committee added:

As wee have above directed you to endeavour to make such Contracts wth. the Indians in all places where you settle as may in future times ascertain to us *all liberty of trade & commerce and a league of friendship & peaceable cohabitation*, So wee have caused Iron marks to be made of the figure of the Union Flagg wth. wch. wee would have you to burn Tallys of wood wth. such ceremony as they shall understand to be obligatory & sacred, The manner whereof wee must leave to your prudence as you shall find the modes & humours of the people you deal with, But when the Impression is made, you are to write upon the Tally the name of the Nation or person wth. whom the Contract is made and the date thereof, and then deliver one part of the Stick to them, and reserve the other. This wee suppose may be sutable to the capacities of those barbarous people, and may much conduce to our quiet & commerce, and secure us from forreign or domestick pretenders.[3]

Subsequently, the governor and committee repeated this instruction to other post commanders during the 1680s. When planning to build York Factory, then referred to as Port Nelson, John Bridgar received this order on 15 May 1682:

There is another thing which wee thinke of greate Moment and therefore recommend to your particular care and that is that you Endeavor to make *such Contracts with the Natives* for the River in & above Port Nelson as may in future times ascertain to us a right & property therein and the Sole Liberty of trade & Comerce there, and to make Leagues of friendship & peaceable Cohabitation with such Ceremonies as you shall finde tobee most Sacred and Obligatory amongst them.[4]

The same year the directors dispatched these orders to Bridgar, they repeated this instruction to Governor Nixon. They underscored its importance by telling him, "Wee have formerly Given our Instructions, and Wee now earnesly press it that you Endeavour to make such Contracts."[5] In other words, in spite of having received title to Rupertsland from the English Crown, the company's directors realized that the grant meant nothing to their customers. The company had to obtain Native approval to occupy portions of their territory.

One way the company's traders fulfilled the orders of the governor and committee to use the religion or custom of the country for the company's advantage was by participating in the First Nations diplomatic customs. All Indian nations had well-developed diplomatic/political traditions for reaching peace and other accords with outsiders. It was a widespread practice in the territory of present-day Canada to cement treaties with the smoking of the calumet, an exchange of gifts that symbolized goodwill, and through arranged marriages. The latter served to extend kinship bonds and the mutual obligations associated therewith to foreigners. Bringing outsiders into the fold in this way was especially important when First Nations wanted to establish long-term relations with each other. Historians of the fur trade have noted that Indian nations wishing to draw Europeans into their trading networks or political alliances did so partly through marriages. The French referred to such fur trade unions as marriages *à la façon du pays*.

In short, the HBC acknowledged Aboriginal peoples' possession of the territory of Rupertsland and the need to obtain their consent to occupy trading sites within it. Likewise, the company appreciated the need to obtain this consent by taking part in Aboriginal diplomatic and religious ceremonial practices.

TRADE CEREMONY

The most complete descriptions of the HBC's diplomatic/trading ceremonies are contained in documentary records pertaining to York Factory, the HBC's most important post throughout most of the eighteenth century. Its hinterland included most of the Nelson River basin and the upper portions of the Churchill River.

By the mid-eighteenth century, the visits of trading parties to York Factory had become very elaborate affairs. According to company officers, most notably James Isham and Andrew Graham, trading parties from inland territories rallied behind a leader, whom company men referred to as a "trading captain," and his allied elders, who were called "lieutenants."[6] Just before reaching York Factory, the trading captain collected one or two skins from each of his followers to present on their behalf to the post commander, who was known as the governor or chief factor. The Cree term for this gift was *puc'ca'tin'ash'a'win*. Graham described the elaborate welcoming ceremony that followed: "soon after [they] appear in sight of the Fort, to the number of between ten and twenty [canoes] in a line abreast of each other. If there is but one captain his station is in the centre, but if more they are in the wings also; and their canoes are distinguished from the rest by a small St. George or Union Jack [flag], hoisted on a stick placed in the stern of the vessel."[7]

When the flotilla of canoes drew near York Factory, "Several fowling-pieces [were] discharged from the canoes to salute the Fort, and the compliment [was] returned by a round of twelve pounders."[8] After landing, the visitors set about making camp while the trading captains and lieutenants walked inside the fort to pay their respects to the company's officers. Graham described what happened next:

The Governor being informed what Leaders are arrived, sends the Trader to introduce them singly, or two or three together with their lieutenants, which are usually eldest sons or nighest relations. Chairs are placed in the room, and pipes with smoking materials produced on the table. The captains place themselves on each side of the Governor, but not a word proceeds from either party, until everyone has recruited his spirits with a full pipe. The silence is then broken by degrees by the most venerable Indian, his head bowed down and eyes immovably fixed on the floor, or other object. He tells how many canoes he has brought, what kind of winter they have had, what natives he has seen, are coming, or stay behind, asks how the Englishmen do, and says he is glad to see them. After which the Governor bids him welcome, tells him he has good goods and plenty; and that he loves the Indians and will be kind to them. The pipe is by this time is renewed and the conversation becomes free, easy and general.[9]

Graham noted that near the close of the smoking of the pipe, the captain and his lieutenants received outfits of clothing, which he described them as follows:

A coarse cloth coat, either red or blue, lined with baize with regimental cuffs and collar. The waistcoat and breeches are of baize; the suit ornamented with broad and narrow orris lace of different colours; a white or checked shirt; a pair of yarn stockings tied below the knee with worsted garters; a pair of English shoes. The hat is laced and ornamented with feathers of different colours. A worsted sash tied round the crown, an end hanging out on each side down to the shoulders. A silk handkerchief is tucked by a corner into the loops behind; with these decorations it is put on the captain's head and completes his dress. The lieutenant is also presented with an inferior suit.[10]

The company presented the captain and the lieutenants with uniforms for several reasons. Company officers understood that the political organizations of the First Nations were fundamentally different from those of England. In particular, they recognized that leadership was fluid among the Indian nations that ventured to Hudson Bay to trade, in the sense that the people followed those who were best suited to lead. As Graham described it:

When several tents or families meet to go to war, or to the Factories to trade, they choose a leader; but it is only voluntary obedience. Everyone is at liberty to leave him when he pleases; and the notion of a commander is quite obliterated when the journey or voyage is over. Merit alone gives the title to distinction; and the possession of qualities that are held in esteem, is the only method of obtaining affection and respect out of his own house. Thus, a person who can make long harangues [is a diplomat], is an expert hunter, is a conjurer [has spiritual powers] and has a family of his own; such a man will not fail of being followed by several Indians … They follow him down to trade at the settlements, style him Uckimow, that is a great man, chief or leader; but he is obliged to secure their attendance by promises and rewards of too weak a nature to purchase subjection.[11]

By giving suits of clothing to chiefs and headmen, HBC traders acknowledged the leadership positions of First Nations trading captains, and they sought to win their loyalty. Company traders also understood that allied First Nations leaders would be in a better position to retain or expand their following inland if these chiefs received generous treatment at the posts. After all, well-endowed captains had more goods to redistribute as gifts to their followers. In this way, a symbiotic relationship developed between the company traders and First Nations chiefs, or *Uckimow* (*Okimâw*). The success of each depended on the sustained goodwill of the other in the partnership.[12]

After the presentation of the captain's and lieutenants' coats, the final phase of the pre-trade gift-exchange began: "The guests being now equipped, a basket of bread and prunes is brought and set before the captain, who takes care to fill his pockets with them before it goes out to be shared amongst his followers; together with a two gallon runlet of brandy, tobacco, and pipes."[13] The participants now moved to the Native camp outside of the fort:

Everything being prepared he is conducted to his tent with a procession. In the front are the spontoons [halberds] and ensigns, next the drummer beating a march, then several of the Factory servants bearing the bread, prunes, etc. Then comes the captain, walking quite erect and stately, smoking his pipe and conversing with the Governor and his officers; then follow the Second, and perhaps a friend or two who was permitted to come in with the Chief. The tent is all ready for their reception, and clean birch-rind or beaver coats are spread on the ground for the chief to sit on; and before him are deposited the prunes etc. The Chief then makes a speech to his followers, and then orders his lieutenant, or some respectable person, to distribute the presents, never performing this himself. I must take notice that the women and children are last served.[14]

Graham observed that before any trading could take place, the "league of friendship" had to be renewed by smoking the calumet:

As the ceremony of smoking the calumet is necessary to establish a confidence, it is conducted with the greatest solemnity, and every person belonging to that gang is admitted on the occasion. The captain walks in with his calumet in his hand covered with a case, then comes the lieutenant and the wives of the captains with the present [*Puc'ca'tin'ash'a'win*], and afterwards all the other men with the women and their little ones. The Governor is genteely dressed after the English fashion, and receives them with cordiality and good humour. The captain covers the table with a new beaver coat, and on it lays the calumet or pipe; he will also sometimes present the Governor with a clean beaver toggy or banian to keep him warm in the winter. The *Puc'ca'tin'ash'a'win* is also presented. Then the Governor sits down in an arm-chair, the captain and chief men on either hand on chairs; the others sit round on the floor; the women and children are placed behind; and a profound silence ensues.

The calumet being lighted by the Governor, a servant holding the bowl and applying the fire, it is pointed towards the east, south, west, and north parts of the hemisphere, also to the zenith, and nadir. Every man takes a certain number of whiffs as fixed by the owner of the pipe, and thus it passes round the circle. When out, it is delivered again to the Governor who repeats the manoeuvres as when he lighted it; at which all the men pronounce the monosyllable Ho! which is expressive of thanks.[15]

Graham also noted that it was customary to present medicines to the Aboriginal doctors: "The captains and several others are doctors, and are taken singly with their wives into a room where they are given a red leather trunk with a few simple medicines such as the powders of sulphur, bark, liquorice, camphorated spirit, white ointment, and basilicon [ointment of 'sovereign' virtues], with a bit of diachylon plaster [an ointment made of vegetable juices]."[16] This practice would have had symbolic and practical significance to First Nations. Through this act the company displayed a willingness to share its special healing powers in secret ("singly" in a room) with Aboriginal healers. Also, the act signaled the company's willingness to help them deal with sickness.

Graham reported that at York Factory in the eighteenth century the trading captains received another gift, comprising a wide variety of luxury and staple goods, after members of their trading party had nearly completed their business. The size of the parting gift that a captain received depended on the volume of trade he had brought to the post. Likewise, the captains who brought the largest trading parties to the fort received preferential treatment during the course of their visit. Graham made the following remarks about this practice:

The [HBC] traders have bargow [oatmeal porridge] made for them [the trading captains], and prunes given them every day, and the leader gets a small bag of oatmeal and prunes at his going away, and if the person is a leader of fifteen or twenty canoes he dines every day with the Chief [in charge of the fort] and officers, and receives the above present [parting gift of goods] in full. But if otherwise several articles and indulgences are curtailed, and if he brings less than ten canoes, or any misfortune has befallen him, he is still looked on by the Chief in the former light as when he brought his former complement of canoes, which conduct in the Chief [post commander] is a sure means of keeping up the Company's trade, and ingratiating himself into the natives' favour, who are a good natured people and very susceptible of wrongs done them.[17]

These practices were a further recognition by the HBC traders of their need to sustain positive relations with the leaders of their First Nations clientele. Graham reported that trading captains expressed their approval or disapproval of the company's treatment at the close of trade in the following manner: "Each leader leaves his grand calumet at the Fort he trades at unless he is affronted, and not designed to return next summer, which is sometimes the case, each Factor [trading post manager] laying every scheme to enlarge his trade by seducing leaders from other Forts."[18] In other words, when a trading captain left his calumet, it was as a sign that he believed that the officer in charge of the fort had lived up to the spirit of the mutual accord they had reached previously. If the latter had failed to do so, the captain withdrew his calumet, thereby symbolizing the termination of their agreement. This indicates that First Nations regarded their accord with the company as an ongoing relationship that had to be renewed annually.

When the HBC moved inland, beginning in 1774 with the establishment of Cumberland House, the welcoming ceremonies described by Graham for York Factory became a feature at inland posts, albeit in modified forms. For instance, in 1852 Reverend Abraham Cowley visited Fort Pelly to observe the work of Native catechist Charles Pratt. While he was there, a Cree trading party arrived at the fort. Cowley described the welcoming ceremony:

The Crees halted at Pratt's, as I believe is their custom, to dress, & prepare to appear at the Ft. This gives Charles an opportunity to speak with them. When painted etc to their satisfaction they left Pratt's on their way to the Ft. firing salutes at intervals as they advanced but no flag or salute replied from the Ft. Still they fired as they proceeded, till they reached the Ft. where they arrived in due marching order & were met & welcomed by Mr. Buchanan. In the same stately order they proceeded through the yard & into the room where I was sitting. The Chief walked first, an old Ojibwa followed & after him all the rest in single file & very stately. This seemed remarkable as I had never seen anything like it among Indians before; there was a dignity in their deportment which was quite imposing. The room had been previously prepared for their reception & they took their seats in the same dignified manner in which they had hitherto conducted themselves. Tobacco was on the table & the Intrerpreter [McKay] filled & handed a pipe to the Chief, who having smoked a little while passed it on to the next, meanwhile the Interpreter filled another pipe for him which he used as before.[19]

Significantly, all the major components of pre-trade gift-exchanges – the calumet rite, the presentation of outfits of clothing to Aboriginal leaders, and the distribution of food – were carried over into the treaty-making process in the late nineteenth century. The promise to give medicine (in times of need) was incorporated into Treaty 6.

In the early fur trade, maintaining the goodwill of Aboriginal leaders and their followers through these ceremonies was the key to success for the HBC and its rivals. As the HBC would learn, First Nations regarded any attempts to alter these customs unilaterally as a breach of faith that put these living accords in jeopardy. As Graham put it, they were very sensitive to "wrongs being done to them." Those who believed they had been ill-treated withdrew their custom. Once the gift-exchange ceremony was concluded, trade commenced.

From the earliest days of the fur trade, credit was used extensively as an aspect of the barter that followed the gift-exchange ceremonies. It was common practice for traders to give "outfits" of goods to their Aboriginal clients as credit against their next year's returns. In the early eighteenth century, an outfit normally consisted of staple items needed for hunting and trapping, as well as a few luxuries, most notably Brazil tobacco. Usually Native clients were able to pay off their debts every year and have enough left over to buy a few additional items. This system was compatible with Native customs of sharing among close relatives, a practice economic anthropologists refer to as general reciprocity.[20] If poor hunts, outbreaks of disease, or other catastrophes resulted in a shortfall of returns, traders normally extended their lines of credit over two or more years.[21] Sometimes traders wrote off bad debts. In this way, the credit system provided a safety net for Aboriginal people, who became progressively more reliant on European goods. Of key importance, Aboriginal people who remained loyal to the HBC believed that they were entitled to receive credit. They regarded it as a demonstration of the company's good faith toward them.[22] For this reason, subsequent attempts by the company to curtail credit in order to reduce business expenses, as during the period after 1821, generally failed. In essence, credit losses were one of the social overhead costs of doing business that the company had to accept.

INTERDEPENDENT LIVELIHOOD RELATIONSHIPS

The above discussion shows how Europeans and Aboriginal people accommodated each other's economic and political traditions in the fur trade, thereby setting the stage for the development of interdependent relationships between them. It is important to recall that from time immemorial, economic/ecological flexibility had been a key survival strategy of Aboriginal peoples, because game, fur bearers, and fish and waterfowl populations are subject to largely predictable, cyclical fluctuations and to sudden changes caused by grassland and forest fires, droughts, epidemic diseases, and other natural calamities. Aboriginal people responded to these periodic problems by shifting the focus of their livelihood quest and by moving within, or beyond, their traditional territories to gain needed supplies of food and other resources. These practices continued after groups became involved in the fur trade, but then they had to take into account additional economic and ecological factors. The increasing incorporation of European technology and goods into their economies, especially in the primary production sector, meant that it became essential to maintain at least some commercial production from the land to survive. To achieve this goal, Aboriginal people had to factor in short- and long-term fur and game depletion problems resulting from over-hunting, fluctuating prices, and local employment opportunities. In other words, it was more essential than ever to maintain a diversified economy that facilitated the exploitation of local opportunities and guarded against local calamities. Consequently, over time the relative economic importance of hunting, trapping, fishing, gathering, and wage labour varied, as did the relative balance of commercial and subsistence activity, even though these two spheres had become inseparably linked. The change in their economies also meant that their commodity output mix varied spatially and temporally according to changing economic and ecological circumstances.

Aboriginal people had an additional reason to maintain commercial links to trading posts. Post managers offered relief to their steady clients whenever calamities thwarted local peoples' best efforts to obtain the commodities or earn the wages they needed to buy their basic necessities.[23] They were able to do so because trading companies, most notably the Hudson's Bay Company and the North West Company (NWC), built transportation networks that allowed them to move surplus food to places where it was scarce. From the European perspective this was a sound business strategy, because it enabled them to promote Native trapping in productive fur areas that suffered from short- or long-term food shortages. The advantage for Aboriginal people was that they did not have to haul food surpluses by foot or dog sled in winter. Of great significance for Aboriginal people, this meant, further, that the fur trade generated an internal market for what the traders termed "country produce." The term covered a growing array of foodstuffs, as well as other products trading companies needed to carry on their operations.

Epidemics, the vicissitudes of the fur trade, and various other factors meant that the precise nature of Aboriginal-HBC relations was fluid. Normally, gift giving and credit/barter accounted for most economic intercourse, with the latter form of exchange being paramount. During the high point of HBC and NWC competition (from about the late 1780s to 1821), gift exchange became an ever larger component, as European rivals found themselves in a bidding war for the Native customers.[24] Also, they extended credit lavishly in the hope of laying claim to the future returns of Native hunters and thereby preventing them from falling into the hands of their arch-opponents. Depletion of local fur stocks was one of the negative results of the easy credit, lavish gift giving, and competitive fur buying during this era.[25] Following the merger of the HBC and the NWC in 1821, the amalgamated firm sought to place the operations of its Northern Department on a more economical footing under the direction of George Simpson (later

Sir George). Simpson believed that more restrictive credit policies were needed, and he wanted to eliminate gift exchanges. On 31 July 1822 he addressed these issues in a letter to the governor and the committee:

In regard to the proposed reduction on the standard of Trade, no question exists that it would be much to the interest of the concern and beneficial to the Indians could it be effected, if at the same time the system of giving presents and treats was abolished, but it will be difficult and require a great length of time and much caution to bring such a reform about. During the heat of opposition in some Districts, it was necessary to give Indians expensive presents in Clothing, guns, etc., whether they made a hunt or not in order to attach them to either party ... This ruinous practice has been discontinued and nothing beyond Tobacco and Ammunition in some parts and a few trifles such as Firesteels, needles, Vermillion, etc., in others have been given and occasionally a dress to a Chief or Indian of considerable influence ... Heavy Debts are ascertained to be injurious to the trade and of little benefit to the Indians, it is therefore understood that no more shall be given than there is a reasonable prospect of being repaid.[26]

Although the governor wanted to eliminate gift giving altogether, he failed. At best, he managed only to curtail the lavishness, because the company's compacts with Aboriginal groups were renewed annually and gifts symbolized the peaceful intent of these unwritten accords.

Simpson's debt reduction scheme was also unrealistic. The trade was built on the understanding that the two parties would help one another in times of need, and extending credit was one of the principal ways of doing so. Consequently, Aboriginal people steadfastly resisted the governor's efforts to unilaterally alter such a fundamental aspect of their relationship with the company. There is little doubt they would have regarded his attempt to do so as a breach of faith and trust. Furthermore, contrary to Simpson's claim that debt was of little benefit to the Indians, access to credit remained essential for them. Indeed, it became more essential because of the depletion of fur resources, the subsequent decline of bison populations, and the periodic ravages of epidemics. Finally, over time, the credit system had come to provide traders with a means to express the degree to which they respected and trusted their clients. The individuals whom traders held in the highest esteem received the most generous lines of credit. Withdrawing credit to them would have conveyed a very negative message.

In any event, in the Saskatchewan District (largely corresponding to the Treaty 4, 6, and 7 territories) the company had to move cautiously with reforms because the Plains Cree and their neighbours had access to the American posts on the Missouri River. Any changes that undermined Aboriginal loyalties to the company would have increased their traffic with these opponents. Partly for these reasons, the company's trade in the parkland area changed little in spite of Simpson's wishes.

Even the rather ruthless Simpson had to recognize, however, that the elderly, incapacitated, and sick had to be looked after. Therefore, he authorized the continuation of the established company practice of giving gunpowder and shot to these people, on the understanding that they would seek the support of good hunters who would hunt for them in exchange for this ammunition.[27] Thus, before 1870 the economic safety net of the mercantile fur trade remained in place for the HBC's Aboriginal customers, in the form of the debt system, which was to address the short-term problems its able-bodied clients faced from time to time in earning their livelihood. It also continued as sick and destitute relief for the chronically infirm. Additionally, whenever local hunts failed, the company supplied food (rations).

Besides responding to Aboriginal needs and pressures, the HBC was also concerned about the welfare of its Native clients, because the British parliament periodically monitored its operations. It did so because in 1821 it had granted the amalgamated HBC and NWC exclusive rights to trade with the Aboriginal peoples of Rupertsland and the Northwestern Territory (the western Arctic drainage area and the territory of present-day British Columbia), in order to restore order to these regions. The ruinous competition of the preceding thirty years had resulted in violence, a rampant alcohol trade, and the economic ruin of many Aboriginal groups through fur and game depletion.[28] Although Parliament was no longer disposed to grant trading monopolies by the early nineteenth century, granting one to the reorganized company saved the government from the financial burden of establishing a colonial government with policing powers to bring peace to the region.

These considerations led Parliament to stipulate the elimination of the alcohol trade as a condition of the HBC's 1821 license, which was subject to renewal at least every twenty-one years. The company was therefore aware that Parliament's periodic reviews would seek to determine how Aboriginal people were faring at its hands. Indeed, Parliament called the HBC to account at hearings in 1837 and again in 1857.[29] On both occasions committee members asked a series of questions aimed at finding out if the company was acting as a good steward.

During the 1857 hearings Colonel John Lefroy, who was inspector general of Army Schools and had spent two years in Rupertsland making magnetic observations for the British Royal Society, was one of the witnesses the parliamentary committee queried. They also called Governor Simpson. After they had asked Colonel Lefroy a series of questions about the demographic trends of the Aboriginal people living in HBC territory, committee member Adderley asked him:

In your opinion how have the Company generally treated the Indians?
[Lefroy in reply] It is necessary in answering that question to draw a distinction between the Company in its corporate capacity as a body of non-resident shareholders and the Company as a body of resident Traders and servants. The Traders almost without exception as far as my observation went treated the Indians with signal kindness and humanity, –

many instances of their relieving them in their distress and taking great pains to do so came to my knowledge. But then their means of doing so are in some degree contingent upon the financial arrangements of the Company at large over which they have no control or but little.

The committee chairman then asked, "What is the general character of the Agents of the Hudson's Bay Company as far as you could observe were they respectable men?" Lefroy replied: "Very generally so. I never mingled with a body of men whose general qualities seemed to me more entitled to respect. They are men of simple primitive habits leading the most hardy lives, generally speaking, contented, doing their duty faithfully to their employers, and in many instances taking sincere interest in the welfare of the Indians around them and doing all they can to benefit them, but the Indian is a very difficult subject." The chairman then asked Lefroy if he thought the HBC traders acted considerately towards Aboriginal people. Lefroy replied, "I think so most eminently."[30]

Lefroy's comments about HBC officers highlight a key element of the traditional fur trade. Traders developed close economic and social bonds with their Aboriginal clientele (often through marriage). They consequently looked after their clients' needs, but in return the officers expected loyalty.

In the 1870s Isaac Cowie summarized the qualities of a good trader in ways that help explain why Lefroy held these men in such high regard. His observations also give us insights into the fundamental nature of Aboriginal/HBC socio-economic relations on the eve of the treaties:

Any officer who neglected to personally meet and talk with the Indians, and arrange for their requirements in accordance with their needs and abilities, and consider the prospects of the grounds upon which they hunted or planned to hunt, in fact, to acquire a sympathetic knowledge of the Indian, his character and capabilities, was no good as an Indian trader. For to be a successful one he had to judiciously furnish in advance the outfit required by the Indian if he were to be successful in his winter and summer hunting. The trader having arranged how much of the vital essentials – such as ammunition, guns, axes, and traps, and such luxuries as blankets, tea and tobacco – without which he would be miserable, – the Indian should get on credit, he was allowed to take a few other things for his personal adornment.[31]

In other words, Lefroy's and Cowie's remarks make it clear that the fur trade was sustained by the reciprocal bond that had developed between traders and their Aboriginal clientele. Traders made sure Aboriginal people had what they needed; in return these Whites expected Native loyalty and their help when necessary.

After taking Lefroy's testimony, the committee called Governor Simpson. Before returning to the issues they had raised with Lefroy, the chairman and Simpson had the following exchange:

[QUESTION NO. 983, BY THE COMMITTEE CHAIRMAN] Will you state to us the system under which the Country is managed with regard to trade and Government with reference to the Indian populations – in short the machinery which is employed. How many Officers and Servants altogether are employed by you in the management of the territory of the Hudson's Bay Company?

[ANSWER BY SIMPSON] There is a Governor in Chief to begin with, there are 16 Chief Factors who are principal Officers forming the members of our Council – being 29 Chief traders, 5 Surgeons, 87 Clerks, and 67 Post Masters.[32]

After asking the governor how many Aboriginal people the company employed, the chairman raised the issue of the general well-being of Aboriginal people in the company's domain by asking a series of questions about demographic trends (similar to the questions the committee had asked of Lefroy). In reply to these queries Simpson indicated that he thought the population of the prairie nations was declining due to intertribal warfare and the ravages of smallpox. In contrast, he thought that the population of woodland peoples, with whom the company was more influential, was increasing.[33]

The chairman then probed into the nature of the HBC's trading relations with its Aboriginal clients:

[QUESTION NO. 1008, CHAIRMAN] What is your system with regard to the Indians in connection with the fur trade?

[ANSWER BY SIMPSON] Our mode of management is this – The Indians are usually outfitted from the establishment in the fall of the year with such supplies as will enable them to get through the winter in comfort and make their hunts.

[QUESTION NO. 1009, CHAIRMAN] How do you pay them for the furs which they bring?

[ANSWER BY SIMPSON] We pay them by barter entirely – money is not known in the country ... it is a barter trade on a tariff of very old standing, varied from time to time according to circumstances.[34]

After exploring a number of other topics,[35] the committee returned to trading practices when committee member Kinnaird asked:

[QUESTION NO. 1127] Is not the Company pledged to them [Indians] by payments in advance?

[ANSWER BY SIMPSON] Decidedly that is to say an Indian to make his hunt must be provided with certain necessaries to enable him to live during the Winter. He requires a Gun – he requires ammunition – he requires blanketing.

[QUESTION NO. 1128] Are they not to all intents and purposes your own Servants hunting for you for what you pay them in advance?

[ANSWER BY SIMPSON] There is no contract – there is an understanding that they will pay us if they can. If the Indian is sick we lose the outfit.

[QUESTION NO. 1129, BY KINNAIRD] You make him payments in advance then you settle with him after the hunt and in the event of any illness or sickness or of old age you
undertake to provide for them?

[ANSWER BY SIMPSON] We consider that [the debt] a dead loss.[36]

In other words, the governor indicated that it was company policy to use the debt
system as a means of providing relief when necessary. Sometimes traders issued
credit knowing that the recipient could not pay. The resulting "bad debts" were
written off. This policy of issuing credit as relief continued into the twentieth
century.[37]

The committee then turned its attention to exchange rates and the practice of
giving Aboriginal people gratuities:

[QUESTION NO. 1614, BY MR ROEBUCK] You say that in different parts of the territory
different prices are charged by the company for the goods they sell to Indians.

[ANSWER BY SIMPSON] Yes.

[QUESTION NO. 1618, BY MR ELLIS] That is to say that you give less for the furs [along
the lower Mackenzie River than the Red River].

[ANSWER BY SIMPSON] We give less for the furs.

[QUESTION NO. 1619, BY ELLICE] You take more furs in fact for an article.

[ANSWER BY SIMPSON] Yes our system of dealing is this. Indians require certain necessary supplies to enable them to hunt and these we provide them with.[38]

Thus, Governor Simpson acknowledged that the HBC understood that Aboriginal
people required certain European tools and weapons to earn their livelihood from
the land. These had to be provided even when the incomes that Aboriginal hunt-
ers/fishers earned from the commercial activities were not sufficient to buy these
essential items.

The parliamentary committee next raised the issue of gift giving.

[QUESTION NO. 1620, BY MR ROEBUCK] Do you know the quantity of beads which you
have imported per annum?

[ANSWER BY SIMPSON] I do not they are not an article of trade they are given as presents.

[QUESTION NO. 1621, BY MR ROEBUCK] You never give so many beads for so many
skins?

[ANSWER BY SIMPSON] Never – they are entirely gratuities – beads are never traded to my
knowledge – if they are it is quite contrary to instructions.[39]

[QUESTION NO. 1622, BY ROEBUCK] Do you know the amount of Marten skins imported last year?

[ANSWER BY SIMPSON] I do not I cannot tell from recollection. Awls, gun flints, gun
worms, hooks, needles, thread, beads, knives, gartering, ribbons, &c are given as gratuities about 20 percent of the outfit in those articles are given as gratuities.

[QUESTION NO. 1623, BY ROEBUCK] So that a good knife is not considered an article of commerce at all?

[ANSWER BY SIMPSON] No it is given as a gratuity.[40]

Simpson's testimony here is significant, since he had tried to make substantial curtailments in gift-giving practices in his economizing reforms of the 1820s. Although he had managed to eliminate the elaborate presentation ceremonies of the earlier years, clearly gift exchange had remained a central aspect of the business. Furthermore, the company now used the practice as an additional means of providing essential economic help by presenting basic staples as gifts.

At this point in the inquiry the committee asked Governor Simpson about the merits of extending the HBC's fur trading monopoly:

[QUESTION NO. 1643, BY THE COMMITTEE CHAIRMAN] As fur traders do you consider monopoly as essential to the conduct of a trade of that description?[41]

[ANSWER BY SIMPSON] Decidedly.

[QUESTION NO. 1644, BY CHAIRMAN] What do you believe would be the consequence of supposing the trade was thrown open indiscriminately to any body who chose to pursue it?

[ANSWER BY SIMPSON] I think the fur bearing race would be in a very short time destroyed and the Indians left to poverty and wretchedness.

[QUESTION NO. 1645, BY CHAIRMAN] Would there be anybody then who would have any interest in preserving the fur bearing animals and who would not on the contrary have an interest in destroying them as fast as possible with a view to immediate returns?

[ANSWER BY SIMPSON] Decidedly not.

[QUESTION NO. 1646, BY CHAIRMAN] Were you acquainted with that country when there was a contest in trade and I am afraid a contest awful in violence and acts of outrage carried on between the North Westers Company and the Hudson's Bay Company in that country?

[ANSWER BY SIMPSON] Yes, I was there the last year of the contest.

[QUESTION NO. 1647, BY CHAIRMAN] What were the effects of that contest?

[ANSWER BY SIMPSON] The demoralization of the Indians. Liquor was introduced as a medium of trade throughout. The peace of the country was disturbed, there were riots and breaches of the peace continually taking place and the country was in a state of great disorganization.[42]

The line of questioning of the hearing makes it abundantly clear that the parliamentary committee wanted to make sure that the HBC was fulfilling its obligation to protect the well-being of Aboriginal people before it recommended extending the company's trading monopoly. In the end, the committee concluded that this was the case, and, based on that understanding, it recommended continuing the HBC's trading privileges beyond those areas that were suitable for colonization.[43]

Shortly after this hearing the character of the HBC changed substantially when land speculators bought up the majority of its shares in 1863 and put the future direction of the company in doubt. The vast majority of the new shareholders were not interested in the fur trade, which remained its primary source of income. It was uncertain when its residual land holdings in old Rupertsland would be of any value. To plan for the future, on 30 November 1870 the directors of the HBC asked Cyril C. Graham (later Sir Cyril), vice-president of the Transatlantic Telegraph Company, to travel across Canada, assess the company's operations and business prospects, and make comprehensive recommendations for its future. Among the items the governor and committee asked Graham to consider was a request to find ways to reduce the cost of operating the company. When he filed his report at Fort Garry, Manitoba, in March 1871, Graham wrote:

Another source of present expenditure arises from your system of dealing with the Indians. To secure their good will and their patronage you are in the habit of making them advances, a certain percentage of which may be redeemed, but on the whole leaving behind a large average of bad debts. Yet in the present state of the country no change should be introduced abruptly, and indeed I should at any time be sorry to see an inflexible rule laid down with them. Those who have been found honest and faithful should be trusted as before, and in the years of dearth or scarcity of furs the officer in charge should have discretionary power to be indulgent with defaulters.

Again the custom of giving presents to friendly chiefs and those who are regular in their payments, should not to my mind be discontinued. Such tokens of goodwill are rarely wasted, and a small mark of distinction conferred upon the punctual man easily leads others to imitate his example.[44]

One reason why Graham warned the directors not to make any abrupt changes in policy with regard to the treatment of Aboriginal people was that he was anxious to avoid the bloodshed that was taking place in the western territories of the United States. He thought that the HBC could play a major role in preventing such violent disturbances by maintaining good relations with its Aboriginal customers.

Although the London directors adopted most of Graham's suggestions, they nevertheless opted to try to cut fur trade operating costs in a fashion reminiscent of Simpson's scheme of the 1820s. In his very insightful observations on the fur trade of the Saskatchewan District in the 1870s, company trader Cowie expressed the view that these business reforms, particularly orders to curtail credit, were adding to the already considerable instability in the region. He first addressed in a general way the problems caused by the company's reforms:

After the alleged "Reorganization," under Mr. Donald A. Smith, as Chief Commissioner, most stringent orders were issued to officers in charge to cease advancing the Indians on their hunts. In this matter the officers in charge of districts had a certain amount of discretion, but I was ordered to summarily cease to supply the plain [*sic*] Indians with the means of existence which their inherent improvidence and poverty demanded on credit every fall and spring. The omniscient beings composing the London Board had viewed with alarm the annual increase of "Outstanding Indian Debts" placed on inventory, but not valued as assets, every spring. The increase of uncollectable debts was chiefly due to the lack of proper control over native post-masters, interpreters and traders, whose personal sympathy with the Indians and desire to be popular amongst them often led them into being partial at the Company's expense. But instead of taking measures to prevent this indiscriminating practice of sowing the seed broadcast and on barren and unprofitable subjects to obtain the harvest in furs, the Board in its wisdom and justice decreed that the whole system of credit in the Indian trade must cease, forgetting that the universal application of such a principle to any commerce in the world would mean its ceasing to exist.

He then commented on the difficulties that the new policies created in the Saskatchewan region:

Great care had always been taken at Fort Qu'Appelle, under Mr. McDonald, in giving advances to deserving Indians at the fort, and he exercised rigorous criticism over any which our people on the plains had been induced, or perhaps, virtually compelled, to give. Only a small proportion of those trading at Qu'Appelle were deemed worthy, and their paying up depended not only on their luck in hunting, but also on their good fortune in preserving their lives from the enemies who encompassed them.

But in framing the selling prices of goods and fixing those for the purchase of furs and provisions every possible risk had been taken into consideration, thereby providing an insurance fund, which the London Board, in its wisdom, chose to ignore. And so, forgetful also of the loyalty of the Indians and their effective aid in preventing Fort Qu'Appelle from falling ignominiously to be pillaged by the Métis, it was decreed that all advances whatsoever by me to those Indians should be stopped.

Next, Cowie explained how he dealt with the threat to peace that the HBC's directives had created:

The wiser Indians then made their plea for advances in very plausible and respectful form. So, as the policy of the Company was always to yield as a favour what the Indians would otherwise take by force, putting all the blame on Zenith for the warlike preparation with which the gathering had been met, I said, while refusing them advances on their personal accounts, that I had authority to present to them as a favour what they had no right to, and let them divide the supplies amongst them according to need. And so the trouble ended that time.

He ended his commentary by heaping scorn on the London directors for their short-sighted reforms:

The fact that "tobacco" to smoke in council was being sent around by messengers of the malcontents [Siouan refugees] to every chief and influential person among our Indians soon was noised abroad. Our Crees, however, were not to be either cajoled or intimidated by the machinations and magnitude of the alliance. The Saulteaux, while we could not so fully rely on them as the Crees, had from time immemorial been at war with the Sioux, with only armistices intervening, and they as followers of and later intruders than the Crees into the Blackfeet territory, deeply resented the proposal that an asylum should be given, in the hunting grounds so occupied by them, to the new friends and allies of the Métis, who had come in such large numbers, so unwelcomely and with modern repeating rifles, to more speedily exterminate the already woefully depleted numbers of the buffalo. It was our policy and duty to sustain the Crees and Saulteaux in this attitude; yet the orders from the gentlemen in London, who sat at home in ease and considered themselves all-wise, were calculated to destroy our influence over and our ancient alliance for mutual protection with these tribes, by abolishing the "system of Indian debts."[45]

Thus, Cowie rightly noted that the "ancient alliance," which was symbolically renewed every year through an exchange of gifts and the ceremony of the pipe, was the key to the HBC's success and to peace in the region. Changes to the fundamental nature of the old mercantile fur trade being introduced by industrial-age capitalists, particularly the pressures to curtail gift giving, threatened to undermine peace and order. As we will see below, the HBC's increasing interest in its land holdings was another sign of the changing times. These developments deeply disturbed the Plains Cree and other First Nations and encouraged them to renegotiate their relationship with Whites through treaties with the Canadian government.

CHAPTER TWO

The Selkirk Treaty, 1817

There was at least one major occasion in western Canada before 1870 when First Nations–European diplomacy did not have as its primary objective the facilitation of peaceful trading relations. It took place in 1817, when the Ojibwa and Cree of the Red River concluded a treaty with Thomas Douglas, the fifth earl of Selkirk. The accord, which is now widely known as the Selkirk Treaty, aimed to provide for the peaceful continuation of the first European agricultural colony in western Canada. To date, historians have largely ignored this agreement, because Treaty 1 supplanted it in 1871. As a result, they mostly regard the Selkirk Treaty as a curiosity because it included a map that displayed the totem symbols of the signatory chiefs, a feature it had in common with the early-nineteenth-century agreements of present-day southern Ontario. The Selkirk Treaty warrants serious consideration, however, for several reasons. It is the first document that specifically recognizes Aboriginal title in western Canada. Also, it involved HBC officials during the fur trade era and therefore affords further insights into Native-European diplomatic relations at the time. Finally, First Nations raised the accord as an issue at the time of Treaty 1 negotiations. Thus, in the minds of Aboriginal people it had direct relevance to late-nineteenth-century treaty-making.

The Selkirk Treaty was associated with the hostile competition between the NWC and the HBC, which in 1816 had provoked the violent clash between the Métis and settlers at Seven Oaks. William Bacheler Coltman and John Fletcher were given commissions of peace by Governor Sir John Coape Sherbrooke for the "Indian territory of the northwest." They held a dispatch from Lord Bathrust ordering the end of hostilities, restitution of property, and the arrest of Lord Selkirk. They also conveyed a proclamation from the Prince Regent announcing the government's intentions. Coltman investigated the causes of the hostilities and suggested means to resolve the conflict. To facilitate this investigation into the disturbances in the Indian Territories, Coltman received a commission as lieutenant-colonel in the Indian Department.[1]

Correspondence between Selkirk and Coltman provides crucial contextual information on the treaty. Early in July, Selkirk suggested certain priorities for Coltman's investigation, and, at the same time, he informed Coltman that Indians were interested in meeting with him:

> I have been requested by one of the principal Indian chiefs in this neighbourhood, the request that as early as you conveniently can you will admit a few of their leading men to a conference, in which they wish to state some matters of importance conceiving it better to communicate their sentiments in that manner than in presence of a mixed multitude: The individuals who are named as desirous to wait upon you are 5 or 6 of the Santoux [Ojibwa] Nation comprehending the chiefs of the most considerable bands that frequent the Red River & also two chiefs of the cree [*sic*] nation whose bands frequent the lower parts of Ossiniboine R – They may be considered as representatives of about 200 Warriors the greater part of the population of the country extending from the L of the Woods [Lake of the Woods] to Brandon House or R La Souris [Souris River]. – I have ventured to suggest that in the event of your acceding to their request they ought to select an Interpreter for themselves & to state my opinion that you would not object to any one whom they may prefer whether he belongs to one party or the other.[2]

Evidently, the leading chiefs had concerns and wished to speak formally with a representative of Lower Canada. The request for a meeting involved Coltman in a process that eventually led to the Selkirk Treaty. From this point onward, he participated in development of the treaty.

Several days later, Selkirk communicated to Coltman:

> Mr. Allan has communicated Lt. Col. Coltman's observations respecting the proposed meeting with the Indian chiefs. Ld S [Lord Selkirk] is fully satisfied that such a communication of these sentiments cannot have the same degree of weight, as it would have if recorded in the presence of a Govt Interpreter: but he thinks it of material consequence not to delay hearing these people; of course it must be left to Lt. C. C. [Lt. Col. Coltman] to judge according to the best information he can obtain, how far these individuals are to be considered as entitled to speak in the name of the Indians at large. – With respect to the fidelity of the Interpretation, a method has occurred to Ld. S. which appears to him to afford a complete check. There is a young man here, an English half-breed, who acts as Interpreter for the H.B.Co. & who does not understand French. Every speech of the Inds therefore, after being interpreted in Fr [French] may be again interpreted in E. [English] & the comparison of the two will afford an accurate criterion for judging of their accuracy.[3]

Through this early phase Selkirk, who was concerned about problems of translating, suggested that a comparison of separate French and English translations of Indian dialogue would act as a check. Agents of the NWC were kept informed about the possibility of a treaty. On 16 July 1817, when Coltman attended an Indian council, he expressed reluctance to sign the treaty as a representative of the government.[4]

On 16 or 17 July, Lord Selkirk assured Coltman that he was present only to witness the agreement. Because of what Selkirk deemed to be great misrepresentations about the colony, he wanted Coltman to witness the fairness of the proposed transaction. At the same time Selkirk gave assurances that the NWC posts could remain until the Sovereign's pleasure was known. Selkirk also indicated that a draft deed existed and that the terms of the deed were known: "This may perhaps obviate the necessity of altering the draft of this Deed. The Quit rent specified in it, the Draft of Deed has been spoken of to the Inds some weeks ago, and it is the opinion of every one who is acquainted with the Indian character, that it would have a very bad effect, if any alteration were now to be made."[5] Evidently, discussions about the quit rent had occurred before the formal meetings.

On 17 July Selkirk communicated to Coltman his general intentions with respect to the treaty, and more importantly, he reviewed the relationship between an annual payment in tobacco and the lands needed by the colonists. Since Coltman was still meeting with the Indians, Selkirk asked Coltman to propose the question concerning land for settlers to them.

You are aware that one of the allegations which have been made in vindication of the N.W.Co. is that the outrages committed here, have arisen from the jealously of the native Indians against agricultural settlements, & their resentment against my Settlers for having taken possession of their lands without their consent or any purchase from them. – I believe you have already heard enough to satisfy you how little foundation there is for any such idea. But it would be still more satisfactory if the sentiments of the Indians on that point were explicitly & formaly declared in your presence, & still more so, if they would consent to a specific cession of a portion of their lands to be set aside for the express purpose of agricultural settlements.

With a view to obviate misrepresentation & to show in a more decided manner their sense of the benefits likely to arise from agricultural Settlements, I would propose to them not a sale, but a Gift. If a large quantity of goods were offered for the purchase it might be said that the temptation of immediate advantage had induced them to sacrifice their permanent interests. I would therefore purpose to them merely a small annual present, in the nature of a quit rent, or acknowledgment of their right: – & having specified what I intend to give in this way, I would leave it to themselves to specify the boundaries of the lands which they agree to give up on that consideration, & to appropriate to me for the exclusive use of the Settlers.[6]

Clearly Selkirk wanted Coltman to raise the issue of a land treaty and to investigate Indian views on the agricultural colony. Rather than an outright, once and for all purchase, Selkirk suggested a small annual quit rent. Selkirk also argued the relevance of a treaty in light of challenges to the validity of the large grant (the Selkirk Grant) from the HBC to Lord Selkirk's colony: "I am aware that such a cession from the Indians can be of no avail unless the grant of K. [King] Charles 2nd to the H.B.Co be found to include this country. But at all events the transaction would serve to facilitate the Settlement of the Country under Crown grants, in the event of my title being found defective."[7] In this instance, Selkirk indicated a necessary connection between the Charter of 1670 and the capacity to take a cession of Indian interests in land.

At the same time Selkirk indicated the desirability of having an interpreter from the Indian department, but he also wanted the treaty to be pursued while Coltman was at the Red River colony because "during the very limited period of time which you propose for the Commission to remain here, there is no probability that so many of the leading men of the Indian Tribes can again be assembled here."[8] He added, "I would therefore purpose that a Deed should be now executed as a record of whatever may be agreed to," and that "If you approve of this suggestion I will transmit without delay for your revisal, a draft of such a Deed as may answer the purpose."[9] Clearly Selkirk felt some urgency to conclude a treaty at the time that the leading men and Coltman were both at Red River.

After a meeting with the Indians, Coltman wrote to Selkirk and confirmed a number of Selkirk's assertions:

Nothing could be more satisfactory than all that I have heard of the sentiments expressed throughout this conference by the Indians in general even by some among them who are considered as the most attached to the NWCo. & it is particularly pleasing to observe that they consent to make the proposed cession of land for a direct & nominal consideration of trifling value, it is because they form a just estimate of the collateral advantages which they will obtain from a progress in the arts of civilized life.

My Lord

It appears to me as far as I can yet see that the Indians wish the Settlement for their own advantage & would scarcely require any consideration for allowing to the Settlers an exclusive possession of a reasonable portion of land something will however perhaps be expected as the subject has been so much talked of & certainly an annual present seems best, as it is evident that the interests of the colony would require the Indians friendship to be ensured in this manner even if they gave their lands voluntarily.[10]

Here Coltman reported that Indians were interested in providing land for the colony, since they regarded such a development as being in their own interests. The Indians agreed to a low annual rent, which Coltman and Selkirk considered trifling, because they anticipated receiving ongoing "collateral advantages" out of the arrangement. Coltman was also aware that a voluntary treaty would be of mutual advantage to Indians and settlers, since "the interests of the colony would require the Indian's friendship." He also informed Selkirk that "The Cree Indians have agreed that the Saulteurs may treat for the lands as far as the River aux Champiquans [Rivière des Champignons]. The latter have always appeared to me disposed towards the Sales but I have not heard a word from them as to terms or boundaries: something however they evidently will expect."[11]

Apparently Coltman had to deal with questions concerning the effect the treaty would have upon the antagonistic relations between the trading companies:

I am about to tell them [Indians] the Princes order as to both parties being permited to occupy their old Stations, & to state to them your wish to treat for some presents to be given them yearly to compensate any loss they may experience by the occupation of a part of their lands by the Settlers, & shall recommend them to listen to the proposals of your Lordship who was encouraged by the great Father to send out the Settlers. I think it would be well that your Agents should be at hand after this discourse to propose specific terms, respecting which I can be no judge, nor otherwise interfere than as a Witness of the good faith & fairness of the transaction without any pledge on the part of the Government.[12]

He also had to explain the Crown's approval of settlement and offered "proof of the Kings approbation of the Settlement & as to the terms of the bargin."[13] On 18 July, the day of the treaty, he advised Selkirk of his discussions with the Indians:

my recommendation not to be unreasonable in their demands seeing the advantage to themselves of the settlement & a caution to take care in their bargain to avoid offending or causing trouble with the Crees or driving the Metifs [Métis] to despair either of which might lead to fresh troubles which it was the particular object of my mission to prevent. Finding that all the Indians have attended the meeting & that it is considered by them as public, I have notified the North West Agent to attend & should be glad some Agent of your Lordship was also present at my Speech.[14]

Thus for Coltman and Selkirk, dealing with the land question would promote peace among the various Indigenous nations, colonists, and traders. After the treaty, the two-mile belt along the rivers was surveyed and occupied.

Coltman supported the treaty, but did not want to involve the government of Lower Canada in the actual treaty-making. He reported to Sherbrooke:

At the period of my leaving Red River, in September last [1817], the number of settlers, chiefly Europeans, remaining there, might be from 100 to 150 men, of whom many had families. It was principally on account of these people, that I thought it right to give some encouragement to the inclination existing on the part of the Saulteaux Indians, to convey a portion of their lands to the Earl of Selkirk for an annual quit-rent; the particulars of this transaction, and of the precautions I took to avoid the possibilities of my committing the Government, I have already the honour of stating … The interests of the British fur trade, as well as the political connections with the Indians, might also probably be best promoted

by leaving this portion of the country in the hands of the Earl of Selkirk, or the Hudson's
Bay company; as the intercourse they are forming by the route of the Red River, with the
Sioux Indians ... may hereafter become an object, both of commercial and political conse-
quence.[15]

Although Coltman tended to sympathize with the North West Company's version
of the disturbances, he recognized that security for Lord Selkirk's colony was in
the best interest of the British fur trade. Clearly, commercial and political consequences could be achieved through "connections with the Indians."

Significantly, although Lord Selkirk referred to the 18 July 1817 agreement as
a "Deed", the treaty essentially was a "surrender" of lands adjacent to the Red
and Assiniboine Rivers in exchange for an annual present of tobacco. Specifically, the Selkirk Treaty provided the following: "Witnesseth, that for and in
consideration of the annual present or quit rent hereinafter mentioned, the said
Chiefs have given, granted and confirmed, and do, by these presents, give, grant
and confirm unto our Sovereign Lord the King all that tract of land adjacent to
Red River and Ossiniboyne [Assiniboine River]."[16]

The land treated for included a two-mile strip adjacent to both banks of the
Red and Assiniboine Rivers (except at Fort Douglas where it extended out six
miles). On the Red River this strip extended from the mouth of the river south-
ward to the mouth of the Red Lake River (Grand Forks, North Dakota). Along
the Assiniboine River the land treated for extended from the Forks of the Assiniboine and Red westward to Rivière des Champignons (also known then as Musk
Rat River). According to Lieutenant-Governor Alexander Morris, the distance
back of the river was explained to the Indians in a particular fashion: "They were
made to comprehend, the depth of the land they were surrendering, by being
told, that it was the greatest distance, at which a horse on the level prairie could
be seen, or daylight seen under his belly between his legs."[17]

The written treaty also stipulated the following:

together with all the appurtenances whatsoever of the said tract of land, to have and to hold
forever the said tract of land and appurtenances to the use of the said Earl of Selkirk, and
of the settlers being established thereon, with the consent and permission of our Sovereign
Lord the King, or of the Earl of Selkirk. Provided always, and these presents are under the
express conditions that the said Earl, his heirs and successors, or their agents, shall annually pay to the Chiefs and warriors of the Chippeway or Saulteaux Nation, the present or
quit rent consisting of one hundred pounds weight of good and merchantable tobacco, to
be delivered on or before the tenth day of October at the forks of the Ossiniboyne River –
and to the Chiefs and warriors of the Killistine or Cree Nation, a like present or quit rent of
one hundred pounds of tobacco, to be delivered to them on or before the said tenth day of
October, at Portage de la Prairie, on the banks of the Ossiniboyne River.[18]

Lord Selkirk treated under the authority of the Crown. The payment of an annual quit rent of 200 pounds of tobacco to the Ojibwa and Cree was part of the agreement. This treaty specified when and where the quit rent would be paid.

Although the treaty secured a land base for a small agricultural colony whose existence had previously been threatened by North West Company harassment, the treaty also made provision for the fur traders: "Provided always that the traders hitherto established upon any part of the above-mentioned tract of land shall not be molested in the possession of the lands which they have already cultivated and improved till his Majesty's pleasure shall be known."[19] Thus any existing posts in the lands set aside for the colony were secured. The treaty was signed by Lord Selkirk, Mache Wheseab (Le Sonnant), Mechkaddewikonaie (La Robe Noire), Kayajieskebinoa (L'Homme Noir), Pegowis (Peguis), Ouckidoat (Le Premier);[20] and was witnessed by Thomas Thomas, James Bird, Captain F. Matthey, Captain P.D. Orsonnens, Miles MacDonell, Jean Baptiste Charles De Lorimier, and Louis Nolin (interpreter).

Following the conclusion of the Selkirk Treaty, other observers from this era provided details about the treaty and the treaty relationship that ensued. In September 1818 Captain F. Matthay, a witness to the treaty, reported: "I must stay untill the quit Rent Tobacco is paid to the Indians, who claim something else, which I remember was just mentioned but nothing stipulated – Rum of course, but they expect goods which we must endeavour to confine to Chiefs."[21] Apparently the fur trade custom of gift giving and the Selkirk Treaty quit rent overlapped. Duncan Graham, stationed at Fort Douglas, recommended to Lord Selkirk in September 1818 that "that it would be very requisit that a Large medal with a Silk flag with the Company's arms on it if possible should [be] sent to the Little Corbeau & I beg that your Lordship would take the trouble to procure them as it is necessary not only for the interest of the Company but that of the Colony."[22] Alexander MacDonell informed Selkirk in December 1817 that "Lagemoniere was out in the plains the other day, and he says that he had been told by the premiers['] son, that tho' they had sold the lands in the neighborhood of Red River they did not sell the lands more out on the plains."[23] The records imply that the quit rent might have involved more than tobacco and that in the same period it was suggested that medals and the company's flag would be given to a leading Indian. Moreover the lands out on the plains and the river lands were distinguished in terms of possession.

Peter Fidler, in his 1819 report on Brandon House recorded that

These chiefs all received medals from the Colony last fall [1818] along with their annual present of Rum Tobbacco ammunition & clothing. Altho' the agreement signed by Lord Selkirk & the 5 Chiefs only specify that the Sateaux [Saulteaux] shall annually receive as a quit Rent 100 lb Tobbacco & the Crees the same quantity but the Crees have not as yet received any part. No proper officer having been sent out to meet them at the Portage De

Prairies belonging to the Colony but next October it is fully intended that the Crees shall have the stipulated quantity distributed amongst them the 2 or 3 principal men of that Tribe.[24]

It seems that in 1819 the Cree had still not received their compensation in tobacco. Although rum, medals, flags, and goods for the chiefs are not mentioned in the written treaty, these items were part of the relationship. In 1875 a medal associated with the Selkirk Treaty was shown to Alexander Morris at Portage La Prairie.[25]

The 1817 Selkirk Treaty was an issue for contemplation in 1870 when the Canadian government came to consider Indian title following the transfer of Rupertsland. In the 1860s the status of land title for the Red River Settlement was a matter of general anxiety, and Chief Peguis argued that Indian title had not been extinguished properly.[26] Some sort of treaty was entered into between James McKay on behalf of the Kenneth McKenzie settlement at Musk Rat Creek with Yellow Quill.[27] In an 1870 letter to Secretary of State Joseph Howe explaining the disposal of Crown lands in Manitoba, Lieutenant-Governor Adams G. Archibald reported that

The Indian Title to these tracts is released by a deed of which I send you a copy ... I do not now enter into the question of genuiness or validity of this Deed. The Indians dispute both. They say at one time, that the Chiefs never executed such a Deed. They say at another time that if the Chiefs did sign a Deed they did not intend to sign one to this effect. That they never sold their rights but merely lent the land for a season, and even then, did not lend according to the boundaries set forth in the Deed.

At another time they say that the Chiefs who pretended to sell, had no right, as they were not Chiefs of the tribes in actual occupation.[28]

In 1870, the status of the Selkirk Treaty and the question of title were challenged. The documentary records hint that more opposition to the Selkirk Treaty was expressed by the Cree than by the Ojibwa.[29] Archibald added: "On the other hand it is quite certain that the Chiefs of the Crees have annually received at Portage Laprairie, and the Chiefs of the Saulteaux at Fort Garry the 100 lbs. of Tobacco named in the Deed as the consideration for which they respectively sold their claims. Be this as it may, the Indian Title has here always been assumed to be extinguished to the Tract of Land skirting these two main Rivers of Manitoba, except only as to that portion of it already referred to and considered as an Indian Reserve.[30] Archibald's real problem with the Selkirk Treaty was understanding how the band led by Chief Peguis came to occupy St Peters parish, the northernmost of the river lot parishes, since the Selkirk Treaty specifically took possession of a two-mile strip of land adjacent to each bank of the Red and Assiniboine Rivers.

This problem led Archibald to instruct Molyneux St John, legislative clerk, to investigate the origins of the St Peters Indian settlement and the Selkirk Treaty. St John's report to Archibald recorded a number of details concerning the Selkirk Treaty and the two-mile strip along the river.

The History of its origin as an Indian Reserve I derive from Mr. Andrew McDermitt who was resident in the settlement at the time the treaty [was] being made between the Earl of Selkirk and the Indian Chiefs from whom the land was purchased –

Mr. McDermitt says that, when the proposal to purchase was made by the Earl of Selkirk the Indians showed great reluctance to comply with his request, arguing that they were not the true proprietors of the country, and making at the same time a counter-proposal to the effect that he, the Earl of Selkirk should lease the land for twenty years instead of buying it for ever. The Earl of Selkirk refused to accept this proposal and eventually succeeded in persuading the Indians to accept the offer and terms he had made to them.[31]

Indian acquiesence, according to St John, did not last.

Three days after the treaty had been signed the Indians held a council amongst themselves at which the action they had taken in selling the land was condemned and the fact that they were now shut out from the river commented upon. It was determined at this council that Peguis one of the Chiefs who had signed the treaty on behalf of the Seauteux Tribe should with others wait upon the Earl of Selkirk and endeavour to obtain a portion of the land they had sold, as a Reserve for their people.

On hearing their request the Earl of Selkirk granted to Peguis for his people the land from Sugar Point Northward to Lake Winnipeg; and to another Chief the land between the fork of the Assiniboine and the Red River, and a creek situated a short distance to the North of this confluence.

St John was of the opinion that it was uncertain

whether the creek in question is that one immediately to the South, or the one immediately to the North of the house now occupied by Mr. McDermitt.

When a survey was made of the Red River Settlement, a few years subsequent to the purchase by Lord Selkirk, the Surveyors under Mr. Kemp took "Sugar Point" as their terminus on the Northern side, thereby affording an indirect testimony to the alleged concession of the Earl of Selkirk.

In the course of some years the land referred to in the vicinity of the confluence of the Assiniboine and Red Rivers being required for experimental farming, Mr. Christie then Governor of the Hudson's Bay Company repurchased it from the Indians, giving in its stead a piece of land across the Assiniboine, and another piece on the North side of the same river a little above a place where St. James Church now stands.

Once more, according to St John, Aboriginal groups turned against the arrangements.

After a time the Indians became dissatisfied with these places on account of their distance from the Fort and the inconvenience of crossing the river, and returned to their old camping ground. The Hudson's Bay Company then sold the two pieces of land relinquished by the Indians to various settlers.

A Third Chief was given a piece of land in the neighbourhood of Portage la Prairie but Mr. McDermitt is unaware of the circumstances under which this reverted to the Hudson's Bay Company.

The Reserve from "Sugar Point" to Lake Winnipeg was occupied by the Indians; "lots" varying in size were also sold by the Hudson's Bay Company, and "lots" also by the son of Peguis – the chief known as Henry Prince.

The concession made to the Indians was verbal, but it was thoroughly understood to have been made, and Mr. McDermitt accounts for the Survey made by Mr. Kemp being commenced at Sugar Point by the fact of the lands lying being to the North of that being the property of the Indian Tribe represented by Peguis at the time of the treaty.

As indicated by Archibald's letter to Howe, the authority to treat for land was a matter of contention. Yet according to McDermitt an agreement was reached in 1817. Apparently, Lord Selkirk was willing to change the treaty in accordance with the Peguis band's need for access to the Red River, and subsequently an entire parish was reserved for this band. Several other "reserves" existed, even though the written treaty made no provision for reserves.[32]

The correspondence between Selkirk and Coltman provides details of the historical process leading up to the Selkirk Treaty, information that cannot be obtained from the written treaty. The Selkirk Treaty was negotiated with the Crown's authority and was very much associated with the tense conflict of the competitive era of fur trade history. The treaty, which provided a land base for a tiny colony to develop into a large settlement, conceived of the compensation for Indian title in terms of an annual quit rent. Since the provision of tobacco was regarded as a quit rent by the Europeans but as an annual payment by the Ojibwa, the problem of ownership would emerge. The lands set aside for agricultural settlement were later adjusted so that Indian bands would have "reserves" within the two-mile strip referred to in the written treaty. Along with the quit rent, the signatories expected to benefit through an association with the incoming settlers. The legitimacy of this treaty was later disputed, but the historical records do not specify where the opposition to the Selkirk Treaty came from. It also seems that First Nations and government officials held different interpretations about the status of Aboriginal title in the treaty area. Since certain land tenures of the Red River settlement were affirmed by the deed of surrender and confirmed by the Manitoba Act, 1870, the treaty should be taken seriously.

Although Charles II had granted the HBC title to Rupertsland and monopoly trading rights within that territory, the company understood that it was required to negotiate access and trading rights with the First Nations nonetheless, in order to carry on a peaceful and profitable business. It did so by adopting the appropriate First Nations protocols, most notably by participating in gift exchange and calumet ceremonies and through the intermarriage of officers and men with local Native women. On this basis, the First Nations welcomed the company's representatives as kin and expected them to act accordingly. The obligation to share and provide mutual support was a fundamental social norm among close kin in First Nations and, therefore, they expected the HBC men, as well as any other European fur traders with whom they had forged relations, to abide by this fundamental rule. Consequently, it became common practice for European fur traders to provide for the basic needs of their First Nations clients whenever they were sick or economically destitute as a consequence of a scarcity of fish and fur or game animals, or of weak fur markets. The Selkirk Treaty was a compact in keeping with the understanding the HBC had reached much earlier with First Nations whereby it had gained peaceful entry into their territories. However, because it entailed an understanding concerning tenure for agriculture and because it was a written treaty, it shared elements of the later treaties with the Dominion of Canada.

CHAPTER THREE

Precedents from Early Eastern Treaties

We have seen that their long association with the Hudson's Bay Company con-ditioned the western First Nations' approach to treaty talks with the Queen's Canadian government. In turn, the Crown's earlier relations with First Nations in the eastern half of North America shaped the Dominion of Canada's attitudes and response.[1] Prior to the negotiations for the numbered treaties, imperial and colonial officials had developed a policy of treating with Aboriginal peoples living in eastern North America for access to their lands for development pur-poses. This policy was rooted in the Royal Proclamation of 1763 and in impe-rial and colonial practices in the future southern Ontario between the 1770s and 1850.

THE ROYAL PROCLAMATION OF 1763
AND TREATIES MADE BEFORE 1850

Although the Royal Proclamation has become significant as a legal and consti-tutional document, its origins were much more prosaic and its intent more lim-ited. A royal proclamation is an instrument of the royal prerogative, one of the three direct sources of law in the British system. (The other two are the com-mon law and the statutes.) Under British legal principles, prerogative instru-ments have the force of statutes of a legislature or a parliament in regions that do not have representative legislative bodies, as was the case where the Royal Proclamation of 1763 was to apply.[2] Of course, these considerations were not necessarily present in the minds of imperial officials who developed the instru-ment that was used in 1763.

The background to the Royal Proclamation was the unease of imperial plan-ners over growing restiveness of Aboriginal peoples west of the Appalachian mountains. The problem was that groups in the Ohio Valley and other portions of this territory resisted the invasion of land speculators and settlers from the Thirteen Colonies. Since the colonial governments proved unable or unwilling to restrain these expansionists, with resulting clashes between First Nations and intruders, Britain began to develop a policy to prevent conflict. The need for such an instrument was heightened when Pontiac's War erupted in the spring of 1763, the Ottawa chief Pontiac leading a coalition of First Nations that attacked and took a series of British posts in the interior.[3] As the violence born of First Nations resistance to dispossession became a horrible reality, the government of the United Kingdom issued its Royal Proclamation on 7 October 1763. In 1764 William Johnson followed up the proclamation with a conference attended by some two thousand chiefs at Niagara, at which the superintendent of the Northern Indians explained the promulgation, made commitments of noninterference to the leaders, and secured First Nations agreement. The compact was recorded in a belt of two-row wampum.[4] In the 1990s John Borrows made a strong argument that the proclamation, when read together with the solemn agreement made shortly thereafter at Niagara, constituted a treaty between First Nations and the Crown that positively guarantees First Nations the right of self-government.[5]

Although focused upon Britain's colonies of Quebec, East Florida, West Florida, and Grenada, the Royal Proclamation was to have an enormous impact throughout North America. What the proclamation did, among other things, was to define the western boundary of what is now known as the province of Quebec, approximately along the Ottawa River, and to establish a barrier, usually referred to as the Proclamation Line, that prohibited settlement beyond the Appalachian mountain chain. Western regions were henceforth Indian territory, and legal access to them could be obtained only by the Crown:

And whereas it is just and reasonable, and essential to our Interest, and the security of our Colonies, that the several Nations or Tribes of Indians with whom We are connected, and who live under our protection, should not be molested or disturbed in the Possession of such Parts of Our Dominions and Territories as, not having been ceded to or purchased by Us, are reserved to them or any of them, as their Hunting Grounds – We do therefore, with the Advice of our Privy Council, declare it to be our Royal Will and Pleasure, that no Governor or Commander in Chief in any of our Colonies of Quebec, East Florida, or West Florida, do presume, upon any Pretence whatever, to grant Warrants of Survey, or pass any Patents for Lands beyond the Bounds of their respective Governments ...

And We do further declare it to be Our Royal Will and Pleasure ... to reserve under our Sovereignty, Protection, and Dominion, for the use of the said Indians, all the Lands and Territories not included within the Limits of Our Said New Governments, or within the Limits of the Territory granted to the Hudson's Bay Company ...

And We do hereby strictly forbid, on Pain of our Displeasure, all our loving subjects from making any Purchase or Settlements whatever, or taking Possession of any of the Lands above reserved, without our especial leave and Licence for the Purpose first obtained ...

And Whereas Great Frauds and Abuses have been committed in purchasing Lands of the Indians, to the Great Prejudice of our Interests, and to the Great Disssatisfaction of the said Indians; In Order, therefore, to prevent such Irregularities for the future, and to the End that the Indians may be convinced of our Justice and determined Resolution to remove all reasonable Cause of Discontent, We do, with the Advice of our Privy Council, strictly enjoin and require, that no private Person do presume to make any Purchase from the said Indians of any Lands reserved to the said Indians ... if at any Time any of the said Indians should be inclined to dispose of the said Lands, the same shall be Purchased only for Us, in our Name, at some public Meeting or Assembly of the said Indians, to be held for the Purpose of the Governor or Commander in Chief of our Colony respectively within which they shall lie.[6]

In other words, the Royal Proclamation provided Crown recognition that lands occupied by First Nations beyond Britain's existing North American colonies were in some sense Indian lands and prescribed that access and title to these lands could legally be obtained only by the Crown. The objective was to avoid conflict with First Nations by halting speculators' invasions of their territories and by regulating future acquisitions of their lands.

Although imperial and colonial governments did not always follow the requirements of the Royal Proclamation, between the American Revolution and the middle of the nineteenth century its terms were implemented so frequently in southern Ontario that the proclamation became a binding precedent covering acquisition of First Nations lands. Following the American Revolution and the War of 1812, and also in response to heavy immigration from Britain to Upper Canada (southern Ontario) between 1815 and 1850, the United Kingdom had to negotiate with the Mississauga for access to lands for former military allies, both First Nations and non-Native. Until the 1820s, the treaties that resulted covered relatively small territories and included one-time compensation payments to the First Nation. From the 1820s onward, however, these one-time payments were replaced with annual payments – annuities – from the Crown to the Native peoples who had signed these treaties.[7] Under this scheme annuity payments essentially helped finance purchases of Aboriginal title. By the 1820s the eastern Ojibwa were rapidly running out of lands to which they could retreat as White settlement advanced. They needed reserves. As a result, by the end of the decade, provisions for reserves became a common feature of the land surrenders. By means of a succession of such pacts concerning access to land, most of southern Ontario was covered by treaty by the middle of the nineteenth century. This practice was extended, with important modifications concerning reserves and hunting rights, in the two Robinson Treaties of 1850.

The accumulation of precedents from the 1770s to 1850 meant that by Confederation the practice of negotiating with First Nations before entering and utilizing their lands was so firmly established in central Canada as to be almost unavoidable. Also, from the late nineteenth century to the present, it became increasingly important in Canadian legal circles because clauses of the Royal Proclamation of 1763 recognized the inherent territorial rights of First Nations and made explicit the Crown's desire to protect those rights. These clauses have never been repealed, and, therefore, they still have the force of law.[8]

THE ROBINSON TREATIES, 1850

The Robinson Treaties simultaneously brought the treaty-making process to a peak in eastern Canada and established precedents for treaty-making in the West.[9] Although the Robinson Treaties directly concerned the Ojibwa of the upper Great Lakes region of Ontario, indirectly they would apply to northwestern Ontario and to the Plains Nations of the West.

The Ojibwa, who had lived in the lands north of Lake Huron and east of Lake Superior from time immemorial, became directly involved in the fur trade during the first half of the seventeenth century. Thereafter, they developed a mixed economy that integrated subsistence fishing, hunting, and trapping with commercial production. Also, after the fall of Huronia in 1649 some Ojibwa bands – especially those who were living at Garden River – took up farming to meet their domestic requirements and for sale to traders and others. In addition, they produced a variety of so-called country produce for sale to fur trading companies, most notably the HBC and the NWC. Native men also participated in the labour market the Eurocanadian fur trade provided, serving mostly as seasonal workers in capacities such as boat and canoe men, fishers, hunters, and unskilled general labourers.

In spite of this diversity, Aboriginal people faced economic problems. Throughout the first half of the nineteenth century the hunting and trapping sector of the economy experienced recurrent crises as a result of chronically depleted large game and fur stocks. This was particularly vexing for the Aboriginal peoples living in the interior, away from Lake Huron and Lake Superior, who were forced to rely on hare – a species whose population fluctuates widely. Low points in the hare cycle often left Aboriginal peoples facing the threat of starvation unless they had access to a good fishery. Inadequate fur stocks, coupled with low beaver prices in the late 1840s, meant that Aboriginal trappers needed to find alternative sources of income to buy the Euroamerican goods they needed and wanted.

New economic developments in the upper Great Lakes area, especially mining exploration and development beginning in 1846, offered First Nations and Métis a new opportunity to address their economic problems through an expanded regional labour market.[10] The possibility of gaining income by leasing lands to miners and other newcomers or through treaty annuities in exchange for relinquishing their Aboriginal title to the land offered another possibility. Local

Indian bands were familiar with the concept of leasing land, having engaged in the practice as early as 1790, when they granted a concession to the NWC (subsequently assumed by the HBC in 1821) at Sault Ste Marie, on the understanding that the company would distribute presents to them annually in return.[11] Also, prior to the signing of the Robinson Treaties they had granted mining leases of their own, most notably to Allan Macdonnell.[12] They were mindful of the benefits of annuities, since their southern Ojibwa relatives in Canada and the United States already were under treaty. Also, the treaties made in the Great Lakes territory of the United States provided land grants to "Half Breeds."[13]

Given these interests and needs, it is understandable why the Native people became alarmed and angry when the colonial government of Canada awarded sixty-eight lakeshore tracts (two miles by five miles) in the upper Great Lakes region between 1845 and 1850, in violation of the terms of the Royal Proclamation of 1763.[14] Besides denying Native people the benefits of any economic gains from the disposal of their lands, the government practice also posed a potential threat for Ojibwa and Métis lakeshore settlements. Indeed, one of the mining leases the government granted included the Ojibwa and Métis settlement at Garden River. Without proper safeguards, the local people risked losing their familial homesteads. Natives raised all these concerns with government agents before and during the negotiations that resulted in the Robinson Treaties of 1850.[15]

First Nations began to take measures aimed at advancing their economic interests in April of 1846, when Chief Shinguakonce (Little Pine) of the Garden River Ojibwa threatened a Crown land surveyor. In June he followed up this action with a petition to Governor-General Lord Elgin demanding he and his followers receive money for their lands and a share of whatever was found on them.[16] At first the government balked at even considering the chief's demands, or those of other Natives. Lord Elgin decided, however, that the issue needed to be explored, and he dispatched two parties to the area to investigate. One departed in 1848 and was led by Thomas Gummersall Anderson of the Indian Department; the second headed for the region in 1849 under the direction of land surveyor Alexander Vidal, with Captain Anderson acting as second in command.

While these government probes were under way, in November of 1849 an armed party of Indians and Métis seized the Quebec Mining Company property at Mica Bay. Historians generally agree this event prompted the government to come to terms with the Native people as quickly as possible. The HBC post manager at Sault Ste Marie, William Mactavish, who later served as governor of Assiniboia and Rupertsland at the time of the Red River resistance in 1869–70, provided an extended description of events leading up to this incident and of the confrontation itself. On 12 November 1849, just before the clash occurred, Mactavish wrote to HBC Governor Sir George Simpson telling him that

There is considerable excitement here at present regarding an expedition nominally led by the two Indian Chiefs but the real leader, no one doubts, is Mr Allan McDonell assisted by his Brother Angus & a Mr. Metcalfe … some say they are to plunder the Mining Establishment at Mica Bay, others that they intend carrying on the works under their own management, but it would appear from what they said to me when I urged them to desist that their intention is to put the Indians not in possession but to carry on the mining operations under the superintendence of the present Mining Captain, removing Mr. Bonner [present manager] altogether from the Mines. But it is questionable if they will be able to restrain their party to that line of conduct.[17]

In other words, it seems that Macdonnell's interest in attacking Mica Bay and the interests of the Native people who backed him were not identical. For the latter, it was an issue of Aboriginal title, rather than a question of who should manage the mining operation.

On 20 November 1849 Mactavish dispatched another letter to Governor Simpson in which he provided more details about the raiding party: "They gave out themselves as numbering 100 men at present on the works, but only find that 33 accompanied vizt: 2 American Indians, 5 American half breeds, 12 Indians from this side & 13 half breeds & 1 Canadian."[18] Of particular importance, the composition of the party underscores that Indians and Métis from both sides of the border obviously believed they had a stake in the land title issue that had flared up. This belief is to be expected, given that familial ties reached across the border.

Indeed, they may have sent out a call for support from their relatives in western Canada in the event additional armed clashes took place. For instance, in his 14 December 1849 letter to Governor Simpson, Mactavish stated: "My last letter I think correctly stated the attacking force which wonder makers had swelled most prodigiously. The latest news [gossip at Sault Ste Marie] is that 2,000 Red River half breeds are to be down in spring to act as allies of Shingwâkonce's, having sent him a wampum belt with a message to that effect this autumn."[19] Apparently Mactavish doubted the story. Nonetheless, it suggests that there was enough solidarity among the Native people to enable them to use the rumour as a credible threat when bargaining.[20]

Once the disturbance ended, HBC Chief Trader John Swanston, who was in charge of the company's post at Michipicoten and the father of a Métis family, made the following comment about the Mica Bay incident: "The Indians I believe had no intention of injuring any of the mining party, but they were determined I fancy to stop the work and drive all off the grounds, in which they succeeded, without much difficulty, when led on by the Messrs McDonnells and Metcalfe. Had the government attended to the petitions of the Indians, and purchased the lands which they are now proposing to do at this *Eleventh hour,* the disgraceful attack would never have taken place, nor the government put to the expense of sending tropes [troops] to pass the winter uselessly."[21] In any event, the government decided to act on this issue, and in 1850 it dispatched William Robinson at the head of a government negotiating team that reached an accord with the Native people of Lakes Huron and Superior.[22]

The traditional written histories of the treaty, most notably that of Robert Surtees, emphasize the land rights issue that the colonial government had provoked by granting mining leases without first clearing Aboriginal title according to the principles of the Royal Proclamation of 1763.[23] As the above discussion makes clear, this issue certainly was a rallying point for the people. To properly understand the negotiations, however, a whole range of economic issues has to be taken into account.

In order to simplify the discussion of the negotiating process, we have listed the key participants in table A1, indicating their position and the interests that they represented. These individuals, and others, addressed a number of key issues in the preliminary treaty negotiations (which began with T.G. Anderson's "survey" of the area in 1848 and Anderson and Vidal's survey of 1849) and final bargaining sessions in 1850. A major topic of the negotiations concerned the extent of land cessions the people would make. Initially the government wanted only to clear Aboriginal title to the lands it had granted in mining leases. When Vidal and Anderson visited the region to survey Native attitudes on this crucial topic, they discovered that the Aboriginal leaders expressed an interest in "surrendering" a much larger area. In their official report of 1849, the two commissioners noted, "there is a general wish expressed by the Indians to cede their territory to the Government provided they are not required to remove from their present places of abode – their hunting and fishing not interfered with, and that compensation given to them be a perpetual annuity."[24] Pursuing this topic further, Vidal and Anderson recommended that

it will not be advisable to propose the cession of a narrow strip upon the Lake shore, merely including the present mining tracts, as there is a general wish on the part of the Chiefs to cede the whole, with the exception of small reservations for the use of the respective bands. Little if any difference need be made in the terms offered, for all that is known to be of value [from the government's perspective] is situated on the front, and they will still retain undisturbed possession of their hunting grounds in the interior: – in fact, whatever may be given to them for the surrender of their right, they must be gainers, for they relinquish nothing but a mere nominal title, they will continue to enjoy all their present advantages and will not be the poorer because the superior intelligence and industry of their white brethren are enabling them to draw wealth from a few limited portions of their territory, which never were nor could be, of any particular service to themselves.[25]

There is little doubt that one of the primary reasons why the Native people wanted to reach an agreement that included the inland sections of the territory was that concluding treaties only for the lakeshore tracts would not have benefited the people most in need of income to supplement that derived from the hunting and trapping activities. Robinson accepted Vidal and Anderson's perspective on this matter. Thus, he accommodated the Native people's wish to bring the interior under treaty, even though the hunting/trapping ranges of the various groups apparently overlapped.

The two other issues of major importance to all the Native people of the region were closely intertwined – the level of financial compensation they should receive for their surrendered lands and the continuation of traditional economic rights in the surrendered territories.

Apparently Natives expected substantial remuneration. Vidal noted this in the diary he kept during his 1849 survey. While making his first stop at Sault Ste Marie, he wrote that it was not "practicable to commit to paper the unbounded expectations of almost all classes to participate in the benefit of the 'Treaty Money' for they have persuaded themselves that a very large number of kegs containing $1000 in each will be distributed at this place and there will be fine *pickings* for the time being."[26]

After traveling to Fort William, Anderson and Vidal returned to Sault Ste Marie and held a council with Shinguakonce and his followers on 16 October. Apparently it was a fractious meeting. As Anderson described it, "at 10 [A.M.] the Council again commenced [from the previous night] ... on asking Shinguakonse party whether they were inclined to sell their land and what they expected for it – they obstantely [sic] refused to answer except thro' Allan McDonnell, Esq., – we objected to his acting as their Agent and closed our proceedings with them – after which he made a most inflamatory speech to the Indians in my presence which astonished me not a little – as soon as he had done the Indians retired."[27] In his diary, Vidal offered the same interpretation of the meeting and also cast McDonnell as a troublemaker.[28]

HBC manager Mactavish's reports to Governor Sir George Simpson painted a somewhat different picture of this meeting and provided more details about it. Mactavish said that one of the reasons relations between Anderson and Vidal and the Native people became strained was that the latter apparently had expected the government to settle with them in 1849. Thus, Mactavish noted, "the Indians feel disappointed at seeing the Commissioners arrive without money."[29] He added that just before the meeting "The Commissioners returned from Fort William on the 13th Inst [October] and appear to think that although in one or two instances they made somewhat unreasonable demands the Indians up the Lake will be very easily dealt with and at *least said* that they [the Commissioners] attributed this to the good management of the HBCo. Le Peau du Chat [a Fort William Chief] asked from Government in compensation for the Mineral Lands a payment to every Indian of $30 p ann in perpetuity."[30]

The demands of the Lake Superior Ojibwa proved to be much lower than those of their southern relatives. According to Mactavish, the latter held out for much higher annuities:

> & one of the Michipicoten Indians demanded $100 p ann. Mr. Vidal thinks however that they will reduce the *demand* & take in lieu a small amount in annual presents besides Government supporting two or three stations with schools &c attached for the instruction of the Indians at least it is the course he intends recommending in his report to the Government. He speaks a little bitterly of Mr McDonell whom the Indians have chosen for their agent, but whom Mr Vidal has had private instructions not to recognize as such. Mr Vidal says Mr McDonell is doing all in his power to prevent a settlement. It is said he sent up a message to the Fort William Indians that they should not have anything to say to the Commissioners as they were averse to doing the Indians justice in consequence of which they were very averse to stating their claims to the Commissioners, but that after some time they agreed to leave the matter in the Commissioners hands as they thought Mr McDonell had given them ill advice, & had actually deceived them.[31]

Mactavish then provided a lengthy description of the meeting that eventually took place. Apparently, on the first day the talks commenced by focusing once again on the issue of who had the right to speak for the local Aboriginal people and also on the nature of the HBC's tenure at Sault Ste Marie:

> Since writing you on the 15 Inst [October] the Commissioners held a Council here which was broken up on the second day, from the Indians declining to answer any of the Commissioners' questions except through their agent Mr Allan McDonell to which the Commissioners would not agree. On the first day the Indians had not been I suppose well enough schooled and answered all the questions at once except as to what remuneration they expected for the cession of their lands, when the oldest Chief here ("Shinguakonce") said that as that was a most important question he would take to the following day to think of his answer, as it was necessary he should consult with his people.
>
> Mr Vidal among the first questions asked if the Indians had given to the H.B.Co a block of land round this Establishment. This was answered by the two chiefs in the affirmative. Mr Vidal then asked if they wished this grant to be confirmed when they again said they did, but a useless scoundrel rose up and said that the H.B.Co had not fulfilled their part of the agreement, as part of the bargain was that the Indians were annually to receive a feast on the arrival of the first canoe from Montreal, which had not been given for many years past.[32]

The discussions then shifted to the contentious issue of the mining and right-of-way leases that the local chiefs had granted to their spokesman, William McDonell:

Mr Vidal then asked some questions regarding Mr McDonell's leases of Michipicoten Island, and Mamainse. These questions were answered in such a way that Mr Vidal said the Indians did not understand the leases they were said to have granted, while Mr McDonell said they did not understand the questions put by Mr Vidal. There were a few high words & probability of higher when Captain Anderson proposed an adjournment to next day. Mr McDonell's leases are so framed as to bind him to work the lands leased within five years & secure to the Indians 2 p cent of the nett profits & are for 999 years. But in answer to Mr Vidal's the Indians said Mr McDonell's lease only existed for a term of 5 years.

The second day of the talks proved to be even more fractious because of McDonell's continuing presence and his ties to the local Aboriginal community:

On the 2nd day Mr Vidal asked some questions, regarding Mr McDonell's lease of land for a railway on the portage here, having accidentally omitted to mention it on the first day, one of which it [*sic*] intended to run through the H.B.Co's lot, but could not obtain any answer from the Indians beyond that he must apply to Mr McDonell for their views on the subject they [*sic*] answer being returned to several more questions. Mr Vidal informed them that he had not come there to confer with Mr McDonell but with them, but if they pursued the course they were taking Government would have nothing to do with them, but would treat with the other Indians that they had leased lands to Mr McDonell which were not their own without consulting the Michipicoten Indians to whom they belonged. Shinguakonce & Nepinagootchin the Chiefs here claim the land from Puckuswaw River between the Pic & Michipicoten to the Grand Batture below the Bruce Mine. He then asked the Indians if they had more confidence in Mr McDonell or any other man than in the Government to which they answered certainly they had.

At this point, Vidal stormed out of the meeting in anger because of McDonell's interventions on behalf of his Aboriginal backers:

Mr McDonell then proposed to speak & on Mr Vidal objecting to this he told him he might either listen or put his fingers in his ears, neither of which Mr Vidal would do but gathered up his papers a little a [?] he declared the council over & walked out. Captain Anderson remained to hear I suppose what would go on, & Mr McDonell made a flaming speech blaming the Government for the manner in which they had treated the Indians, in procrastinating & in not sending up Cash or payment of some kind this season, reflecting also on the rather singular position of the Commissioners, they not being authorized to make any definite proposals, & declaring that the government would be compelled to give fair compensation instead of buying up the land for a trifle as they evidently intended. He also read a letter from Mr Price of the Crown Land Department acknowledging him to be the agent for the Indians. Mr McDonell says he will publish the whole proceedings together with the terms on which the Indians are prepared to treat with the

Government. He told me that the first stipulation was to be that the H.B.Co & all the settlers here were to have free grants of the lots they at present occupy. Mr Vidal says that
the first stipulation is that Mr McDonell's leases are to be recognized but Mr McDonell
himself says that if the Indians can obtain better terms he will have great pleasure in giving them (the leases) up. So stands the matter at present.

Mactavish closed with the suggestion that the local chiefs were seeking to protect their role in any future negotiations: "The Commissioners intend going
down Lake Huron to see the Indians as far as Sawenawgaiu within 70 miles of
Penetanguishene in a Canoe. Report says that the Chiefs here have sent a canoe
to bring up some of the neighbouring Chiefs here to form a council among themselves as they say but I suspect mainly to prevent the Commissioners seeing
them." It is clear that the reason Vidal lost his patience was that the local chiefs
wanted substantially more compensation for their concessions than he believed
were reasonable.

In their official report of their 1849 discussions, Vidal and Anderson stated
that they doubted Native leaders were capable of deciding what their lands were
worth: "Where they are not influenced by the counsels of designing whites the
chiefs candidly declare their perfect ignorance of the value of their lands and are
quite content to leave it to the government to determine."[33] Of the more demanding people from the Garden River and Sault Ste Marie, who were represented by
McDonell, the commissioners said, "These simple minded Indians have been led
to believe that this person is more desirous and better able than the Government
to protect their interests."[34] Vidal and Anderson concluded their discussion of
this topic with the observation that "With reference to the terms on which the
treaty of cession should be made, your commissioners are of [the] opinion that
the Indians themselves are quite incompetent to negotiate them: – confessedly
ignorant of the value of the lands, and having no proper idea of large sums of
money … This incapacity on their part while it renders it necessary for the government to fix the terms, entitles the Indians to the most liberal consideration and
a scrupulous avoiding any encroachment upon their rights."[35] This was, of
course, a self-serving interpretation. The land had no inherent value. It was
worth whatever the government was prepared to offer for it, given that no one
else had the legal right to purchase Aboriginal lands.

In any event, the fact that important Native leaders had high expectations
meant that government negotiators had to come up with a scheme that would
persuade Aboriginal people to accept much lower rates of compensation. Because the colonial government's primary objective was to secure title to mining
properties, its agents quickly seized on the idea of explaining the reasonableness
of their offer on the grounds that they would be able to continue their traditional
economic practices on all of their ceded ancestral lands, excepting developed
mining properties, and receive a bonus income in the form of annuity payments.

This was Robinson's negotiating strategy. In his 1850 report to the superintendent of Indian Affairs about the treaty negotiations, Robinson said he told the chiefs their claims were extravagant:

I explained to the chiefs in council the difference between the lands ceded heretofore in this Province, and those then under consideration, they [the former] were of good [agricultural] quality and sold readily at prices which enabled the Government to be more liberal, they were also occupied by the whites in such a manner as to preclude the possibility of the Indian hunting over or having access to them: whereas the lands now ceded are notoriously barren and sterile, and will in all probability never be settled except in a few localities by mining Companies, whose establishments among the Indians, instead of being prejudicial, would prove of great benefit as they would afford a market for anything they may have to sell, and bring provisions and stores of all kinds among them at reasonable prices.[36]

In other words, Robinson, following the lead of Vidal and Anderson, claimed a treaty would create a "win-win" situation (to use a modern expression) for Native people. They would be able to continue their traditional subsistence and commercial fishing, hunting, trapping, and other economic pursuits, but with the benefit of expanded commercial opportunities for the fruits of their labour and more competitive prices for the Euroamerican goods they wanted.

Granting reserves and unfettered hunting and fishing rights to the Native people appealed to Robinson for an additional reason. He believed that these key economic concessions would protect the government from any future claims Natives might bring forward for loss of traditional income: "In allowing the Indians to retain reservations of land for their own use I was governed by the fact that they in most cases asked for such tracts as they had heretofore been in the habit of using for purposes of residence and cultivation, and by securing these to them and the right of hunting and fishing over the ceded territory they cannot say that the government takes from their usual means of subsistence and therefore have no claims for Support, which they no doubt would have preferred, had this not been done."[37]

In the end this negotiating strategy worked. The Lake Superior chiefs, anxious to settle, were not willing to hold out while Shinguakonce pressed for a more lucrative agreement. So, on 7 September 1850 they signed the treaty. Their actions and strong dissent among his own people – many of whom wanted to follow suit – forced Shinguakonce to accept essentially the same terms two days later. It was the differing economic agendas of the Lake Superior and Lake Huron Ojibwa in 1850 that largely explain why the area treated for by Robinson is covered by two treaties instead of one.

The two treaties each provided lump sum payments of £2,000 colonial currency and annuities of £500 (Robinson Huron) to £600 (Robinson Superior) per year (which were to be increased if government revenues from the land exceeded expectations), and they gave Aboriginal people the livelihood right to have "the full and free privilege to hunt over the territory now ceded by them, and to fish in the waters thereof, as they have heretofore been in the habit of doing; saving and excepting such portions of the said territory as may from time to time be sold or leased to individuals or companies of individuals, and occupied by them with the consent of the Provincial Government."[38] The prerogative of the Royal Proclamation of 1763 was not particularly respected in 1849. The colonial state authorized economic development without first dealing with First Nations, and it was the resistance by Aboriginal peoples that led to the treaty-making process.

The Robinson Treaties of 1850 and Treaties 1 to 3 set the precedents for the Saskatchewan treaties of the 1870s and later years. Fur trading activities had led to chronic fur and game depletion problems in the inland districts of the Upper Great Lakes region by the beginning of the nineteenth century, and these problems persisted at least until the signing of the Robinson treaties. The local Ojibwa developed a mixed economy involving subsistence and commercial fishing, hunting, trapping, collecting (maple sugar in particular), and, especially in the case of some of the lakeshore Ojibwa, small-scale farming. The expansion of the mining frontier into the region led the colonial government of the province of canada into the area when it began granting lakeshore mining leases in the late 1840s, before it had negotiated over Native title to those lands. The Natives objected and demanded that their Aboriginal rights be addressed through treaties in ways that met their immediate economic needs. The government responded by granting the Ojibwa unfettered "traditional" economic rights on all ceded lands that were not actually developed by white settlers. This right included the subsistence and commercial use of fish, fur, and game resources on the understanding that this justified offering the Aboriginal people much lower annuities than they had demanded in treaty negotiations.

CHAPTER FOUR

The Rupertsland Transfer:
Expanding the Dominion of Canada

The HBC Territory, which encompassed Rupertsland and the North Western Territory, was incorporated into the Dominion of Canada before western First Nations and Canadian officials began negotiating treaties. Aboriginal people were aware that the spatial contraction of HBC authority and the Dominion of Canada's expansion westward and northward had major implications for them.[1] For instance, they regarded the terms by which the HBC surrendered its chartered rights in Rupertsland to be a highly contentious issue during the treaty negotiations of the 1870s.[2] HBC and Canadian officials also knew Indian title and Indian interests would be affected. The negotiations that led to the Rupertsland Order, facilitating the transfer, make this abundantly clear. The deed of surrender, the specific instrument by which the HBC agreed to give up its claims, also addressed these vital First Nations interests. For instance, term 14 of this deed acknowledged that Aboriginal people likely would have valid claims for compensation for the lands that Canada wanted for settlement. The transfer that followed did fundamentally alter the traditional relationship between the HBC and First Nations. It also became part of the foundation on which Canada built a new association with these people. For all of these reasons, a detailed discussion of the negotiations and agreements between the Imperial and Canadian governments and the HBC regarding Rupertsland is needed, to provide the background that is essential for a proper understanding of the treaty negotiations that began in the 1870s. This analysis must begin with a consideration of the HBC's charter, which was the focus of the negotiations between Canada and the company in the late 1860s and an issue in First Nations–Canadian treaty talks in the 1870s.

ACQUIRING AN INTEREST IN RUPERTSLAND:
INVESTING IN THE COMPANY'S CHARTER

The Royal Charter of 2 May 1670 incorporated the HBC, and, in the eyes of the English Crown, gave the small group of merchant adventurers who comprised the new company title and benefits to the lands of a vast and distant area where the company "at all times hereafter shall be, personable and capable in law to have, purchase, receive, possess, enjoy and retain lands, rents, privileges, liberties, jurisdictions, franchises and hereditaments, of what kind, nature or quality soever they be, to them and their successors; and also to give, grant, demise, alien, assign and dispose lands, tenements and hereditaments."[3] The charter also gave the new company monopoly trading rights in this immense territory.[4] In the late nineteenth century the company's authority to give up its proprietary rights and benefits proved to be a more valuable charter right than its monopoly trading privilege, which had proved to be largely unenforceable.

Traditionally, the company asserted its territorial claims in the European sphere of diplomacy based on the right of "discovery." In Rupertsland, on the other hand, we have seen that the company did not make territorial claims to the exclusion of Aboriginal land tenure. In the late seventeenth century the London directors ordered their HBC post officials to negotiate rights of access for trading purposes, which included the acquisition of sites for the construction of posts. In the early nineteenth century the company exercised its right to assign its proprietary interests to a third party, by making a land grant to Lord Selkirk. The treaty he subsequently negotiated with the Red River District Ojibwa for the sake of his agricultural colony recalled the company's late-seventeenth-century practices. In this instance, the Selkirk Treaty formally acknowledged Aboriginal title through a treaty. As long as the company's relationship with Indian and Métis peoples emphasized trade, the Aboriginal peoples' use and occupancy of land beyond the Selkirk colony did not become an issue until the 1850s and 1860s.

Problems began to surface at this time when some of the residents of the Red River settlement began to express their opposition to company rule. One reason was that the parliamentary select committee of 1857, which had been convened to consider renewing the company's charter, provided no direction for the future development of the Red River settlement. This left the fate of the indigenous inhabitants of Rupertsland to the schemes of railroad financiers and those who had plans for a nation state to facilitate their business schemes.

By 1863 various financial and political interests coalesced, making it possible for those seeking profits from land, and not commercial gain through trade, to buy control of the HBC. As a result, the company's charter rights fell into the hands of men interested in colonizing the "fertile belt."[5] Edward Watkin (later Sir Edward) was a key promoter of transcontinental railroad and telegraph schemes. His plans depended on the acquisition of Rupertsland. He was closely allied with the duke of Newcastle, who was a very influential colonial secretary at the time. HBC historian E. E. Rich commented on the interlocking nature of their political and economic objectives: "the statesman and the railway magnate were of one mind on the need to complete the Intercolonial line and to reach out towards the Pacific with railways which would be a preliminary necessity to the union of all provinces and territories into 'one great British America.' "[6] Watkin's plan to alleviate the existing railroad debt problems by extending railroads, telegraphs, or even wagon roads across the company's territory, thereby connecting British Columbia with the pre-Confederation Canadian provinces, generated considerable financial and political interest.

From 1859 the HBC was willing to sell its monopoly rights, but the Imperial government was not interested in buying them.[7] Aware that grand proposals for colonial infrastructure were based on a partial surrender of the company's rights to Rupertsland (the fertile lands and rights of way), company governor Berens retorted, "If these gentlemen are so patriotic, why don't they buy us out?"[8] Watkin eventually agreed to Berens' price of £1.5 million for the HBC, even though HBC stock was valued at only £500,000 at that time. According to the terms of the sale, Watkin and his group, who had recently established the International Financial Society (IFS), gained control of the HBC. Subsequently, the IFS raised the old stock of £500,000 to £2 million through a widely subscribed public issue.[9] The details of this stock watering remain obscure even today. In 1869 puzzled Canadian government officials described the financially restructured company: "The stock of the old Company, worth in the market about £1,000,000, was bought up, and by some process which we are unable to describe, became £2,000,000."[10] More importantly, the HBC had been taken over by interests not involved in the fur trade who were motivated by a desire to secure title to Rupertsland for colonization purposes.

The IFS's buy-out of the HBC foretold fundamental changes in the political and economic realities the inhabitants of Rupertsland faced. The duke of Newcastle, secretary of state for the colonies, was aware of these serious implications. When he learned of the IFS takeover, Newcastle predicted "that a new era was about to open in the north-west, and the wild animals and fur traders [would] retreat before the march of 'European' settlers."[11] After all, the new stockholders who bought shares in the IFS-controlled HBC thought they were investing in land. The 1863 prospectus stressed that the company lands would be opened up for European colonization and mining development.[12] After 1863 the company was under the control of men whose priority was "to realise [sic] the values of the southern parts of Rupert's Land rather than to manage a trade to the north."[13] At Red River, the buy-out, which occurred without consultation with the residents, created the belief among the fur trade elite that "they had all been sold 'like dumb driven cattle.' "[14] In the end, those who hoped to profit from the sudden change were frustrated and angered by how long it took for the reorganized company to begin to profit from the sale of its landed estate. Before this could happen, a period of difficult negotiations had to take place with Canadians that delayed somewhat the disruptions to their lives that Aboriginal people and fur traders would experience in the process.

NEGOTIATING AND LEGISLATING THE TRANSFER

Between 1863 and 1869 neither the company nor Canadians could proceed with colonization. There were several reasons for the delay. The new owners of the HBC had to determine the best way to realize the value of their proprietary interests in Rupertsland as expeditiously as possible. One course of action would have involved undertaking the development costs of colonization. After lengthy consideration, the company ruled out this option as too expensive and time consuming. The alternative strategy was to sell its estate to a developer. The unwillingness of the British government to buy Rupertsland meant that Canadians represented the only alternative. But until Confederation the colony of Canada lacked the financial resources to make the purchase on its own. Another problem was that Canadians, before and after Confederation, wanted to annex the fertile belt without compensating the company, on the premise that the charter had no validity. The British government rejected this argument, forcing Canadians to negotiate with the company. The Colonial Office acted as an intermediary and proposed solutions to the impasse.

The HBC had initially sought a large cash payment, a substantial grant of land, and royalties from any mineral wealth that might be developed. The new speculative shareholders had expected to receive as much as £1 million for the sale of Rupertsland.[15] Company negotiators also wanted to retain a stake in the land, asking for grants of six thousand acres around each post and five thousand acres out of every fifty thousand acres alienated by the government (i.e., one-tenth). They also sought protection for HBC fur trade operations. The company stubbornly fought for concessions on these issues.

The Imperial government, which was represented by the Colonial Office, was anxious to have the talks succeed, because it wanted British North America to be politically unified. This was to be done through confederation and by respecting the HBC's Royal Charter of 1670. The British North America Act, 1867, helped accomplish one of these goals. It created the Dominion of Canada and set the stage for the new country's westward expansion, through section 146, which provided that an address from the Canadian Parliament would "admit Rupert's Land and the North-western Territory, or either of them, into the Union, on such Terms ... as the Queen thinks fit to approve."[16] Canada followed up on this provision with the Address of 1867. This address also argued that the transfer of the HBC territory to the Dominion "would promote the prosperity of the Canadian people, and induce to the advantage of the whole Empire."[17] Furthermore, the Address of 1867 expressed clearly the economic objective of expansion: "That the colonization of the fertile lands of the Saskatchewan, the Assiniboine, and the Red River districts; the development of the mineral wealth which abounds in the region of the North-west; and the extension of commercial intercourse through the British possessions in America from the Atlantic to the Pacific, are alike dependent on the establishment of a stable government for the maintenance of law and order in the North-western Territories."[18] The problem was that Canadian officials argued that section 146 of the act and the Address of 1867 were all that was required for them to bring about the transfer, after which any of the company's territorial claims to Rupertsland could be decided in a Canadian court.

This proposition was unacceptable to the Imperial government, and it became legally untenable when the British parliament passed the Rupert's Land Act of 1868. The purpose of this statute was to provide for the transfer of Rupertsland, but it also acknowledged that the charter of 1670 had "granted or purported to be granted" land and rights to the company.[19] Once Canada addressed those rights, the Rupert's Land Act permitted the surrender of the company's charter to the Queen, who, after receiving an address from the Canadian Parliament, would admit Rupertsland into the Dominion. The passage of the Rupert's Land Act essentially forced Canada to negotiate in good faith with the HBC.

Complicated three-way negotiations commenced on 1 October 1868 and lasted until the end of March 1869. The parties made little headway from October until the end of January 1869. At the beginning of February, Canada's leading negotiators, George E. Cartier and William McDougall, wrote to the colonial undersecretary to restate the traditional Canadian position about the 1670 charter, but they left it to the Colonial Office to determine "whether this Company is entitled to demand any payment whatever, for surrendering to the Crown that which already belongs to it." The Canadians argued that the company's claim was nothing more than a "nuisance suit." Worse, they asserted that the HBC's occupation of Rupertsland jeopardized the sovereign rights of the Crown and obstructed Imperial and colonial policy. Cartier and McDougall emphatically rejected the stated principle of compensating the company through future revenues.[20] In support of their position the Canadian negotiators provided the colonial office with calculations that appraised the HBC territorial claims as being worth only £106,431.[21] Cartier and McDougall once again requested that the British government act on Canada's Address of 1867.

In order to move the deadlocked talks forward, Colonial Secretary Lord Granville proposed a series of terms to HBC and Canadian delegates on an accept-or-reject basis. These were that the HBC surrender its rights to Rupertsland and other areas of British North America as directed by the Rupert's Land Act; that Canada pay the company £300,000 when Rupertsland was transferred to the Dominion; that the company select blocks of land around posts, up to a maximum total of fifty thousand acres; that the company select, within fifty years, one-twentieth of the land set out for settlement in the area defined as the fertile belt; that all land titles conferred by the company before 8 March 1869 be confirmed; and that the company would be free to carry on the trade without exceptional taxation.[22] Granville threatened that if either party rejected his detailed proposal, he would have the Judicial Committee of the Privy Council examine the rights of the Crown and the company.

Both parties expressed enough interest in Granville's plan to proceed with face-to-face negotiations without further involvement of the Colonial Office. The HBC and Canada finally reached an agreement that they detailed in memoranda dated 22 and 29 March 1869. The provision that is most relevant here (term 8) specified that Canada would be held responsible for any future Indian claims.[23]

In April 1869 the Colonial Office wrote to HBC governor Sir Stafford Northcote, conveying Granville's sentiment "that the transfer which Her Majesty will then be authorized to effect will prove a source of increasing prosperity both to the inhabitants of that Dominion and to the proprietors of the HBC."[24] Certainly, the prosperity of the company had been secured. The crucial terms provided for a payment of £300,000 ($1.5 million Canadian) to the company. It retained fifty thousand acres of land around its posts, and, over a fifty-year period, the company was entitled to select one-twentieth of the land in the townships of the fertile belt. The agreement conferred titles to all the lands the company had granted before 8 March 1869, and it relieved it of the liability for any future Indian claims.[25]

Shortly after they achieved these concessions, the owners of the HBC resolved "to surrender to Her Majesty's Government all this Company's territorial rights in Rupert's Land, and in any other part of British North America not comprised in Rupert's Land, Canada or British Columbia."[26] On 20 May 1869 the company's solicitors prepared a deed of surrender. Term 14 restated clause 8 of the 22 March 1869 memorandum: "Any claims of Indians to compensation for lands required for purposes of settlement shall be disposed of by the Canadian Government in communication with the Imperial Government; and the Company shall be relieved of all responsibility in respect of them."[27]

In resolutions and an address to the queen on 29 and 31 May 1869, Canada stated its acceptance of the transfer arrangements. The Imperial order-in-council, known as the Order of Her Majesty in Council Admitting Rupert's Land and the North-Western Territory into the Union (hereafter the Rupertsland Order), stipulated the terms for the incorporation of HBC territory into the Dominion of Canada.[28] Through this order the British Crown accepted the surrender of Rupertsland from the HBC and then passed it, and the North-Western Territory, to the Dominion of Canada. The order could not be issued until 23 June 1870, however, because of the Red River Resistance of 1869, which forced the government of Canada also to negotiate terms of union with Louis Riel's provisional government. The Manitoba Act was the outcome of these talks.

"INDIAN TITLE" AND THE TRANSFER OF RUPERTSLAND

The question of Aboriginal rights was never central for the negotiators of the surrender agreement, even though the interests and rights of the Indigenous inhabitants of the HBC territory were involved. Aboriginal title was mentioned as early as the 1867 address to the Queen, however. The question of Indian title was raised in the third term of this document: "And furthermore that, upon the transference of the territories in question to the Canadian Government, the claims of the Indian tribes to compensation for lands required for purposes of settlement will be considered and settled in conformity with the equitable principles which have uniformly governed the British Crown in its dealings with the aborigines."[29] This commitment did not change in the course of the 1868–69 talks. The Canadian delegates reiterated these terms during the negotiations and added that they were among the "only terms and conditions which, in the opinion of the Canadian Parliament, it was expedient to insert in the Order in Council, authorized by the 146th section."[30] Clearly, the Canadian position acknowledged the principle of compensation for what Prime Minister John A. Macdonald later would describe as Indian title.

On 10 April 1869, Colonial Secretary Lord Granville officially notified the governor-general of Canada, Sir John Young (later Lord Lisgar), that the proprietors of the HBC had accepted the terms of surrender. The bulk of his communiqué was, however, directed at Indian interests and the expectations of Her Majesty's government. He urged the Canadian government to consider the merit of the company's relationship with Indians: "On one point which has not been hitherto touched upon, I am anxious to express to you the expectations of Her Majesty's Government – They believe that whatever may have been the policy of the Company, and the effect of their Chartered rights upon the progress of settlement, the Indian Tribes who form the existing population of this part of America have profited by the Company's rule." Granville added, "They have been protected from some of the vices of civilization, they have been taught to some appreciable extent, to respect the laws and rely on the justice of the white man, and they do not appear to have suffered from any causes of extinction beyond those which are inseparable from their habits and their climate."[31] The extent of benefit that Indians obtained from the fur trade is a matter of ongoing scholarly debate. However, the colonial secretary drew attention to the relationship that Indians had had with the HBC, and he suggested the need for a continuity with HBC policies following the transfer.

On the question of future relations with First Nations, Granville advised: "That Government I believe has never sought to evade its obligations to those whose uncertain rights and rude means of living are contracted by the advance of civilized men. I am sure that they will not do so in the present case, but that the old inhabitants of the Country will be treated with such forethought and consideration as may preserve them from the dangers of the approaching change, and satisfy them of the friendly interest which their new Governors feel in their welfare." By characterizing the pending changes in terms of a danger for the old inhabitants of the country with a "rude means of living" from the "advance of civilizing men", he attempted to stress the need for the Canadian government to take a serious interest in Indian livelihood. Granville also warned, "I am sure that your Government will not forget the care which is due to those who must soon be exposed to new dangers, and in the course of settlement be dispossessed of the lands which they are used to enjoy as their own, or be confined within un-wontedly narrow limits."[32] Clearly, the colonial secretary had anticipated that the Transfer of Rupertsland would affect Indians and that the Canadian govern-ment had obligations to maintain their livelihoods.

Yet Granville did not let his concern for Indian interests detract from the nego-tiations involving the HBC claims to Rupertsland. For he also wrote on 10 April 1869 that "This question had not escaped my notice while framing the proposals which I laid before the Canadian Delegates and the Governor of the HBC. I did not however even then allude to it because I felt the difficulty of insisting on any definite conditions without the possibility of foreseeing the circumstances under which those conditions would be applied, and because it appeared to me wiser and more expedient to rely on the sense of duty and responsibility belonging to the Government and people of such a Country as Canada."[33] In effect, these ne-gotiations did not have to reconcile the competing Aboriginal and company terri-torial claims. During the negotiations, serious consideration of Indian title would have led to a comparison of the HBC claim to Rupertsland with Indian entitle-ment. Clearly, the question of Indian title was not a mere oversight; there was a deliberate effort by the Imperial government to avoid complicating the already convoluted negotiations. This letter suggests that the colonial secretary was not fully aware of term 8 of the memorandum of 22 March 1869, nor that this term had been repeated in the deed of surrender as term 14.

Indian interests were again acknowledged when Canada requested the transfer of Rupertsland and the North Western Territory. The address of the 29 and 31 May 1869 stated the Canadian intention that "upon the transference of the territories in question to the Canadian Government it will be our duty to make adequate provision for the protection of the Indian tribes whose interests and well-being are involved in the transfer."[34] By acknowledging the importance of the transfer to Indians, this address also seems to acknowledge Granville's rec-ommendations of 10 April 1869. In any event, in both addresses to the Queen, the Canadian parliament acknowledged Indian interests. Despite the Colonial Office's unwillingness to raise the question of Indian interests until Lord Granville's letter of 10 April 1869, as we have seen, HBC and Canadian negotia-tors already had dealt with the issue in term 14 of the deed of surrender. This clause is often cited as being recognition of Aboriginal rights.

A textual exegesis of term 14 alone is insufficient for a full understanding of the intent and meaning of that term. Rather, it is also necessary to consider it within the larger context of the transfer negotiations. Clearly, this term relieved the company of any costs associated with Indian title. A legal opinion prepared for the HBC's land commissioner in 1917 cited correspondence from Donald

A. Smith in the 1870s that suggested the company had intended to safeguard their land grants from the complications of Indian title. This legal brief also stated, "The correspondence between the Company and the Government leading up to the surrender indicates that at that time there were *a great many Indians under the care of the Company* and it was necessary that provision be made in the surrender for the compensation of the claims of the Indians to the lands required for settlement."[35] Thus, the company's legal advisors connected the social and economic responsibilities of the pre-1870 company for livelihood to the legal title of First Nations.

The concept of Aboriginal title did not enter into the talks until the face-to-face negotiations between the company and the Canadian delegates. The Aboriginal title concept appears only after the Colonial Office ceased to participate actively as an intermediary. Moreover, Granville clearly stated that he had decided not to raise Indian claims in his 9 March list of terms; he did not raise the general issue of Indian interests until 10 April 1869. Therefore, the Imperial government cannot be credited for the drafting of term 8. Either the Canadians or the company sponsored this stipulation in the surrender, or possibly both parties initiated different portions of the term.

Other documents immediately connected with the negotiations allow us to trace the development of the concept of Aboriginal title among Canadian delegates and HBC officials during their talks in March 1869. Drafts of the memorandum of 22 March 1869 are contained in the HBC London correspondence with Her Majesty's government. We have noted that term 14 of the deed of surrender was based on term 8 of the memorandum of 22 March 1869, both of which were attached to the Rupertsland Order. Term 8 went through two stages of drafting before the negotiators finalised it. The first draft reads, "It is understood that any arrangements which should be made for the satisfaction of Indian claims on the land shall be made by the Canadian Govt. in communication with the Colonial Office, and that the Company shall not be considered to be responsible for them."[36] In this version the Canadian government acknowledged sole responsibility for Indian claims. Only one change was made between the first and second drafts. The second version reduced the commitment to Indian title by substituting "should be made" with "may be necessary."

The final version that appeared as the memorandum of 22 March 1869 contained some very important additional changes. The drafters tied the idea of Indian title to the concept of compensation; thus, they substituted "satisfaction of Indian claims on the land" for "claims of Indians ... for lands required for the purposes of settlement." This rewording points to a conscious effort to link compensation for Indians to a specific change in land use. Another modification entailed substituting "Colonial Office" for "Imperial Government." The final change firmed up and broadened the company's expectations for the post-1870 period. The expression "the Company shall not be considered to be responsible for them" was changed to "the Company shall be relieved of all responsibility in respect of them." The use of "them" is ambiguous: it could mean "compensation" or "Indians" or "claims." The indirect expression "shall not be considered" is firmed up with the direct wording "shall be relieved." The term "all responsibility" broadens the disengagement of the HBC from its traditional obligations to Indians. The wording "relieved of all responsibility" acknowledges the existence of certain real responsibilities that the HBC was giving up. In terms of how the drafters handled term 8, Indian livelihood was closely connected to the issue of Indian title.

These archival records concerning drafts of term 8 provide no direct indication of which party desired a term on Aboriginal title in the memorandum of March 22. Clearly the company gained: in the post-1870 period it could reduce its social obligations to the livelihood interests of the indigenous inhabitants of Rupertsland, maintaining that they had become a government responsibility.[37] It seems unlikely that the Canadians felt a need to indicate their intentions towards Indian claims. Their intentions were already outlined in the Address of 1867, and certainly the Imperial government did not force the Canadians to commit to Indian claims. While it is not entirely clear how this term was arrived at, the HBC secured some flexibility in its legal obligations towards the Indian population. Since the HBC was giving up its monopoly trading rights, HBC officials no longer felt solely responsible for the well-being of Indian trappers. Ultimately, term 8 may have had the effect of reconciling the ambiguous HBC claim to Rupertsland with Indian livelihood interests.

THE MANITOBA ACT (1870)

The opposition of the people of Red River to the Dominion of Canada's annexation of the Northwest upset the timetable for the transfer of Rupertsland and the Northwestern Territory to the Dominion of Canada. Led by Louis Riel and his provisional government, the people of Red River forced Canada to address their major concerns in the Manitoba Act of 1870, which provided for the entry of the province of Manitoba into Canada. Although Riel had expressed a strong dislike of the concessions the HBC had won for the surrender of its claims, he approved section 34 of the Manitoba Act, which upheld the transfer agreement. This portion of the act stated that "Nothing in this Act shall in any way prejudice or affect the rights or properties of the HBC, as contained in the conditions under which that Company surrender Rupert's Land to Her Majesty."[38] Thus, the arrangements made with the company were enclosed within the Canadian constitution, beginning with section 146 of the British North America Act, 1867, and closing with section 34 of the Manitoba Act, which was validated by the BNA Act, 1871.

Both the background leading to the Manitoba Act and the drafting of its provisions forced the federal government to ponder and articulate its understanding of

Aboriginal rights to territory. As early as 1864, Simon Dawson, the surveyor of the route from Fort William to Fort Garry that bore his name, had warned Canada that the local Ojibwa would block any attempt to open "a highway without any regard to them, through a territory of which they believe themselves to be the sole lords and masters."[39] The Ojibwa demonstrated the accuracy of Dawson's prediction in 1869, when one of their spokesmen reportedly said:

We are not afraid of the white man; the people whom you go to see at Red River are our Cousins as well as yours, so that friendship between us is proper and natural. We have seen evidence of the power of your Country in the numerous warriors which she has sent forth. The soldiers have been most orderly and quick and they have held out the hand of friendship to the Indians. We believe what you tell us when you say that in your land the Indians have always been treated with clemency and justice and we are not apprehensive for the future, but do not bring Settlers and Surveyors amongst us to measure and occupy our lands until a clear understanding has been arrived at as to what our relations are to be in the time to come.[40]

The following year Colonel Garnet Wolseley, who was leading a military expedition through the North West Angle en route to Manitoba, encountered opposition from disgruntled Ojibwa. The fear of trouble led Colonel Wolseley to distribute presents to them.[41]

The Red River Resistance of Louis Riel and the Métis during the winter of 1869–70 also underlined the importance of recognizing and accommodating Aboriginal title to territory. Riel's negotiators pressed for the establishment of a land base for the Métis, and succeeded in getting included in the Manitoba Act a clause that set aside 1.4 million acres from which the lieutenant-governor would make land grants to "the children of the half-breed heads of families residing in the Province at the time of the said transfer to Canada."[42] The introduction to the clause was explicit about the justification for this allocation of land to the Métis: "And whereas, it is expedient, towards the extinguishment of the Indian Title to the lands in the Province, to appropriate a portion of such ungranted lands, to the extent of one million four hundred thousand acres thereof, for the benefit of the families of the half-breed residents."[43]

In explaining the provision to the House of Commons during the debate on the Manitoba Act, Prime Minister John A. Macdonald was equally clear about the relationship between the Métis land base and Aboriginal title. In language that reflected the assumptions of the government and the times, Macdonald said:

With respect to the lands that are included in the Province, the next clause provides that such of them as do not now belong to individuals, shall belong to the Dominion of Canada, the same being within boundaries already described. There shall, however, out of the lands there, be a reservation for the purpose of extinguishing the Indian title, of 1,200,000 acres.

That land is to be appropriated as a reservation for the purpose of settlement by half breeds
and their children of whatever origin on very much the same principle as lands were appropriated to U.E. Loyalists for purposes of settlement by their children. This reservation,
as I have said, is for the purpose of extinguishing the Indian title and all claims upon the
lands within the limits of the Province ... It is, perhaps, not known to a majority of this
House that the old Indian titles are not extinguished over any portion of this country, except for two miles on each side of the Red River and the Assiniboine.[44]

Later in the debate Macdonald again acknowledged Aboriginal territorial
rights of First Nations. In explaining why the eastern boundary of the new province was drawn where it was, he observed that

The line was fixed at 96 degrees, because a large body of the Sioux Indians, who were
friendly of the Canadian Government, but opposed to the Red River authorities, dwelt to
the east of that line and to hand them over to the new Province would not tend to promote
friendly feelings towards the Canadian Government, or give a peaceful passage to the
troops through their country. If those Indians were handed over without any treaty being
made with them, or without consulting their rights or wishes, they might cut off, or seriously interfere with, communication between the head of Lake Superior and Fort Garry.
For that reason they fixed the eastern boundary at the 96th meridian.[45]

As these incidents and quotations illustrate, the government of Canada reflected upon and articulated its recognition of Aboriginal territorial rights both
before and during the fashioning of the Manitoba Act.

The International Financial Society's takeover of the HBC in 1863 signalled the beginning of fundamental changes that would greatly affect the society that had developed in the fur trade country over the previous two centuries. In the European
sphere of diplomacy, the Rupertsland Order recognized the existence of certain obligations, and, not surprisingly, later in the European/First Nations sphere of diplomacy treaty-making, livelihood obligations, and land were discussed. The transfer
of Rupertsland in 1870 foretold a shift between the fur trade era and the treaty-
making period. Under HBC rule, the relationship between Indians and Whites had
been primarily a socioeconomic one. In April of 1869, Colonial Secretary
Granville had communicated the "expectations of Her Majesty's Government,"
not the least of which was that responsibility for the Indian population was to be
shifted from the HBC to the Canadian government.

In effect, two claims to the HBC territory existed in the 1860s: one based on
Aboriginal occupation prior to European arrival and the other on the 1670
charter. The two claims to Rupertsland were not given equal consideration. During the three-party negotiations of 1869 and 1870, the English and Canadians

gave priority to the HBC's territorial claims and the remuneration that the company was to receive for yielding them. The compensation proved to be substantial. Between 1905 and 1922 the company yielded hefty dividends for its shareholders, ranging from 20 to 50 percent, largely because of land sales.[46] From 1891 to 1930 these sales earned net profits of $96,366,021, well in excess of the £2 million shareholders had invested in 1863.[47] Likewise, the HBC's land sales were far greater than the £1 million value that the Colonial Office had put on the company's claim to Rupertsland in 1869. Finally, it is noteworthy that the HBC land grant was significantly larger than the lands set aside for Indian reserves. There is no doubt that the "equitable principles" referred to in the Address of 1867 were not reflected in the manner in which the two claims were recognized.

CHAPTER FIVE

Precedents from Treaties 1, 2, and 3

After the Rupertsland Order and the Manitoba Act, 1870, took effect, Indians lobbied officials representing the dominion government in Manitoba about the land
question. In the treaty talks that followed, the use of land for the pursuit of a livelihood took on new political and legal meanings. In the early 1870s Treaties 1
(Stone Fort), 2 (Manitoba Post), and 3 (North West Angle) established a treaty relationship between the Dominion of Canada and various Cree and Ojibwa nations. Geographically, these treaties covered parts of what is now southern
Manitoba and northwestern Ontario. In both historical and geographical terms,
Treaties 1, 2, and 3 are relevant to treaties subsequently made in Saskatchewan.[1]
The lieutenant-governor of Manitoba, Alexander Morris, who negotiated Treaties
3 through 6, commented on the historical significance of Treaty 3: "This treaty
was one of great importance, as it not only tranquilized the large Indian population affected by it, but eventually shaped the terms of all the treaties, 4, 5, 6 and 7,
which have since been made with the Indians of the North-West Territories – who
speedily became apprised of the concessions which had been granted to the
Ojibbeway nation."[2] Certainly the written versions of these earliest "numbered"
treaties framed the terms offered at later treaty talks. The experience of negotiating these treaties also shaped the approaches that Crown treaty commissioners
took. And as Morris indicated, natives spread word of the terms of treaties to their
kinfolk in "unceded" territories.

For the above reasons, an analysis of the treaty-making process in southern
Manitoba and northwestern Ontario before 1874 is pertinent to understanding
the Saskatchewan treaties. We will focus on identifying the pattern of negotiations and highlighting the issues that Indian nations and the Crown were concerned about during the treaty-making events that created Treaties 1, 2, and 3.
Our analysis is not organized chronologically, nor are the separate treaties our
units of analysis. This is because these treaties are interrelated; Treaties 1 and 2
are nearly identical, and several attempts to get the Ojibwa of Treaty 3 to treat
occurred at the same time that the Crown was dealing with the Cree and Ojibwa

of Manitoba. The emphasis here is on analyzing the written records related to treaty-making between 1870 and 1875 and not the terms of the written treaties. The 1875 revision to Treaties 1 and 2 is also considered. In particular, we present information that is relevant to understanding the interrelationship between Indian title and future livelihood.

For Treaties 1 and 3 considerable documentation exists; however, little exists for Treaty 2. In essence the records pertaining to Treaty 1 are directly relevant to Treaty 2. Indian Commissioner Wemyss McKenzie Simpson, who negotiated Treaties 1 and 2, reported laconically on the Manitoba Post Treaty: "but on my speaking to the leading men of the bands assembled, it was evident that the Indians of this part had no special demands to make, but having a knowledge of the former treaty, desired to be dealt with in the same manner and on the same terms as those adopted by the Indians of the Province of Manitoba."[3] In contrast with the Stone Fort Treaty talks, Simpson noted that "The negotiations with these bands therefore occupied little time."[4] Interestingly, the version of Treaty 1 that had been conveyed to the Indians in the Treaty 2 area was acceptable to Simpson.

THE WRITTEN TERMS OF TREATIES 1, 2, AND 3

Each of the western or numbered treaties began by stressing "the desire of Her Majesty, to open up to settlement" a particular tract of country by obtaining the consent of "her Indian subjects inhabiting the said tract" through a treaty resulting in "peace and goodwill" between the Indians and Her Majesty, since they could be assured of "Her Majesty's *bounty and benevolence.*"[5] In effect, this language indicates the objectives of the treaty-making process: opening areas for settlement in exchange for the Crown's bounty and benevolence, thereby ensuring peace and goodwill.

After lengthy talks, Treaty 1 was signed at the HBC post Lower Fort Garry on 3 August 1871. Wemyss M. Simpson, Indian commissioner, signed for the Crown; the treaty was witnessed by Adams G. Archibald, lieutenant-governor of Manitoba and the North-West Territory, and James McKay, among others (a full list of Indian signatories and other witnesses is given in table A2).[6] Treaty 2 was concluded at the Manitoba House post on 21 August 1871. Simpson signed for the Crown, and Mekis, Sonsense, Masahkeeyash, and François and Richard Woodhouse signed for their bands. Archibald, McKay, and Molyneux St John witnessed this treaty. Treaty 3 was signed at the North West Angle on 3 October 1873. Lieutenant-Governor Alexander Morris, and Indian Commissioners J.A.N. Provencher and S.J. Dawson signed for the government.[7] The twenty-four Indian signatories are listed in table A2. Witnesses who played active roles in the Treaty 3 negotiations included James McKay, M. St John, Robert Pether, Charles Nolin, and Pierre LeVieller.[8]

The written terms for Treaties 1, 2, and 3 and the 1875 revisions to Treaties 1 and 2 are summarized in table A3. Treaty 1 pledged Indians subject to the treaty to maintain perpetual peace between themselves and Whites and to neither interfere with property nor molest Her Majesty's subjects. Treaty 2 and subsequent treaties added that Indians should behave as good and loyal subjects of Her Majesty; respect, obey, and abide by the law; maintain peace and good order between themselves and other Indian tribes; not interfere with any person passing through the said tract; and assist officers in bringing justice and punishment to any Indian offending the treaty or Her Majesty's laws. Despite concessions that increased the size of reserves (from 160 to 640 acres), the written version of each new treaty tended to reinforce government control over reserve lands and resources. Treaties 1 and 2 discussed the location of reserves with respect to specific bands and chiefs, whereas subsequent treaties did not imply specific reserve sites but stated only that reserves will be located "where it shall be deemed most convenient and advantageous" for Indian bands by officers for the government and that "such selection shall be so made after conference with the Indians."[9] The government was also given authority in the later treaties to decide about conflicting claims. These treaties also specified that reserve surrenders could occur for public works but that such surrenders could not occur without Indian consent.

Treaties 1 and 2 do not refer to hunting or fishing rights. In Treaty 3, Her Majesty agrees with the Indians that they "shall have right to pursue their avocations of hunting and fishing throughout the tract surrendered."[10] While the written treaty acknowledges this right, it is "subject to such regulations as may from time to time" be made by the government and excludes areas "taken up for settlement, mining, lumbering or other purposes."[11]

The revisions to Treaties 1 and 2 increased the annuities, so as to conform to the provision for annuities in Treaty 3. The government agreed to provide items that had been agreed to at the Treaty 1 talks, while the Indians agreed to "abandon all claim whatever against the Government in connection with the so-called 'outside promises' other than those contained in the memorandum attached to the treaty."[12]

FACTORS INFLUENCING A DOMINION TREATY POLICY

When the Dominion of Canada began to think about establishing a framework for "surrendering" Indian title in western Canada, it looked to the HBC for advice. Immediately following the 1870 transfer of Rupertsland, for instance, the Canadian government asked the company for information on the First Nations population and sought policy advice.[13] In June 1871, HBC governor Stafford Northcote reported a communiqué from Prime Minister John A. Macdonald: "I am very anxious, indeed, that we should be able to deal with the Indians upon satisfactory terms. They are the great difficulty in these newly civilized countries. They are the great difficulty with which the Americans have to contend in their new countries. The Hudson's Bay Company have dealt with the Indians in a thoroughly satisfactory way. The policy of Canada is also to deal with the Indians in a satisfactory manner."[14] Macdonald intended no departure from the relationship that the HBC had established with First Nations.

Macdonald was also aware that the HBC had the administrative capacity to maintain a relationship with Indians on behalf of the dominion and therefore suggested that the HBC could assist with the implementation of treaties: "It would be of advantage to us, & no doubt it would be of advantage to you, that we should be allowed to make use of your officers & your posts for the purpose of making those payments to the Indians which will have to be made annually by the Government of Canada in order to satisfy their claims & keep in good humour. The Indians had a title to some of these lands which is now extinguished – upon which certain terms involve annual payments; & it would be of great advantage that we should be able to employ officers, who are known to these Indians in order to make these payments & keep the Indians in good humour."[15] While the dominion government chose to set up its own bureaucracy, Macdonald's suggestions to Northcote indicate that he recognized that maintaining the existing relationship between the Indians and the HBC was a desirable objective.

The pre-Confederation treaties in Upper Canada, especially the Robinson Treaties of 1850, influenced the process in western Canada. Lieutenant-Governor of Manitoba and the North-West Territories and treaty negotiator Alexander Morris commented in 1880 that the Honourable William B. Robinson "discharged his duties with great tact and judgment, succeeding in making 2 treaties, which were the forerunners of the future treaties, and shaped their course."[16] The deputy superintendent general of Indian Affairs in the early 1870s, William Spragge, had negotiated the Manitoulin Island Treaty in 1860. He acknowledged the purpose of the treaty approach to Aboriginal title when he pointed out that "the inconvenience and danger of attempting to pass over the territorial rights" had been avoided.[17]

These Upper Canada treaties helped inform the government's basic approach to Indian title in Rupertsland, and the connections between treaty-making in the former Rupertsland and Upper Canada were explained to Indians during the Treaty 1 talks. Secretary of State Howe provided Indian Commissioner Simpson with a copy of the Robinson Treaty along with his instructions.[18] Lieutenant-Governor A.G. Archibald stated during Treaty 1 talks that the Queen "can do for you no more than she has done for her red children in the East. If she were to do more for you, that would be unjust for them."[19] Despite the Robinson Huron-Superior treaties and the Manitoulin Island treaty, a comprehensive approach to Aboriginal rights in western Canada had not been worked out in advance of the annexation of Rupertsland. The differences between these two groups of treaties can be explained by the particular bargaining strategies adopted by First Nations.

The provisional nature of Indian policy at the time of the Rupertsland Transfer is evident in the instructions to the "first" lieutenant-governor appointed by the dominion. On 28 September 1869, W. McDougall was directed to "make a full report upon the state of the Indian tribes now in the Territories – their numbers, wants and claims; the system heretobefore pursued by the Hudson['s] Bay Company in dealing with them – accompanied by any suggestions you may desire to offer with reference to their protection, and to the improvement of their condition."[20]

The particular circumstances of Indians, their relationship to the HBC, and their claims were relevant information for Ottawa officials. Significantly, protection of Indians and "improvement of their condition" was of interest to dominion politicians. These instructions were consistent with the Rupertsland Order, and Donald A. Smith, who was sent out to represent the dominion government's intentions to people of Red River was also instructed to report on "the most advisable mode of dealing with the Indian Tribes in the North-West Territories."[21]

Similarly, the first actual lieutenant-governor of Manitoba and the North-West Territories, Adams G. Archibald, had some input into the treaty process, since he was to "ascertain and report to His Excellency the course you may think most advisable to pursue, whether by treaty or otherwise, for the removal of any obstruction that may be presented to the flow of population into the fertile lands that lie between Manitoba and the Rocky Mountains."[22]

These instructions reveal the dominion government's priorities more clearly: the entire process was subordinated to the settlement of the West. Moreover, the government was willing to consider alternatives to treaties in order to deal with the perceived obstruction that Indians represented to expansionism. J. Howe advised the Privy Council that Indian Commissioner Simpson was to "be instructed to confer, from time to time, with the Lieut. Governor of Manitoba, who will consult and co-operate with him."[23] The instructions to McDougall, Smith, and Archibald suggest that obtaining information on Indians and establishing a relationship with Indian nations were high priorities for the assertion of a dominion presence in the old territory of Rupertsland.

Treaties 1, 2, and 3 did not merely duplicate the Robinson, Huron-Superior, and Manitoulin Island treaties. The instructions to the lieutenant-governors help explain why. They also reveal that government negotiators needed information from local sources and solicited it. For instance, Lake Superior politician S.J. Dawson advised the government on treaty matters. His knowledge of the Fort Francis area led him to recommend setting aside exclusive fisheries and gardens for Indians who lived there and to suggest marking off vast areas as Indian hunting territories. The timber and mineral wealth of these tracts also would ensure a fund for Indian annuities.[24] In effect, Dawson had proposed a scheme that would secure Indian livelihoods, provided that resource industries continued to generate revenues and royalties.

Secretary of State of Canada Joseph Howe pointed out to Indian Commissioner W.M. Simpson that the "powers intrusted [sic] to you are large" and that the government depended "upon the exercise of your judgment in fixing the price." Simpson was to secure terms favourable to the government and at a maximum cash payment of twelve dollars per annum for a family of five.[25] Thus representatives of the Crown had the power to negotiate an agreement.

Just before Treaty 1 a conference had taken place between Archibald, Simpson, S.J. Dawson, Robert Pether, and Hon. James McKay.[26] Dawson and Pether had accompanied Simpson through northwestern Ontario, and they had met with the Ojibwa about the need to treat. (Later they participated in the negotiation of Treaty 3.) James McKay, a member of the Executive Council of Manitoba, was described by Morris as "a half-breed intimately acquainted with the Indian tribes, and possessed of much influence over them."[27] Among personnel participating in treaty-making, McKay is a central figure. His name and signature usually appear immediately after Archibald or Morris on Treaties 1, 2, 3, 5, and 6. He was also involved in the ratification of the revisions to Treaties 1 and 2. The text of several treaties indicates that the treaties were signed and witnessed after "having been first read and explained by the Honorable James McKay." Morris frequently acknowledged McKay's important role in the treaty process. For example, in 1875, after meeting with the Portage band, he reported to the minister of the interior that "In conclusion I have to express my obligations to the Hon. Mr. Mckay for the valuable services he rendered me. The Indians told me they would not have come into the Stone Fort Treaty but for him, and I know it was the case."[28]

McKay has been recognized as an interpreter, but he was more than that. Reverend Henry Cochrane was in fact the government's interpreter at Treaty 1 talks.[29] But on 12 August 1871, early on in the negotiations, the Manitoban reported that "The Commissioner [Simpson] explained, and Hon. Mr. McKay, at the request of the Governor [Archibald] and the Indians, also entered into very full explanations in Indian." Later McKay played an essential role when the Treaty 3 talks broke down. Thus, McKay might also be regarded as an important influence on Canada's treaty policy.

Canada's approach to Indian title and the future of the Indian population was not cast in stone with the unfolding of the 1870 transfer. Basic information and advice on the Indian populations of the newly acquired Rupertsland were required by Ottawa-based decision makers. The fact that it was soliciting information from locals and providing negotiators with "large powers" indicates that the dominion government did not have an inviolable draft treaty. The Indian nations therefore had scope to influence the relationship created by treaty negotiations. Because they had an economic and social agenda for securing a future livelihood, the details of the terms of the treaties had to be negotiated. Otherwise an agreement would not have been reached.

TERRITORY AND RESOURCES:
GOVERNMENT PRIORITIES IN TREATIES 1, 2 AND 3

The territorial dimension of the treaty process was based on the government's geographical interest in particular areas and the particular priorities of Indian nations after 1869 with regard to treating with the Crown, as a response to the influx of settlers. The government's appraisal of the diverse and potential wealth of these territories established the parameters for the timing and location of treaty talks. Although often defined in ambiguous terms, the written terms provide boundaries defining a particular territory in which title was to be ceded.

The dominion's main interest in formally treating with Indians – to clear what it understood to be "Indian title" to facilitate an agricultural and commercial frontier – is well known. But not all the land ceded in territories of Treaties 1 and 2 was prime agricultural land, and Treaty 3 was not of particular agricultural significance.

Before initiating Treaty 1 talks, Archibald reported to Howe, "We were all of opinion that it would be desirable to procure the extinction of the Indian title, not only to the lands included within the Province, but also to so much of the timber grounds east and north of the Province, as were required for immediate entry and use, and also of a large tract of cultivable ground, west of the Portage, which, having very few Indian inhabitants, might be conceded with very little additional cost."[30] Consequently, Archibald recommended "negotiations at the Lower Fort with the Indians of the Province, and certain adjacent timber Districts."[31] Thus the commercial rationale for Treaties 1 and 2 was the acquisition of agricultural land and timber resources.

The Indians east of Manitoba came under Treaty 3, but the dominion had formerly acknowledged their rights when presents were given to them in 1870 so that Colonel Wolseley's troops could pass through their lands en route to the Red River settlement. Several efforts to negotiate a treaty for this territory had failed; nonetheless, obtaining this area was a priority for the Crown. A corridor between Thunder Bay and Fort Garry, along with any land that could be thrown "open to settlement" and that might be "susceptible of improvement and profitable occupation" were the dominion government's main reasons for wanting a treaty with Indians in what became known as Northwestern Ontario.[32] Lieutenant-Governor Alexander Morris recalled that Treaty 3 resulted in the opening up of a territory "of great importance to Canada, embracing as it does the Pacific Railway route to the North-West Territories ... and, as is believed, great mineral resources."[33] From the beginning, government officials knew that various forms of commercial wealth could be obtained from Indian lands.

Despite the dominion's resource and location priorities, a certain territorial ambiguity with respect to treaty boundaries is evident. Consequently, the particular traditional hunting grounds of some bands are not well represented by the territory defined by the treaty text. In some areas only a portion of the Indians occupying the territory were included in the original treaty negotiations. Morris was alert to the possibility that if boundaries were not properly defined, Indian title to some areas might be left unextinguished.[34] The northern boundaries of Treaties 1 and 2 were problematic, since they ran along the east shore of Lake Winnipeg and included the hunting territories of bands not participating in the negotiations. Some bands made use of lands on both sides of Lake Winnipeg and the islands in between. In 1875, the surveyor-general was not certain whether or not the islands around Grindstone Point on Lake Winnipeg had been surrendered.[35] The Berens River band had been invited to Treaty 1 negotiations and their hunting territory had been partly ceded by this treaty. A mix-up had occurred: members of the band got hungry waiting for the commissioner, which had somewhat soured their interest in negotiating a treaty.[36] Similarly, some Indians occupying lands just west of the Interlake in an area clearly described by Treaty 2 were not party to that treaty and ended up signing Treaty 4.

OUTLINE OF TREATY PROCESS AND GOVERNMENT APPROACHES TO NEGOTIATIONS

The dominion's intent to treat with the Indians in the province of Manitoba was formalized with a proclamation of 18 July 1871 that called upon various Indians "to enter into negotiations on the subject of an Indian Treaty" with the commissioner of Her Most Gracious Majesty, the Queen.[37] The talks held at the Stone Fort in the summer of 1871 were a major event in the early political history of the province of Manitoba. Towards the end of July 1871, Indian bands gathered at the Stone Fort, or Lower Fort Garry, an HBC post, but negotiations were delayed for a few days.

A correspondent from the local newspaper, the *Manitoban*, provided a description of the site of the treaty on 29 July 1871, just before the talks began:

This accession to the encampment, which immediately adjoins Lower Fort Garry, will increase the number of tents to 100 or 120, and make a very lively scene. The encampment is in the form of a semicircle, with the chiefs' lodges – near which a handsome flag flies – in the centre. Of the followers, it must be said that they are apparently very comfortable. Most of their lodges are of birch bark, but a considerable number have good tents. Each lodge or tent has a fire in front or inside, where the Indian women are everlastingly baking bread or making tea. Any number of horses and dogs roam through the camp, and along in the afternoons one or more large crowds gathered near the tents.

According to a 1926 map, the negotiations were conducted at the northeast corner of the fort, just outside the stone walls. At times, more than a thousand Indians participated, and many White and Métis residents of Red River also attended.

Representatives of the dominion were aware that their authority had to be evident. Troops were on hand, in part to prevent trade in liquor and in part because, according to Lieutenant-Governor Archibald, "Military display has always a great effect on savages, and the presence, even of a few troops, will have a good tendency."[38] Secretary of State Joseph Howe advised the Privy Council that the Indian commissioner should "be allowed to wear an uniform, without which they [Indians] are slow to believe that any one, having the Queen's authority, can be sent to treat with them."[39] A uniform might seem to have been an unnecessary affectation; however, Indians needed to be assured that they were entering into negotiations with individuals possessing the authority to negotiate a treaty. Given a legacy of misrepresentation of intentions with respect to Indian title during the colonial era, a problem that the Royal Proclamation of 1763 acknowledged, the appearance of authority was a means to confirm the Crown's intentions.

Other protocols were evident. Morris reported on the beginning of the North West Angle Treaty: "On arriving, the Indians, who were already there, came up to the house I occupied, in procession, headed by braves bearing a banner and a Union Jack, and accompanied by others beating drums. They asked leave to perform a dance in my honor, after which they presented to me the pipe of peace."[40] Morris's party reciprocated, and provided the Indians with provisions. Similarly, at the Treaty 1 talks Chief Henry Prince (Miskookenew) "made a speech in which he expressed strong attachment to the British flag."[41]

An important step once the Indians had gathered was to get them to formally select chiefs and headmen for each band so that the treaty could be negotiated. This procedure was considered essential to avoid the problem of the Selkirk Treaty (1817), since, according to Archibald, some "Indians now deny that these men ever were chiefs or had authority to sign the Treaty."[42] Clearly, the Selkirk Treaty had not been forgotten, and the representatives of the Crown wanted to be sure that the Indians that they were dealing with had the authority to treat.

With respect to the pre-Saskatchewan treaties, a useful official document that provides extrinsic evidence concerning the process was titled "Memorandum of an Address to the Indians by the Lieutenant-Governor of Manitoba." This statement by Archibald to the Indians assembled at the Treaty 1 talks reveals important features of the government's intent. In effect, it is the Crown's initial position with respect to Indian title in what had been Rupertsland. On one level, the tone seems patronizing and makes frequent use of the expressions "red children" and "Your Great Mother, the Queen, [who] wishes to do justice to all her children alike."[43] On the other hand, such metaphors might not have been regarded as Eurocentric paternalism in 1871; rather, with such symbolic language, the Queen's representative assured the Indians that a treaty would create an enduring relationship with the Crown, since "mother" and "children" are kinship terms.

Archibald's address provided additional meaning to the terms of the treaty. On the question of reserves, he stated: "Your Great Mother, therefore, will lay aside for you 'Lots' of land to be used by you and your children forever. She will not allow the white man to intrude upon these Lots. She will make rules to keep them for you, so that, as long as the sun shall shine, there shall be no Indian who has not a place that he can call his home, where he can go and pitch his camp, or if he chooses, build his house and till his land."[44]

Once they were assured that they would not be dispossessed outright, Archibald explained to the Indians what was meant by a reserve: "These reserves will be large enough, but you must not expect them to be larger than will be enough to give a farm to each family, where farms shall be required. They will enable you to earn a living should the chase fail, and should you choose to get your living by tilling, you must not expect to have included in your reserve more of hay grounds than will be reasonably sufficient for your purposes in case you adopt the habits of farmers."[45]

Interestingly, in his opening address, Archibald did not state exactly what was to be surrendered or given up. The nature of Aboriginal title, according to the Crown, was never made explicit. The general impression was left that room was being made for White settlers and that Indians would not be dispossessed and that they could continue to hunt over much of the country as they always had. In this sense, his address did not comport with the language used in the written treaty to the effect that Indians forever cede, release, surrender, and yield up all lands.

During Treaty 1 negotiations, the government's position stressed that Indians would not have to make drastic changes or a sudden economic transition. Archibald stated that the Queen would only recommend adopting the security of agriculture. Consequently, Archibald indicated, "the Queen, though she may think it good for you to adopt civilized habits, has no idea of compelling you to do so. This she leaves to your choice, and you need not live like the white man unless you can be persuaded to do so with your own free will."[46] Archibald then drew attention to the agricultural pursuits of the St Peters Indians to indicate a viable livelihood.

Thus, rather than getting into legal theories of Aboriginal title, Archibald presented the early treaties as a way of allowing Indians to adjust to changing times: the outcome of treaty with the Crown would not be disruptive for Indian nations; very little would be given up, the Queen would be benevolent, reserves would provide security, the traditional livelihood would continue; Indians could continue to hunt, if they chose to do so but they would be given the opportunity of pursuing agriculture. In effect, Archibald, as a representative of the Crown, gave verbal assurances, documented by the memorandum of his address, that a viable future livelihood was the main intent of the treaty. Apparently, Indians accepted this objective of the treaty process. In his official report on Treaties 1 and 2,

Simpson recorded that the Indians "are fully impressed with the idea that the amelioration of their present condition is one of the objects of Her Majesty in making these treaties."[47] Clearly, Indian Commissioner Simpson did not regard the treaty simply as a narrowly conceived land transaction.

During the Treaty 1 talks, the relationship between Indian livelihood and land was not fully appreciated by dominion officials. With regard to the Indian demand for large reserves, the Queen's representatives maintained a less than conciliatory position. According to Archibald,

In defining the limits of their reserves, so far as we could see, they wished to have about two-thirds of the Province. We heard them out, and then told them it was quite clear that they had entirely misunderstood the meaning and intention of Reserves. We explained the object of these in something like the language of the Memorandum [Archibald's opening address] enclosed, and then told them it was of no use for them to entertain any such ideas, which were entirely out of the question. We told them that whether they wished it or not, immigrants would come in and fill up the country; that every year from this one twice as many in number as their whole people there assembled, would pour into the Province, and in a little while would spread all over it, and that now was the time for them to come to an arrangement that would secure homes and annuities for themselves and their children.[48]

Rather than giving careful calculation to the livelihood needs of Indians in a post-treaty-making era, dominion officials spoke of the inevitability of White settlement. Simpson recalled that at Treaty 1 talks "the peculiar circumstances surrounding the position of the Indians of the Province were pointed out" and "the future of the country predicted."[49] However, White settlement of Indian lands without Indian consent was inconsistent with the Royal Proclamation of 1763 and the commitments that the dominion had made during the transfer of Rupertsland. The threat of unrestrained White settlement was also a development that government officials had sought to avoid since the Mica Bay incident of 1849. Nevertheless, there were clearly limits to how much land Indians could reserve following treaties, and thus the scope of bargaining and negotiation was restricted.

Agents of the Crown employed other strategies, such as exploiting differences among the Indians, to bring treaty talks to a conclusion, strategies that became more apparent during more difficult talks. An example is provided by the Treaty 3 negotiations with the Ojibwa of northwestern Ontario, which were extremely trying for the government officials. At one difficult point the talks had reached an impasse, and in response, Lieutenant-Governor Alexander Morris had stated tersely, "Then the Council is at an end."[50] The Ojibwa had also refused to give in, and one chief had stated, "Our chiefs have the same opinion; they will not change their decision."[51] However, Morris had detected a split between the Ojibwa bands that had gathered for Treaty 3, and he had reasons to suspect that

not all the chiefs were of the same opinion.[52] When he had indicated a willingness to break off the talks, the chief from Lac Seul had responded that he was
willing to treat with Morris. Morris countered that he would rather treat with the
whole nation but that if that was not possible, he was willing to treat with individual bands. He suggested that all the Indians council among themselves and
that he would remain another day.

A council was held in the evening. The next morning, certain well-known Red
River Métis – James McKay, Pierre LeVieller, Charles Nolin, and a Mr Genton –
were sent to attend and advise the Indian council. Shortly thereafter Indian Commissioner J.A.N. Provencher and Molyneux St John, a member of Morris's
party, joined the council and interviewed the chiefs, after which the treaty conference was reconvened.[53] The Ojibwa agreed to the treaty, and after the terms
had been discussed, the Fort Francis chief told Morris, "I wish you to understand
you owe the treaty much to the Half-breeds" – a reference to the Red River Métis
members of Morris's delegation.[54]

Thus, in this example of government strategy, Morris used threats, exploited a
split among the Ojibwa bands, and then had the help of influential Métis to bring
both Indian factions together to accept the treaty. Significantly, what McKay, the
other Red River Métis, and the chiefs said at the Ojibwa council is not a matter
of record.

Generally, once the parties reached an agreement, government officials prepared the treaty for signing; at Treaty 1, payments had commenced the day after
the signing. Morris explained that once an agreement had been reached in Treaty
3, Chief Mawedopenais came forward and stated, "And now, in closing this
council, I take off my glove, and in giving you my hand, I deliver over my birth-
right, and lands, and in taking your hand I hold fast all the promises you have
made, and I hope they will last as long as the sun goes around, and the water
flows, as you have said."[55] Morris replied, "I accept your hand, and with it the
lands, and will keep all my promises, in the firm belief that the treaty now to be
signed will bind the red man and the white man together as friends forever."[56]
The conference adjourned, the treaty was prepared, and then it was signed and
witnessed. The Ojibwa were paid the next day.

INDIAN PRIORITIES: LAND AND LIVELIHOOD

Treaty-making involved an unequal meeting of two property systems. Unfortunately, this aspect of the process has not received much attention, and it is poorly
understood, in part because the terms describing ownership, land use, and occupancy are used in an imprecise way in the historical records and scholarly literature. Furthermore, conflicting scholarly theories about the nature of Aboriginal
tenure systems add to the confusion. What the documentary record pertaining to
treaty negotiations does make clear is that Indian chiefs were well informed about

land and resource issues, both in terms of their own needs and of the values Whites placed on them. Significantly, Indians wanted to establish treaty relations with the Crown to address their Aboriginal interest in the land.

Shortly after the signing of Treaties 1 and 2, Native clergyman James Settee observed, "The Indian family in general were always under the impression that the foreigners were usurpers [and] destroyers of their race and Country; that is this land belonged to them exclusively; that they had sole claim to the rock[,] ground, grass, timber[,] the fish & its water; that all these things were created for them only."[57] Settee's observation underlines the Indians' strong sense of exclusive resource ownership. His reference to the Indian family suggests a hunting-territory tenure system based on family stewardship. Significantly, problems of livelihood and land predate the treaty talks with foreigners, who were seen as usurpers and destroyers. Not only did Indians claim to own a full range of resources, but they believed these resources were created specifically for them.

In his address opening Treaty 1 talks, Lieutenant-Governor Archibald alluded to how Indians expressed a desire for a treaty shortly after his arrival in Manitoba. Manuscript sources recording the period between the establishment of an administration in Manitoba and the signing of Treaty 1 substantiate this point. Shortly after his arrival he received word from John Schultz that Chief Henry Prince of St Peters was anxious to meet with the lieutenant-governor. A week later, Prince raised the issue of a treaty with Archibald, but the lieutenant-governor responded that he was too busy to treat with the Indians.[58] He successfully stalled talks for almost a year.

In the fall of 1870, Archibald corresponded about the necessity of dealing with Indian title and the disorganization at Red River; however, he was not ready to treat with Indians until he was "in possession of information as to the occupation and rights of the different Tribes, facts that the Indians disputed among themselves and of which the Whites could not be expected to be very well informed."[59] Chief Prince was not alone in his desire for a treaty. A memorial from seventy Fairford Indians to Archibald indicated a willingness to sell the land, as "the above named Indians as in Council do agree to Sell by Treaty when the appointed time for such Sale shall arrive all such Lands as may be desired by Your Excellency and Council save this our Reserve."[60] (A large reserve area was indicated by map.) Moreover, the memorialists claimed a property right by asking Archibald, as a representative of the Dominion of Canada "to take cognizance of this our Notice to the prevention by your Excellency's Notice of all infringements on our Reserve Rights of Fishing, Hunting cutting timber and taking up of Claims on this our Reserve by the Hudson's Bay Company or any other Individuals so Trespassing."[61] By claiming a large area as a reserve, these Fairford Indians sought a treaty to recognize their property and looked to the Crown to protect them from trespass.

Indian anticipation of the impact of settlers predates the transfer of Rupertsland and the demise of the buffalo. Research by Richard Daniel has revealed that

Indians were even preparing for a treaty prior to the transfer of Rupertsland; Sault-eaux and Cree chiefs of Assiniboia had met in the winter of 1868–69 to establish boundaries for their specific territorial claims.[62] Pressure for a treaty was created by Portage la Prairie Indians when they denied settlers use-rights to resources. In May of 1870 Indians from Portage complained about settlers taking their wood and requested a treaty.[63] In June of 1871 Indians posted a notice on a church door informing settlers that "we have not yet received anything for our lands, therefore they still belong to us."[64] The notice also stated, "Why we speak to day, is because we are poor but we still hold the land for our children that will be born after-wards."[65] The Portage band's concerns about pre-treaty settler encroachment were further alluded to by Alexander Morris in 1875: "In 1868 a number of Ontario farmers had settled on Rat Creek. Yellow Quill's band drove them off and trouble was impending. [HBC] Governor McTavish [Mactavish] sent Mr. [James] McKay up to arrange the difficulty, in anticipation of the advent of Canadian power. He made a lease for 3 years of their rights, assuring them that before that time the Canadian Government would make a treaty with them and recognize the tempo-rary arrangement, and in consequence the settlers were unmolested."[66]

The Musk Rat Creek area was the western limit of the settlement lands cov-ered by the two-mile strip provided for in the Selkirk Treaty. Archibald had suc-ceeded in delaying a treaty, but he noted, "as soon as the spring opened they became anxious about the Treaty. They have sent repeated messages enquiring when the Treaty was to come off, and appeared very much disappointed at the delay."[67] The Portage band in particular articulated property rights and took ac-tion to protect them from trespass. Thus, the actions of the Portage and Fairford bands suggest that Indians were looking to a treaty with the Crown as a means to protect their rights.

The question of Indian title was not simply of interest to the dominion offi-cials. All versions of the lists of rights from the provisional government at Red River (1869–70) called for treaties with Indians. On 1 February 1870 the Convention of Forty agreed to article fifteen of the Bill of Rights, which read, "That treaties be concluded between the Dominion and the several Indian tribes of the Country," and in the course of discussion William Bunn, with support from Louis Riel and Reverend Cochrane, had "as soon as possible" added. James Ross, leader of the English-speaking Métis, had further suggested that the wording "with the view of satisfying them with respect to their claims to the lands of this Country" be added.[68] The need for a treaty was recognized by all the long-term residents of Red River, especially those who had settled on lands based on a tenure originating with the Selkirk Treaty of 1817.

Other sources make it clear that some Indians had been thinking in terms of economic and social change, future livelihood, and Aboriginal title for some time. The prospect had been foreseen by Henry Prince's father, Chief Peguis, when he wrote to the Aborigines Protection Society (ca. 1857): "We are not only willing but very anxious after being paid for our lands, that the whites would come and settle down among us, for we have already derived great benefits from their having done so, that is, not the traders, but the farmers. The traders have never done anything but rob and keep us poor, but the farmers have taught us how to farm and raise cattle."[69]

Chief Peguis' interest in a treaty follows the treaties made between Robinson and the Ojibwa of the north shores of Lakes Huron and Superior (1850). No doubt Chief Peguis was aware of development among the Ojibwa of the Robinson Treaty territories in the 1850s.[70] Significantly, he wrote this request long before any proposals for western treaties with the Dominion of Canada, but at a time when HBC monopoly rule was uncertain. Peguis understood that the land belonged to Indians as property that could be paid for prior to widespread settlement. He also expressed an awareness of the advantages and disadvantages of agriculture and trapping and demonstrated an understanding of the dangers and prospects of White settlement well before the end of company rule. He suggested that "before whites will be again permitted to take possession of our lands, we wish that a fair and mutually advantageous treaty be entered into with my tribe for their lands."[71] HBC historian E.E. Rich noted that Peguis had demanded a rent in wheat from the colony's settlers, a proposition that assumed a sense of ownership or right.[72]

In 1871 Indian Commissioner Simpson reported that "Indians were anxiously awaiting my arrival, and were much excited on the subject of their lands being occupied, without attention being first given to their claims for compensation."[73] Settlers were also anxious for a treaty; as Simpson explained, "an uneasy feeling existed, arising partly from the often-repeated demands of the Indians for a Treaty with themselves."[74] Because the scope of land claims would have been narrowed had White settlement preceded the consideration of the question of Indian title by the Crown, the political pressure Indians mounted was focused on the question of land and resources, and a desire to treat as soon as possible was expressed. Thus, the treaties did not catch First Nations unprepared, and they played a forceful role in initiating the process.

Statements attributed to Indians during treaty negotiations illustrate that they believed they had Aboriginal property rights. Treaty 3 records provide important documentation on the Indian approach to the negotiations. Before the Treaty 3 talks began, the chiefs had wanted to be "recompensed" for building houses on a section of the route connecting Lake Superior and Red River and for steamboats and wood, which they claimed as theirs. This grievance was referred to as "past promises" by the Ojibwa and was raised before they would entertain any discussion of the treaty.[75] To dispute these claims, Morris suggested that "Wood and water were the gift of the Great Spirit, and were made alike for the good of both the white man and red man."[76] In effect, Morris was suggesting that resources were to be shared.

Although Morris argued that "We are all children of the same Great Spirit, and are subject to the same Queen," in order to undermine exclusive claims to land and resources, the Ojibwa continued to press their rights.[77] A Treaty 3 chief made the point that "it was the Indian's country, not the white man's."[78] Chief Mawedopenais stated, "We think where we are is our property. I will tell you what he [the Great Spirit] said to us when he planted us here; the rules that we should follow – us Indians – He has given us rules that we should follow to govern us rightly." And Chief Mawedoponais understood the context of the treaty: *"The sound of the rustling of the gold is under my feet where I stand; we have a rich country*; it is the Great Spirit who gave us this; where we stand upon is the Indians' property, and belongs to them."[79]

Furthermore, Chief Mawdopenais made it clear to Morris that Indians would not take a passive position on the question of title, stating, "If you grant us our requests you will not go back without making the treaty." However, "The white man has robbed us of our riches, and we don't wish to give them up again without getting something in their place."[80] In the Treaty 3 area, Indians obviously held a sense of tribal territorial ownership, which included the idea that Indians had the right to surrender or transfer that ownership and to benefit from their resources.[81] Mawedopenais stated, "and it is riches that we ask so that we may be able to support our families as long as the sun rises and the water runs."[82] The idea that Indians considered treaties as a means towards an economic transition indicated that title and livelihood were intertwined.

The split among the Ojibwa at the Treaty 3 talks, which Lieutenant-Governor Morris so effectively detected, can be understood in the context of "past robberies" and future possibilities. During the 1873 negotiations, it was reported that "The Rainy River Indians were careless about the treaty, because they could get plenty of money for cutting wood for the boats, but the northern and eastern bands were anxious for one."[83] Those bands were locked into the fur trade, did not have "plenty of money," and were interested in the support a treaty would bring for agriculture. Hence the Lac Seul chief was willing to treat with Morris on terms more or less acceptable to the Crown. The Rainy River Indians, on the other hand, were not so much careless about a treaty as they were free of economic pressures that nurtured concessions.

Furthermore, the idea that Indians considered that treaties might afford an alternative to their economic circumstances is supported by the emphasis government negotiators gave to certain terms. Simpson reported that "The system of an annual payment in money, I regard as a good one, because the recipient is enabled to purchase just what he requires when he can get it most cheaply ... The sum of 3 dollars does not appear to be large enough to enable an Indian to provide himself with many of his winter necessaries, but as he receives the same amount for his wife or wives, and for each of his children, the aggregate sum is usually sufficient to procure many comforts for his family, which he would otherwise be compelled to deny himself."[84]

In fact, the wording of Treaties 1 and 2 stated the value of the annuities in terms of a total family income and not as a per capita figure or an individual payment. The conception of annuities as a total family income indicates that this treaty term was part of the government's recognition that future Indian liveli-hood required cash. Annuity payments were not based on any sort of valuation of the land or resources, but seemed to be based on sufficient cash for necessities. The use of annual payments and not once-and-for-all payments permitted the winter outfitting of Indian families. Traditionally, this had been the HBC's obligation.

The features of the treaty that supported the traditional livelihood were an en-during commitment. At difficult points during the negotiations, Morris stressed the ongoing nature of the annuities: "I think you are forgetting one thing, that what I offer you is to be while the water flows and the sun rises."[85] Similarly, with respect to support for the traditional economy, he stressed that "The ammu-nition and twine will be got at once for you, *this year*, and that will be for every year."[86] In a sense, the responsibilities of preexisting Indian-European economic and social relations were expanded and reenforced by the treaties.

Written versions of Treaties 1, 2, and 3 are inadequate for fully presenting First Nations views, but to a certain extent their positions can be gleaned from government records and newspaper accounts. Indians attempted to hold on to as much land as possible, and Simpson reported with respect to Treaty 1 that "the quantity of land demanded for each band amounted to about 3 townships per In-dian, and included the greater part of the settled portions of the Province." At these talks Indians were not quick to give in; Simpson documented that "when their answer came it proved to contain demands of such an exorbitant nature, that much time was spent in reducing their terms to a basis upon which an arrange-ment could be made."[87] Archibald's report corroborates Simpson's record: "Furthermore, the Indians seem to have false ideas of the meaning of a Reserve. They have been led to suppose that large tracts of ground were to be set aside for them as hunting grounds, including timber lands, of which they might sell the wood as if they were proprietors of the soil."[88] Simpson's statement demon-strates that the problem during treaty negotiations was not that Indians lacked an understanding of their property rights. Rather, chiefs expressed firm notions of occupancy, but representatives of the Crown believed that Indian claims were ex-cessive. Indians also perceived commercial opportunities, such as selling wood, from their resources. Apparently, Indians accepted the limitations on the size of the reserves because of the promise of ongoing access to natural resources.

Indian efforts to define the nature of the treaties are apparent in Treaty 3 docu-ments, which record portions of their dialogue. Morris reported that the negotia-tion for Treaty 3 "was a very difficult and trying one, and required on the part of the Commissioners, great patience and firmness."[89] Morris estimated that their initial demands would annually amount to $125,000. Even after a basic agreement had been worked out, Treaty 3 Indians raised demands for an assortment of tools, free passage on the railway, mineral rights, reserves as marked out by Indians, fishing rights, and lumber.

Despite the importance of the treaty to both the Crown and Indians, limits were put on the scope of the bargaining and negotiations. Morris reminded the Ojibwa that "I wish you to understand we do not come here as traders, but as representing the Crown, and to do what we believe is just and right."[90] Decades of fur trade bargaining gave Indians considerable experience in dealing with European commercial impulses and in seeking the satisfaction of their livelihood needs. Ultimately, Morris was forced to limit the scope of the negotiations by placing the treaty on the basis of some kind of trust: a belief in the Queen's good intentions.

TREATY 1: RESOLVING LAND AND LIVELIHOOD

A close examination of the Treaty 1 talks gives us instructive insights into the interrelationship between land and livelihood. The negotiations for Treaty 1 spanned nine days. The Winnipeg weekly newspaper, The *Manitoban*, covered the treaty talks at Stone Fort and documented the dialogue between dominion officials and Ojibwa chiefs.[91] The detailed coverage makes it possible to establish the differing views of land and the changing bargaining positions of the two sides. Basically, both the Crown and the Indians accepted the premise that a treaty was a means to address the issues of Indian title and livelihood.

Before the talks could progress Ayeetapepetung announced: "I can scarcely hear the Queen's words. An obstacle is in the way. Some of my children are in that building (pointing to the jail). That is the obstacle in the way which prevents me responding to the Queen's words. I am not fighting against law and order; but I want my young men to be free, and then I will be able to answer. I hold my own very sacred, and therefore, could not work while my child is sitting in the dark."[92] Ayeetapepetung was referring to four Indians who had broken employment contracts with the HBC and had been imprisoned because they had been unable to pay fines levied against them.

Archibald asked if they were not liable to the law. Ayeetapepetung replied that "I am not defying the law, but would wish to have the Saulteaux at present in jail, liberated."[93] Archibald responded:

When I was here at the Lower Fort before, I stated that the Queen knew no distinction between her subjects. If a man does wrong, whether a white man or an Indian, he has to suffer for it. If a white man makes a bargain with an Indian, and does not fulfil it, the Queen will punish the white man. If, on the other hand, an Indian does wrong to an Indian or white man, the law is the same he will be punished. I wish you to understand that all men, whether white or Indian, must obey the law. But if, on account of this Treaty, the Indians wish me to clear away the obstacle spoken of as in the way, I am willing to grant such a request as a matter of favor, not as a matter of right.[94]

Apparently, "Ay-ee-ta-pe-pe-tung and the Indians expressed their gratitude, and requested as a matter of favor that the incarcerated Indians should be set free"[95]

In his official correspondence on 29 July 1871 Archibald also reported on this event:

On learning the facts I told the Indians that I could not listen to them if they made a demand for the release of the Indians as a matter of right, that every subject of the Queen, whether Indian, half-breed or white, was equal in the eye of the law; that every offender against the law must be punished whatever race he belonged to; but I said that on the opening of negotiations with them the Queen would like to see all her Indians taking part in them, and if the whole body present were to ask as a matter of grace and favor, under the circumstances, that their brethren should be released, Her Majesty would be willing to consent to their discharge; she would grant as a favour what she must refuse if asked for on any other ground. They replied by saying that they begged it as a matter of favour only … I explained again, that there might be no misunderstanding about it, that henceforth every offender against the law must be punished. They all expressed their acquiescence in what I said.[96]

Thus, the account by the *Manitoban* and the official record of Archibald are similar.

Lieutenant-Governor Archibald and Indian Commissioner Simpson began the talks by very generally outlining the Crown's intentions. With respect to reserves, Simpson stated, "The different bands will get such quantities of land as will be sufficient for their use in adopting the habits of the white man, should they choose to do so." With respect to Indian lands with little agricultural potential Simpson actually said that in the rocky swamp areas, "in treating with the Indians from such districts, the Government are [*sic*] in fact giving them presents – not purchasing from them land of great value. When I was on my way through here, I tried all I could to impress on the Indians living in the district between Fort William and Rainy Lake, that their land being unfit for settlement, what they would get for it was, in fact, a present; and so it is in the case of similar lands within the Province – that which the Indians receive for them, is in reality a present from the Government."[97]

With respect to the areas not suited for agriculture (boreal forest/Pre-Cambrian Shield) the government's intentions are not clear. Simpson might have been intending to say that the lands were not of any interest and that Indians were not required to sell the lands, but merely accept the government's presents. The government set aside 160 acres per family of five, which it justified on the basis of a fair policy for Indians and Whites; in Archibald's words "your Great Mother making no distinction between any of her people."[98] The Crown's representatives supported their bargaining positions by making comparisons with the Queen's treatment of Indians in the East. Although the area of 160 acres was a subdivision of land used by the Dominion Lands Survey system, the size of the reserve allocation was based on an agricultural use of reserve lands.[99] Both Archibald and Simpson stated that the need for extensive hay lands could not be used as a reason for large Indian reserves. Clearly, therefore, Indians were not expected to derive their entire livelihood from small reserves.

To make a distinction between possible land uses and the needs Indians would have for land, Archibald said that "you will still be free to hunt over much of the land included in the Treaty. Much of it is rocky, and unfit for cultivation; much of it that is wooded, is beyond the places where the white man will require to go, at all events, for some time to come. Till these lands are needed for use, you will be free to hunt over them, and make all the use of them which you have made in the past."[100] Archibald's position is independently verified by the *Manitoban*, which reported that on 28 July, "His Excellency explained that reserves did not mean hunting grounds, but merely portions of land set aside to form a farm for each family. A large portion of the country would remain as much a hunting ground as ever after the Treaty closed."[101]

Indian Commissioner Simpson also indicated that in many places Indian lands would not be encroached upon by White men for many years: "I would remind them that a large section of the country beyond here is of a rocky swampy character, and such as they need not expect to see inhabited by white settlers. Not in the lifetime of the present generation will farming settlements of white men be seen in such quarters as Fort Alexander."[102] This position conveys the impression that settlers were being accommodated in a way that would not drastically disrupt the existing livelihood. A hunting right was being acknowledged, not encumbered, by hunting regulations. Moreover, Archibald's words quoted in the previous paragraph – "and make all the use of them which you have made in the past" – would include fishing, gathering, trapping, and free access.

The problem of Treaty 1 hunting rights illustrates the difficulty of written and oral versions of the treaty. Treaty 1, as a narrowly conceived, written document does not recognize traditional livelihood rights; yet other documents record a written version of Archibald's opening spoken address that affirms the right to hunt. There are no indications that Indians would be prevented from making a living.

The initial response by Indians to the Crown's proposal for reserves did not acknowledge the restriction on size. Kamatwakanasnin conveyed that "As for the reserves, the Indians wish it to be distinctly understood that they are to have a voice in that alone."[103] On 29 July, after being assured that they could select the locations of reserves and after the method of annuity payments was explained, the chiefs laid out claim for lands they wished to be reserved. Despite the fact that an effort was made by the Crown's representatives to distinguish hunting territories and reserves, claims were made to vast areas that probably reflected traditional areas of occupancy. When Ayeepepetung advanced his claim, he stated: "I understand you are going to buy this land from me. Well God made me out of this very clay that is besmeared on my body. This is what you say you are going to buy from me. I live far away where it is silvery. When you first found me naked, with the fur-bearing animals by me, I traded with the white man, and saw what he got for his fur. With regard to land within the Settlement, I have nothing to say, as I am on the outside."[104] Thus, Ayeepepetung evaluated the Crown's intentions by drawing upon his experience with the white men in the fur trade. However, after the various claims were stated, little area was left open for settlement. The Reverend H. Cochrane and James McKay responded, indicating that the Indians' claims were preposterous, and urged them to curtail their demands.

The Crown's representatives then repeated their arguments. Archibald tried to persuade Indians of the good intentions of the Crown by arguing that Indians in the east "were living happy and tranquil, enjoying all the rights and privileges of white men."[105] Simpson reminded Indians that annuity payments were not terminated, unlike the cash payments in the American Indian treaties. In essence, it was suggested that the Crown's relations with Indians in Ontario and the future commitment to cash would secure a livelihood for Treaty 1 Indians. Simpson pointed out that the land grant of 160 acres per family was twice the size of the existing family lots in the Indian parish of St Peters. Archibald then issued an ultimatum: the Crown had laid out its propositions; at the next meeting (the fifth day of negotiations), the Crown expected to learn whether Indians would accept or reject the terms.

Nonetheless, the concerns of the Indians did not cease. Ayeetapepetung, of the Portage Indians, protested:

But God gave me this land you are speaking to me about, and it kept me well to this day. I live at the end of the Settlement, in a clean place (unsettled); and as I travelled through the Settlement, I looked on nothing but my property! I saw pieces of land high up (meaning bridges) – these are my property! When I went into the houses by the wayside, these too I considered my property – (laughter)! I have turned over this matter of a treaty in my mind and cannot see anything in it to benefit my children. This is what frightens me. After I showed you what I meant to keep for a reserve, you continued to make it smaller and smaller. Now, I will go home to-day, to my own property.[106]

Generally, Ayeetapepetung held a firm position against the officials, arguing that the commissioner could take the lands if he wished and stating, "Let the Queen's subjects go on my land if they choose. I give them liberty. Let them rob me. I will go home without treating."[107] Another Portage Indian stated, "what puzzled his band was that they were to be shut on a small reserve, and only get ten shillings each for the balance. They could not understand it."[108] In effect, reserve lands and cash annuities did not seem to be adequate for future needs. Commissioner Simpson then tried to undermine the Ojibwa claims by reminding them that the Cree had previously occupied Manitoba. He also argued that the time had come for the land to be cultivated.

Although the reporting by the *Manitoban* is incomplete and even crucial commentary is not on the record, a number of issues were raised that indicate that the broad agreement referred to more than the final written treaty text. Under the heading "Providing for Posterity", the *Manitoban* reported Chief Wasuskookoon's concern: "I understand thoroughly that every 20 people get a mile square; but if an Indian with a family of 5, settles down, he may have more children. Where is their land?"[109] This is a significant question, because it raises the problem of future land needs. The dominion government's response conveyed the impression that reserves could expand to meet the needs of the Indian population. According to Archibald, "Whenever his children get more numerous than they are now, they will be provided for further West. Whenever the reserves are found too small the Government will sell the land, and give the Indians land elsewhere."[110] The Crown's representatives clearly put forward the general principle that the future land needs of the Indian population would not be confined by the proposed reserve sizes. Certainly it did not suggest that reserves were a fixed and final, once-and-for-all-time ratio of land to population.

Towards the close of the negotiations, the positions of the various Indian speakers shifted. At the end of the fifth day, Ayeetapepetung indicated that he wanted to take a winter to think about the treaty. Subsequently, James McKay "made an eloquent speech in Indian, explaining matters" – the substance of which was not documented.[111] Ayeetapepetung then said that he would accept the treaty for an annuity of $3 per person. (Apparently, this was a slight increase over the offer of ten shillings.) The commissioner agreed to this demand, but the agreement was short-lived and not generally acceptable. Again Simpson threatened to end negotiations if an agreement was not forthcoming.

On the sixth day, Chief Henry Prince, the senior chief of the region, took a more active role and raised some objections to the treaty terms, stating, "The land cannot speak for itself. We have to speak for it."[112] Once it was clear that the large reserves could not be obtained but that Indians could continue to hunt on lands outside reserves, new demands were made with regard to the use of reserve lands for livelihood purposes. The Indians took advantage of the government position that the size of the reserves was defined by the reasonable needs of a family farm. Prince announced. "the Queen wishes the Indians to cultivate the ground. They cannot scratch it – work it with their fingers. What assistance will they get if they settle down?"[113] According to the *Manitoban:* "His Excellency entered into a lengthy statement showing that the Queen was willing to help the Indians in every way, and that besides giving them land and annuities, she would give them a school and a schoolmaster for each reserve, and for those who desired to cultivate the soil, ploughs and harrows would be provided on the reserves."[114] At this point some concessions had been made. Significantly, the talks had shifted from the size of reserves to future livelihood needs.

Livelihood and land were linked in the Treaty 1 talks. When it was abundantly clear that larger areas were not to be reserved, traditional Indian livelihood was jeopardized. However, the Crown's rationale for small reserves was based on a fair amount of land for a family farm, and because the adoption of an agricultural mode of life was voluntary, Indians had to have continuing access to off-reserve lands future for their livelihood. The assurances that hunting could continue off reserve, that annuities would be increased, and that assistance would be provided for agricultural and educational pursuits were significant substantive points in the negotiations.

Indians continued to make demands on the sixth day of talks. Again a property right was asserted; compensation for the road that ran between the Red River Settlement and Lake of the Woods was requested. Then Prince and several other chiefs came forward and Wasuskookoon addressed the Commissioner Simpson:

First, in the early part of every spring, we want all the children to be clothed with fine clothes! In the fall of the year they are to be clothed from head to foot with warm clothing! Whenever an Indian wants to settle, a house is to be put up for him fully furnished, and a plough, with all its accompaniments of cattle, &c., complete is to be given him! We want buggies for the chiefs, counsellors and braves, to show their dignity! Each man is to be supplied with whatever he uses for hunting, and all his other requirements; and the women in the same way!! Each Indian settling on the reserve is to be free from taxes![115]

Simpson rejected these demands by suggesting that he would be better off as an Indian. Nonetheless, in his opening address, discussed above, Archibald had informed the Indians that the Queen was interested in their welfare; she "wishes her red children to be happy and contented. She wishes them to live in comfort."[116]

At this point, the Portage Indians indicated that were going to leave, and it appeared that other Indians would depart as well. James McKay then requested the Indians to stay over one more night and to meet next day with the commissioner. He promised in the interval to "try and bring the commissioner and Indians closer together."[117] The next day, 3 August, a treaty was signed. According to the *Manitoban* the Indians were in better humour and a cash present of $3, a pair of oxen for each reserve, and buggies for each chief were added. Regrettably very few details of the crucial last day of Treaty 1 talks have been recorded. How James McKay brought the two sides closer together may not have been captured in the written text of Treaty 1.

Although demands for housing and clothing must have been viewed as excessive in the late nineteenth century, by the norms of the society that had commissioned Archibald and Simpson to treat, Indians were looking either to hold on to significant amounts of land or to receive economic compensation for the loss of their property. On the second day of the talks, Sheoship addressed the Queen, "begging her to grant me wherewith to make my living."[118] In both Treaty 1 and Treaty 3 James McKay played a pivotal role. Complicating any full understanding of the treaty process is the fact that important negotiations occurred in between the public meetings, and these meetings were off the record.

REVISING WRITTEN TREATIES: VERBAL ASSURANCES AND THE "OUTSIDE PROMISES"

The controversy around the so-called outside promises of Treaties 1 and 2 illustrates the problems of verbal understandings reached at the time of treaty talks, as well as the possibilities of a noncorrespondence between written records about treaty-making and the written version of the treaty. The words "outside promises" refer to specific verbal commitments made by government officials during Treaty 1 negotiations. They have been dubbed "outside" because the written treaty relied upon by senior dominion officials made no reference to these commitments. (The use of "outside" does not imply that there were promises outside the agreement reached at the treaty talks). Official reluctance to deal with commitments made during Treaty 1 and 2 talks indicates that even when written evidence corroborated several features of an oral version of a treaty, the dominion government sought refuge in the written version of the treaties. Although a number of the verbal agreements reached at the Treaty 1 talks were listed in a memorandum of 3 August 1871 signed by Simpson, St John, Archibald, and McKay and attached to the treaty, the Privy Council approved a version of Treaty 1 that did not contain all of the terms that had been agreed to by the Indian nations and Crown towards the conclusion of the talks.

There were no significant government obligations to assist Indian agriculture in the written versions of Treaties 1 and 2. However, Simpson's report on the treaty negotiations (3 November 1871) lists a number of additional terms, largely related to agriculture, which were not part of the official treaty text.[119] Simpson reported that "it had been agreed, at the signing of the treaty as before mentioned, to give certain animals as a nucleus for stocking the several reserves, together with certain farming implements." Later in the same report, he explained "Then, and by means of mutual concessions, the following terms were agreed upon ... As each Indian settled down upon his share of the reserve, and commenced the cultivation of his land, he was to receive a plough and harrow. Each Chief was to receive a cow and a male and female of the smaller kinds of animals bred upon a farm ... On this basis the treaty was signed by myself and the several Chiefs.[120]

Thus, the so-called outside promises were listed in Simpson's official report summarizing the treaty agreement: clearly, in the view of the Indian commissioner, the terms that were discussed and agreed upon towards the end of the talks were not outside the treaty.[121] The record of the *Manitoban* with respect to the verbal commitments was corroborated by the *Canadian Illustrated News*, which reported that the terms of the treaty were liberal and included providing "to every one of the reserves set apart for each tribe some ploughs and harrows, and a pair of oxen to enable the Indians to cultivate the soil."[122] Despite a memorandum attached to Treaty 1 that listed promises "outside" of the treaty and Simpson's official report, Ottawa officials were extremely slow to recognize and to act on these treaty commitments. The delay in implementing some important treaty promises occurred in part because the Privy Council approved Treaties 1 and 2 before receiving Simpson's report of 3 November 1871. Occasionally some of the outside promises were implemented before the government formally admitted the validity of these verbal commitments.[123] Indians held that the promises included a plough and harrow for each family, a yoke of oxen, a farmer, blacksmith, and carpenter to teach them, wheat seed, clothing, and food in the winter.[124]

Discontent grew over the nonfulfillment of the verbal treaty terms, and the new Indian commissioner, J.A.N. Provencher, reported in 1873 that the Indians

do not perfectly agree as to the nature of these promises, and some Chiefs have announced the most exaggerated pretensions on this subject. They think that the Government has undertaken to furnish them first-class residences; clothes of a superior quality, and provisions of their own choice for them and their families; but putting aside what is impossible and absurd in these different rumors, it is undoubted that by an interpretation put by the Indians on the words of the Commissioners, that they who were present at the treaties Nos. 1 and 2, were led to expect many more benefits than were expressed in those 2 treaties; and in the meantime they almost accuse the representatives of Canada of obtaining their consent under false pretences.[125]

Such sentiments were verified by Indian Agent Molyneux St John, who reported in 1873 that they "are not content with the terms of the Treaty, and are unanimous in the belief that they have been deceived and promised more than they have received."[126] St John forwarded the Indians' list of promises to the department's deputy superintendent. In a petition forwarded by John Schultz in 1873, the St Peters Indians stated their position: "That promises made to them at the Treaty of 1871 have not been fulfilled. And that a state of general dissatisfaction exists in consequence; that they find it quite impossible to supply their most ordinary wants with the present Annuity of 3 dollars; that game has become very scarce and their reservations is [sic] found to be small and insufficient for their use."[127] The more favourable terms of Treaty 3 only reinforced the dissatisfaction among Manitoba Indians' who pointed out that their prairie land was more valuable than the rock and muskeg of Treaty 3 lands.[128] In 1873 there was some difficulty in getting Indians to accept annuities. John Schultz wrote to Ottawa explaining that "I am led to believe that the Indians have just grounds for their present dissatisfaction," and he pointed out that such dissatisfaction might influence the Plains Cree to the west.[129]

Moreover, dissatisfaction with treaty implementation caused the Portage band to warn Saskatchewan Indians about the problems with the treaty. Morris noted that in 1874 the Portage band twice sent to Qu'Appelle "to prevent the making of the treaty there."[130] Morris wrote to the minister of the Interior stating, "and you are aware of their intimate relation with the 'Plain Indians,' and the difficulty their message to Qu'Appelle, 'that the white man had not kept his promises,' caused us then."[131] The problems of implementing verbal treaty commitments had implications for Saskatchewan treaties.

The discontent concerning the outside promises was eventually resolved in 1875 when the government agreed to acknowledge the terms listed on the memorandum of 3 August 1871, which, as mentioned, was attached to Treaty 1. An order-in-council of 30 April 1875 acknowledged "the very unsatisfactory state of affairs arising out of the so called 'outside promises'" and authorized the inclusion of the terms of the memorandum with the treaty.[132] This revision to Treaties 1 and 2 also increased the annuities from $3 to $5 per person, increased the annuities for chiefs and headmen, and included an agreement to "abandon all claims whatever against the government in connection with the so-called 'Outside Promises,'" apart from those terms included in the memorandum.[133] Written acceptance of the revisions to Treaties 1 and 2 was obtained by Morris, McKay, and Provencher. In the summer of 1875 most of the bands of Treaties 1 and 2 signed acceptances of the revision of the treaties as laid out by the order-in-council. In the following summer the Portage bands signed the revision. However, Treaties 1 and 2 were not changed so as to increase the size of reserves or to incorporate the hunting and fishing livelihood rights.

The documents around the outside promises issue demonstrate that Indians had made specific demands during the negotiations that were designed to secure a future livelihood. We have seen that there is a well-documented divergence between the agreement that was made on 3 August 1871 and the written version of Treaty 1. The revision to the treaties, in line with the memorandum of 3 August 1871, indicates that even the written text of a signed treaty is not the final representation of the agreement reached at treaty talks. The oral version of a treaty, features of which are verified by a variety of extrinsic written records, is crucial in understanding the contemporary meaning of treaty rights. Most of the outside promises recognized by government were intended to provide the means for an agricultural economy, an issue raised by Chief Prince. The historical records show that Indian political pressure – petitions, rejection of annuities, and the use of Schultz as a political agent – succeeded in gaining some changes in the 1870s.

Despite the complications raised by the revisions to Treaties 1 and 2, Lieutenant-Governor Morris indicated a positive outcome for the Crown: "The experience derived from this misunderstanding, proved however, of benefit with regard to all the treaties, subsequent to Treaties 1 and 2, as the greatest care was thereafter taken to have all promises fully set out in the treaties, and to have the treaties thoroughly and fully explained to the Indians, and understood by them to contain the whole agreement between them and the Crown."[134] Certainly, at subsequent talks agents of the Crown did not compose memoranda documenting verbal understandings of the terms of treaties.

Soon after the signing of pre-Saskatchewan treaties disputes arose. Undoubtedly one of the key reasons was that the written terms of a given treaty could easily miss the points of agreements reached at the talks that led up to it. Usually these talks raised a variety of complex issues. The varied documentation pertaining to these negotiations examined above offers a wider perspective than is contained in the treaty.texts. For example, Treaty 1 provided a reserve for the Portage band, stating that there would be "for the use of the Indians, of whom Oo-za-we-kwun [Yellow Quill] is Chief, so much land on the south and east side of the Assiniboine, about twenty miles above the Portage, as will furnish one hundred and sixty acres for each family of 5, or in that proportion for larger or smaller families, reserving also a further tract enclosing said reserve, to comprise an equivalent to twenty-five square miles of equal breadth, to be laid out round the reserve."[135]

Complications that resulted from divisions within this band over leadership and reserve locations were raised in 1875 when Treaty 1 was revised. Morris explained the problems he encountered when attempting to implement the reserve provision of the treaty:

I produced the plan of the reserve, as proposed to be allotted to them, containing 34,000 acres, but Yellow Quill said it was not in the right place, and was not what was promised, and moreover it was not surrounded by the belt of five miles, mentioned in the treaty, but was only partially so, and did not cross the river. I told them they could get no more land than was promised in the treaty. They appealed to Mr. McKay whether the Reserve was not promised to be on both sides of the river, and he admitted that it was. I told them it was not so written in the treaty, and that if the Government should allow it to cross the river, the rights of navigation must be conserved, but I would consult the Queen's Councillors.[136]

The Portage band's problem was that, because he had not negotiated Treaty 1, Morris interpreted the reserve location according to the written treaty, which failed to grant lands on both sides of the Assiniboine River, as promised. Luckily for the Portage band, James McKay, who had been the Crown's interpreter at the treaty talks, remembered that Oozawekwun had been promised a reserve on both sides of the river.

In this chapter we have considered the development of treaty policies, especially the federal government's policy toward specific territorial and resource interests. The terms of the written treaties were influenced by the pre-Confederation Upper Canadian treaties, information and suggestions provided by Ottawa agents and friends in the Northwest, the relationship between the HBC and Indians, and Indian bargaining strategies and the demands they made during the negotiations. Recognizing that Indians made claims to property is essential for understanding their aspirations at the treaty talks. By the 1860s various forms of land tenure existed among Indians, some of whom engaged in significant farming activities, whereas others depended almost exclusively on collecting, hunting, fishing, and trapping. It is not surprising, therefore, that some, such as the St Peters farming village, held land as individual river lots. Those heavily engaged in the commercialized trapping economy, on the other hand, were accustomed to common property and family hunting-territory arrangements. In any event, although Indian concepts of Aboriginal tenure differed from those of the Eurocanadians, Indians were able to express their notions sufficiently clearly to formulate bargaining positions.

In Treaties 1, 2 and 3, some sort of understanding also existed between treaty commissioners and First Nations with regard to reconciling the rights and livelihood needs of Indians vis-à-vis incoming settlers. At Treaty 3 talks in 1873, Chief Mawedopenais provided a clear statement of the Indians' future needs: "It is your charitableness that you spoke of yesterday – Her Majesty's charitableness that was given you. It is our chiefs, our young men, our children and great grand children, and those that are to be born, that I represent here, and it is for them I ask for terms."[137] From the written records it would seem that First Nations expected that treaties would secure their future. Similarly, Morris urged a future-oriented perspective during the Treaty 3 talks: "I only ask you to think for yourselves, and your families, and for your children and children's children."[138]

Indian motivation for accepting a "surrender" of Aboriginal title can partly be understood as a desire, by some Indians, to secure a means to become agriculturists, to secure an economic alternative or adjunct to the fur trade, and also to ensure that provisions of the treaty would support the traditional economy. In the case of Treaty 3, annual payments in ammunition and twine and relief rations, as well as annuities, were a means to maintain a viable livelihood based on participation in a commercial hunting economy. Indians used the treaty negotiations to advance their own economic and social program, which sought to diversify their own economy.

In these ways, a detailed reconstruction of the talks at Treaty I serves to provide a context and to broaden the comprehension of treaties beyond the narrow
legal terminology contained in the official treaty texts. Aboriginal title was not
explained, the significance of reserves was blurred by assuring Indians of an ongoing access to lands not taken up, and concerns about land needs and livelihood
were placated by invoking the Queen's good intentions. The delay in fulfilling
important terms of the agreements made with respect to Treaties I and 2 demonstrates that the written version of these treaties was not complete.

CHAPTER SIX

Saskatchewan on the Eve of Treaties

The context needed to understand Treaties 4, 5, and 6 includes more than instruments of Crown policy and earlier precedent-setting treaties in eastern and western Canada. Equally important parts of the setting in which the Saskatchewan treaties were negotiated were the major social, economic, and demographic developments that western First Nations were experiencing in the middle decades of the nineteenth century.

ABORIGINAL SOCIETIES AND ECONOMIES

The ethnohistorical geography of Saskatchewan is very diverse.[1] Generalizing broadly, it encompasses two distinctively different cultural/economic realms of Aboriginal Canada. The northern boreal forest section (subsequently included in Treaties 8 and 10) lying to the north of the Saskatchewan River valley is part of a vast area that anthropologists have identified as the Subarctic. This was the world of hunters, fishers, and gatherers, who, at the initial European contact, included the Dene, Woodland Cree, and Woodland Assiniboine.

Today scholars hold different opinions about the relative contributions that large-game hunting and fishing activities made to Subarctic economies, but they do not dispute that both were important. Moose and woodland caribou were the most consequential large-game animals living in the full boreal forest. Male hunters stalked these nonherding creatures in small hunting parties and killed them at close range with bows and arrows and lances. Large game animals yielded big rewards. A moose provided up to 500 pounds of dressed meat; caribou yielded 100 to 150 pounds. These quarry also provided women with the essential hides they needed to make clothing, footwear, and summer lodge covers.

Barren-ground caribou roamed along the boreal forest–tundra boundary. During the winter, herds of these animals browsed in the sheltering woods and in the summer moved out onto the open tundra. The Aboriginal groups who depended on these animals, such as the Dene speakers known as the Chipewyan, developed a number of ingenious hunting techniques that took advantage of the predictability of herd movements. The Chipewyan, for instance, worked in large parties to build brush enclosures, called surrounds or pounds, in places where particular herds normally wintered. The hunters set snares inside these pounds to catch the hapless caribou they drove into them. They also built barricades across the trails regularly used by caribou, placing snares in the gaps left in these "deer hedges." During the open-water season Chipewyan parties herded caribou into rivers and lakes, where fellow hunters speared them from canoes with ease.

Woodland groups employed a wide variety of snares and deadfall traps to kill an assortment of furbearers. More common and widespread were those used to take beaver, muskrat, and hare. Men did most of the trapping, but women and children also took part. The beaver coat, which the Aboriginal peoples wore with the hair side against their bodies for warmth, was the key article of winter clothing; hare blankets and coats also were very important. The meat of some of these small animals – most notably beaver – was a crucial food. An adult beaver, for example, could provide a hunter and his family with up to forty pounds of meat – or about one-third the amount of a woodland caribou. The Cree even considered unborn beaver to be a gourmet delight.

Freshwater fishing was a very important activity during the warmer months. At the end of winter several hunting groups who used adjacent territories normally came together at a good fishery, where they camped for several weeks or more. The composition of the catches varied considerably from one locale to another, but sturgeon, whitefish, and lake trout were among the leading species taken. The Subarctic fishers used different techniques, depending on the site and species sought. Their gear included hook and line, spears, dip nets, and fences, or weirs. Fish were the mainstay of the diet for many groups between late spring and early autumn. Also, the women usually dried and smoked a small surplus to carry them into the winter. They used the swim bladders of sturgeon to make glue, which they mixed with paint to fix the colours that decorated everything from their bodies to dwellings.

During the spring and autumn the subarctic teemed with millions of waterfowl. At these times the hunters took prodigious numbers of ducks and geese, which were a welcome seasonal addition to the diet. During the autumn hunters preserved large numbers of these birds simply by letting them freeze in the cold air. The main difficulty with this procedure was that the occasional protracted winter thaws sometimes spoiled these larders.

Close relatives worked in teams. The men made their own weapons and fishing gear, fashioned snowshoe frames, built canoes and sleds, and did most of the hunting, trapping, and fishing. The women kept busy butchering the meat, collecting firewood, gathering canoe-building and repairing supplies (birch bark, spruce root, and tar); processing and cooking the food; scraping and tanning the bear, deer, and moose hides and fur pelts; making the clothing and household equipment; and stringing snowshoes. During the winter the women carried most of the gear when the hunting parties trudged from camp to camp by snowshoe and sled. Pack and sled dogs often helped, but most families could not afford many of these creatures because they had voracious appetites. Fish – particularly white fish – was the ideal dog food, and often the quality of the winter fishery determined the number of animals a group could sustain. Some Dene groups fed their animals caribou meat. In most areas, families could support only a single two-dog team. Obviously, summer movement by canoe was much less taxing for the women. A typical canoe could hold a family with one or two children and about 250 pounds of cargo.

Subarctic people typically had an egalitarian socio-political organization. Most of the year people lived in small, mobile hunting groups comprised of a few closely related hunters and their families. Typically, these families in-cluded grandparents, parents, and children. Political leadership was fluid in the sense that band members followed the man who was best suited to lead them in the task immediately at hand. Normally the "situational leader" was a married elder who was a superior hunter, a generous man, a skilled orator, and a good conciliator. When a number of local hunting groups came together to form a summer camp, the winter headman who commanded the greatest respect usu-ally was paramount. Effective leaders were those who were skillful at molding a consensus.

Arctic and Subarctic hunting groups returned to the same territories every year. The principal exceptions to this practice usually occurred when natural calami-ties, such as forest fires, temporarily ruined hunting or trapping prospects, thereby preventing bands from returning to their home territory. On these occasions hunt-ing parties obtained permission from neighbouring groups to use portions of their traditional land. There was little need for sharply demarcated territories before European contact; everyone belonged to a band, and these in turn were knit to-gether by regional kinship networks, since individuals had to marry outside their winter group. Thus, before contact with Europeans, Subarctic hunters had a vested interest in husbanding the resources of their own lands as well as those of their neighbouring kin, who could be depended on in times of need. What was crucial was to establish social bonds, not physical boundaries.

The part of the province of Saskatchewan that lies beyond the boreal/subarctic area was part of the northern plains (parkland/grassland) region. Here, bison hunters predominated. These people included the Plains Assiniboine, Cree, Blood, and Gros Ventre. By the early nineteenth century, the latter two groups had withdrawn from the grassland region of Saskatchewan, leaving the Plains Assiniboine and Cree in control of most of this territory. Woodland and Plains Ojibwa, who were allies of the Assiniboine and Cree, moved into some of the eastern districts of the province that subsequently were included in Treaties 4 and 5.

Bison had been the main focus of the Plains peoples' economies since the great ice age. The adult male weighed up to two thousand pounds and could provide the hunter with as much as a thousand pounds of dressed meat; females yielded much less, about four hundred pounds. Plains people preferred the meat from the females because it was more tender. Bison tongues and bosses (the fatty humps located between the shoulders) were special delicacies. Plains hunters also depended on bison for an array of essential raw materials. For instance, the heavy winter coats served as warm robes for bedding and outer wear. The hides secured during the summer molting season were ideal for making lodge coverings, *parflèches* (leather containers), clothing, hide and leather strips for *babiche* (leather cording), and rawhide war shields. The men and women worked bison bone into a variety of tools, and the women used the paunch as a cooking and storage container. In short, this one animal provided the foundation for their way of life.

Bison hunts were major, all-consuming enterprises, akin to military campaigns. When the summer rutting season approached, the bison gathered into enormous herds; as the autumn winds grew chilly, they scattered into smaller herds and headed for the shelter of the parklands to face the oncoming winter. Herd movements were highly predictable, and the hunters devised a number of strategies to take advantage of them. During the winter they pitched camp in sheltered locations near places the bison frequented. Under the direction of the "poundmaker," or winter village chief, they constructed a circular brush enclosure close to their settlement with a fenced chute leading to the nearby prairie. When a herd approached, skilled hunters often met them disguised as bison or wolves. These human decoys lured the unsuspecting bison into the chute, where other kinfolk, hidden behind the fence, helped drive the animals into the pound by spooking them. Once the animals were inside, they were killed by men, women, and children with lances, bows, and arrows. The pounds, if well maintained, lasted for many years.

Before Spaniards reintroduced horses to North America, the cliff drive was the most important summer bison-hunting technique. Hunters stampeded the animals over precipices to their death by using fire drives. When everything worked according to plan, a carefully set blaze terrorized the bison and sent them thundering to the planned cliff-kill site. Aboriginal people frequently built an enclosure at the base of the precipice to make it easier to dispatch any animals that did not die in the fall. Precontact "bison jump" sites dotting the prairie landscape and spanning thousands of years testify to the effectiveness of this technique.

The "surround" was yet another hunting strategy, in which a group of hunters approached and surrounded part of a herd on foot. Subsequently, the hunters drew themselves into an ever-smaller circle while killing as many animals as possible until the herd broke through and ran away. Clearly this practice demanded nerves of steel and required a lot of experience, considering that the pedestrian hunters always faced the risk of being trampled by their jittery quarry.

All of the important bison-hunting techniques involved a communal effort. Although men played the major role, women, and even children, often participated. In the case of pound-hunting, for instance, women and children often were among those who stood behind the fences and helped spook the animals. As in other regions, the Plains women did most of the butchering and processed the hides and robes. Furthermore, they made one of the most famous Indian foods – pemmican. This highly nutritious product was a mixture of dried and pulverized bison meat and melted fat flavored with berries – usually Saskatoon berries. The women poured the pemmican into *parflèches* to congeal. Each container held about ninety pounds and its contents had an extremely long "shelf-life." Pemmican was the ideal traveling food for this reason and because it was extremely concentrated. A single *parflèche* held the equivalent of nine hundred pounds of fresh meat, or that of two adult female bison. Every summer and autumn Plains Nations accumulated a stock of pemmican for the winter and for trade. This food would become the staple provision of the Western fur trade after contact.

Plains hunters took a variety of other quarry. Wapiti, which weighed up to eleven hundred pounds and lived in the bordering woods, was an important "back-up food" when the bison herds failed to leave the open grasslands. This commonly happened during exceptionally mild winters. The Plains Nations also took moose in the woods. Those Plains people who were relatively recent immigrants from the woodlands, such as some of the Plains Cree and Ojibwa Nations, still relished moose meat. In addition, Plains hunters preyed on packs of wolves, which stalked the bison herds, and pursued a variety of fur bearers – most notably beaver and muskrat – in the aspen woods bordering the rivers and countless lakes that dot the prairie landscape. Migrating waterfowl abounded during the spring and autumn and attracted the hunters.

Plains Indian's attitudes towards fish were divided. For some groups, fishing was very important in the spring and autumn. The Assiniboine and Cree, for instance, built weirs in the spring to catch sturgeon and other fish. The Saulteaux also relied on fish.

The socioeconomic organization of the Plains bison hunters varied with the seasons. The winter bison-pound village, for instance, numbered from twenty-five to one hundred or more, which was about the same size as the summer encampments of the boreal forest groups. During the late summer, on the other hand, the bison-hunting and Sun Dance camps could include over one thousand inhabitants.

A chief and an informal council of elders, who were recognized for their prowess in war, their skill as hunters, their generosity, and their ability as orators, oversaw the affairs of the summer and winter camps.[2] When several bands gathered during summer, the oldest and most respected winter chief assumed the paramount position and acted as spokesman for the combined group. As in the subarctic region, in the parklands and plains decision making by consensus prevailed, and persuasion rather than coercion was the preferred way for elders to implement their individual and collective wills. Men's warrior or police societies provided enforcement of rules when needed. Maintaining tight control was particularly important during the summer, because this was the time of the mass bison hunts, when hostile raiding parties posed a constant threat. Warrior society members could seize a defiant individual's property and impose physical punishment. This was rarely necessary, however.

In Saskatchewan, as in most other areas of precontact North America, civil or peace chiefs and war leaders (individuals could serve in alternative capacities) guided relations with nonkin groups. In order to establish or renew peaceful relations with outsiders, chiefs called councils for that purpose. To symbolize the intended goodwill, a ceremonial exchange of gifts took place and the calumet ceremony was performed. It should be noted here that among the Cree one major responsibility of a chief was to maintain peace and order among his followers. A primary way he accomplished the latter objective was by giving gifts to individuals who had been injured by other members of his camp. Such acts of chiefly generosity ended disputes and enhanced his prestige. This method of internal dispute resolution was extended to the realm of external relations as gift exchange.

The solemnity of a peace council was signaled by the calumet ceremony. Here it should be noted that ceremonial pipestems and the smoking of tobacco were extremely powerful symbols and acts for many First Nations. Anthropologist David Mandelbaum noted that among the Plains Cree, for example, elders carefully selected men to hold the office of sacred pipestem bundle bearer. The bundle *(oskitci)* contained a pipestem three or four feet long, elaborately decorated with quills, beads, fur, and feathers. Sweetgrass, tobacco, and an ornamented pipe tamp were also included. The pipestem had no bowl; in fact, the stem was not used for smoking.[3] According to Mandelbaum,

No intemperate action could occur in the presence of the Pipestem ... A man bent on avenging the death of a relative could not continue in his purpose if confronted with this Pipestem. When peace was to be made with a hostile tribe, the Pipestem Bearer led the way. When the enemy saw the pipe, they recognized it and respected its sanctity.

The owner of the bundle had to intervene in all intertribal disputes, a duty often hazardous when the men were beside themselves with anger. The Bearer himself could not engage in quarrels no matter how greatly he was provoked and in all things his conduct had to be exemplary.[4]

Mandelbaum's Cree informants said that before the bundle was ritually unwrapped, those who were assembled drew another filled pipe through sweetgrass smoke and then passed it amongst themselves so that each of them could smoke it in turn.[5] By taking part in this sacred ceremony, the participants committed themselves to telling the truth during the course of diplomatic negotiations.[6]

As noted earlier, First Nations managed to incorporate their diplomatic traditions into their trading relations with the HBC. Through gift exchanges and participation in the rite of the calumet they annually renewed their partnership with the company and granted it the right to share their territory for trading purposes. This arrangement was in keeping with the kinds of accords that groups such as the Cree routinely reached with neighbouring First Nations. For instance, they formed a long-lasting alliance with the northern Ojibwa whereby the latter people gained peaceful entry into ancestral Cree territory in northern Ontario, Manitoba, and eastern Saskatchewan.[7] Also, during most of the eighteenth century the Cree served as one of the primary middleman groups supplying the Blackfoot and their allies with HBC trading goods. Accordingly, the Blackfoot granted the Cree peaceful access to their lands for trading purposes. They permitted the Cree, and their Assiniboine allies, to hunt in Blackfoot territory provided they did not trap beaver, which the Blackfoot reserved for themselves for trading purposes.[8]

THE DEMOGRAPHIC, ECONOMIC, AND POLITICAL SITUATION ON THE PLAINS AND IN THE PARKLANDS

Increasing pressure on the buffalo resource, compounded by losses resulting from epidemic diseases, threatened the Plains way of life. This was not a new problem on the eve of the treaties. The proliferation of trading posts and the development of a transport system to supply them and export returns provided local Aboriginal people with markets for provisions and seasonal employment opportunities. In addition to the rise and collapse of the commercial and subsistence buffalo hunt, other developments adversely affected the lives of First Nations in the Treaty 6 area and adjacent territories beginning in the late eighteenth century. The increasing frequency of epidemic diseases was one of the most disastrous. Unfortunately, the trading system facilitated the spread of European diseases.

The first major epidemic of record took place in 1780–81, when a devastating outbreak of smallpox swept the area, decimating all the nations in the western interior. Additional epidemics of this deadly scourge took place before treaty-making commenced in Saskatchewan. One took place during the autumn and winter of 1837–38. The quick response to the first news of the outbreak by Dr William Todd, who was in charge of Fort Pelly, saved most of the Cree and others who lived to the north of the Qu'Appelle valley. In keeping with the practice of sharing medicines, noted earlier, Todd shared his powers by teaching local Cree healers how to vaccinate their people. He attributed the success of the program partly to their efforts. The Assiniboine who lived in southern Saskatchewan chose not to take part in the vaccination scheme and were devastated. Significantly, the HBC continued its practice, begun in the eighteenth century, of offering medical assistance, to the extent that local circumstances permitted, until this responsibility was transferred to Canada.

On the eve of the treaty-making era in Saskatchewan, smallpox swept the prairies once more. The outbreak began in the late summer of 1870 and extended at least until mid-winter in most districts. Again, the Plains Cree of the Saskatchewan district were hit very hard. On 12 September 1870 Father Albert Lacombe wrote from his mission to the Cree at St Paul to Bishop Taché in Winnipeg, saying that "I am alone with Indians disheartened and terrified to such a degree that they hardly dare approach even their own relations." Lacombe added: "Poor Indians; what a pitiful sight they then offered and still offer, as a great number still labour under this painful disease. Every one implored my aid and charity. Some for medicine, others for the benefit of the last Sacraments ... This dreadful epidemic has taken all compassion from the hearths of the Indians. These lepers of a new kind are removed at a distance from the others and sheltered with branches. There they witness the decomposition and putrefaction of their bodies several days before death."9

HBC district manager W.J. Christie reported that the epidemic had erupted in the Fort Carlton area by early autumn and had already killed many people. By the time the epidemic had run its course, it had "swept away one-third of the population of the Saskatchewan district."10 According to Christie, "Every precaution shall be taken in Spring to prevent the spread of the epidemic from infected articles."11

The government of Manitoba and the appointed governing council for the North-West Territory made a concerted effort to deal with the 1870 smallpox crisis through the actions of the board of health and by legislation. Collectively, the government's initiatives aimed to check the spread of smallpox by banning the shipment of buffalo robes and other articles that could carry the contagion. The government set up hospitals and quarantine areas, and it sent medicine and doctors. Unfortunately the worst phases of the pestilence had already passed by the time the government was able to act.

Other scourges, most notably measles and influenza, spread through the area with increasing frequency in the nineteenth century, often taking a heavy toll. High mortality rates were the direct effect of the disease and the indirect consequence of malnutrition, because hunters were too sick to pursue their quarry or reach trading posts for relief. The collapse of the HBC robe and hide returns in the Saskatchewan district in 1871, for instance, was caused by the smallpox epidemic mentioned above. Many White observers commented on the terrible suffering that Plains nations had to endure as a result of these outbreaks.

By the 1870s, significant buffalo hunting was largely restricted to the prairies around the Cypress Hills.12 Significant trade in buffalo robes had ended by 1880. As the ranges contracted toward the Cypress Hills, clashes between First Nations escalated as they competed for the dwindling resource that had defined their essence since time immemorial. Historian J. Milloy refers to this period as the time of the buffalo wars.13 Isaac Cowie, who served as an HBC trader in the

Saskatchewan district during the late 1860s and 1870s, provided a first-hand account of the problem: "Already in 1867 Mr. [Archibald] McDonald's absolute fearlessness and vehement energy had conferred upon him the post of honor on the frontier [where Fort Ellice was located], back from which the Crees and Saulteaux were pushing the Blackfeet as they followed the buffalo into the country of the latter further west, while the Assiniboines of Wood Mountain and along the Missouri to the south, although nominally friendly, were a greater source of anxious uncertainty than the Blackfeet, who were open and certain enemies."[14]

Although the Blackfeet and their allies were friendly to the Whites at Edmonton and Rocky Mountain House, they considered Fort Carlton House and the posts at Touchwood Hills and Qu'Appelle, along with the trading and hunting parties belonging to all of them, as allies of their enemies, the Crees, and as objects of attack, as such, because they supplied arms and ammunition to the aggressive invaders of the hunting-grounds of the Blackfeet.[15]

Significantly, even though many aspects of the buffalo hunt had been commercialized beginning in the late eighteenth century, it remained a communal enterprise, as is made very clear by Peter Erasmus' description of a hunt made in 1858 by the Pigeon Lake Cree, who lived to the southeast of Fort Edmonton.[16] According to Erasmus,

We were continuously on the move as the band followed the buffalo. At one time we must have been almost three hundred miles east of Pigeon Lake and our range covered possibly one hundred miles south of the North Saskatchewan River. Our stay at one place was about a week, seldom more than twelve to fifteen days, then we moved the camp to some other location.

Contrary to the stories I have heard of idleness among Indian tribes, I found this band very industrious. They never killed more buffalo than they could use without waste ...

There was a definite assignment for each member of the tribe. The elder men acted as guards and buffalo hunters. The young men were given regular duties scouting or locating buffalo or enemy camps ... The women were always busy tanning hides or making moccasins, leather clothing for the men, and their own clothes ...

It was around the first of September when the Indians finally decided to make their way back to Pigeon Lake. They now had prepared quite a quantity of pemmican. The women had tanned the buffalo hides of the animals killed and made countless pairs of moccasins, gloves, leather coats, and other parts of their wardrobe. The making of teepees was a community affair in which a number of women took part under the direction of one of the older women. The pack horses would be well loaded when they got home.[17]

The complex buffalo-reliant way of life was soon to come under attack by forces representing potential agricultural settlers.

The lobbying of developers and speculators led the Canada West and British governments to back separate, well-publicized scientific expeditions to the region in the late 1850s to assess its economic potential. The Canadian excursion, led by Henry Youle Hind, and the British-sponsored party, commanded by Captain John Palliser, provided solid information about the Prairie Nations and those of the southern Canadian Rocky Mountains. These expeditions also made detailed descriptions of the agricultural promise of the prairies, gave accounts of coal and other mineral deposits, and discussed possible transcontinental transportation routes.[18] Additionally, the Hind report addressed the issue of Aboriginal title, which is discussed below.

Politicians and would-be developers and speculators paid little attention to Hind and Palliser's ethnographic works, but they were thrilled by their discussion of the economic potential of the sprawling region. The information circulated widely and had an impact well beyond Canada.

Aboriginal people strongly feared that the sale of Rupertsland would hurt their economic and political interests. They distrusted immigrants from Canada, in no small part because of a small but vociferous group of settlers led by Dr John Christian Schultz, who championed the annexation of the Northwest to the province of Canada. He used the *Nor'Wester*, a newspaper that he published from 1865 to 1868, to promote this outlook.

Hind was acutely aware of the problems of settlement. Much earlier he addressed them at length in his 1857 report. After a considerable discussion of troubled relations on the expanding frontier in the United States, he warned:

In Canada much trouble, great expense, and endless inquiry have been created by Indian claims, which even now remain in part unsettled, and are a source of many incidental expenses to the Government, which might have been avoided if proper arrangements had been made at the right season. In Rupert's Land, where disaffected Indians can influence the savage prairie tribes and arouse them to hostility, the subject is one of great magnitude; open war with the Sioux, Assiniboines, Plain Crees or Blackfeet, might render a vast area of prairie country unapproachable for many years, and expose the settlers to constant alarms and depredations. The Indian wars undertaken by the United States Government during the last half century, have cost infinitely more than the most liberal annuities or comprehensive efforts for the amelioration of the condition of the aborigines would have done; and in relation to the northern prairie tribes, war is always to be expected at a day's notice.[19]

In short, Hind was convinced that the government should address the legitimate concerns of First Nations. He had no doubt that this would minimize the risk of bloodshed and that in the end, it would also be the least costly approach for the government to pursue.

Hind went on to predict, accurately, that American policies would erupt into violence in Dakota country. He also expressed the worry that the Sioux, old enemies of the Canadian Assiniboine, Cree, Métis, and Ojibwa, might be driven to an alliance with the latter people.[20] This could have dire consequences for the settlement of the Canadian West. Regarding this potential threat, he wrote,

The country of the Dakotahs [Sioux] borders on British territory, some of the tribes ... are the confirmed enemies of the half-breeds and Ojibways of Red River; peace has often been made, but as often broken again upon trivial and even accidental grounds.

The frontier tribes can muster at least two thousand warriors by uniting with several of their more southern allies. Being the most warlike and numerous Indians in the United States territories, and their hunting grounds interlocking with those of the Crees in British America, they will probably yet play an important and active part in the future of the colony and the new adjoining territory of Chippewa [Dakotah territory and a portion of Nebraska].

Thickwood Crees [Woodland Cree], Swampy Crees, Plain Crees, and Ojibways are the Indian nations who now occupy that part of Rupert's Land where settlements would first be made. These nations are friendly to one another and hostile to the Sioux. They are, in fact, the hunters of the Hudson's Bay Company, and consequently friendly with that body, who have never sought to extend the settlements of the white race in Rupert's Land; but of late years since the questions relating to title to lands, annuities, and compensation have been raised, they are becoming dissatisfied, suspicious, and untrustworthy.[21]

In these comments Hind raised a critical issue. The Indigenous people of Rupertsland had welcomed the HBC as a trading partner and had given it access to their territories on that basis. For instance, in the nineteenth century Thunderchild recalled that at Fort Carlton the HBC "gave one boat load of goods for the use of the Saskatchewan River."[22] But the growing interest in land development by Canadian settlers and the company was beginning to undermine this long-established socio-commercial bond. Aboriginal people were becoming suspicious of the intentions of the HBC. Subsequently, they would raise these and other concerns about their relationship with the HBC during treaty negotiations with Canada. But already in 1857–58, as we have seen, Hind feared, with good reason, the spectre of an alliance between Canadian Plains groups and the Sioux, unless the government addressed their concerns about their lands and their future in the new economic order that was dawning.

Under these volatile circumstances it was imperative that the HBC move cautiously with reforms of its operations. Pressures for change had been building with the company since 1863. Several factors determined the pace and nature of treaty negotiations in parkland/grassland sections of Saskatchewan. One of these was the possibility of a frontier war. The HBC and government agents in the West were particularly sensitive to this danger. For instance, on 28 December 1870 HBC trader Richard Hardisty wrote a lengthy letter to William J. Christie, who was in charge of the company's Saskatchewan District,[23] about the state of Indian affairs there:

With reference to your letter of 15th November respecting the Indians, I will now give you my opinion as far as it has come under my own observation, as regards their trade and their present disaffection towards the Whites in the Saskatchewan District.

In the present unprotected state of the Country, the trade with the plain Indians is a dead loss to the Concern. As it had been customary before the introduction of Free Traders into the district to advance these Indians with Supplies, it has been continued more or less up to the present time; as long as the Indians had none but the Company to look to for supplies, they were, in some measure Kept in check and would make some attempts to pay up their Debts. At present, they demand supplies without any intention of ever paying them and even go so far as to threaten the Shooting of our animals and even further if refused.[24]

Hardisty thought that other forces were making the relations with the First Nations even more difficult:

For the last few years a great many dissatisfied Halfbreeds have lived among the Indians and done all they could to sow seeds of discord in the Indian minds, and again as the Buffalo have been scarce for some years, many have been ready to catch at the idea that whites coming into the Country have been the cause of the absence of Buffalo, and that the Company are to blame for this change. If they could prevent the settlement of whites in the Country they would gladly do it.

The plain Indians as far back as I can recollect have always considered the whites and Halfbreeds as aggressors on their lands when parties have gone to the plains to make provisions, but as it has always been our policy to have staunch men from among them-selves as Guides and Hunters, no very serious collision has ever taken place, but latterly, the aspect of things has changed considerably, and as I have mentioned above, the disturbances in Red River, have sensibly affected the Indian mind in this part of the Country, and again the small pox having carried away so many of their friends for which they blame the whites there appears to be a careless indifference as to the future not caring how soon troubles may commence.

In the month of October when the Victoria freemen [Métis] were out on the Plains, a party of Plain Crees came to their Camp with the deliberate intention of pillaging them and even going further if necessary, but when the Crees saw that the freemen armed themselves and were determined to resist them, they considered it useless to attempt anything. If the Crees party had been larger it would likely ended in bloodshed.

All these factors – buffalo scarcity, difficult Métis-First Nations relations – made Hardisty apprehensive for the future: "It is my opinion that, as soon as an influx of whites comes to the Country and especially of miners and if there is no protection speedily sent into the Country or law enforced, which will be wanted as much for the Indians as the white man, and even more so, the Country will be embroiled in Indian troubles which none of us may live to see the end of." Christie shared Hardisty's concerns. He was anxious to have the government respond with a treaty, fearing bloodshed would be the result if they failed to do so.

On 13 April 1871 Chief Sweetgrass, a prominent Plains Cree, dictated a letter to Christie asking the territorial government for a treaty and asking Christie to forward the letter to Lieutenant-Governor Archibald. Christie did so and attached a memorandum to the letter warning,

Had I not complied with the demands of the Indians – giving them some little presents – and otherwise satisfied them, I have no doubt that they would have proceeded to acts of violence, and once that had commenced, *there would have been the beginning of an Indian war, which it is difficult to say when it would have ended.*

The buffalo will soon be exterminated, and when starvation comes, these Plain Indian tribes will fall back on the Hudson's Bay Forts and settlements for relief and assistance. If not complied with, or no steps taken to make some provision for them, they will most assuredly help themselves; and there being no force or any law up there to protect the settlers, they must either quietly submit to be pillaged, or lose their lives in the defence of their families and property, against such fearful odds that will leave no hope for their side.

Gold may be discovered in paying quantities, any day, on the eastern slope of the Rocky Mountains. We have, in Montana, and in the mining settlements close to our boundary line, a large mixed frontier population, who are now only waiting and watching to hear of gold discoveries to rush into the Saskatchewan, and, without any form of Government or established laws up there, or force to protect whites or Indians, it is very plain what will be the result.

I think that the establishment of law and order in the Saskatchewan District, as early as possible, is of most vital importance to the future of the country and the interest of Canada, and also the making of some treaty or settlement with the Indians who inhabit the Saskatchewan District.[25]

Government officials in the territory, including Lieutenant-Governor Morris, shared Christie's concerns. For example, on 2 August 1873 Morris wrote to Alexander Campbell, minister of the interior, warning him of possible trouble and proposing a way to avoid it:

The numbers of Indians west of Fort Ellice (up to which point treaties have been made with the Indians) are formidable. I have made enquiries of persons likely to know the numbers, such as Bishop Granden, Pere Andre, Honble Pascal Breland, Honble J. McKay, and others. From these sources of information, I estimate the number dwelling in the Plain country as follows: – Blackfeet, (a very warlike tribe, well armed and supplied horses) 7000. Plain Crees (another warlike tribe, at present at peace with their hereditary foes, the Blackfeet) 5000. Assiniboines 2000. = 14000.

But these numbers are liable to be largely increased at any time by members of these tribes, and others, such as the Sioux in the u.s. who cross the line for hunting purposes.

The number of children in Indian families is small, averaging probably three per family, so that in the event of hostilities arising, I believe the Indians could place in the field 5000 mounted warriors, well armed.

If large numbers of Plains warriors were the danger, what was the solution? Morris wrote,

The Americans are obliged to maintain a large force in the adjoining State and Territories By pursuing a policy of conciliation, I believe the Dominion might secure the preservation of peace by maintaining, in addition to the proposed Police force, a Military Force of 500 men in the N.W. This I regard as absolute necessity. Already the Indian Tribes have formed a very low estimate of the Military power of Canada, and believe that about 3000 warriors could drive the Canadians from the country. *If there were no force here the results would be disastrous and at any moment the scenes of Massacre, plunder, and violence enacted in Minnesota, might be repeated here.*[26]

In other words, Morris recommended a two-fold course of action that would involve extending peaceful overtures through treaties while also making a display of force. In the letter just quoted he recommended promptly making two treaties, one with the Plains Cree and the other with the Blackfoot.

On 6 August Campbell replied to Morris that "I myself was in favor of going on with the treaty this year ... because I conceived it would be easier to deal with the Indians now than hereafter, and also that dealing with them now would be the means of preserving peace amongst them, but Sir John Macdonald and all my colleagues were of the other opinion holding that there was no use making a treaty so long in advance of our requiring the land."[27] Morris was very disappointed with the delay and increasingly worried that trouble would arise in the Saskatchewan District. He was particularly concerned that delays in making treaties were giving the Métis opportunities to persuade their Indian relatives not to come to terms with Canada. On 23 October 1873 he cautioned Campbell about this problem:

I have inc. copy of a confidential statement, given to me by Mr. Bell, of the Geological Survey, at my request. He has just returned from the Territories, and reports to me that a very bad feeling exists among the Indians, as also that the Half-Breeds at Lake Qu'Appelle, claimed that there is no visible government there, and no policy, and that they did not wish strangers to enter the country. I transmitted to the Government, on the 5th June last, a letter from the Half-Breeds there, presented by one [Mr] Fisher, and my reply. Fisher then stated that they did not want any strangers to come into the country; but I told him that the country was open to all, but that they would be dealt with justly. I am led to fear, from various sources of information, some movement there which may give trouble, and think that the Government should reconsider their decision as to making a Treaty with the Indians in the region I indicated to them in my dispatch of July 26th.[28]

Clearly, mounting White development pressures were cause for alarm in the absence of the treaties.

On 6 March 1874 Morris wrote a private letter to David Laird, minister of the interior under the new Liberal/Reform government of Alexander Mackenzie, to complain that he did not think that Ottawa was taking Indian Affairs seriously enough.[29] There was an additional reason to worry about the risks of armed conflict. Americans were trading new repeating rifles to Plains nations, such as the Blackfoot. On 22 March 1874 HBC trader John Bunn wrote from the Bow River area to Richard Hardisty at Fort Edmonton, noting: "As you are aware these repeating Combines have been for some years traded to the Blackfeet by the Americans, the propriety of supplying them with so formidable a fire arm in their present wild & lawless state may be questionable (in my opinion it is) should the like opinion be held by those in authority, then the sale of them to the Indians should be prohibited altogether."[30]

While Morris lobbied for treaties in the Treaty 4, 6, and 7 regions, the territorial government expressed support for his efforts. On 8 September 1873 council members resolved

That the Council of the North-West are of opinion, that in view of the rapid increase of Settlement in the North-West Territories, and the present disturbed condition of the Indians and their anxiety as to the future, it is imperatively necessary that a Treaty should be concluded with the bands of Indians living between the Western Boundary of that portion of the Territory in which the Indian Title has already been extinguished, and Fort Carlton or thereabouts.

The Council are of opinion that to defer the negotiation of a Treaty of this nature beyond the earliest time possible in the year 1874 would be attended with unfortunate results.[31]

On 16 March 1874 the council adopted the report of its Committee on Indian Affairs, which included the following observations:

2 That a sufficient force be sent to secure the collection of the Customs duties and the repression of the trade in liquor by the American traders and outlaws in the Belly and Bow River Districts, and that such force should consist of such a number of trained men as the Military authorities are of opinion will be necessary to reduce the outlaws to order estimated at 300 men in view of the possibility of their effecting an Indian Alliance, and of their having fortified posts.

3 That in view of the danger of an Indian War and of International complications which might embroil, at any moment the British and American people in war, the Privy

Council should ask that a British Regiment should be stationed and maintained in the North West to act in support of the Civil authorities and in concert with the Dominion forces.

4   That the Council are of opinion that the existing Provisional Infantry and Artillery are of urgent necessity.[32]

On 1 June 1874, the councillors noted "That in view of the unsettled state of the Cree and Blackfeet Indians, the Council of the North West Territories recommend that the first Treaty advised by the Council, otherwise known as the Qu'Appele [sic] Treaty [Treaty 4], be made, and that Messengers be sent to the rest of the Crees and the Assiniboines, informing them of the treaty and of the intentions of the Government in regard to them, before the occupation of their Country by the Mounted Police."[33] The councillors passed a resolution to implement this recommendation and also decided that they "would be glad if the other Treaties suggested by them [covering Treaty 5 and 6 areas] also be made this year if possible." They also stated that they were "of opinion that a Messenger should precede the Police Force to explain the object of their coming into the North-West Territories, and to inform them that a Treaty will be made with the Indians of the Qu'Appele [sic] region this year and also with the other Indians as soon as practicable." In other words, the council for the North-West Territories believed that treaties were urgently needed for the peaceful resettlement of the prairie West and made every effort to expedite the process.

The conclusion of Treaty 4 in 1874 (and Treaty 5 the following year) would make the Plains nations who remained outside of treaty increasingly restive. In 1876, David Mills, minister of the interior and Indian affairs, reported:

Official reports received last year from His Honor Governor Morris and Colonel French, the officer then in command of the Mounted Police Force, and from other parties, showed that a feeling of discontent and uneasiness prevailed very generally amongst the Assiniboines and Crees lying in the unceded territory between the Saskatchewan and the Rocky Mountains. This state of feeling, which had prevailed amongst these Indians for some years past, had been increased by the presence, last summer, in their territory of the parties engaged in the construction of the telegraph line, and in the survey of the Pacific Railway line, and also of a party belonging to the Geological Survey. To allay this state of feeling, and to prevent the threatened hostility of the Indian tribes to the parties then employed by the Government, His Honor Governor Morris requested and obtained authority to dispatch a messenger to convey to these Indians the assurance that Commissioners would be sent this summer, to negotiate a treaty with them, as had already been done with their brethren further east.[34]

The territorial council understood that Indian nations objected to any kind of survey of unsurrendered land. For instance, on 1 October 1873 it had resolved

That the Council of the North West having been informed that the Boundary Commission [Canada/United States] is about to proceed Westward and being aware of the jealousy with which their advance is likely to be viewed by the Indians, and also, of the feelings of animosity which the Sioux entertain towards the American portion of the Survey, and being also of opinion that if the Indians were thoroughly informed as to the real objects of the Survey they would not attempt to impede its onward progress, the Council recommend that Commissioners should precede the Survey to explain matters to the Indians, and also that a competent person should accompany the Survey for the same purpose.[35]

The missionary George McDougall delivered Morris' message to the Plains Cree in the autumn of 1875. In a letter to the lieutenant-governor, describing his visit, McDougall wrote:

I was also informed by these Indians [a group of Cree near Fort Carlton] that the Crees and Plain Assiniboines were united on two points: 1st That they would not receive any presents from Government until a definite time for treaty was stated. 2nd Though they deplored the necessity of resorting to extreme measures, yet they were unanimous in their determination to oppose the running of line, or the making of roads through their country, until a settlement between the Government and them had been effected. I was further informed that the danger of a collision with the whites was likely to arise from the officious conduct of minor Chiefs who were anxious to make themselves conspicuous, the principal men of the large camps being much more moderate in their demands. Believing this to be the fact, I resolved to visit every camp and read them your message.[36]

McDougall was particularly worried about the Ojibwa. In the course of his letter to Morris, he observed:

In a word, I found the Crees reasonable in their demands, and anxious to live in peace with the white men. I found the Big Bear, a Saulteaux [he was a Cree with Ojibwa ancestry on his paternal side], trying to take the lead in their council. He formerly lived at Jack Fish Lake, and for years has been regarded as a troublesome fellow. In his speech he said: "We want none of the Queen's presents; when we set a fox-trap we scatter pieces of meat all round, but when the fox gets into the trap we knock him on the head; we want no bait, let your Chiefs come like men and talk to us." These Saulteaux are the mischief-makers through all this western country, and some of them are shrewd men.[37]

Other Whites in the region reconfirmed the urgent need to conclude a treaty and establish government authority. For instance, on the eve of Treaty 6 (2 May 1876) Lawrence Clarke, who was in charge of Fort Carlton, wrote to Morris stating the problem:

Because a written information was laid before me, as justice of the Peace by five Freemen that whilst in the peaceable pursuit of their business on the prairie country, they were forcibly robbed by a party of forty armed men headed by one Gabriel Dumont.

Because a Government expedition under the charge of Mr. Ells of the Geological Survey of Canada was turned back from the Elbow of the North Saskatchewan River by Indians who would not allow the party to carry out their instructions. A copy of Mr. Ells letter to me was addressed to your Honor.

Because the Indians openly threaten to prevent the working of the Telegraph Company unless a treaty or a promise of a treaty was first made with them, and did actually turn back a party of the Company Freighters South of Fort Pitt and would not allow them to proceed any farther.

Having fully reported to your honor the circumstances of the trouble here last Summer in my dispatches of 10th/20th July last, I remarked that unless we have a certain protection force stationed at or near Carlton, I cannot answer for the result of Serious difficulties [that] will arise and life and property to be endangered. Leaving it to your Excellency to take what steps you deemed most advisable to meet the danger, and I repeat that the expedition sent to Carlton was the only effective measure that can have been adopted.[38]

Clearly the possibility of bloodshed was real; the conditions Hind had warned about had come to pass. The Blackfoot and Cree had reached a peace accord in 1871. The Lakota (Sioux) led by Sitting Bull had been making peaceful overtures to Canadian Plains groups throughout the 1870s in the hope of building a military alliance with them.[39] As Sweet Grass and McDougall had made plain, the chiefs were having trouble controlling those among their followers who wanted to take up arms. The government did not have sufficient manpower in the field to offer anything more than token resistance against a general uprising or to prevent destitute First Nations people from taking what they needed from settlers and the HBC. Concluding a treaty offered the prospect of avoiding the high financial and human costs that inevitably would result from an outbreak of hostilities. This consideration played a major role in persuading the government to come to the bargaining table.

On the eve of treaty-making, Saskatchewan held challenges for both First Nations and the Crown. Plains Nations were devastated by disease and declining resources. These difficulties, which were the consequences of First Nations heavy reliance on the land and its resources, are well known. The political and military instability inherent in the pending changes were conveyed to government by senior HBC officials and missionaries. For its part, Canada, though now aware of the challenges facing Plains First Nations, still feared the military strength of these people.

CHAPTER SEVEN

Qu'Appelle Treaty, or Treaty 4

Connections and similarities existed between Saskatchewan treaties and the preceding Robinson Treaties and Treaties 1, 2, and 3. Alexander Morris, in his 1880 publication *The Treaties of Canada*, considered the similarities, pointing out that the Robinson agreements and the first three treaties served as the blueprint for those that followed: "The treaties are all based upon the models of that made at the Stone Fort in 1871 and the one made in 1873 at the north-west angle of the Lake of the Woods with the Chippewa tribes, and these again are based in many material features, on those made by the Hon. W. B. Robinson with the Chippewas dwelling on the shores of Lakes Huron and Superior in 1860 [1850]."[1] He noted that the treaties had seven common features:

1 A relinquishment ... of all their right and title to the lands covered by the treaties, saving certain reservations for their own use, and

2 In return for such relinquishment, permission to the Indians to hunt over the ceded territory and to fish in the waters thereof, excepting such portions of the territory as pass from the Crown into the occupation of individuals or otherwise.

3 The perpetual payment of annuities of five dollars per head to each Indian – man, woman and child. The payment of an annual salary of twenty-five dollars to each Chief, and of fifteen dollars to each Councillor, or head man, of a Chief (thus making them in a sense officers of the Crown), and in addition, suits of official clothing for the Chiefs and head men, British flags for the Chiefs, and silver medals ...

4 The allotment of lands to the Indians, to be set aside as reserves for them for homes and agricultural purposes, and which cannot be sold or alienated without their consent, and then only for their benefit; the extent of lands thus set apart being generally one section for each family of five.

5 A very important feature of all the treaties, is the giving to the Indian bands, agricultural implements, oxen, cattle (to form the nuclei of herds), and seed grain ...

6 The Treaties provide for the establishment of schools, on the reserves, for the instruction of the Indian children. This is a very important feature, and is deserving of being

pressed with the utmost energy. The new generation can be trained in the habits and ways of civilized life – prepared to encounter the difficulties with which they will be surrounded, by the influx of settlers, and fitted for maintaining themselves as tillers of the soil ...

7 The treaties all provide for the exclusion of the sale of spirits, or "fire-water" on the reserves ...

Such are the main features of the treaties between Canada and the Indians, and, few as they are, they comprehend the whole future of the Indians and of their relations to the Dominion.[2]

Not surprisingly, Morris understood the treaty relation between Indian nations and the Crown only in general terms. For example, Treaties 1 and 2 did not express a hunting or fishing right, yet his summary of the common features stated that the Indian right "to hunt over the ceded territory and to fish in the waters" was central to all the treaties.

PRELIMINARY TALKS AT FORT QU'APELLE

Although Treaty 4[3] was not, strictly speaking, the first of the Saskatchewan treaties (Treaty 2 of 1871 includes the southeastern corner of Saskatchewan), in practical terms the 1874 discussions that led to this accord initiated the treaty-making process in the territory that became Saskatchewan.[4] These talks brought together an impressive cast of characters. Alexander Morris, a lawyer and lieutenant-governor of Manitoba and the North-West Territory and David Laird, minister of the Interior and superintendent general of Indian Affairs in the Alexander Mackenzie government (1873–78) led the Crown's party. These two officials were accompanied and assisted by retired Hudson's Bay Company factor for the Saskatchewan District, W.J. Christie; a future Indian agent, M.G. Dickieson, who acted as secretary to the proceedings; an official interpreter, Charles Pratt, who was a member of the Cree-Assiniboine band known as the Young Dogs and also a catechist of the Church of England; and a military escort consisting of Canadian militia.[5] For reasons that are not explained in Alexander Morris' account, two other men also acted for a time as interpreters: William Daniel at Qu'Appelle and Joseph Robillard at Fort Ellice (see table A4).

Alexander Morris, who for a variety of reasons was to be the most influential of the government's representatives at Qu'Appelle, was anxious to achieve a successful conclusion to the negotiations. Appointed lieutenant-governor of Manitoba and also of the North-West Territories in 1872, Morris had, after much difficulty negotiated Treaty 3, the North West Angle Treaty, in 1873. In the autumn of 1873 he informed Alexander Campbell, minister of the Interior and superintendent general of Indian Affairs, that "unsatisfactory accounts of the state of affairs in the Territories" made him "regret much that the Treaties I proposed were not carried out." He was alarmed at the restiveness of "the Metis at Lac Q'Appelle," who were reported as "wishing to resist the coming of any settlers & saying there is no law there." What was worse, "They [the Métis] are also I am told exciting the Indians, telling them their lands are to be taken from them."[6] Morris tied "the future of the North West and the Indian question" together, apparently recognizing that failure to solve the latter dimmed the former.[7]

Morris kept up his campaign with Ottawa for more treaties to the west of Treaty 2, and in the spring told the minister of justice that "I am glad that you have obtained a sum for a Treaty this summer. A Treaty covering the region of the Qu'Appelle Lakes is of great importance and would have a very beneficial effect in the North West."[8] Morris clearly saw treaties in the prairie region west of Treaty 2, including the Qu'Appelle Treaty, as essential to avoid unrest among Plains First Nations – unrest made worse by discontented Métis, perhaps, and unrest that would deter potential settlers and retard the agricultural development of the Northwest.

The First Nations negotiators whom Morris and the other government representatives met spoke for both the Plains Cree and the Saulteaux groups from the Qu'Appelle Valley and surrounding area, as well as the Fort Pelly district. The man who articulated the Cree point of view was Kakushiway (Loud Voice), while Meemay (Gabriel Coté) and Otahaoman (the Gambler) took the lead for the Saulteaux party.[9] Other prominent chiefs who were present included Pisqua (Pasqua, the Plain), who did speak at one point, and Kawacatoose, who did not.[10] All in all, thirteen leaders would give their approval of the treaty after many days of difficult argument and negotiation.[11]

Treaty 4 is unique among the Saskatchewan treaties for two things that preceded the actual discussion of treaty terms. First, neither the Plains Cree nor the Saulteaux who were present appeared to have carried out the pipe ceremony or other important rituals that marked other negotiations.[12] Morris was not slow to notice the absence of ceremony and what the omission signified. To The Gambler, the Saulteaux spokesman, he critically contrasted the behaviour of the Saulteaux at Qu'Appelle in 1874 with that of their countrymen at the Treaty 3 talks held at the North West Angle a year earlier: "I held out my hand but you did not do as your nation did at the Angle. When I arrived there the Chief and his men came and gave me the pipe of peace and paid me every honor."[13] The Gambler told Morris that those of his people whom he represented were offended that the government had located its militia tents on the HBC site. Also, he was angry that Morris had not shaken the hand of a Métis when introduced, but it emerged over several days that the underlying cause of Native discontent went much deeper than these perceived slights.

"SOMETHING IN MY WAY"

For four days of preliminary discussions and part of the fifth day, Saulteaux negotiators refused to engage in substantive discussions with the government negotiators because they resented the Dominion of Canada's dealings with the HBC over
land that the First Nation regarded as Saulteaux territory. During 1869–70, the
Dominion of Canada had, as explained earlier, paid £300,000 for the company's
interests in Rupertsland, except for lands adjacent to its posts and a share of lands
located in the fertile belt. The Gambler's and other Native objections to the location of Canada's militia camp has to be understood as an objection to this transfer
agreement. This is why they immediately objected to Morris' intention to hold
treaty talks on HBC land; this is also why they complained about Morris and his
fellow commissioner, David Laird, being lodged in the HBC quarters during the
talks.[14] These concerns were of great symbolic importance. For the first two days,
the Saulteaux Chief, Coté, refused to come to the table, leaving the Gambler to
articulate his deep reservations. When Coté finally attended on the fourth day, he
initially would not talk. He deferred instead to Plains Cree chief Loud Voice, who
pointedly told Morris that "there is something in my way" that was preventing serious discussions from taking place.[15]

When the Saulteaux finally expressed openly what was troubling them, they
made it clear that they did not accept the company's pretension that it had the
right to dispose of First Nations lands to Canada. Likewise, they resented the
surveying of the tracts that the company claimed according to the terms of the
1869–70 transfer agreement.[16] This subject had already been raised briefly
and in a rather narrow context during Treaty 3 talks. Indians near Fort Francis
had been angry that the company was claiming lands that they wanted for
their reserves. The Fort Francis Ojibwa chief had asserted that the land belonged to him. Morris had dealt with this problem by saying that he would
look into the matter and assured the Ojibwa that their interests would be dealt
with fairly.[17]

At Fort Qu'Appelle in 1874, the Gambler demanded to know who was responsible for the surveying that had gone on around the HBC fort:

I have understood plainly before what he (the Hudson Bay Company) told me about the
Queen. This country that he (H.B.Co.) bought from the Indians let him complete that. It is
that which is in the way. I cannot manage to speak upon anything else, when the land was
staked off it was all the Company's work. That is the reason I cannot speak of other things.

The Company have stolen our land. I heard that at first. I hear it is true. The Queen's
messengers never came here, and now I see the soldiers and the settlers and the policemen.
I know it is not the Queen's work, only the Company has come and they are the head, they
are foremost; I do not hold it back. Let this be put to rights; when this is righted I will answer the other.

When one Indian takes anything from another we call it stealing, and when we see the present we say pay us. It is the Company I mean.

Lieut. Gov. Morris – What did the Company steal from you?

The Gambler – The earth, trees, grass, stones, all that which I see with my eyes.[18]

Later in the same confrontation the Gambler spelled out even more plainly that the Saulteaux regarded the company's survey of land as presumptuous and an affront:

Lieut-Gov. Morris – What do you complain of? I can not tell.

The Gambler – The survey. This one (pointing to an Indian) did not say so, and this Saulteaux and he was never told about it. He should have been told beforehand that this was to have been done and it would not have been so, and I want to know why the Company have done so. This is the reason I am talking so much about it.[19]

And again he made the point that

The Company have no right to this earth, but when they are spoken to they do not desist, but do it in spite of you. He is the head and foremost. These Indians you see sitting around report that they only allowed the store to be put up. That is the reason I was very glad when I heard you were coming. The Indians were not told of the reserves at all[.] I hear now, it was the Queen gave the land. The Indians thought it was they who gave it to the Company, who are now all over the country. The Indians did not know when the land was given.[20]

The climax of this confrontation came soon after, when Pasqua, in exasperation, pointed at an HBC man and said, "You told me you had sold your land for so much money, £300,000. We want that money."[21]

Pasqua's brother-in-law, the reporter F.L. Hunt, quoted an unidentified negotiator as saying to Morris: "A year ago these people [the company] drew lines, and measured and marked the lands as their own. Why was this? We own the land; the Manitou [or Great Spirit] gave it to us. There was no bargain; they stole from us, and now they steal from you."[22]

Commissioner Morris refused to entertain these demands, arguing that the Canadian government did not have any particular responsibility for the HBC and that the Queen could dispose of the lands as she saw fit. He tried to resolve the issue by stating that the Queen had the right to grant lands to the company just as she did to the Indians. He said that "the Company are nothing to her except that they are carrying on trade in this country,"[23] and he added that the company needed land to carry on its trading operations and the Queen had granted the reserves to the company for that purpose. Morris also stressed that the Queen would not break her promises to the company, just as she would not break them with the Indians. And in an attempt to undermine The Gambler's position, Morris pointed out that the Saulteaux, the Gambler's people, were newcomers to the territory and that their ancestral homelands lay to the east. Thus, argued Morris, the Gambler's people were like the HBC. The Cree had given both of them permission to live in the area.

Morris offered another dubious counterargument to The Gambler:

I told you that many years ago the Queen's father's father gave the Company the right to trade in the country from the frozen ocean to the United States boundary line, and from the Atlantic Ocean to the Pacific. The Company grew strong and wanted no one to trade in the country but themselves. *The Queen's people said, "no, the land is not yours, the Queen's father's father gave you rights to trade, it is time those rights should stop."* You may go on and trade like any other merchant, but as it was worth money to you to say to this trader you shall not buy furs at any post, the Queen would not act unjustly to the Company. She would not take rights away from them any more than from you; and to settle the question, she took all the lands into her own hands and gave the Company a sum of money in place of the rights which she had taken from them.[24]

Although Morris told the Indians that the £300,000 paid to the HBC was intended solely to compensate it for withdrawal of its monopoly trading privileges, he must have known that the payment was for the purchase of the company's charter title to Rupertsland, given that the terms of this transaction had been the subject of protracted negotiations between the HBC and the Canadian and British governments during the late 1860s. Even more misleading was Morris' statement that the Queen had taken all of the lands into her hands. After all, the HBC retained one-twentieth of the territory of the fertile belt, as well as the developed lands (the reserves) around its posts. The latter concession amounted to 45,160 acres, of which 42,170 was located in the old Northern Department. Of the latter figure, the Saskatchewan District comprised over half with 25,700 acres.[25] Morris could not have been ignorant of the terms of the sale of Rupertsland, given the public offices he held. More likely, he was attempting to conceal these aspects of the transaction from the Indians.

After Morris rebuffed them about the HBC-Canada transfer, First Nations negotiators advanced other demands related to the company. On behalf of the Saulteaux, The Gambler demanded an agreement to restrict Hudson's Bay Company activities to their posts: "The Indians want the Company to keep at their post and nothing beyond. After that is signed they will talk about something else ... The Company is not to carry anything out into the country, but are to trade in the Fort. That is what we want signed on the paper; then we will talk on other subjects."[26] When Morris said that he could not sign such an agreement, Chief Coté began to talk of leaving Fort Qu'Appelle and returning to his home territory: "You wanted me to come here and I came here. I find nothing, and I do not think anything will go right. I know what you want; I cannot speak of anything here concerning my own land until I go to my own land. Whenever you desire to see me I will tell you what you are asking me here. Now I want to return."[27] Coté desisted only when Morris intimated that the chief's departure would be interpreted as rejection of the Crown's overtures and that it might well be a long time before another opportunity for treaty talks occurred:

If that be the message that, your conduct to-day is going to make us carry back, I am sorry for you, and fear it will be a long day before you again see the Queen's Councillors here to try to do you good. The Queen and her Councillors may think that you do not want to be friends, that you do not want your little ones to be taught, that you do not want when the food is getting scarce to have a hand in yours stronger than yours to help you. Surely you will think again before you turn your backs on the offers; you will not let so little a question as this about the Company, without whom you tell me you could not live, stop the good we mean to do.[28]

In response, The Gambler implied that the Saulteaux were not leaving, and that Chief Coté would enter into discussions.

When talks resumed the next day, the sixth day of meetings, the First Nations negotiators were still not ready to let go of the Hudson's Bay Company issue. Kamooses, a Cree spokesman, tried by an indirect means to obtain some benefit from the HBC-Canada transfer: "Now, I am going to ask you that the debt that has been lying in the Company's store, I want that to be wiped out. I ask it from the great men of the Queen."[29] Morris suggested that such a course of action would not be appropriate. Surely, he asked, if someone owed a chief a debt it would be wrong for someone else to cancel the obligation? Moreover, he had no authority to wipe the ledger clean: "I would be very glad if we had it in our power to wipe out your debts, but it is not in our power. All we can do is to put money in your hands and promise to put money in the hands of those who are away, and give you money every year afterwards, and help you to make a living when the food is scarce."[30] Both Cree and Saulteaux would have to satisfy themselves with these promises of annuities and support for subsistence in the future.

TREATY 4 NEGOTIATIONS

In light of the protracted preliminary arguments that revolved around the issue of who owned the territory that the treaty was to cover, perhaps it is not surprising that Morris' and First Nations elders' accounts of this aspect of the talks are in sharp contrast. Even according to his own secretary's version of the talks, the commissioner said relatively little about the land. On the other hand the elders' recollections of what the treaty negotiations had to say about the land are sharp and consistent. The commissioner asserted a Crown title when justifying the HBC transfer to Canada. "All the ground here is the Queen's and you are free to speak your mind fully," he told Cree spokesmen at the beginning of the third day's meeting.[31] During his argument with the Gambler over the HBC on the fourth day, Morris denied that the Indians' lands had been stolen, because "it is not stealing to use the gift of the Great Spirit. The lands are the Queen's under the Great Spirit."[32] And later in the same set-to, Morris said, "We are here to talk with you about the land."[33]

However, through all the many days of talks, Morris was never very specific about what the future status of the lands to be embraced by the treaty would be. For example, on the first day he told the Cree, "We want to speak to you about the land and what the Queen is willing to do for you."[34] And on the fifth day he tried to counter Saulteaux charges that the land had been "stolen" by the HBC and Canada with an argument that implied the government wanted to share the territory as First Nations had done earlier: "We have two nations here. We have the Crees, who were here first, and we have the Ojibbeways, who came from our country not many suns ago. We find them here; we won't say they stole the land and the stones and the trees; no, but we will say this, that we believe their brothers, the Crees, said to them when they came in here: 'The land is wide, it is wide, it is big enough for us both; let us live here like brothers'; and that is what you say, as you told us on Saturday, as to the Half-breeds that I see around. You say that you are one with them; now we want all to be one."[35] Commissioner Morris' vague language stands in sharp contrast to the full and precise language in the government's printed version of Treaty 4: "The Cree and Saulteaux tribes of Indians, and all other the Indians inhabiting the district hereinafter described and defined, do hereby cede, release, surrender and yield up to the Government of the Dominion of Canada for Her Majesty the Queen and her successors forever, all their rights, titles and privileges whatsoever to the lands included within the following limits [which are then described]."[36]

For most of the other aspects of Treaty 4, the talks were relatively brief, principally because the First Nations negotiators were prepared to accept the terms that Ojibwa had agreed to a year earlier in the North West Angle Treaty. On the final day of talks, Kamooses, speaking on behalf of Loud Voice of the Cree "and for the other chiefs," told the commissioner, "We want the same Treaty you have given to the North-West Angle." When Morris inquired, "Who are you speaking for? Is it for the whole of the Indians?" the assembly, according to Morris' account, "expressed their assent."[37] This concurrence left the commissioner with the rather delicate task of explaining to those at Fort Qu'Appelle why he proposed to pay them eight dollars per person, whereas he had given the Ojibwa of northwestern Ontario twelve dollars as an initial payment. His explanation implied that prior usage of the Treaty 3 region by non-Natives had justified a higher payment: "You must know that the steamboats had been running through their waters, and our soldiers had been marching through their country, and for that reason we offered the Ojibbeways a larger sum than we offered you. Last year it was a present, covering five years; with you it was a present for this year only. I paid the Indians there a present in money down of twelve dollars per head."[38]

Morris also implied that the higher payment in Treaty 3 was justified by the greater difficulty and longer time it took to negotiate that agreement.[39] Whatever his supposed justification for a lower initial payment in Treaty 4, the final document contained a provision for payment "for every other man, woman and child [other than chief and headmen], twelve dollars in cash."[40] The commissioner explained that the payment was augmented to the same level as Treaty 3 "rather than not close the matter [i.e., conclude the treaty]."[41] In addition, each chief received twenty-five dollars and each head man, to a maximum of four in a band, fifteen dollars, and a coat. Each chief would also receive "a Queen's silver medal."[42]

Most other terms in Treaty 4 were identical to those in Treaty 3. For annuities, each chief would receive twenty-five dollars, each headman fifteen dollars; and both chiefs and head men would receive a commemorative suit of clothes every three years. Each chief was also to receive "in recognition of the closing of the treaty, a suitable flag." After a census of the people had been taken, each man, woman, and child would receive five dollars per year forever.[43] Kamooses, a Cree spokesman, had tried during negotiations to improve these terms: "I want ... all my children around me, something more on the top. For my chief thirty dollars, for my four chief head men twenty dollars, and each of my young children fifteen dollars a year." However, Morris accused him of trying to renege on the commitment to accept the same terms as had been agreed upon in Treaty 3 and refused to change the article of the treaty.[44]

"THE CUNNING OF THE WHITE MAN"

Treaty 4 also contained provisions for reserves that were the same as those of Treaty 3: "And Her Majesty the Queen hereby agrees, through the said Commissioners, to assign reserves for said Indians, such reserves to be selected by officers of Her Majesty's Government of the Dominion of Canada appointed for that purpose, after conference with each band of the Indians, and to be of sufficient area to allow one square mile for each family of five, or in that proportion for larger or smaller families."[45] For both the First Nations and the Crown, the reserves were related to a possible transfer to a sedentary, agricultural economy. Said Morris:

The Queen knows that you are poor; the Queen knows that it is hard to find food for yourselves and children; she knows that the winters are cold, and your children are often hungry; she has always cared for her red children as much as for her white. *Out of her generous heart and liberal hand she wants to do something for you, so that when the buffalo get scarcer, and they are scarce enough now, you may be able to do something for yourselves* ... What the Queen and her Councillors would like is this, she would like you to learn something of the cunning of the white man. When fish are scarce and the buffalo are not plentiful she would like to help you to put something in the land; she would like that you should have some money every year to buy things that you need. If any of you would settle down on the land, she would give you cattle to help you; she would like you to have some seed to plant. She would like to give you every year, for twenty years, some powder, shot, and twine to make nets of ... We are ready to promise to give $1,000 every year, for twenty years, to buy powder and shot and twine, by the end of which time I hope you will have your little farms.[46]

The following day Morris repeated this offer. Once again he referred to the problems they faced as buffalo hunters: "She [the Queen] knows that her red children, their wives and children, are often hungry, and that the buffalo will not last for ever and she desires to do something for them."[47] First Nations negotiators also related the reserve allocations to treaty terms covering the means with which to begin farming. Kamooses, for example, said to Morris, "We ask that we may have cattle." To this the commissioner replied that "We offered you cattle on the first day, we offered your Chief cattle for the use of his band – not for himself, but for the use of his band; we gave the same at the Lake of the Woods. We can give no more here."[48]

Beginning with Treaty 1 discussions, government representatives had agreed to give Indians a "once and for all" gift of equipment and livestock when they commenced farming operations. These were among the "outside promises" not included in the original copies of Treaties 1 and 2. The numbered treaties that followed included these "once and for all gifts" to promote Indian agricultural efforts, and each succeeding treaty was somewhat more generous in these terms. In the government's printed version of Treaty 4 the commitment on cattle was part of a broader clause covering support for farming:

It is further agreed between Her Majesty and the said Indians that the following articles shall be supplied to any band thereof who are now actually cultivating the soil, or who shall hereafter settle on these reserves and commence to break up the land, that is to say – two hoes, one spade, one scythe, and one axe for every family so actually cultivating; and enough seed, wheat, barley, oats and potatoes to plant such lands as they have broken up; also one plough and two harrows for every ten families so cultivating as aforesaid; and also to each Chief, for the use of his band as aforesaid, one yoke of oxen, one bull, four cows, a chest of ordinary carpenter's tools, five hand-saws, five augers, one cross-cut saw, one pit saw, the necessary files, and one grindstone; all the aforesaid articles to be given once for all, for the encouragement of the practice of agriculture among the Indians.[49]

Significantly, no explicit undertaking was made in the treaties to provide agricultural instruction. Indians asked for it, however. When Lieutenant-

Governor Morris returned to Fort Garry following the signing of Treaty 6, he made a series of recommendations to the Canadian government that included a recommendation to respond positively to the Indians' request for such instruction. According to Morris,

In the year 1876, I reported to the Minister of the Interior, the Hon. David Mills, after my return from the negotiation of the treaties at Forts Carlton and Pitt, "that measures ought to be taken to instruct the Indians in farming and building."

I said "that their present mode of living is passing away; the Indians are tractable, docile and willing to learn. I think that advantage should be taken of this disposition to teach them to become self-supporting, which can best be accomplished by the aid of a few practical farmers and carpenters to instruct them in farming and house-building."[50]

Also related to these farming provisions was a promise of schools, the two being linked by a concept that the treaty commissioner used more than once in the discussions, as we have seen. The Queen, Morris said, was offering the Plains Cree and Saulteaux "the cunning of the white man," if they chose to adopt it.[51] And shortly thereafter, the commissioner offered that "Whenever you go to a Reserve, the Queen will be ready to give you a school and a schoolmaster."[52] Accordingly, Treaty 4 promised that "Her Majesty agrees to maintain a school in the reserve, allotted to each band, as soon as they settle on said reserve, and are prepared for a teacher."[53]

As important as the promises of assistance in making a transition to agriculture and in learning the cunning of the white man were, they were offers of voluntary, not compulsory, change. When Commissioner Morris returned to this theme on the fourth day of talks at Fort Qu'Appelle, he spelled it out: "The Queen wishes her red children to learn the cunning of the white man and when they are ready for it she will send schoolmasters on every Reserve and pay them. We have come through the country for many days and we have seen hills and but little wood and in many places little water, and it may be a long time before there are many white men settled upon this land, and you will have the right of hunting and fishing just as you have now until the land is actually taken up."[54]

The government text of the treaty was more restrictive, however, than Morris' words during negotiation: "Her Majesty agrees that her said Indians shall have right to pursue their avocations of hunting, trapping and fishing throughout the tract surrendered, subject to such regulations as may from time to time be made by the Government of the country acting under the authority of Her Majesty, and saving and excepting such tracts as may be required or taken up from time to time for settlement, mining or other purposes under grant, or other right given by Her Majesty's said Government."[55] To support continuing hunting and fishing Morris offered what had been given to the Ojibwa in Treaty 3: "We promised there that the Queen would spend $1,500 per year to buy shot and powder, ball and twine. There were 4,000 of them. I offered you $1,000 although you are only one-half the number, as I do not think that you number more than 2,000."[56]

"THE QUEEN'S KINDNESS"

Beyond the precise terms of the government's text of Treaty 4, there was another important aspect of the pact that took precedence over such details: Treaty 4, as Morris' record of the First Nations negotiators' words makes clear, would establish a relationship between the Plains Cree and Saulteaux and the Queen. Cree leader Loud Voice began the sixth day's discussions with an allusion to this fact: "We see the good you wish to show us. If you like what we lay before you we will like it too. Let us join together and make the Treaty; when both join together it is very good."[57] And a little later Kamooses sought clarification of the party the First Nations were being asked to join hands with:

Is it true you are bringing the Queen's kindness? Is it true you are bringing the Queen's messenger's kindness? Is it true you are going to give my child what he may use? Is it true you are going to give the different bands the Queen's kindness? Is it true that you bring the Queen's hand? Is it true you are bringing the Queen's power?

Lieut-Gov. Morris – Yes, to those who are here and those who are absent, such as she has given us.

Kamooses – Is it true that my child will not be troubled for what you are bringing him?

Lieut-Gov. Morris – The Queen's power will be around him.[58]

It is possible, though there is no documentary evidence on the point, that uncertainty about the identity of the people asking them to make treaty – were they representing the Queen or the company? – underlay First Nations concern about the obviously close ties between Morris and the HBC, symbolized by Morris lodging at the HBC post. Morris' reassurances during the substantive negotiations followed on earlier comments that he came on behalf of the Queen to establish a relationship with the Cree and Saulteaux. On the first day he had explained that the previous year at the North West Angle "I took her children there by the hand, and the white man and the red man made friends for ever."[59] On the second day Morris had said, "What I want, is for you to take the Queen's hand, through mine, and shake hands with her for ever."[60] On the third day the message continued: "The Queen cares for you and for your children, and she cares for the children that are yet to be born. She would like to take you by the hand and do as I did for her at the Lake of the Woods last year."[61] On the fourth day Morris said, "The Queen has to think of what will come long after to-day. Therefore, the promises we have to make to you are not for to-day only but for to-morrow, not only for you but for your children born and unborn, and the promises we make will be carried out as long as the sun shines above and the water flows in the ocean[62] ... In our hands they feel the Queen's, and if they take them the hands of the white and red man will never unclasp."[63]

During the fifth day's discussions, the relationship with the Queen was linked more explicitly to promises of protection and equal justice:

In this country, now, no man need be afraid. If a white man does wrong to an Indian, the Queen will punish them. The other day at Fort Ellice, a white man, it is said, stole some furs from an Indian. The Queen's policemen took him at once; sent him down to Red River, and he is lying in jail now; and if the Indians prove that he did wrong, he will be punished. You see then that if the white man does wrong to the Indian he will be punished; and it will be the same if the Indian does wrong to the white man. The red and white man must live together, and be good friends, and the Indians must live together like brothers with each other and the white man.[64]

Probably because of the importance of relationship in treaty-making, the commissioner found it necessary as discussions drew to a close on the sixth day to explain why the chief's flag that was promised would not be forthcoming immediately: "each Chief on signing the treaty will receive a medal and the promise of a flag. We cannot give you the flag now, as there were none to be bought at Red River, but we have the medals here."[65] The government text of Treaty 4 embodied the notion of relationship in its statement of purpose in the opening paragraph: "and to make a treaty and arrange with them so that there may be peace and good-will between them and Her Majesty, and between them and Her Majesty's other subjects; and that her Indian people may know and be assured of what allowance they are to count upon and receive from Her Majesty's bounty and benevolence."[66] Though imperfectly, the government's text captured the treaty relationship that Commissioner Morris had repeatedly held out, a link that Saulteaux and Cree negotiators obviously considered important.

The other relationship that First Nations negotiators at Fort Qu'Appelle clearly considered significant was their tie to the Métis. On two occasions during the six days of talks, First Nations leaders asked for consideration for their mixed-blood kin. On the fourth day, the Gambler complained that the commissioner had slighted a Métis who was presented to him. All that Morris said in response was, "you may leave the Half-breeds in the hands of the Queen who will deal generously and justly with them."[67] And near the end of talks on the sixth day, Kamooses said to Morris, "we ask that the Half-breeds may have the right of hunting." To this Morris responded, "As to the Half-breeds, you need not be afraid; the Queen will deal justly, fairly and generously with all her children."[68] The First Nations negotiators did not succeed in obtaining any explicit commitment to their mixed-blood friends.[69] A few days later, a group calling themselves the "half-breeds of Lake Qu'Appelle" petitioned Morris formally, asking that their customary land holdings be recognized by the government, that they retain their fishing and hunting rights, and that the Roman Catholic mission in their midst retain its possessions.[70] After consulting the minister of the Interior, David Laird, who was a member of the treaty party, Morris provided reassuring responses without committing the government to any specific course of action.[71]

Finally, Morris' account demonstrates a strong concern among First Nations leaders that they receive a copy of the treaty agreement. For example, at the end of the fourth day's meeting Morris assured the Gambler, Pasqua, and others that "Mr. Pratt [the interpreter] will tell you so that there may be no mistake as to what we have promised. He has it written down so that it may not be rubbed out."[72] On the next day Morris explained how the previous year he had given the Ojibwa signatories of Treaty 3 a copy of the agreement, "and I told him when I went home to Red River I would have it all written out, a true copy made on skin, that could not be rubbed out, that I would send a copy to his people so that when we were dead and gone the letter would be there to speak for itself, to show everything that was promised; and that was the right way to do. I did so, and sent a copy of the treaty written in letters of blue, gold, and black to the Chief 'Maw-do-pe-nais,' whom the people had told to keep it for them."[73] And on the final day at Fort Qu'Appelle Morris made a similar commitment to the Plains Cree and Saulteaux:

Since we went away we have had the treaty written out, and we are ready to have it signed, and we will leave a copy with any Chief you may select and after we leave we will have a copy written out on skin that cannot be rubbed out and put up in a tin box, so that it cannot be wet, so that you can keep it among yourselves so that when we are dead our children will know what was written.

Kamooses – Yes, we want each Chief to have a copy of the treaty.[74]

TREATY 4 ADHESIONS

Six days after the conclusion of talks at Fort Qu'Appelle, Morris and Laird met at Fort Ellice with Chief Waywasecapow (the Man Proud of Standing Upright) and headman Otamakoooewin (the Man Who Stands on the Earth), also identified as Shaponetung's first son, representing "thirty tents who were not at Qu'Appelle, and ten who were there." Morris offered this group the same terms as had been accepted a week earlier, explaining, "What we offer will be for your good, as it will help you, and not prevent you from hunting." Chief Long Claws responded, "My father – I shake hands with you, I shake hands with the Queen." Shaponetung's son asked of the proffered agreement, "does it take in all my children?" Morris responded, "Yes," requested the names of chiefs and headmen, and asked, "Now I want to know will you take my hand and what is in it." At this, the leaders "came up and shook hands." After further explanations of the terms, the treaty adhesion was signed.[75] (For data on these and other adhesions to Treaty 4, see table A5).

The last phase of treaty-making in Treaty 4 during the 1870s concerned adhesions of further Plains Cree, Assiniboine, and Saulteaux groups. On 8 September 1875 Cheecuck signed at Qu'Appelle for an unspecified number of Saulteaux and Assiniboine; and the next day at the same location Wahpeemakwa (White Bear), Okanese, Piapot (He Who Knows the Secrets of the Sioux), Le Crou de Pheasant (Pheasant Rump), and Kitchikahmewin (Ocean Man) adhered to the same terms as negotiated in 1874.[76] White Bear, Pheasant Rump, and Ocean Man all led groups who resided in the area covered by the earlier Treaty 2. On 24 September 1875 at Swan Lake, Owtahpeekakaw and Kiishikouse signed for Cree and Saulteaux communities at Shoal River, while the next day at Fort Walsh, Teepee Hoska (Long Lodge) and Wichawostaka (The One that Fetched the Coat) adhered on behalf of Assiniboine groups. And with that, the nineteenth-century phase of negotiating Treaty 4 concluded (see table A4).

The negotiations over Treaty 4 in 1874 illustrate a number of important points, while hinting at others whose meanings are less clear. First, the talks at Fort Qu'Appelle illustrate yet again what an important formative influence the HBC had been in the experience of the Western First Nations. The symbolism of the location on which the parleys were to take place – on HBC land or away from the post? – obviously was considered important by the Saulteaux representatives in particular. Furthermore, the resentment of Plains Nations over the terms of the Rupertsland transfer obviously still was strong. Again, it was Saulteaux negotiators who held up talks in 1874 for several days as they sought to secure some benefit from the dealings with the HBC, the United Kingdom, and Canada.

The same HBC relationship also provides tantalizing hints of issues or forces that might have been at work. As noted, Commissioner Morris complained at the negotiations that the First Nations representatives refused him the honour of traditional pipe ceremonialism, although the anonymous author of "Memories of the Treaty of 1874" described at some length the equestrian ceremonialism that took place.[77] Furthermore, Morris later asserted that the Portage band of Saulteaux "twice sent messengers with Tobacco [the usual Indian credentials for such messengers] to Qu'Appelle to prevent the making of the treaty there," because of their unhappiness with Canadian reluctance to implement the promises in Treaty 1 that had been given orally but omitted from the government text of the treaty. After the dispute over "outside promises" was resolved in 1875, Morris observed that satisfying the aggrieved group was important for government relations with other First Nations: "You are aware of their intimate relations with the 'Plains Indians,' and the difficulty their message to Qu'Appelle 'that the white man had not kept his promises,' caused us then."[78] Morris and others also contended that Saulteaux unhappiness over the transfer issue was so much greater than the unhappiness of the Plains Cree that there was a split between the two nations at Qu'Appelle in 1874, a split that might have been reflected in who spoke and who did not during the first few days of oral fencing.

CHAPTER EIGHT

Lake Winnipeg Treaty, or Treaty 5

Three Saskatchewan First Nations – Cumberland House, Shoal River, and Red Earth – belong to Treaty 5, even though the original agreement and subsequent adhesions (1908, 1909, 1910), essentially pertained to present-day Manitoba.[1] Unlike the large treaty meetings involving several First Nations that took place on the prairies, the Treaty 5 commissioner dealt individually with regional bands. In comparison to Treaties 3 and 4, Treaty 5 provided fewer benefits to Indians (see tables A6 and A7). This chapter reconstructs the making of Treaty 5, concentrating on the details relevant to the three Saskatchewan bands. Unfortunately, the official records for Treaty 5 provide very few details on the issues that were discussed at the treaty talks or the goals of the Indian chiefs. And unlike Treaties 1, 3, 4, 6, and 8, there are no third-party accounts of these talks.

THE CROWN'S TERRITORIAL IMPERATIVES AND THE RATIONALE FOR TREATY 5

On 25 June 1874 Chief Rundle and several other Native leaders petitioned North-West Territories Governor Alexander Morris. The petition from Indians of the Norway House probably offers us the clearest insight into the First Nations' interest in having a treaty with the Crown, and, for this reason, it is substantially reproduced here:

We the Christian Indians of Rossville and Nelson River wish to present our humble and Christian regards to your excellency, and to submit the following questions.

i. As our Christian friends of Manitoba and other sections of the country have been treated with by the government in regard to their temporalities, we wish to know if it is the intention of the Government to make a treaty with the Indians in this section of the country also.

The reason why we ask this question is because the country is becoming too thickly peopled to find a sufficiency of the necessities of life to prevent much suffering among them in the future.

ii. Have we who now live in this section the same privilege as any other of Her Majesty's subjects, of going to any part of the country either Manitoba up the Saskatchewan or wherever we may find good farming country to form a settlement, in order to help our children from suffering hunger and the better to provide for our necessities.

The reason why we ask this question is because the Tripping to York Factory which has been carried on by the Honourable Hudson's Bay Company for very many years, will cease after this summer and by this means nearly two hundred of our people are thrown out of employment, and we have no way of our own, in this country, to procure the clothing and food which was thus earned by us and received from the Honourable Hudson's Bay Company during the past; this makes us feel that we must do something ourselves and if possible to obtain help from Her Majesty's Government at this time to meet the necessities of the future.

Submitting to your clemency, and feeling confident that you will do that which Providence has placed in your power to do for us, we and all our brethren, remain your humble obedient subjects.

> David Rundell x chief
> Quisko Nipinwaskum x
> James Cochrane x asst. chief
> William Cochrane x
> Abel Frayer x
> James Kesekastawaknum x
> Nelson McKay x
> George Kekeekesus x
> Thomas Kennedy[2]

The petitioners pointed out that obtaining a livelihood had become difficult in two crucial respects: the population density exceeded the country's capacity to provide the necessities of life, and changes to the fur trade transport system, including the deployment of steamboats, meant that a number of men were facing unemployment and that their families would suffer as a consequence. They recognized that a treaty and assistance from the government offered potential remedies for the declining economic circumstances associated with the post-1870 era. They argued that the hunting economy needed assistance, and they sought to move to a location where farming might be pursued. Furthermore, they made it clear that the loss of boat work generated the kind of insecurity that the Plains Indians felt in anticipation of the collapse of the buffalo economy. Seasonal labour associated with the fur trade had long been an important source of income for the local economy.

Previously, Morris had ruled out the need for a treaty covering the Norway House area, saying, "the country lying adjacent to Norway House is not adapted for agricultural purposes" and "there is therefore no present necessity for the negotiation of any treaty."[3] By November 1874, Chief Rundle had still not received a response from him regarding the petition.[4] After Treaty 5 had been concluded, Morris, taking a retrospective view of it, stated that the need to deal with the Norway House situation had been one of the rationales for making the covenant: "A band of Indians residing at Norway House, who had supported themselves by serving the Hudson's Bay Company as boatmen on the route from Lake Winnipeg to the Hudson Bay, by way of the Nelson River, but whose occupation was gone, owing to supplies being brought in by way of the Red River, desired to migrate to the western shore of Lake Winnipeg, and support themselves there by farming."[5]

If these concerns actually motivated Morris to reach an agreement, it means that Treaty 5 was an instance where the "Queen's benevolence" was used to address a livelihood problem created by the obsolescence of Indian and Métis labour that resulted from the deployment of modern steam power. This was unusual, since in most other areas, the government's primary interest in concluding treaties was to make way for avaricious Euro-Canadian settlers. In any event, Canada did have development interests in the region, and ambiguity about the position of the northern boundaries of Treaties 1 and 2 meant that the tenure for a proposed Icelandic settlement on the southwest shore of Lake Winnipeg was in doubt. One reason was that the Berens River people, who had been informed that they would be treated with in 1871 as part of Treaty 2, had been overlooked. In 1874 Morris argued for a limited treaty around Lake Winnipeg to deal with this and other development problems. Treaty 5 addressed this problem. It covered part of the Manitoba Interlake, the lower Saskatchewan River, and the Canadian Shield country around Lake Winnipeg. For a variety of reasons it also extended as far west as Cumberland House and as far north as Cross Lake.

In 1874, Morris did recommend a treaty with the Berens River Indians, since "trading, sailing of vessels and steamers will be carried on and probably settlement of the shore."[6] The resource potential of the Lake Winnipeg region permitted Morris to justify a much larger treaty by arguing that "the prevalence of timber suitable for fuel and building purposes, of lime and sandstone, of much good soil, and natural hay lands on the west shore of the Lake, together with the great abundance of white fish [sic], sturgeon and other fish in the Lake, will ensure, ere long, a large Settlement."[7] Additionally, plans to develop steam navigation on Lake Winnipeg and the lower Saskatchewan River meant that the government was interested in securing a navigable right of way. Morris had foreseen that until the completion of the railroad "the lake and Saskatchewan River are destined to become the principal thoroughfare of communication between Manitoba and the fertile prairies."[8] Several economic reasons suggested a treaty covering a large region.

Morris provided a number of technical reasons for including the Swampy Cree bands of the Lower Saskatchewan River and Norway House in a treaty that was

originally intended to cover territory and bands that had not been properly covered by Treaties 1 and 2:

1st   The extension of the boundary carries the treaty to the western limits of lands claimed
      by the "Saulteaux and Swampy Cree Tribes" of Indians, and creates an eastern base
      for the treaties to be made with the "Plain Crees" next year.
2nd   The "Swampy Cree" at the "Pass", on the Saskatchewan, would otherwise have had
      to be included in the western treaties. –
3rd   That the extension of the boundaries will add some 600 to the number of the Indians
      in the suggested limits, of whom 300 at "Wahpahhuha" or the "Pass" on the
      Saskatchewan would have had to be treated with, owing to the navigation of the
      Saskatchewan, and in any event, –
4th   The inclusion of the "Norway House Indians" in the treaty, and the surrender of their
      rights, involved a larger area of territory.
5th   That a number of the "Norway House" Indians came from Moose Lake and the
      Cumberland region, and possessed rights there which have been included in the
      boundaries.
6th   Unless the boundaries had been properly defined, in conformity with known geographi-
      cal points, a portion of the country lying between the territories formerly ceded and
      those comprised in Treaty No. 5, would have been left with Indian title unextinguished.[9]

If the proposed treaty had been confined to Lake Winnipeg, the Swampy Cree
bands on the Saskatchewan River would have been positioned on unceded lands
between Treaties 5 and 6, and consequently, the rights of navigation by steamboats would have been unclear. In this respect, a right of way for steamboats was
a priority for the Crown, not unlike the development of steam railroad on the prairies. Morris understood that Indians who had moved to new locations could retain
rights to unceded territory traditionally occupied. He was also alert to the potential problems arising from the geographical ambiguity of treaty boundaries.

Finally, a comprehensive economic rationale for Treaty 5 was provided by
Lieutenant-Governor Morris: "The progress of navigation by steamer on Lake
Winnipeg, the establishment of Missions and of saw milling enterprises, the discovery of minerals on the shores and vicinity of the lake as well as migration of
the Norway House Indians all point to the necessity of the Treaty being made
without delay."[10] Morris' reasoning for a treaty covering Lake Winnipeg clearly
demonstrates that agricultural development was not the sole concern of the government. Even at this early date, the potential resources of the boreal forest were
attracting the attention of agents of the Crown. Moreover, for the bands of Indians that soon settled at Fisher River, a treaty was a means to obtain a livelihood.

While most conventional rationales for the southern treaties centre on land for
settlement, a more complex and diverse set of reasons lead the Crown and
Swampy Cree and Ojibwa nations to negotiate Treaty 5.

TREATY-MAKING, 1875–1876

The original negotiation of Treaty 5 was carried out during the open water seasons in 1875 and 1876. In 1875 Morris and the Honourable James McKay represented the Crown at negotiations at Berens River, Norway House, and Grand Rapids. For this treaty, McKay served as a commissioner, but he also translated for the Crown. Thomas Howard was the paymaster and secretary. This treaty party traveled from one end of Lake Winnipeg to the other on the HBC steamboat *Colville*, but they relied on the chief and councillor to safely pilot the craft to the Berens River post.[11]

The *Colville* was the first steamboat to visit the HBC posts and communities of Berens River and Norway House. Indians from the Berens River band met the treaty party at the Methodist Mission School at 4 P.M. on 20 September 1876. Morris' account of treaty-making at Berens River was curt: "The question of Reserves was one of some difficulty, but eventually this was arranged, and the Indians agreed to accept our offer, and the indenture of treaty was signed by the chiefs and head-men about 1, m [1 P.M.]. The payment of the present of $5 per head, provided by the treaty, was immediately commenced by Mr. McKay and the Honorable Thomas Howard, who accompanied me as Secretary and Pay Master, and was continued until 1 a.m., when the payment was concluded."[12] It seems from this observation that the treaty-making at Berens River did not entail drawn-out discussions. The signatories included Alexander Morris, James McKay, Nahweekeesickquahyash (Chief Jacob Berens), and two councillors. There were several witnesses (table A6).

The day after the agreement was completed the treaty party left for Norway House, and after some delay en route Morris reported that "We arrived at Norway House at 3 o'clock and were welcomed there by the Indians, who fired a salute."[13] As explained earlier, such a discharge of firearms was a well-established tradition originating with the annual trade ceremony at York Factory nearly two hundred years earlier. Here the Crown's representatives recognized the Norway House and Cross Lake bands. The parties agreed to the terms of the treaty and discussed the location of reserves. The desire of part of the Norway House Band to locate in the Interlake was discussed. Morris reported, "The treaty was then signed and the medals and uniforms presented. The chiefs, on behalf of their people, thanked Her Majesty and her officers for their kindness to the Indian people, which I suitably acknowledged, and the payment of the presents was commenced by Messrs. McKay and Howard, and completed on the 15th [25th?]."[14] When the treaty party departed, the natives fired another salute.

At Norway House Alexander Morris and James McKay signed the treaty for Canada, and Chief David Rundle and three councillors did so for the Norway House band. Representing the Cross Lake band were Chief Tapastanum (Donald William Sinclair Ross) and two councillors. There were nine witnesses to this treaty (table A6).

After boarding the *Colville*, Morris, McKay, and the rest of the treaty party headed for Grand Rapids, at the mouth of the Saskatchewan River. The discussion of the treaty, which occurred near the chief's house, revealed a Crown negotiating strategy: Morris reported that "We took a similar course as at 'Norway House' in severing the question of terms of the treaty and Reserves, and with like satisfactory results, after a lengthy discussion the Indians agreed to accept the terms, and we then entered upon the difficult question of the Reserves."[15]

At Grand Rapids the Indians complained of the "reserve" set aside for the Hudson's Bay Company and disputed its strategic monopolization of the portage. As elsewhere, Morris defended the awards made to the company under the terms of the transfer of Rupertsland: "we explained whatever had been promised the Company would be given just as promises made to them would be kept."[16] Morris would not provide the Grand Rapids band with a reserve on both sides of the river since "the locality they had hitherto occupied is so important a point, controlling as it does the means of communication between the north of the river, and the head of the rapids, and where a 'tram-way' will no doubt ere long require to be constructed, presenting also deep-water navigation and excellent wharfage, and evidently being moreover the site where a town will spring up."[17] Eventually, Morris got the band to agree to a reserve on the south bank of the river, and according to Morris, once this agreement about the location of the reserve was made, the treaty was signed. However, the Grand Rapids Band was brought into Treaty 5 as an "Adhesion of Saskatchewan Indians" on 27 September 1875. This adhesion was signed by Morris, McKay, and Chief Peter Beardy and two councillors. There were seven witnesses to the adhesion (table A6).

On the way back to Red River, the treaty party encountered a party of Indians at Doghead. Thickfoot spoke for this group of Indians, which was one of several small bands that occupied the islands and adjacent shores at the narrows of Lake Winnipeg. This band knew about the treaty that had recently been negotiated. Morris reported that "Eventually we decided on paying these Indians – took 'Thickfoot's' adhesion to the treaty, of which I enclose a copy, and authorized him to notify the Indians to meet at the 'Dog Head Point' next summer, at a time to be intimated to them, and to request them in the mean time to select a Chief and Councillors. 'Thickfoot' expressed gratitude for the kindness of the Government, and his belief, that Indians of the various Islands and of 'Jack Head Point' would cheerfully accept the Queen's benevolence and settle on a Reserve."[18]

The agreement between Morris and Thickfoot was documented as a memorandum in which Thickfoot indicated that he accepted payments under treaty. The use of the term adhesion here is ambiguous, since a formal adhesion to Treaty 5 of Thickfoot's band and the other Island Bands was completed in the following year (table A6). After being approved by an order-in-council (3 December 1875), Treaty 5 was registered with the Office of the Registrar General on 21 December 1875.[19]

In the summer of 1876, several necessary adhesions to Treaty 5 were carried out.[20] Commissioners Thomas Howard and J. Lestock Reid conducted these adhesions, and as it happened, Rev. Henry Cochrane was available to translate.[21] Reid carried out an adhesion of the various island bands (Bloodvein River, Big Island, Sandy Bar, and Jackhead), including Thickfoot's band, on 26 July 1897.[22] on 4 August 1876, an Ojibwa band living at the narrows or rapids of the Berens River accepted Treaty 5 at the schoolhouse at Berens River. This band's desire to have a reserve at Little Grand Rapids was noted in the adhesion.

The adhesion of The Pas bands was carried out by Thomas Howard, who first visited the Grand Rapids band to pay annuities, deliver implements, and settle compensation for their relocation from the north to the south bank of the river. When Howard arrived at Grand Rapids,

To my surprise, the Chief at once expressed his astonishment at my saying that the treaty had been made last year, and said he had only a talk then with the Governor preliminary to making the Treaty this year, and that they were only then prepared to be treated with. I explained to the Band how I had been present myself when it was made, and that I would have it read to them. I accordingly requested Mr. Cochrane to do so, explaining it thoroughly; yet, it was only after a great deal of talking on their part, during which they made most unreasonable demands, and many explanations on my part, that the Indians were satisfied that a treaty had been made, when they requested me to go on with the payments; at the same time a number of them stated that they had been misled by one of the counsellors, Joseph Atkinson by name. I then paid the annuity, distributed the provisions, tools, implements, &c., and gave the Chief a copy of the treaty, and, arranging to meet them again on Monday.[23]

Apparently, an effort to reopen the treaty was attempted. An adhesion to Treaty 5 had already been signed, but the Grand Rapids band may have been dissatisfied with Treaty 5.

Howard then traveled up the Saskatchewan River and met the Moose Lake Band at Chemawawin, but he was unwilling to treat with them there. When he came into view at Devon Mission, or The Pas, "a salute was fired, the like of which, I was subsequently told, had never been heard in the 'Ratty Country.' "[24] (Muskrats were the main fur produced in the vast wetlands covering the lower Saskatchewan River between Cumberland House and Grand Rapids.) Some five hundred Indians had gathered at The Pas. For the purposes of the adhesion, Howard recognized chiefs for Moose Lake, The Pas, and Cumberland House bands. He provided few details about the adhesion: "I stated the object of my mission to them, and was at once assured of their desire to accept of, and their gratitude for, the Queen's bounty and benevolence."[25]

As at Grand Rapids, Howard encountered resistance to Treaty 5 at The Pas: "and having been presented to the Chiefs and Councillors I proceeded to explain the terms of the treaty that I desired to receive their adhesion to. The Chiefs immediately stated that they wanted to make a treaty of their own, and it was only after great difficulty that I could make them understand that in reality it was a new treaty they were about to make."[26]

But "in reality" an adhesion to the original Treaty 5 that had been negotiated at Berens River and Norway House in 1875 was all that was being offered by Commissioner Howard. What he meant by "a new treaty" is perplexing. Beyond discussions of reserve locations, the terms offered to the Swampy Cree gathered at The Pas were the same as the terms presented at Berens River and Norway House in 1875.

The Indians' desire for a new treaty was understandable. In fact, the Swampy Cree were well-informed: "They had heard of the terms granted the Indians at Carlton [Treaty 6], and this acted most prejudicially at one time against the successful carrying out of my mission; but I at last made them understand the difference between their position and the Plain[s] Indians, by pointing out that the land they would surrender would be useless to the Queen, while what the Plain Indians gave up would be of value to 'Her' for homes for 'Her white children.'"[27] But if the lands being surrendered were useless to the Queen, it is hard to understand why more of this "useless" land could not be reserved for Indians. The character of the land in the Treaty 5 territory is similar to the lands of Treaty 3, but reserves in Treaty 3 were based on a larger per capita acreage than the Treaty 5 reserves.

CROWN NEGOTIATING STRATEGY IN TREATY 5

With experience, Crown negotiators developed a strategy of separating the acceptance of a treaty involving a land surrender from the particular problems relating to the location and the size of reserves. Treaties 1 and 2 actually indicated the locations of future Indian reserves. The references to reserves in Treaty 5 came about differently. In the 1875 negotiations Morris succeeded in severing the basic idea of a treaty from the problem of reserves. The 1876 adhesion to Treaty 5 followed the same strategy, since Commissioners Thomas Howard and J. Lestock Reid reported that the bands were "anxious that the places where they are in the habit of living should be granted" as reserves and mentioned in the treaty; "but as our instructions were positive on this point, we refused."[28]

A central aspect of the government's approach to treaties was to split the general idea of a treaty from the specific delineation of the reserves, obtaining acceptance of the treaty from the Indians and then making as few commitments to the particulars of the location of reserves as possible. Such a tactic would have the effect of gaining general acceptance for a treaty by circumventing the Indian demand for large reserves. Why reserves in Treaty 5 were smaller than the reserves provided for in Treaties 3, 4, and 6 was not justified. Separating the idea of a treaty concerning Aboriginal title from the specifics of reserves also served to disconnect the ongoing use and occupancy of vast hunting territories from the future ownership of small, enclosed reserves. In this manner, the agents of the Crown gained maximum flexibility in deciding future land tenures for particular regions.

In certain respects, Treaty 5 was as much about water as it was about land. Morris explained: "The necessity for it had become urgent. The lake is a large and *valuable* sheet of water, being some three hundred miles long."[29] One of the purposes of the Crown was to secure navigation rights, and to this end it was unwilling to give the Grand Rapids band a reserve with strategic advantages. The bountiful fisheries were also well known. Regrettably, the written records do not provide details of the talks. However, a record of an 1890 meeting between Lieutenant-Governor John Schultz and the Berens River band provided a glimpse of the agreement made in 1875. Chief Berens reasoned, "When we made this Treaty, it was given us to understand that although we sold the Government these lands, yet we might still hunt in the woods as before, and the fish and the waters should be ours as it was in our Grandfathers' time."[30] Although this statement was made some fifteen years after the treaty negotiations at Berens River, it was made by a participant in those negotiations, and it is therefore strong evidence that assurances were made about livelihood.

For Treaty 5, concerns about livelihood are illustrated by the Crown's willingness to assist a section of the Norway House band in dealing with declining economic opportunities. The Crown's response demonstrates that treaties were not a mere formality quieting an Indian interest in "hunting grounds." Although the Crown was willing to consider the desires of the Norway House band, there were limits whereby treaty relations were timed to assist Indians. Commissioner Reid reported in 1876 that "Whilst at Norway House I was waited upon by a Chief and four Councillors from the vicinity of Oxford House, who were anxious to know if the same bounties would be extended to them as were being extended to their brethren of Norway House and Cross Lake, and also whether they could obtain a Reserve on Lake Winnipeg, as the country in which they were living was totally unfit for cultivation, and that they had the greatest difficulty in procuring a livelihood."[31]

Some thirty years of petitioning for a treaty would pass before the Crown would establish a treaty relation with Indians in Manitoba north of the 1875 Treaty 5 boundaries.

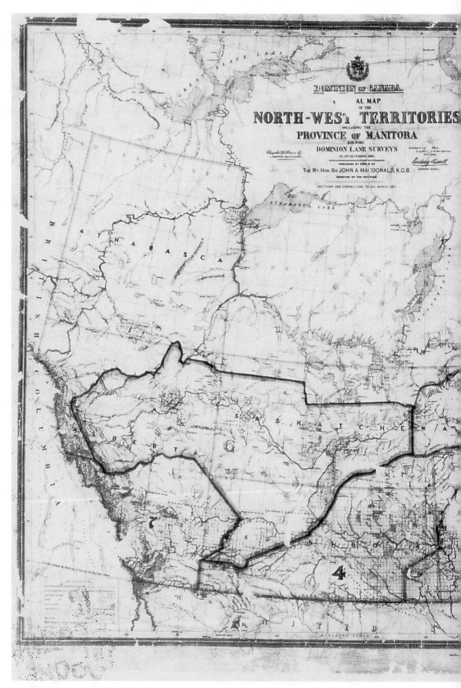

Dominion map of treaty areas 1–6, 1883. The map also shows the townships that had been sur-

veyed to that date. Courtesy of National Archives of Canada, NMC 11630

Chief Kapetekoos (Thunderchild) wearing Treaty 6 coat and medals. He did not join the treaty until 1879.
Courtesy of National Archives of Canada, PA 28839

Chief Mosomin (The Grandfather Berry). In 1876 his Chief, Yellowsky, refused to take treaty. In 1879 Mosomin and 123 followers, mostly Cree, took treaty and their reserve (named after Mosomin) was surveyed in 1881. Courtesy of Provincial Archives of Saskatchewan

Chiefs in council at Thunderchild First Nation, 1922. The chiefs are wearing Treaty 6 coats and medals. Courtesy of Provincial Archives of Saskatchewan

Treaty Commissioner David Laird "discussing" the terms of Treaty 8 in 1899. Commissioner Macrae, who returned to the region the following year to make adhesions, stated he spent much of his time explaining the treaty to those who had signed it previously. Courtesy of Glenbow Archives

Generic treaty medal (blank). Once treaty preparations commenced, the treaty number and date were added. Courtesy of National Archives of Canada, C 70758

Northwest Mounted Police in Treaty 8 area at Grand Rapids, Athabasca River, 1899. First Nations leaders objected to the presence of the police prior to the treaty because they symbolized the authority of the Crown. Courtesy of RCMP Museum

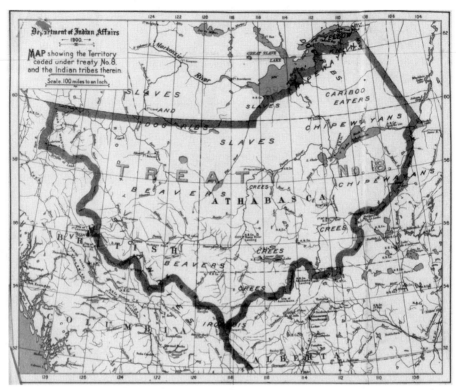

Map of Treaty 8, 1901. This map was published with Treaty Commissioner J. A. Macrae's 1900 report of his expedition to gain adhesions to the treaty. The western boundary is at variance with the verbal description contained in the treaty. Courtesy of National Archives of Canada, NMC 12251

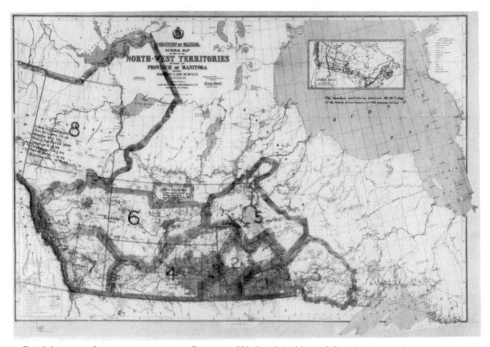

Dominion map of treaty areas, ca. 1900. Courtesy of National Archives of Canada, NMC 11690

Joe McKay and Mistawasis. Mistawasis signed Treaty 6 at Fort Carlton. Courtesy of Provincial Archives of Saskatchewan

Big Bear captured, 1885. During treaty 6 talks Big Bear expressed doubts about the sincerity of Canada's promises to his people and called for government conservation measures to protect the dwindling buffalo herds. Courtesy of National Archives of Canada, c 1873

Four Saskatchewan chiefs visiting Brantford, Ontario, in 1886 for the unveiling of a statue of Joseph Brant. Standing left is Ojibwa chief Louis O'Soup (Treaty 4) and three Plains Cree chiefs, Mitawasis [Mistawasis] (seated to the right) and Ahtahkakoop (seated on the left). The latter two chiefs had been prominent in the 1876 negotiations and met Governor General Lorne at Fort Carlton in 1881. Courtesy of National Archives of Canada, C 19258

Chipewyan chiefs who accepted Treaty 8 at Fond du Lac, 1899. Chief Maurice Piche is in the centre flanked by headman Laurent Dzieddin and Toussaint. Courtesy of National Archives of Canada

CHAPTER NINE

Treaties at Forts Carlton and Pitt, or Treaty 6

Treaty 6 negotiations extended the dialogue between the Crown and the Plains Cree that had begun in earnest with the Treaty 4 talks. Although most of the issues the Cree had raised earlier were brought up again at Forts Carlton and Pitt, they placed much greater emphasis on the issues of famine relief and medical assistance. This reflected the fact that the more northerly Plains Cree already were suffering acutely from the continuing decline of the bison and that they seemed to have suffered most severely from the smallpox epidemic of the early 1870s. Nonetheless, in seeking guarantees of government help in times of need, the Plains Cree, in effect, were seeking merely to obtain an agreement with Canada that would provide for their basic security in the dawning industrial age, security that was compatible with what they had had with the HBC during the previous mercantile era.

CREE PERCEPTIONS OF THE SITUATION IN 1876

The documentary record explains only imperfectly what First Nations believed they were giving up in exchange for government promises.[1] Most likely, they envisioned the treaty as a pact through which they agreed to share the portions of their ancient territory that lay beyond the boundaries of reserves. This notion would have been consistent with the repeated assurances of government negotiators that the First Nations could continue to use off-reserve lands as they were accustomed to do, provided that they did not interfere with the economic activities of White settlers. This belief also would have been in keeping with the notion the government's chief negotiator, Alexander Morris, conveyed: that they should regard the treaty as a "gift" from a beneficent Queen mother, a negotiating strategy Morris had used so effectively during Treaty 4 talks. They would have the use of their lands "as before," but with the addition of presents, annuities, and other benefits. Morris expressed it in this way: "What I have offered does not take away your living, you will have it then [after treaty] as you have now, and what I offer now is put on top of it."[2]

At a caucus of Cree negotiators early in the proceedings at Fort Carlton, Peter Erasmus, a Métis, heard the chiefs Ahtakakup and Mistawasis, who had hired him as the interpreter, outline the reasons why they were willing to enter into treaty with the Crown. Mistawasis, for example, countered the arguments that some younger leaders had been making against treaty by reminding his audience of the crisis that would soon be upon them when they could no longer rely upon the buffalo:

I have heard my brothers speak, complaining of the hardships endured by our people. Some have bewailed the poverty and suffering that has come to Indians because of the destruction of the buffalo as the chief source of our living, the loss of the ancient glory of our forefathers; and with all that I agree, in the silence of my teepee and on the broad prairies where once our fathers could not pass for the great number of those animals that blocked their way; and even in our day, we have had to choose carefully our campground for fear of being trampled in our teepees. With all these things, I think and feel intensely the sorrow my brothers express.

I speak directly to Poundmaker and The Badger and those others who object to signing this treaty. Have you anything better to offer our people? I ask, again, can you suggest anything that will bring these things back for tomorrow and all the tomorrows that face our people?

I for one think that the Great White Queen Mother has offered us a way of life when the buffalo are no more. Gone they will be before many snows have come to cover our heads or graves if such should be.[3]

Mistawasis also explained to the caucus that the Crown represented power, power that could protect and assist them in the difficult times that the future was expected to bring:

I, for one, look to the Queen's law and her Red Coat servants to protect our people against the evils of white man's firewater and to stop the senseless wars among our people, against the Blackfoot, Peigans, and Bloods. We have been in darkness; the Blackfoot and the others are people as we are. They will starve as we will starve when the buffalo are gone. We will be brothers in misery when we could have been brothers in plenty in times when there was no need for any man, woman, or child to be hungry.

We speak of glory and our memories are all that is left to feed the widows and orphans of those who have died in its attainment. We are few in numbers compared to former times, by wars and the terrible ravages of smallpox. Our people have vanished too. Even if it were possible to gather all the tribes together, to throw away the hand that is offered to help us, we would be too weak to make our demands heard.

Look to the great Indian nations in the Long Knives' country who have been fighting since the memory of their oldest men. They are being vanquished and swept into the most useless parts of their country. Their days are numbered like those of the buffalo. There is

no law or justice for the Indians in Long Knives' country. The Police followed two mur-
derers to Montana and caught them but when they were brought to the Montana court they
were turned free because it was not murder to kill an Indian.

The prairies have not been darkened by the blood of our white brothers in our time. Let
this always be so. I for one will take the hand that is offered. For my band I have spoken.[4]

Ahtakakup, a senior chief like Mistawasis, then took over the task of making
the case for taking treaty. Ahtakakup argued that change was inevitable, thanks
to the oncoming Whites and the vanishing buffalo; that Mother Earth had always
sustained the Cree; and that they, with the help of the Queen's government
within a treaty relationship, could learn to gain their livelihood from the earth in
a new way:

Can we stop the power of the white man from spreading over the land like the grasshop-
pers that cloud the sky and then fall to consume every blade of grass and every leaf on the
trees in their path? I think not. Before this happens let us ponder carefully our choice of
roads.

There are men among you who are trying to blind our eyes, and refuse to see the things
that have brought us to this pass. Let us not think of ourselves but of our children's children. We hold our place among the tribes as chiefs and councillors because our people
think we have wisdom above others amongst us. Then let us show our wisdom. Let us
show our wisdom by choosing the right path now while we yet have a choice.

We have always lived and received our needs in clothing, shelter, and food from the
countless multitudes of buffalo that have been with us since the earliest memory of our
people. No one with open eyes and open minds can doubt that the buffalo will soon be a
thing of the past. Will our people live as before when this comes to pass? No! They will
die and become just a memory unless we find another way.

For my part, I think that the Queen Mother has offered us a new way and I have faith in
the things my brother Mista-wa-sis has told you. The mother earth has always given us
plenty with the grass that fed the buffalo. Surely we Indians can learn the ways of living
that made the white man strong and be able to vanquish all the great tribes of the southern
nations. The white man never had the buffalo but I am told they have cattle in the thousands that are covering the prairie for miles and will replace the buffalo in the Long
Knives' country and may even spread over our lands. The white men number their lodges
by the thousands, not like us who can only count our teepees by tens. I will accept the
Queen's hand for my people. I have spoken.[5]

Taking treaty – accepting the Queen's hand – meant establishing a relationship
with the powerful people who were inexorably invading their lands, a relationship
that would bring them protection and assistance during a transitional period that
was expected to be very difficult.

TREATY-MAKING AT FORT CARLTON

Since Cree negotiators hoped to link their people's future with their past by means of a treaty relationship with the Crown, it was appropriate that the Treaty 6 talks opened at Fort Carlton with a pipe ceremony. (See tables A8 and A9 for particulars.) The treaty commission's secretary described it as follows:

As soon as the Governor and party arrived, the Indians who were to take part in the treaty, commenced to assemble near the Chief's tents, to the sound of beating drums and the discharge of small arms, singing, dancing and loud speaking going on at the same time.

In about half an hour they were ready to advance and meet the Governor; this they did in a large semi-circle; in their front were about twenty braves on horseback, galloping about in circles, shouting, singing and going through various picturesque performances. The semi-circle steadily advanced until within fifty yards of the Governor's tent, when a halt was made and further peculiar ceremonies commenced, the most remarkable of which was the "dance of the stem." This was commenced by the Chiefs, medicine men, councillors, singers and drum-beaters, coming a little to the front and seating themselves on blankets and robes spread for them. The bearer of the stem, Wah-wee-kah-nich-kah-oh-tah-mah-hote (the man you strike on the back), carrying in his hand a large and gorgeously adorned pipe stem, walked slowly along the semi-circle, and advancing to the front, raised the stem to the heavens, then slowly turned to the north, south, east and west, presenting the stem at each point; returning to the seated group he handed the stem to one of the young men, who commenced a low chant, at the same time performing a ceremonial dance accompanied by the drums and singing of the men and women in the background.

This was all repeated by another of the young men, after which the horsemen again commenced galloping in circles, the whole body slowly advancing. As they approached his tent, the Governor, accompanied by the Hon. W. J. Christie and Hon. Jas. McKay, Commissioners, went forward to meet them and to receive the stem carried by its bearer. It was presented first to the Governor, who in accordance with their customs, stroked it several times, then passed it to the Commissioners who repeated the ceremony.[6]

The secretary concluded his observation with the remark that "The significance of this ceremony is that the Governor and Commissioners accepted the friendship of the tribe." Morris interpreted the rite similarly.[7] But historian John Taylor noted that this perspective shows a lack of understanding that the pipe-stem ceremony was a sacred ritual that was performed before any matter of importance and that it committed the participants to speaking only the truth.[8] It is clear that the ceremony performed on this occasion, which was repeated at Fort Pitt, was similar in many key respects to the one performed at York Factory in the eighteenth century.

One troublesome issue that had to be dealt with involved picking an inter-preter who did not confuse Plains Cree, Swampy Cree, and Saulteaux. A clash over who was qualified to interpret at Fort Carlton highlights this problem of treaty negotiations. The trouble arose because Rev. John McKay (also spelled Mackay) was supposed to interpret for the government team; the assembled chiefs, on the other hand, had selected Métis Peter Erasmus to act on their be-half. Unexpectedly, however, once Morris had completed his opening address, McKay asked Erasmus to interpret it to the assembled First Nations leaders. Ini-tially Erasmus refused to do so saying: "I object, Sir. It is my impression that I am not employed by the government but am acting only on behalf of the chiefs assembled here. Therefore I refuse to interpret the governor's speech; that I consider is the duty of its paid servants."[9]

According to Erasmus' narrative, the chiefs strongly backed him, but McKay remained anxious to have Erasmus interpret nonetheless. Erasmus then ex-plained why McKay was so determined:

I knew that Peter Ballenden [another multilingual individual] had not the education or practice to interpret, and his voice had no carrying quality to make himself heard before all this large assembly. The Rev. McKay had learned his Cree among the Swampy and Saulteaux. While there was a similarity in some words, and I had learned both languages, the Prairie Crees would not understand his Cree … They would be intolerant at being ad-dressed in Swampy or Saulteaux words. I knew that McKay was not sufficiently versed in the Prairie Cree to confine his interpretations to their own language.[10]

According to Erasmus' narrative, McKay then proceeded to translate, but his translation, which mixed words from the three languages, was not well received. Chief Mistawasis, "after listening for a time, jumped to his feet and said, 'We are not Swampy Crees or Saulteaux Indians. We are Plains Crees and demand to be spoken to in our own language.'"[11] This statement led the rattled McKay to stop translating and ask Peter Ballenden to do so. Erasmus, who had felt slighted by the treaty commission was enjoying the debacle. He wrote:

Ballenden was now called up, I was delighted, for I knew the man quite well. He was a good man to interpret personal talks but I knew he would be completely out of his element as an interpreter for such a large meeting, where a man's voice had to carry to reach the men furthest from the stand. Ballenden did exactly as I thought. He made an excellent in-terpretation of the Governor's words but in a voice so low that it could not be heard be-yond the first ten rows of men seated on the ground. The men in the back rows got to their feet and demanded that he speak in a louder voice … Ballenden tried to raise his voice, choked, and then sat down. My revenge at that moment was sweet but I could read con-sternation on the faces of my impolite friends at the table.

The Governor, who I could see was growing exasperated at these frequent interruptions to his talk, said, "All right, Erasmus. Let this be your chance to justify your chiefs' confidence in your work."[12]

Having made their point, Erasmus took over translating responsibilities with the backing of the chiefs.

During Treaty 6 negotiations, the Plains Cree and Saulteaux raised all the issues their neighbours and relatives had discussed in Treaty 4. As mentioned earlier, Morris' account of the treaty talks indicates that the Cree from this region had requested consultations with government representatives as early as 1871. They were concerned about several issues: the stories they had heard that their lands had been sold to Canada, the invasion of their lands by miners and other white settlers, the ravages of smallpox and other diseases, and the rapid decline of the buffalo herds.

As noted above, on 13 April 1871 prominent Cree chiefs visited W. J. Christie at Fort Edmonton to have him draft a letter on their behalf to the government.[13] He wrote that "The object of their visit was to ascertain whether their lands had been sold or not, and what was the intention of the Canadian Government in relation to them. They referred to the epidemic [smallpox] that had raged throughout the past summer, and the subsequent starvation, the poverty of their country, the visible diminution of the buffalo, their sole support, ending by requesting certain presents *at once* , and that I should lay their case before Her Majesty's representative at Fort Garry."[14]

The paramount chief, Weekaskookeeseyin (Sweet Grass) sent a more detailed message:

GREAT FATHER – I shake hands with you and bid you welcome. We heared our lands were sold and we did not like it; we don't want to sell our lands; it is our property, and no one has a right to sell them.

Our country is getting ruined of fur-bearing animals, hitherto our sole support, and now we are poor and want help – we want you to pity us. We want cattle, tools, agricultural implements, and assistance in everything when we come to settle – our country is no longer able to support us.

Make provision for us against years of starvation. We have had great starvation the past winter, and the small-pox took away many of our people, the old, young, and children.

We want you to stop the Americans from coming to trade on our lands, and giving firewater, ammunition and arms to our enemies the Blackfeet.

We made peace this winter with the Blackfeet. Our young men are foolish, it may not last long.

We invite you to come and see us and to speak with us. If you can't come yourself, send some one in your place.

We send these words by our Master, Mr. Christie, in whom we have every confidence. – That is all.[15]

"MAKE PROVISION FOR US AGAINST YEARS OF STARVATION"

Well before negotiations began, the Indians had indicated the range of topics they wanted the government to address. Sweet Grass had made it clear that protection from starvation was a paramount objective. The Cree had instructed the missionary George McDougall, Morris' emissary to them, to

Tell the Great Chief that we are glad the traders are prohibited bringing spirits [alcohol] into our country; when we see it we want to drink it, and it destroys us; when we do not see it we do not think about it. Ask for us a strong law, prohibiting the free use of poison (strychnine). It has almost exterminated the animals of our country, and often makes us bad friends with our white neighbors. We further request, that a law be made, equally applicable to the Half-breed and Indian, punishing all parties who set fire to our forest or plain. Not many years ago we attributed a prairie fire to the malevolence of an enemy, now every one is reckless in the use of fire, and every year large numbers of valuable animals and birds perish in consequence. We would further ask that our chiefships be established by the Government. Of late years almost every trader sets up his own Chief and the result is we are broken up into little parties, and our best men are no longer respected.[16]

Morris' report of his 1876 treaty-making mission stated that most of the Cree were eager to conclude an agreement with him but that there were some who tried to block the proceedings. Métis and Saulteaux were among the dissidents. Nonetheless, even those who supported the treaty had doubts, which Morris had to address before he could get talks underway. Afterwards he reflected, "the Indian mind was oppressed with vague fears; they dreaded the treaty; they had been made to believe that they would be compelled to live on the reserves wholly, and abandon their hunting, and that in time of war, they would be placed in the front and made to fight."[17] He assured them these fears were groundless.

On the day negotiations began at Fort Carlton, the issue of food relief and other assistance became the focus of discussions. Pitikwahanapiwiyin, or Poundmaker, apparently was the first to raise this issue.[18] Morris said I

replied that they had their own means of living, and that we could not feed the Indians, but only assist them to settle down. The Badger, Soh-ah-moos, and several other Indians all asked [for] help when they settled, and also in case of troubles unforeseen in the future. I explained that we could not assume the charge of their every-day life, but in a time of a great national calamity they could trust to the generosity of the Queen ...

At length the Indians informed me that they did not wish to be fed every day, but to be helped when they commenced to settle, because of their ignorance how to commence, and also in case of general famine; Ah-tuk-uk-koop winding up the debate by stating that they wanted food in the spring when they commenced to farm, and proportionate help as they advanced in civilization, and then asking for a further adjournment to consider our offers

... The whole day [12 August 1876] was occupied with this discussion on the food question, and it was the turning point with regard to the treaty.[19]

Morris replied to these requests by "reiterating my statements as to our inability to grant food, and again explaining that only in a national famine did the Crown ever intervene."[20] At this point, James McKay entered the discussion about food relief, telling the assembled Indians that "you have made demands on the Governor and from the way you have put them a white man would understand that you asked for daily provisions, also supplies for your hunt and for your pleasure excursions."[21]

Following McKay's intervention, the chiefs asked for an adjournment to give further consideration to the government offer. When they returned to the treaty talks, they presented Morris with a written list of changes they wanted made, which Erasmus read. According to the lieutenant-governor,

They asked for an ox and a cow [for] each family; an increase in the agricultural implements; provisions for the poor, unfortunate, blind and lame; to be provided with missionaries and school teachers; the exclusion of fire water in the whole Saskatchewan; a further increase in agricultural implements as the band advanced in civilization; freedom to cut timber on Crown lands; liberty to change the site of the reserves before the survey; free passages over Government bridges and scows; other animals, a horse, harness and waggon, and cooking stove for each chief; a free supply of medicines; a hand mill to each band; and lastly, that in case of war they should not be liable to serve.[22]

When talks resumed, several chiefs said that they were being misunderstood on the issue of food relief. One of the leading chiefs (Mistawasis) reportedly said: "We were glad to hear what the Governor was saying to us and we understood it, but we are not understood, we do not mean to ask for food for every day but only when we commence [farming] and in case of famine or calamity. What we speak of and do now will last as long as the sun shines and the river runs, we are looking forward to our children's children, for we are old and have but few days to live."[23]

Still, a number of the Aboriginal people living in the Fort Carlton area were not satisfied. Poundmaker "rose and said he did not differ from his people, but he did not see how they could feed and clothe their children with what was promised."[24] Joseph Toma, speaking for a band of Saulteaux and Red Pheasant's Battle River Cree, wanted "Men to build houses for them, increased salaries to the Chiefs and headmen, etc. He said what was offered was too little; he wanted enough to cover the skin of the people, guns, and also ten miles of land round the reserves as a belt.[25]

Morris understood that he would have to make concessions. Accordingly, he offered to increase the number of cattle and farm implements the government would provide. Also, he again assured them that they would not have to fight in any Canadian wars. Recognizing that the chiefs were very anxious for the government to help their people make the transition from buffalo hunting to farming, Morris made another concession:

You asked for help when you settled on your reserves during the time you were planting. You asked very broadly at first. I think the request you make now is reasonable to a certain extent; but help should be given after you settle on the reserve for three years only, for after that time you should have food of your own raising, besides all the things that are given to you; this assistance would only be given to those actually cultivating the soil. Therefore, I would agree to give every spring, for three years, the sum of one thousand dollars to assist you in buying provisions while planting the ground. I do this because you seem anxious to make a living for yourselves, it is more than has been done anywhere else.[26]

Regarding the central issue of longer-term commitments to food relief Morris warned: "I cannot undertake the responsibility of promising provision for the poor, blind and lame. In all parts of the Queen's dominions we have them; the poor whites have as much reason to be helped as the poor Indian; they must be left to the charity and kind hearts of the people. If you are prosperous yourselves you can help your unfortunate brothers."[27]

Today we can only speculate about how the Cree would have reacted to this statement, given their ancient traditions of sharing. In any event, it did not address the issue they were concerned about: when the buffalo hunt ultimately failed altogether, the hunters would have nothing to share.

As in previous treaties, Morris was willing to commit the government to education. He told them, "I had already promised you that when you settled down, and there were enough children, schools would be maintained."[28]

While these talks were taking place, one group of Cree, those from Duck Lake, led by Kahmeeyestoowaegs, or the Beardy, boycotted the proceedings.[29] They objected to the treaty, preferring instead to lease their lands.[30] However, they did finally agree to meet Morris at a camp five miles away from Fort Carlton. Beardy informed Morris, "I do not want very much more than what has been promised, only a little thing … on account of the buffalo I am getting anxious. I wish that each one should have an equal share [of the buffalo], if that could be managed; in this I think we would be doing good." Another chief added, "I am getting alarmed when I look at the buffalo, it appears to me as if there was only one. I trust to the Queen and to the Governor, it is only through their aid we can manage to preserve them." Beardy added, "When I am utterly unable to help myself I want to receive assistance. I will render all the assistance I can to my brother [the Queen's representative] in taking care of the country."[31] Once more, Morris had to address the issue of government assistance:

I will speak to you in regard to food as I have spoken to the other Indians; we cannot support or feed the Indians every day, further than to help them to find the means of doing it
for themselves by cultivating the soil. If you were to be regularly fed some of you would
do nothing at all for your own support; in this matter we will do as we have agreed with
the other Indians, and no more. You will get your share of the one thousand dollars' worth
of provisions when you commence to work on your reserves.

In a national famine or general sickness, not what happens in every day life, but if a
great blow comes on the Indians, they would not be allowed to die like dogs.[32]

It is clear from this exchange that the Indian nations and Morris were
approaching the issue from very different perspectives. Beardy was essentially
asking for the same kinds of protection that the mercantile fur trading system of
the HBC had provided. Morris seems to have understood the request as asking for
a kind of universal welfare, which was not yet a common feature of emerging
industrial states.

Morris next addressed the issue of conserving the bison: "With regard to the
preservation of the buffalo, it is a subject of great importance, it will be considered by the Lieutenant-Governor and Council of the North-West Territories to
see if a wise law can be passed, one that will be a living law that can be carried
out and obeyed. If such a law be passed it will be printed in Cree as well as in
English and French; but what the law will be I cannot tell."[33] In fact, at its meeting of 23 November 1875 the council for the North-West Territories had discussed this issue. James McKay had proposed regulations that were approved on
24 November 1875.[34]

In the end, Beardy's people agreed to the treaty, and Morris' party left for Fort
Pitt, where negotiations began on 7 September. In his opening address there
Morris told the assembled Indians, "It is six years since the Queen took back into
her own hands the government of her subjects, red and white, in this country; it
was thought her Indian children would be better cared for in her own hand."[35] In
other words, Morris had altered his account of the sale of Rupertsland yet again,
and in a very fundamental way. Now he was telling the Indians of the Fort Pitt
area that the transfer had been arranged for their benefit so that the Queen could
replace the HBC as their guardian and thereby take better care of them. Morris
expanded on this idea by saying, "Now the whole burden of my message from
the Queen is that we wish to help you in the days that are to come, we do not
want to take away the means of living that you have now, we do not want to tie
you down; we want you to have homes of your own where your children can be
taught to raise for themselves food from the mother earth."[36]

Morris' negotiating strategy here would have struck a very resonant chord
with the assembled First Nations. As we have seen, the mercantile fur trade of
the HBC had provided what we today think of as a "social safety net." The company offered aid during times of scarcity, helped the sick and infirm, and offered

medical assistance in times of pestilence. The trouble was that the old mercantile fur trade hinged on a commercial hunting and trapping economy that was about to collapse. Morris held out the prospect of a beneficent "Queen mother" who would look out for her Indian "children" in the troubling times that lay ahead.

These issues had already come to a head at Fort Pitt, which no longer had access in winter to the retreating bison herds. On 19 April 1875 Lawrence Clarke wrote from Carlton House to HBC Commissioner James Graham, informing him that

Mr. W. McRay from Fort Pitt writes that he will not be able to supply us with a single Bag of pemican as the Indians about him are all Starving and he is obliged to sell them provisions for their Furs.

The Buffalo have now evidently forsaken this part of the country for the winter season, as not one head has been seen during the whole winter. The consequence is that the whole population Indian and half-cast are, before the winter is half over, in a same state of starvation; and towards spring have actually nothing whatsoever to sustain life in the shape of Food.[37]

Two weeks later, Clarke wrote Graham again, stating:

It is most desirable for the prosperity of our business that we should have some protection Force in the vicinity of Carlton. Unfortunately we are obliged, from necessity to purchase all the provisions we can acquire in the Autumn and have therefore a large stock Kept in our stores over winter. All the Buffalo have now apparently abandoned the Lower Saskatchewan during winter season and neither the half cast or Indian population are provided enough to [lay] by a store for winter consumption, the whole population throw themselves on us for support during these constantly recurring periods of starvation. This places us in a very unpleasant position for if we either sell or lend even a moderate quantity, we would have the whole of the starving wretches demanding like succour. I am therefore compelled to risk a great deal by refusing to supply any quantity of Pemican. This entails many trying moments and cannot go on for ever, without some disaster occurring.

Graham was worried that food shortages were threatening the peace:

Fearing the dangers that might result from such an assemblage of Indians as contemplated visiting Carlton this spring for the purpose of consulting with regard to the Position they should take up in reference to the Treaty question, I issued instructions to my Fort Managers to use every exertion to prevent this gathering. I am glad to say that the measures thus adopted were successful and the numbers assembled now at this place have dwindled down to about sixty. The trouble these poverty stricken starving wretches give me, speaks only too forcibly of what I might have expected had the greater body assembled as contemplated.[38]

The HBC's report for the Saskatchewan District dated 26 June 1875 reiterated these concerns: "But the real source of loss at Fort Pitt is the actual decadence of the Trade there [.] Five sixths of the Returns are collected at long distance from the neighborhood; and at a very hearty expense ... The trade alone collected in the environs is a mere trifle. Thus the Provisions gathered during summer form a depot for all the starving wretches for miles round, who have little or nothing to give in return for their food supplies [.] I can see no way to put an end to this state of affairs until you have a protective force in the country and an Indian can be treated as any other mendicant."[39] In other words, food shortages in the Fort Pitt area and the increasing inability of the HBC to deal with the problem left the local people increasingly desperate. They had few options. Seizing the company's larder through force would have been a short-term solution at best. Obtaining a commitment for long-term aid from Canada was a better option. Thus, Morris' assertion that Canada, acting as the Queen mother's new representative, would be a better guardian of their welfare than the HBC would have had a great appeal to the anxious Cree and their allies.

TREATY-MAKING AT FORT PITT

The talks at Fort Pitt, which would expose the Cree concerns for maintaining their livelihood in the face of the waning bison numbers, went well until Mistahimusqua (Big Bear) turned up, four days into the proceedings. One of the most influential of the chiefs at Fort Pitt was the venerable Weekaskookeeseyin (Sweet Grass); he was also one of the leaders who had sent a message from Fort Edmonton to the government in 1871 requesting a treaty. Indeed, at Fort Pitt Sweet Grass echoed many of the arguments that Mistawasis and Ahtakakup had made at Fort Carlton the previous month about disappearing buffalo, invading Euro-Canadians, and the desirability of accepting the "other way" that the Queen was offering them. Moreover, chiefs like Sweet Grass, a convert to Christianity, were probably influenced towards taking treaty quickly by the presence and words of Roman Catholic and Methodist missionaries. These factors account for the fact that Sweet Grass and many others had already accepted treaty on terms identical to those reached at Fort Carlton four days after Morris and his party arrived at the more westerly post.[40]

Mistahimusqua was a very different leader from Weekaskookeeseyin, and the differences showed as soon as Mistahimusqua arrived and learned that talks were concluded. Big Bear was no Christian; he had a powerful reputation for his traditional medicine. Moreover, he had earlier demonstrated his suspicion of the Canadian government and its representatives. Two years before, when HBC factor William McKay had trekked out, on behalf of the government of Canada, to a large buffalo-hunting camp that combined the followers of both Sweet Grass and Big Bear, Big Bear's followers had demonstrated their distrust of Canada.[41] McKay had been despatched to reassure the Plains Cree that the mounted police, who arrived on the plains in 1874, and a Canadian-American boundary survey party that was at work to the south meant the Cree and other First Nations no harm. Whether Big Bear found such messages reassuring or puzzling, or both, is not clear. What is certain is that he and some of his followers had their doubts about the Canadians who had sent McKay to them. When the HBC factor distributed presents to impress the Cree about the government's good intentions, two of the families in Big Bear's camp refused the largesse. As William McKay reported, they "objected to receive the present, stating it was a bribe to facilitate a future treaty."[42]

At Fort Pitt in 1876, Big Bear found himself stymied by the fact that agreement had already been reached, and suspicious about the fact that the negotiators had not waited for his arrival. When Sweet Grass addressed him, he replied: "I have come off [the plains] to speak for the different bands that are out on the plains. It is no small matter we were to consult about. I expected the Chiefs here would have waited until I arrived." While he had a mandate to speak for the bands still out hunting, he did not think he had authority to accept the treaty for them and his own followers: "The people who have not come, stand as a barrier before what I would have had to say; my mode of living is hard."[43] When his mentor, Sweet Grass, urged him to talk to Commissioner Morris, Big Bear responded heatedly with words that expressed his differing attitudes to the Hudson's Bay Company and to Canada. Unfortunately, his heat led him to add words that would haunt him till his death: "Stop, stop, my friends, I have never seen the Governor before; I have seen [HBC man] Mr. Christie many times. I heard the Governor was to come and I said I shall see him; when I see him I will make a request that he will save me from what I most dread, that is: the rope to be about my neck (hanging), it was not given to us by the Great Spirit that the red man or white man should shed each other's blood."[44]

Big Bear, a proud example of Plains culture, was using an equestrian metaphor to say that he did not want, like a horse, to be broken to a halter and rope.[45] However, interpreter Peter Erasmus – self-proclaimed translator extraordinaire – got the metaphor wrong and told Commissioner Morris that Mistahimusqua feared that he might be hanged by Canadian authorities. The Commissioner immediately stiffened, responding "No good Indian has the rope about his neck."[46] From that day forward everything Big Bear said and did was inaccurately viewed by Canadian authorities through the broken glass of that tragically mistaken translation.

Perhaps to get away from the topic of hanging, Big Bear shifted the discussion to the declining buffalo and the need to conserve them. Sweet Grass had already raised the issue of joint action to protect the herds with Morris, saying of the proposed treaty, "We will commence hand in hand to protect the buffalo."[47] Now Big Bear returned to that theme: "Then these Chiefs will help us to protect the buffalo, that there may be enough for all." In response Morris informed them of impending action by the territorial government: "The North-West Council is considering the framing of a law to protect the buffaloes, and when they make it, they will expect the Indians to obey it. The Government will not interfere with the Indian's daily life, they will not bind him. They will only help him to make a living on the reserves, by giving him the means of growing from the soil, his food. The only occasion when help would be given, would be if Providence should send a great famine or pestilence upon the whole Indian people included in the treaty."[48] Though important, this statement was not enough to secure Big Bear's signature, but according to Morris, the Cree chief did tell the commissioner that he would come to Fort Pitt the next year and sign the treaty.[49] However, when Mistahimusqua turned up the following year and was met by only a minor functionary, he declined to enter treaty. He would resist the "rope" that he feared in the treaty until starvation forced him to adhere to Treaty 6 in December 1882.[50]

The request of the Plains Cree, Ojibwa, and their other allies for conservation laws to protect the buffalo, as well as annuities, education, food aid, medical assistance "for as long as the sun shines and the river runs," and help to become farmers must be seen in this context. The determination of First Nations negotiators forced Morris to add two critical concessions to Treaty 6. One stated "That in the event hereafter of the Indians comprised within this treaty being overtaken by any pestilence, or by a general famine, the Queen, on being satisfied and certified thereof by her Indian Agent or Agents, will grant to the Indians assistance of such character and to such extent as her Chief Superintendent of Indian Affairs shall deem necessary."[51] The other concession, known today as the medicine chest provision, committed the government to provide medical assistance to the Indians: "That a medicine chest shall be kept at the house of each Indian Agent for the use and benefit of the Indians, at the discretion of such Agent."[52] Again, this provision was in keeping with the two-hundred-year-old traditions of Native-White relations as established by the HBC. Having obtained these crucial concessions, the chiefs signed the treaty.

THE MONTREAL LAKE AND LAC LA RONGE ADHESION TO TREATY 6

Treaty 6 was negotiated primarily with the buffalo-hunting First Nations of the parkland/grassland region. Thirteen years later, in 1889, the people living in the boreal forest lands in the vicinity of Lac la Ronge and Montreal Lake joined the treaty. (See tables A8 and A9 for details.) One of their primary reasons for adhering was that the 1880s were times of low fur prices and poor hunting and fishing.[53] The people of this wooded region hoped, therefore, to obtain some of the economic benefits from treaty that their Plains Cree neighbours had received. Apparently, the Wood Crees of this region had previously requested a treaty.[54]

Officially it was stated that the territorial Adhesion of the Indians of Montreal Lake or Green Lake to Treaty 6 was in the public interest, since that section of the country "was included in the said timber and land district, and complications were not unlikely to occur, owing to the Indians not having surrendered the same."[55] Essentially, the territory of this adhesion brought the northern boundary of the 1876 treaty to conform to the northern boundary of the District of Saskatchewan. An order-in-council of 29 November 1888 appointed Lieutenant-Colonel A.G. Irvine and Mr Roger Goulet as commissioners to negotiate the adhesion and to issue scrip to Métis claimants. Goulet was appointed because he had taken Métis claims for scrip at Green Lake in 1887.[56]

Irvine joined up with Goulet in Prince Albert on 31 December 1888, and because Indians were out trapping, the commissioners made use of HBC officials to contact the Cree. Irvine explained that he employed HBC chief trader McAuley and a Mr Garson and "sent them out at once to the region inhabited by the Indians interested to summon them to meet me at a Council to be held at the point selected."[57] At this time Irvine learned from HBC officials that there "were no Indians at Green Lake who had not been treated with."[58] Arrangements were made to treat on 10 February. Irvine's treaty party was transported by the North-West Mounted Police, and it included Mr McNeill of Indian Affairs, and the venerable archdeacon J.A. Mackay, who served as translator.[59] Irvine was aware that Mackay "had labored most successfully as a Missionary for years among these very Indians and he had also interpreted for the Commissioners when making Treaty No. 6 at Forts Carlton and Pitt, the treaty to which these Indians were to be asked to give their adhesion."[60] The north end of Montreal Lake served as a central locality for the two bands involved. When the treaty party arrived, "The Indians came out on the edge of the Lake to meet us and according to their own custom fired their rifles in honor of our arrival: after that they all filed past taking off their hats and shaking hands with the Commissioners."[61] After this welcome, Rev. Mackay visited the lodges to explain the terms of the treaty.

On the morning of 11 February, the Indians requested Mackay to explain the treaty further, and in the afternoon the negotiations began. The talks began with the recognition of chiefs and councillors (table A8). Mackay then explained Treaty 6. Irvine asked the Indians present if they were satisfied by the selection of chiefs and headmen. According to McNeill's notes, "Treaty No. 6 made at Forts Carlton and Pitt, was then read and fully explained to them in the Cree language by the Rev. Mr. Mackay."[62] An adjournment was requested and Irvine stated that "he did not wish to hurry them nor did he want them to sign anything that they did not thoroughly understand but he could not help thinking that they must understand the terms of the Treaty by this time as Mr. Mackay had spent all Saturday [Sunday] afternoon and evening and this morning with them explaining it to them."[63] Clearly, Mackay played a central role in explaining Treaty 6 and the proposed adhesion.

From the official written records of the talks, the issues raised included the request for a payment of arrears going back to the date of the original treaty in 1876, reserves and surveys, schools, the substitution of some agricultural items for more ammunition and twine, and a request for a farm instructor. With respect to back payment, Irvine explained that he was authorized to pay only twelve dollars to each person. After the adjournment, the provision for agricultural assistance in Treaty 6 was discussed, and fewer cattle, some pigs, and fewer ploughs and fewer scythes were suggested. Similarly, the horses, harnesses, and wagons were not seen as useful by the Wood Cree. McNeill noted "The value for the articles that they wont [sic] receive under Treaty stipulations in ammunition and twine for nets."[64] The chiefs also expected seed potatoes and requested medicines. Councillor Bird asked that "the old and helpless people may get some clothing."[65] McNeill's notes also recorded that "Col. Irvine said that he would recommend to the Government that they should be supplied with the things they have asked for."[66]

After the treaty was signed, each chief was presented with a flag and medal. McNeill's notes recorded that "Col. Irvine then gave the Chiefs some good advice, telling them he hoped as Chiefs they would show a good example, not only by their conduct but by working hard and to try to be independent of assistance from the Government."[67] Irvine noted that "The Indians then gave three hearty cheers for the Queen and the Commissioners."[68] After the signing, Commissioner Goulet dealt with the claims for Métis scrip. On 12 February treaty payments were made: 273 Indians, one chief and four headmen were paid from the Lac la Ronge band; and for the Montreal Lake Band, one chief, four headmen and 94 Indians were paid.[69] After finishing with the scrip claims, the commissioner departed on 14 February and Irvine recorded that "The Indians all shook hands and bid us good-by and fired off their rifles as a parting salute."[70]

The adhesion of 1889 is unique because it added territory to the original territory described as Treaty 6 and because it was conducted during the winter trapping season. The adhesion concerned not only Indian title in the territory described by the adhesion document but also "transfer, surrender and relinquish" of any other lands: "Also all our right, title and interest whatsoever to all other lands wherever situated, whether within the limits of any other Treaty heretofore made or hereafter to be made with Indians, and whether the said lands are situated in the North-West Territories or elsewhere in Her Majesty's Dominions, to have and to hold the same unto and for the use of Her Majesty the Queen, Her heirs and successors forever."[71] The Crown's statement of a broad interest in unspecified lands outside a particular geographic territory of a treaty or a territorial adhesion is known as a "blanket extinguishment clause."[72]

The written language of the 1889 adhesion was linked to the original Treaty 6 by recognizing that the Wood Cree Chiefs had not "been present at the Councils at which the articles of the said Treaty were agreed upon" and by documenting that "We, the undersigned Chiefs and Headmen, on behalf of ourselves and the other members of the Wood Cree tribe of Indians ... had explained to us the terms of the Treaty made and concluded near Carlton on the 23rd day of August and on the 28th day of said month respectively, and near Fort Pitt on the 9th day of September, 1876."[73] Thus the adhesion not only added territory to Treaty 6, but it established a treaty relationship between the Montreal Lake and Lac la Ronge bands based on the terms of the original Treaty 6.

It seems that government offered but the briefest explanations of the terms of Treaty 6 to the Woodland Cree. The oral record of the treaty is extensive, however, and offers us a Cree perspective on this important adhesion. Significantly, the accounts of these Woodland Cree indicate that when their ancestors adhered to Treaty 6 in 1889, their concept of the land was very different from that of the government negotiators and the settler society they represented. For instance, the oral histories convey the deeply held belief that the forebears of these First Nations thought they had yielded only the dry land. This point of view is expressed very clearly in the transcribed interviews from 1970 that were included in *Aski-Puko:The Land Alone*. (Excerpts of these interviews are presented in table A10.) This limited idea about the land is very contrary to the Euro-Canadian notion that title to it conveyed a bundle of resource rights. Given these very different perspectives, it is understandable why the First Nations people of the Lac la Ronge and Montreal Lake region are adamant today that their traditional livelihood practices were not supposed to have been curtailed by articles of Treaty 6. All the Cree who were interviewed in the 1970 study were unanimous on this issue.[74] Typical of their responses was that of Norman Charles of Lac la Ronge: "This was told to me by the old Chief, about the promises of the first treaties. The Chief was told by the Indian Commissioner that the Queen was going to buy the land. So he asked him, 'What about our way of living?' They answered, 'Your way of making a living and hunting rights shall not be taken away. Just the land.'"[75] In other words, the Woodland Cree who adhered to Treaty 6 in 1889 did so to protect their traditional livelihood. Annuities and promised government help in times of famine and pestilence in exchange for the "dry land" were supposed to help them achieve this fundamental objective.

Treaty 6 was the culmination of the treaty-making tradition in western Canada. The Cree and their allies had forged their relations with Whites within the context of the mercantile fur trade, which had been dominated by the HBC in its dual capacity as a trading company and representative of the Crown. In 1876 Indian negotiators approached the talks from this perspective and with the knowledge of the nature of the accords their neighbours and relatives (especially those in the Treaty 4 area) had already struck with Canada. Agents for Canada, on the other hand, operated largely from the context of established treaty-making practices. The Robinson accords and Treaties 1, 2, 3, and 4 provided their crucial blueprint. For the Plains Cree, the imminent collapse of the buffalo-hunting economy and their changing relationship with the HBC drove them to the bargaining table with a sense of urgency. Canada joined them there because of mounting development pressures and the fear that warfare on the frontier would take place if Plains Indian needs and demands were not met promptly.

The documentary records clearly show that during the talks the Cree and their allies sought a partnership with Canada – the Queen's new representative – that provided for their basic socioeconomic security under the new economic realities of the dawning industrial age. In doing so, they were seeking protection that was equivalent to what they had become accustomed to in their mercantile relationship with the HBC, albeit in a different form. Thus, from the First Nations perspective, Treaty 6 would have had many symbolic parallels to the older unwritten accords they had forged with the company. Treaty coats were the equivalent of captain's coats; annuities and other recurring allowances recalled the annual gifts of the fur trade; and government commitments to provide relief, medical aid, and education served the same ends as the HBC's practice of providing liberal credit to the able-bodied and aid to the elderly, sick, and destitute.

CHAPTER TEN

Treaty 8

Treaties 8 and 10 cover most of the boreal forest country of northern Saskatchewan. Treaty 5 and the Montreal Lake adhesion to Treaty 6 of 1889 also cover vast tracts of this region. The geographical and economic factors that drove treaty-making in this region from 1899 to 1910 were very different from those of the 1871 to 1877 era, when the parkland/grassland portions of the old Hudson's Bay Company territory came under treaty. Nation-building projects, such as the transcontinental transport and communication networks, and promoting the agricultural development of the "Northwest" held sway in the 1870s, whereas mining expansion propelled the treaty process at the turn of the century. During both treaty-making eras, Aboriginal people asked the government to come to the bargaining table well before it was prepared to do so.[1] During the closing decades of the nineteenth century, their entreaties raised the difficult question for Canada about who was responsible for the well-being of Indians living beyond treaty areas. The Native requests prompted federal officials to formulate and specify the government's priorities respecting Aboriginal people. The federal position was summarized in two memoranda written in 1887 that offer us crucial insights into evolving treaty relationships in northern Saskatchewan.

Prime Minister and Minister of Indian Affairs John A. Macdonald sent an important policy proposal to the Privy Council (his cabinet) on 19 January 1887. He began by addressing northern First Nations' petitions for treaties and the often-stated demand of the HBC that the government give economic relief to these people:

The undersigned begs to report for the consideration of your Excellency in Council the following facts respecting the Indians inhabiting unceded parts of the North West Territories and in regard to the country claimed by them as their hunting grounds.

Repeated applications have been made by Indians inhabiting the regions situated North of the Northern boundary of Treaty No. 6, which Treaty embraces the district of Saskatchewan, and North East and West of the boundaries of Treaty No. 5; which Treaty comprehends a portion of the District of Keewatin, for Treaties to be made with them by the Government; also applications have been received from time to time from the Hudsons Bay Company for relief to be given by the Government to the sick and destitute Indians of these regions; and quite recently the Hudsons [*sic*] Bay Company has renewed its solicitations in the same behalf, alleging that serious sickness is now prevalent among the Indians of the Peace River district, and that there is an apprehension of there being an insufficiency of food during the Winter in consequence of a prevailing scarcity of rabbits and lynxes on which these Indians are in the habit of depending for a subsistence. The diseases from which they are suffering are stated to be measles and croup.[2]

Macdonald's memorandum then pointed out why the Indians and the HBC believed that Canada should respond to their petitions:

The grounds upon which the Indians claim a Treaty should be made with them are, that exploration with a view to construction of Railways and public works have been made in their country; and the claim that as it is evident that land within the territory inhabited by them is to be used for these purposes, it is only fair that before such appropriations of land are made Treaty stipulations should be concluded with them as the owners of the soil. They also urge that owing to the diminution in the number of fur-bearing animals and of game they require the annuities and other annulments that would be secured to them under Treaty to enable them to subsist. The Hudsons Bay Company allege that, as the Crown has purchased the Company's interest in these regions as well as in the North West generally, the expense of providing and caring for sick and destitute Indians should devolve upon the government as their natural protectors, and that the Hudsons Bay Company should not charge itself with the same.

The memorandum then reviewed government policies toward northern Indians highlighting the fact that development pressures, rather than Aboriginal needs, had set the treaty-making schedule and that economic help had been kept to a minimum: "Considerable correspondence has been had with various parties in respect to this matter. The government has hitherto declined to make Treaties with the Indians referred to, on the ground that the lands within the regions inhabited by them were not required for settlement and with the exception of occasional gifts of twine for fishing nets and ammunition furnished to some of the Indians in the Western part of the region, especially to those being directly North of the boundary line of Treaty No. 6 in the vicinity of Isle la Crosse no other relief has been afforded by the government to the Indians of those regions."

The prime minister then provided an overview of the circumstances prevailing in the unsurrendered woodland territories:

The 60th degree of North Latitude would appear to be the furthest Northern limit to which the Indians of the region referred to interested in Treaties being made with them extend, and the shores of James or Hudson Bay would be the Eastern boundary of those regions, and the East side of the Rocky Mountains the Western boundary.

Within this vast region the Indians are not very numerous. So far as ascertained, those whose hunting grounds lie in the Eastern section of the territory number 4016. The Indians who claim the country in the central part of the said territory are said to number 1441 souls; and those in the Peace River District are said to number 2038.

The Indians inhabiting these regions are Known as the Beaver tribe, Slaveys, Yellow Knives, Cariboo Eaters, Dog Ribs, Chippewayans, Crees, and a few Halfbreeds.

A vast portion of these regions remains unexplored, and the parts that have been explored are reported to be for the most part unsuitable for agriculture with the exception of the Peace River District, wherein cereals of some description and root crops are said to grow successfully.

Acting on Macdonald's request, in January the deputy superintendent-general of Indian Affairs, Lawrence Vankoughnet, also wrote a memorandum about these subjects. He began by visiting the issue of the HBC's continuing responsibilities for nontreaty Indians. Vankoughnet opined that the company still was obligated to provide relief for Northern Indians, because the transfer of Rupertsland to Canada had not hurt its northern fur trading operations. Indeed, in other respects the company had profited from that change. Vankoughnet opened his memo with two rhetorical questions:

In compliance with the request made by the Superintendent General of the undersigned, he begs to submit his views in respect to the application made by the Hudson [*sic*] Bay Company for relief to be furnished to the sick and the destitute Indians in the regions North of the Northern boundary of Treaty No. 6, more especially at the present time to those in the Peace River District, who are stated to be suffering from severe sickness namely, croup and measles.

In considering this question it appears to the undersigned that there are two points to be looked at 1st What were the relations of the Hudson Bay Company to the Indians of these regions previously to the transfer of the North West Territories to the Dominion? 2nd How have those relations been affected by the said transfer?[3]

Vankoughnet answered his questions by saying that in the North, the HBC, rather than Canada, had been the primary beneficiary of the 1870 transfer:

The Hudson Bay Company carried on a fur trade with these Indians long prior to the transfer of the country to the Dominion. The Indians of these regions live by trapping fur-bearing animals the skins of which they sell to the traders. The transfer of the Hudson Bay Company's interest in the country to the Dominion in consideration of value received for the same by the said Company has not practically up to the present time altered in any respect the relations of the Company to the Indians of the portion of the Territories the Indian title to which remains unextinguished. No White settlement has been effected in these regions in consequence of said transfer. Consequently the country still remains as the hunting grounds of the Indians and the game and fur-bearing animals have not been diminished in number through any action of the Government in settling the country. The Hudson Bay Company have, therefore, insofar as those regions are concerned profited by the payment made to them for their interest therein without any benefit having accrued to the Dominion on account of the transfer by the Hudson Bay Company of their interest in those portions of the Territories.

Vankoughnet then went on to argue that the HBC's traditional obligations toward Indians should continue until economic development undermined its fur trading business:

The Hudson Bay Company before the transfer to the Dominion would in the case of sick, aged, and destitute Indians naturally provide for them when they were unable to provide for themselves, and while in the opinion of the undersigned it is quite proper where White settlement has taken place in the portion of the Territories transferred to the Government, and where such settlement has affected the revenue of the Hudson Bay Company by the diminution in the number of fur-bearing animals consequent upon such settlement, that the Government should be at the expense of providing for the sick, aged, and destitute Indians, the undersigned does not, however, see that the Hudson Bay Company can have any equitable claim to be relieved of the care of the sick and aged Indians in those portions of the Territories which they have transferred to the government but where no white settlement has been effected and no interruption to their trade with the Indians has been caused by government works only settlers taking up lands and the Hudson Bay Company, it appears to the undersigned, stands in exactly the same position practically to the Indians of such parts today as it did before the transfer of its interest in the country to the Government.

Vankoughnet closed by repeating the long-held government position, which Macdonald had reiterated in his January memorandum, that development needs, not Indian needs, should set the treaty making agenda:

With regard, however, to the question of making Treaties with the Indians through whose country it is contemplated to construct Railways and other public works, the undersigned is decidedly of opinion that before any such construction takes place, Treaties should be made with the Indians to prevent trouble with them hereafter; and also consistency with the usage adopted in respect to the other portions of the Territories in which public works have been constructed and wherein settlement has taken place, demands that a similar course be followed by in the first place negotiating with the Indians for their title in the soil of the Country wherein it is proposed to construct such works or to effect such settlement.

What is remarkable about these two memoranda is that they clearly state that Canada was responsible for Indian livelihood only when agricultural settlement or government works projects undermined it. This policy was at variance with term 14 of the HBC's deed of surrender, which had relieved the company of its responsibilities in respect to Indians. Likewise, it violated the spirit of the Canadian parliamentary address of 1867 and the expectations of Her Majesty's government as expressed by Colonial Secretary Granville. All of these were abundantly clear that the Dominion's responsibilities for Aboriginal peoples were not limited to areas where agricultural settlers had taken up the land; likewise these obligations were not restricted to areas covered by treaties.

Northern First Nations suffered as a consequence of Canada's refusal to heed their petitions for treaties and its unwillingness to act generously in the discharge of the obligations for their welfare that it had assumed. Although agricultural settlement had not hurt the fur trade in this region by destroying the habitat of fur-bearing animals, the protracted depression of the late nineteenth century sapped trappers' incomes because it sent fur prices plummeting after 1870. Significant recovery did not begin until after the turn of the century.[4] The HBC was unwilling to shoulder the rising relief costs for two reasons. First, it had transferred the legal responsibility for doing so to Canada in 1870. Second, and of more practical importance, the HBC faced ever more competitors after 1870. The newcomers cut into the HBC's profit margins and were unwilling to share the social overhead costs of the business in the form of relief for sick and destitute Indians. Previously, the HBC's ability to support these unfortunate people had been based on its monopolistic and paternalistic control over local economies.[5] In this respect, the transfer agreement of 1870, which included having the HBC yield up its trading privileges, also had a major impact on the North.

PRESSURES FOR TREATY 8

As with the Robinson Treaty area, the expansion of mining and prospecting activities provided the primary catalyst for treaty-making in the region that was eventually encompassed by Treaty 8 (see tables A11 and A12 for details).[6] Prior to the Klondike gold rush, the government of Canada had rejected the requests of the people of the Athabasca, Mackenzie, and Peace River districts for an accord. There were several reasons why these First Nations were anxious to have a treaty. Like other northern Indians who lived outside treaty areas, they wanted the annuity benefits treaties provided, which were a major consideration in the 1870s and 1880s when the worldwide depression sent fur prices tumbling and hunter/trapper incomes plummeted along with them. As noted above in the discussion of Treaty 3 (chapter 5), annuities provided families with enough income to cover their basic needs at the trading post or store. The purchasing power of treaty annuities was actually increasing during these deflationary times, which lasted until the economy rebounded at the turn of the century.[7] The changing nature of the fur trade also posed new problems for the northern hunters. As we have seen, the loss of its monopoly position and responsibility for Indians made the HBC increasingly unwilling to offer relief to the extent it had previously, during the mercantile era. The government, on the other hand, was anxious to control its expenditures and, therefore, resisted giving assistance to non treaty Indians.[8] In spite of this reluctance, however, by the late 1880s petitions on behalf of First Nations groups by the HBC, other fur traders, and missionaries led the Department of Indian Affairs to provide small amounts of aid through these intermediaries.

This modest relief effort still left the people of the Athabasca and Peace River districts feeling that they were at a disadvantage compared to their neighbours in the Treaty 6 and Treaty 7 districts. On New Year's day 1890, a substantial number of them gathered in the Roman Catholic Church at Lesser Slave Lake to discuss the issue. Afterward, a Cree leader, Chief Kinosayoo, asked a local trader by the name of Dieudonne Desjarlais to inform the government of the results of this gathering. On 24 February 1890, Desjarlais' wrote to Edgar Dewdney, minister of the Interior, and informed him that

I have been requested by Chief Kinosayo, of the Crees at Slave lake to inform you that a meeting of the Indians of Lesser Slave Lake was held at the Roman Catholic Mission Lesser Slave lake, on New Years day, 1890, to consider the matter of applying for a treaty with the government. A very few of these present were against the treaty, but a very large majority were in favor of it. After it was over many letters written in Cree characters were received from Indians who were unable to attend, but who wished to have the treaty. The Indians of the upper part of Peace River are also anxious to have the treaty. There are about 177 families of Indians at [Lesser] Slave lake and about 100 in Peace River, not including Vermillion.

The fur in the country is getting scarcer each year and the Indians poorer. Those in Peace River are starving every winter, and need assistance very much. The traders and missionaries assist them as much as they can, but they cannot afford to do it all the time. The government should begin to do something.[9]

Lawrence Vankoughnet, who was, as we have seen deputy superintendent general of the Department of Indian Affairs, did not favour reversing government policy by offering a treaty to the petitioners. Regarding Desjarlais' letter he wrote Dewdney:

With reference to the question of the making of further Treaties with the Indians of the NWT, the undersigned begs to report that on the 27th of May 1884, Sir John Macdonald, the then Supt General, stated as follows in regard to the matter: "I am of opinion that the making of a Treaty may be post-poned for some years, until there is a likelihood of the country being required for settlement purposes."

As respects to the obligation resting upon the Government, to come to the relief of Indians who are in a state of starvation, and with whom no Treaty relations exist, the undersigned is of opinion, that the Government should act towards them, as it would in the case of any of Her Majesty's subjects, be they White or red who might be placed in a similar position, and this has already been done, in so far as the Indians above referred to are concerned ... to the extent, subject to certain limitations, to which the Hudson Bay Company were authorized to grant relief.[10]

In other words, Vankoughnet was merely reiterating the policy statement that he had made two years earlier, but he made an important qualification by acknowledging that the government was obliged to help First Nations beyond treaty areas. Vankoughnet went on to point out, however, that he thought that the crises in the Peace River country had passed, judging from information he had received from the HBC officer at Lesser Slave Lake, who stated that "game and furs were in great plenty" again.[11] Reports from the region suggest that either Vankoughnet was being overly optimistic or he was deliberately downplaying the problem.

In any event, HBC and North-West Mounted Police (NWMP) records indicate that northern Aboriginal peoples continued to face hardships. The HBC inspection reports for Fort St John and Hudson Hope, for example, indicate that fur and game remained scarce.[12] NWMP inspector A. M. Jarvis' patrol reports for 1897 for the Lake Athabasca area recorded that "a large number of Indians, both Crees and Chipewyan, living near Fort Chipewyan, are suffering from hunger on account of the small supply of furs ... The Hudson's Bay Company and Mr. Colin Fraser, before my arrival had advanced a certain amount of assistance to these starving people, some of whom died during my stay at Chipewyan."[13] The following year Inspector W. W. Routledge remarked, "During my stay at Resolution a party of starving Indians from Fond du Lac, Great Slave Lake [Snowdrift] visited me. They were in a wretched state, having travelled some 150 miles on a scanty allowance of fish, to make known the condition of their people."[14]

At Fond du Lac, Father G. Breynat also recounted the terrible plight of the Aboriginal peoples during the winter of 1898–99: "Dogs died of hunger, and people had no more transportation. Some people walked to the village for three days without food ... Some arrived with hands and nose frozen ... Influenza followed famine."[15] Thus, continuing destitution led to calls for a treaty.

Immediately after Vankoughnet's 1890 recommendation to delay making a treaty in the Athabasca, Mackenzie, and Peace River districts, mineral discoveries in the Mackenzie River region forced the government to reconsider the matter. On 7 January 1891 the superintendent general of Indian Affairs prepared a memo for Cabinet stating that

The undersigned begs to report that owing to the discovery, in the District of Athabaska and in the MacKenzie River Country that immense quantities of petroleum exist within certain areas of those regions as well as the belief that other minerals & new substances also of economic value such as sulphur on the South coast of Great Slave lake, & salt on the Mackenzie and Slave Rivers are to be found there the development of which may add materially to the public weal, and the further consideration that several Railway projects in connection with this portion of the Dominion may be given effect to at no such remote date as might be supposed appear to render it advisable that a treaty, or treaties, should be made with the Indians who claim those regions as their hunting grounds, with a view to the extinguishment of the Indian title in such portions of the same as it may be considered in the interest of the public to open up for settlement.[16]

On 26 January 1891 Cabinet responded to this memo with a report that restated the above information and added that the minister of the Interior and of Indian Affairs recommended commencing treaty negotiations

in those portions of the Mackenzie River Country, and in the District of Athabaska, including the Peace River Country, as well as in that portion of [the] country which lies south of the district of Athabaska, and north and west of the Northern boundary of Treaty No. 6, embraced within the following limits ...

Commencing at a point on the Eastern boundary of Alberta, east of the 112 Meridian, where the northern boundary line of Treaty 6 intersects the height of land as shown on a certain map of the Dominion made in the Department of the Interior and dated 1887, thence following said height of Land in a north-easterly direction to the 58 parallel of North Latitude, then easterly along the said 58 parallel to the 105 Meridian, thence north to the 63 parallel, thence following the 63 parallel to the summit of a northern spur of the Rocky Mountains which divides the waters of the Mackenzie River from those of the Yukon River, thence southerly following the summit of the said spur of mountain to the 60th parallel at the northern boundary of British Columbia, thence eastwardly following the northern boundary aforesaid to the North East Corner of the British Columbia boundary at the 120 meridian, thence southerly following the easterly boundary of British Columbia to the Northern boundary of Treaty 7, thence eastwardly along the boundary of Treaty 7 until it intersects the Western boundary of Treaty 6, thence Northwesterly and easterly following the limits of Treaty 6 to the point of beginning, containing approximately 319,900 square miles.[17]

Significantly, the 1891 proposal excluded British Columbia, because development interests were focused on the Mackenzie River valley. Nonetheless, by this time interest in northeastern British Columbia was beginning to develop, because ever since the arrival of fur traders in this region, beginning with Alexander Mackenzie in 1793, the Peace River and Parsnip River had provided an important access route through the Rocky Mountains into the north-central portion of British Columbia, known to Whites as New Caledonia.[18] The fur trade remained the dominant postcontact economic force in the region throughout the nineteenth century, but the gold rush frontier drew ever closer, reaching the Cariboo district to the south in 1860 and the Omineca River country to the southwest by the end of the decade.[19] As gold fever in the Cariboo subsided, Quesnel became an outfitting centre for fur traders and prospectors who headed north and northeast into the Rocky Mountain region and the Peace River district.[20] Prospectors made gold strikes in the Peace River area by the early 1870s. By the 1890s probes of the eastern boundaries of New Caledonia created the expectation that major strikes of gold and other precious metals were likely to be made in the near future.[21] It was at this time that one of the most famous North American gold discoveries – the Klondike – took place far to the northwest in the Yukon region. The ensuing gold rush drew worldwide attention, not only to the immediate area of the diggings but also to the surrounding country, including the whole of northern British Columbia.

There were two primary reasons for this. First, miners and prospectors headed to Dawson and the Klondike fields via several routes that traversed the drainage basins of the Peace, Athabasca, Liard, and Mackenzie rivers. They scoured the country along the way, hoping to find new gold deposits. Second, merchants in British Columbia and Alberta (Calgary and, especially, Edmonton) hoped to profit from the outfitting business the gold rush generated. These developments had major implications for the local Indian population.

The growing number of prospectors in the territory and the arrival of the NWMP made the Indigenous peoples increasingly anxious and resentful of these intruders. This is evident from NWMP inspector J. D. Moodie's journal of his 1897 visit to the region. He described an incident on 9 October that indicated that relations were badly strained between local Indians and Métis and the newcomers: "Saturday, 9th October ... This p.m. a fire was started by a Half-breed, Cunningham, guide to Johnson from Edmonton. We all turned out and saved Bremner's stacks, but could not prevent the fire getting into the bush. Rain at night with wind high. Cunningham will be brought up for trial on Monday. Indians and Breeds rather mad against Johnson, although he was not to blame."[22]

When talking about the need for police protection in the Fort St John area, Moodie remarked: "One of a party of prospectors going through this district shot two stallions belonging to Chief Montaignee, because they were, he said, chasing his horses. On hearing of this the chief sent two parties in different directions to intercept the white men, declaring that if he was not paid for his stallions he would shoot all the prospectors' horses and then the man who killed his. I believe the matter was settled. Another man stole an Indian pony, and the owner followed him to Fort Graham and recovered it."[23] These events underscored the need to address the concerns of Aboriginal peoples about their rights and White encroachment in the middle Peace River area.

Regarding conditions nearby, at Fort Graham, which was located on the Finlay River, Moodie warned that horse stealing by Whites threatened the peace there too:

Mr. Fox [the post manager] informs me that the Indians here at first refused to allow the white men to come through their country without paying toll, and it was only after much talking that they agreed to keep quiet this summer in the hope that the Government would do something to help them. They threatened to burn the feed and kill the horses; in fact, several times fires were started, but the head men were persuaded by Mr. Fox to send out and stop them. A large number of horses have been lost, but whether these have merely strayed or have been driven off it is impossible to say. A guide engaged by several parties (who joined in the expense) deserted a few miles up the river on hearing of a party of St John Indians having come over to intercept the horse killer as above mentioned, at least this is the reason given.[24]

Moodie continued by noting that Indians intended to defend their rights at all costs:

There is no doubt that the influx of whites will materially increase the difficulties of hunting by the Indians, and these people, who, even before the rush, were often starving from their inability to procure game, will in future be in a much worse condition; and unless some assistance is given to them by the Indian Department, they are very likely to take what they consider a just revenge on the white men who have come, contrary to their wishes, and scattered themselves over their country. When told that if they started fighting as they threatened, it could only end in their extermination, the reply was, "We may as well die by the white men's bullets as of starvation." A considerable number of prospectors have expressed their intention of wintering in this neighbourhood and I think it would be advisable to have a detachment of police stationed here, as their presence would go far to prevent trouble. The number of Indians, men, women and children in this District [vicinity of the fort] is about 300.

Reports from other areas indicate that the Indians' hostility toward the intruders was widespread. For instance, F. White, comptroller of the NWMP, forwarded to the superintendent-general of Indian Affairs a patrol report from Fort Smith that said, "The Indians in this locality are very jealous of Whitemen, Trappers and Miners coming in their country and wanted them forbidden to do so."[25] Aboriginal peoples at Lesser Slave Lake shared these sentiments.

As early as 30 November 1897, these problems led NWMP officials to recommend that the government draw up a treaty. On this date Major James Walker wrote to Clifford Sifton, minister of the interior and of Indian Affairs, stating:

Referring to our conversation during your visit to Calgary respecting the necessity of making treaties with the Indians of the Athabasca and the Yukon I would draw your attention to the fact that these Indians have not been treated with, yet I understand that the late Government contemplated treating with the Athabasca Indians some years ago but nothing was done ... From all appearances there will be a rush of miners and others to the Yukon and the mineral regions of the Peace, Liard and other rivers in Athabasca during the next year. Parties are starting North from here almost every day[,] some with the intention of pushing through to the Yukon other[s] to mine in the rivers of Athabasca and British Columbia; others intend to establish stopping places, trading posts, transportation Companies and to take up ranches and homesteads in fertile lands of the Peace River.[26]

Walker bolstered his argument for a treaty by saying it would be cheaper to arrive at an agreement before the mineral potential of the region became common knowledge: "I think you will pardon the suggestion when I state that in the face of this influx of settlers into that country no time should be lost by the Government in making a treaty with these Indians for their rights over this Territory. They will be more easily dealt with now than they would be when their country is overrun with prospectors and valuable mines be discovered. They would then place a higher value on their rights than they would before these discoveries are made and if they are like some of the Indians of the Saskatchewan they may object to prospectors or settlers going into that country until their rights are settled."

The patrol reports that NWMP commissioner L. W. Herchmer had received by autumn of 1897 led him also to recommend that steps be taken to bring the region under treaty. On 2 December he wrote to the comptroller of the force in Ottawa to state:

I have the honour to draw your attention to the advisability of the Government taking some immediate steps towards arranging with the Indians not under Treaty, occupying the proposed line of route from Edmonton to Pelly River. These Indians although few in number, are said to be very turbulent, and are liable to give very serious trouble when isolated parties of miners and travellers interfere with what they consider their vested rights.

At the present time the Half-Breeds of Lesser Slave Lake are dissatisfied with the presence of the Police in that District, and the numerous parties of Americans and others between that point and Peace River will not improve the situation. The Beaver Indians of Peace River and the Nelson are said to be inclined to be troublesome at all times, and so also are the Sicamies [sic] and Nahamies [sic], and the Half-Breeds are sure to influence them ...

Rich mines are liable to be discovered at any time on the Peace, Nelson, and Liard Rivers, when trouble would almost certainly arise.[27]

On 18 June 1898 the superintendent-general of Indian Affairs informed the cabinet of Herchmer's concerns and recommended that a treaty be negotiated. Nine days later the clerk of the Privy Council replied to Indian Affairs saying that cabinet affirmed this recommendation. Cabinet recommended the appointment of A. E. Forget, Indian commissioner for Manitoba and the North-West Territories, and J.A.J. McKenna, of the Department of Indian Affairs, to act as two of the three commissioners.[28] Significantly, the Privy Council also approved the suggestion of the minister of the interior and Indian Affairs that "as to the territory to be ceded, the Commissioners will likewise have discretionary power, for its extent will depend upon the conditions which are found to exist as a consequence of the inroads of white population; but he is of opinion that the territory to be treated for may in a general way be restricted to the Provisional District of Athabaska, and such of the country adjacent thereto as the Commissioners may deem it expedient to include within the treaty."[29]

PLANNING FOR TREATY 8

The federal government faced a dilemma with regard to the size of the territory the treaty should include. As noted above, the 1891 treaty proposal included only the Athabasca, Mackenzie, and Peace River districts lying beyond the British Columbia boundary because mineral exploration had been limited largely to that region. By 1898, however, prospectors were also combing the entire area of northeastern British Columbia. Furthermore, as early as 1891 HBC chief factor McDougall told Indian Affairs commissioner Hayter Reed that it would be very unwise to exclude from the treaty those Indians who lived in the British Columbia territory. Paraphrasing what the chief factor had told him, Reed wrote:

The recommendations included with the information [concerning which groups should be covered] are Mr. McDougall's, and I have not interfered with them, but I may add relative thereto, that the Indians of St. John's and Hudson's Hope although in British Columbia, really belong to the Beavers, who extend from the Mountains to Little Red River.

The Indians at Fort Wrigley, Nelson and Liard also although living in British Columbia, practically form part of bands included in the proposed Treaty, and even should their present hunting grounds be excluded, it will be for the Department's consideration whether it would not be well to include themselves.[30]

Reed attached the boundary description that McDougall had recommended, along with an amendment he proposed. Both included the part of northeastern British Columbia lying beyond the "summit" of the Rocky Mountains. Reed also attached McDougall's explanation for including portions of the latter territory: "The Indians of Dunvegan, St. John's, Hudson's Hope, and other points on the Peace River in the Peace River District, are Beaver Indians ... Should the Indians of St. John's and Hudson's Hope not be included, the Beaver Indians of Dunvegan and a few Crees and Iroquois from Jasper's House would be the only Indians to be dealt with at that point. A few Crees and Half breeds from about Lake St. Annes, and other points to the South of the Athabasca River, have hunted on the Peace River since about 1870 but have no rights in that country as it belongs entirely to the Beavers."[31]

The Privy Council order of 27 June 1898, which gave commissioners the discretion to determine the lands to be included in the treaty, reiterated the statement of the commissioner of the NWMP about the

advisability of steps being taken for the making of a Treaty with the Indians occupying the proposed line of route from Edmonton to Pelly River. He intimated that these Indians – though few in number – were turbulent and liable to give trouble should isolated parties of miners or traders interfere with what they considered their vested rights; that the Halfbreeds of Lesser Slave Lake showed dissatisfaction with the appearance of the Police in that District and that the situation thus created would be made more difficult by the presence of the numerous parties who had come into the country and were scattered at various points between the Lake and Peace River; that the Beaver Indians of the Peace and Nelson Rivers, as well as the Sicamies [sic] and Nihamies [sic] Indians, were inclined to be troublesome, and that the Halfbreeds were likely to influence them in that direction.[32]

In closing their order, the Privy Council noted: "The Minister states that he caused a copy of the Commissioner's report to be transmitted to the Indian Commissioner at Winnipeg, who thereupon reported that the extension of Governmental authority to the Upper Slave Lake and Peace River Districts before the relinquishment of the aboriginal title had been regarded more or less jealously by the Indians and by the large Half-breed population of the Lesser Slave Lake District."

While government officials pondered these various issues, Aboriginal people took steps to pressure them to negotiate. Early in the summer of 1898 about five hundred Indians gathered at Fort St John to block the northward progress of the NWMP, miners, and prospectors until Canada signed a treaty with them. The situation had reached a flash point for several reasons. A scarcity of rabbits and moose during the winter of 1897–98 had led to severe food shortages – even starvation – in the Peace River region. Making matters worse, extensive fires had driven away fur-bearing animals.[33] The Indians blamed the miners for the fires. White intruders caused several other serious problems. They used poison bait when trapping, which killed valuable packing and hunting dogs.[34] And they destroyed the Indians' laboriously constructed log-deadfall bear traps, in order to prevent their pack horses from stumbling into them.[35]

Of major importance, the confrontation at Fort St John received coverage in Canadian and American newspapers. This greatly alarmed federal officials and underscored in their minds the importance of the warnings they had been receiving from the NWMP. Federal and provincial officials also were aware that a major armed clash would generate adverse publicity and undermine their efforts to promote development in British Columbia and the North-West Territories.[36]

HBC officers, who probably understood the situation better than any other Whites, were also alarmed. They thought that current policing was not sufficient, and they expressed their concerns in letters to HBC commissioner C.C. Chipman, who forwarded some of them to the minister of the interior and Indian Affairs, Clifford Sifton, on 2 May 1899. One of these letters was from Chief Factor Ewen Macdonald, who was stationed at Lesser Slave Lake. Macdonald was in charge of the Peace River District, and on 25 March 1899 he had written to Chipman about local policing problems:

I herewith enclose a letter received from Mr. Hamilton [company clerk at Fort St. John] on the agitated state of the St. John's Indians in their relations with the Miners, etc.

I have not, however, much faith in the good that would arise from Police being stationed there unless headed by a competent Officer. Patrols such as we have in this District, without any Officer, are but of little use to the community and seldom act in any case. At the first offset on their arrival in the District, people were a little in awe of them, but familiarity breeds contempt, and no example ever being made of the law breakers the Police are not much dreaded.

Some of the so-called Miners do not treat the Indians with kindness or civility; shoot their dogs, steal their traps, and I have heard instances of stealing fur animals out of the traps, burning the Country, and roaming all over it destroying and frightening game, etc.[37]

The enclosed letter from Hamilton warned that

relations between miners and natives are becoming strained, and in my opinion, there is likely to be trouble.

Indians claim that the whites have stolen and shot their horses, a case of this happening a day or two ago.

The Indians warned the whites that they would shoot if they found whites travelling through their Country; the Miners claim, on the other hand, by the terms of the British Columbia Miners' License which they hold, the right of travelling at will through the Country, and also the protection of the Government. I would strongly advise, especially in view of the coming Treaty, that Police should be stationed here, or else some one with authority to act in the event of any friction between the white and native elements occurring. I of course have cautioned the Indians as to taking the law into their own hands, and warned them as to what may be the result. I have advised them not to take any action, but to wait the arrival of the Treaty Commissioners and state their case to them.[38]

In other words, Hamilton's letter made it abundantly clear that Indians in the Peace River region would not accept the authority of either level of government in the absence of a treaty. Chipman sent these warnings to Sifton, believing that the treaty commissioners should be apprised of the situation. Also, he thought they should be aware that rumours were circulating that these Indians might even refuse a treaty.[39]

Clearly, the federal government faced a complex and explosive situation. Most of the violence between Indians and Whites was taking place in British Columbia territory. This meant that the treaty would have to include a portion of the province. The problem was that British Columbia did not recognize Aboriginal title and it had entered Confederation holding title to crown lands. Since the late 1870s it had been a well-established tradition to provide reserves for Indian nations and to give land, or scrip, to Métis families. Similar concessions would have to be made to the peoples of the Athabasca, Mackenzie, and Peace River districts who signed the treaty. Thus, a new treaty raised potential problems for federal-provincial relations in British Columbia.

Before proceeding with the treaty, however, federal officials had to consider what its terms should be. They conducted their deliberations in the knowledge that many of the Northern Indians would use Treaty 6 as their point of reference. For instance, on 5 December 1898 McKenna wrote to Indian Commissioner Laird about the proposed treaty and informed him that "Mr. J.A. Macrae who at one time held the position of Indian Agent and had in his charge the Indians of Treaty No. 6 intimated sometime ago that the Commissioners might meet a difficulty in the Wood Cree Indians demanding that explicit provision be made in the treaty to secure to them what the Indians of treaty No. 6 have claimed they understood they were entitled to under treaty."[40]

McKenna favoured negotiating a treaty that would be less costly to the government than Treaty 6, but he doubted that the Indians would agree. In his letter to Laird, McKenna made it clear that he and Macrae wanted the government to consider compensation schemes that departed from those of earlier treaties: "He [Macrae] intimated that it would be well, perhaps, to consider whether instead of agreeing to pay a perpetual annuity to the Indians to be treated with some other way of giving them a quid pro quo could not be devised. The annual expenditure incident to the mere paying of the annuity would be considerable; and the [Indian] Department's view appears to be that the paying of annuities to Indians has not produced desirable results."[41]

McKenna agreed with Macrae that alternatives to the traditional annuity approach ought to be considered. Accordingly, on 17 April 1899 he wrote Sifton: "As to the payment of annuity, although Mr. Laird is favorable to it I am rather disposed to the contrary view, and Mr. James Ross with whom I discussed the matter questions its benefit and is of the opinion that the Indians themselves will not place much value on it. I do not know that we have any reason to be desirous of extending the system if it can be avoided. As to the North country, there is the objection that the yearly payment would cost a large sum."[42] McKenna sought to strengthen his argument further by suggesting northern native lands were less valuable than those of the prairies and future development was not likely to seriously disrupt the traditional Indian economies:

Since Treaty Three, the Dominion in all treaties with the Indians has undertaken to pay $5 a year to each Indian in perpetuity, and $15 to headmen and $25 to Chiefs. Now the question arises, what would be fair compensation for the land in the territory now to be treated for. The former land was admirably suited for agriculture. Its settlement was necessary for the real making of the Dominion. The building of the transcontinental railway made the wiping out of the Indian title urgent; and the changing condition interfered with the Indians means of livelihood and mode of life. There were, therefore, good reasons for giving them the maximum compensation. The latter land is not of appreciable value agriculturally. There is no urgent public need of its acquirement. There may be mineral develoopement and some consequent settlement in spots; but this will not bring sudden or great changes likely to interfere to any marked degree with the Indian mode of life and means of livelihood. I think it would not be illiberal to answer the question by saying that half the amount which we agreed to pay under the former treaties would be ample compensation for the Indians who are to be parties to the proposed one. And as the making of the treaty will not be the forerunner of changes that will to any great extent alter existing conditions in the country, and as the Indians will continue to have the same means of livelihood as they have at present, it may fairly be laid down that the object of the Commissioners should simply be to secure the relinquishment of the Indians title at as small a cost as possible.[43]

McKenna's notion that anticipated economic development would not interfere significantly with the existing livelihoods of the Indians in the region was predicated on the idea that mineral exploitation would not be as land-extensive as the expanding agricultural frontier had been on the prairies in the 1870s. In taking this position, it would seem that McKenna was unaware of the problems northern Indians already were experiencing because of miners and prospectors. In any event, the government decided to "proceed upon the usual lines of providing for the payments of annuities to the Indians."[44]

McKenna also gave considerable thought to the reserve issue, paying particular attention to the question of whether reserves lands should be set aside for bands to be held communally or granted to families to be held in severalty. He wrote extensively on this subject in a letter to Sifton on 17 April 1899:

When the Government negotiated for the surrender of the Indian title to the land in the organized territories, it had to deal with Indian nations which had distinct tribal organizations. The communal idea was strong and made necessary the setting apart of reserves for the continuance of the common life until the Indians could be gradually weaned from it.

The most that can be said in favour of the reserve system, however, is that reserves made it easier for the Government to control and feed the Indians in a country where it was necessary to do so. Experience does not favour the view that the system makes for the advancement of the Indians. We should not be anxious to extend it for its own sake; and the conditions of the country to be treated for are not such as make its extension necessary. From the information which has come to hand it would appear that the Indians whom we are to meet fear that the making of a treaty will lead to their being grouped on reserves. Of course, grouping is not now contemplated; but there is the view that reserves for future use should be provided for in the treaty. I do not think this is necessary.[45]

McKenna also understood that social structures among Northern societies were different in crucial ways from those of the Plains Nations, and he thought that planning for reserves ought to take this into account.

From what I have been able to learn of the North country, it would appear that the Indians there act rather as individuals than as a nation, and that any tribal organization which may exist is very slight. They live by hunting, and by individual effort, very much as the half-breeds in that country live. They are averse to living on reserves; and as that country is not one that will ever be settled extensively for agricultural purposes it is questionable whether it would be good policy to even suggest grouping them in the future. The reserve idea is inconsistent with the life of a hunter, and is only applicable to an agricultural country. The most the Indians are likely to require in the way of reserves are small fishing stations at certain points which they might desire to have secured to them. I do not think the Commissioners should go further in the way of general reservations, unless they should find that circumstances compel them. But they should have authority to guarantee to every Indian settled upon, or in occupation of land, an individual title thereto. The limit might be put at 160 acres as the Indians are likely to require very small holdings.

McKenna's stance in favour of granting reserves to individuals also has to be understood in the context of government policies at the time and Indian concerns about possible infringements on their freedom of movement. Beginning in 1886, the DIA had adopted a policy of subdividing reserve lands to discourage communal approaches to economic life and promote individualistic orientations.[46] Giving Indians the option of taking up reserves as individuals near traditional hunting and fishing places was compatible with that severalty policy. Furthermore, McKenna and other government officials knew that many Indians living in the Athabasca, Mackenzie, and Peace River areas were unwilling to make a treaty with Canada because they were afraid they might be restricted to their reserves.[47] This was a frightful prospect for people whose economic life depended on mobility and having access to a range of hunting, fishing, and collecting sites. (Their worries were partly a legacy of the pass system that the Canadian government had used during the Saskatchewan Rebellion of 1885 to block the threat of widespread Indian participation.) That is why McKenna thought, as we have just seen, that the Native peoples' fear of being grouped together at a few locations could be alleviated by giving them the option of living on small individually held reserves that were located close to traditional family hunting and fishing stations.[48]

TREATY 8 NEGOTIATIONS

One of the problems with Treaty 8 is that it was negotiated in haste. The government expected that the commissioners would be able to conduct their negotiations with the various bands in the region in a very short period of time. This is clear from the HBC's tender to supply the treaty commission with the food that it would need to hold talks at various company posts. The tender was based on the government's assumption that no more than a two- to four-day supply would be needed at each conference location.[49] This tight scheduling meant that some Indian nations, whose seasonal cycles could not be altered to accommodate the commissioners' travel plans, would be left out. The most famous example undoubtedly is that of the Lubicon Cree. During the winter of 1898, NWMP inspector W. H. Routledge received one of the notices that the government had circulated throughout the region announcing the forthcoming summer travel plans of the treaty commission. He thought the schedule was completely unrealistic. Accordingly, he wrote from Fort Chipewyan to the commanding officer of G Company, stating, "I have the honour to report, that, as far as I can judge from conversations with the H.B.CO's Officials, Traders, and my own observations, it will be impossible for the Commissioners to be at the various points on the dates stated therein, and very little time seems to be allowed for the Indians to 'talk', a considerable amount of which is done, as you are aware on such occasions."[50]

Routledge's worries proved to be well founded. During the summer of 1899 commissioners Laird, Ross, and McKenna started much later than planned due to bad weather and a shortage of crew to man the party's boats. As a consequence, the negotiations they had been planned to start at Lesser Slave Lake on 8 June did not get under way until 20 June. It is important to note that this was the only place where any extended discussions (two days) took place that had a bearing on the drafting of the written treaty.[51] Subsequently, the commissioners presented the Lesser Slave Lake accord to other groups for their approval (usually doing so in less than a day).[52] To make up for lost time, the commission divided into two groups, with Ross and McKenna heading northwest for Fort St John, while Laird traveled northeast to the Lake Athabasca region. Ross and McKenna's mission failed, because they arrived after the local Indians had dispersed to their hunting grounds.[53] When reflecting on their failure to connect with the Fort St John Indians, Ross and McKenna observed, "what happened was not altogether unforeseen. We had grave doubts of being able to get to St John in time to meet the Indians, but as they were reported to be rather disturbed and ill-disposed on account of the actions of miners passing through their country, it was thought that it would be well to show them that the Commissioners were prepared to go into their country."[54]

Although Laird was more successful in meeting Indians on his sweep through the eastern part of the territory, many groups from the Peace River and other parts of the proposed treaty area did not sign the Lesser Slave Lake agreement. Accordingly, the government dispatched J.A. Macrae, who was an inspector of Indian agencies living in Ottawa, as commissioner to obtain additional adhesions (table A11 shows the communities that the commissioners visited in 1899 and 1900). Of considerable significance, Macrae's report on this work makes it clear that his predecessors had not explained the treaty sufficiently the previous year:

At nearly all the important points the chiefs and more intelligent men who were present at the making of treaty last year, asked for extended explanation of its terms in order that those of their bands who had failed to grasp its true meaning might be enlightened, and that those who were coming into treaty for the first time might fully understand what they were doing. In the course of the councils held for this purpose, it was possible to eradicate any little misunderstanding that had arisen in the minds of the more intelligent, and great pains were taken to give such explanations as seemed most likely to prevent any possibility of misunderstandings in future.[55]

The treaty commissioners' reports for 1899 and 1900 raise a fundamental question. What were the primary topics of discussion between Indians and commissioners, given that the written agreement had been worked out at Lesser Slave Lake on 20–21 June 1899? In their histories of Treaty 8, René Fumoleau and Dennis Madill note that the commissioners had to labour hard to win Indian consent and they needed the help of Catholic missionaries.[56] The commissioner's key strategy involved convincing the Indians that they would remain free to pursue their usual vocations after treaty, which entailed assuring them that Treaty 8 would not restrict them to living on reserves and that any future fish and game conservation measures would be implemented only when necessary and primarily for their benefit. Even with these repeated assurances, many Indians were, in the end, exceedingly reluctant to sign the accord. The people of the Athabasca, Mackenzie, and Peace River countries also wanted more explicit protection for their hunting, trapping, and fishing interests than previous treaties had provided.

The report of 22 September 1899 that Laird, McKenna, and Ross sent to Sifton underscored the extent to which the above issues had dominated treaty talks:

The Chipewyans confined themselves to asking questions and making brief arguments. They appeared to be more adept at cross-examination than at speech-making, and the Chief at Fort Chipewyan displayed considerable keenness of intellect and much practical sense in pressing the claims of his band. They all wanted as liberal, if not more liberal terms, than were granted to the Indians of the plains. Some expected to be fed by the Government after the making of treaty, and all asked for assistance in seasons of distress and urged that the old and indigent who were no longer able to hunt and trap and were consequently often in distress should be cared for by the Government. They requested that medicines be furnished. At Vermilion, Chipewyan, and Smith's Landing, an earnest appeal was made for the services of a medical man. There was expressed at every point the fear that the making of the treaty would be followed by the curtailment of the hunting and fishing privileges, and many were impressed with the notion that the treaty would lead to taxation and enforced military service. They seemed desirous of securing educational advantages for their children.[57]

The commissioners said that they replied to these concerns and requests as follows:

We pointed out that the Government could not undertake to maintain Indians in idleness; that the same means of earning a livelihood would continue after the treaty as existed before it, and that the Indians would be expected to make use of them. *We told them that the Government was always ready to give relief in cases of actual destitution* ... and we stated that the attention of the Government would be called to the need of some special provision being made for assisting the old and indigent who were unable to work and dependent on charity for the means of sustaining life. We promised that supplies of medicines would be put in the charge of persons selected by the Government at different points, and would be distributed free to those of the Indians who might require them ...

Our chief difficulty was the apprehension that the hunting and fishing privileges were to be curtailed. The provision in the treaty under which ammunition and twine is to be furnished went far in the direction of quieting the fears of the Indians, for they admitted that it would be unreasonable to furnish the means of hunting and fishing if laws were to be enacted which would make hunting and fishing so restricted as to render it impossible to make a livelihood by such pursuits. *But over and above the provision, we had to solemnly assure them that only such laws as to hunting and fishing as were in the interest of the Indians and were found necessary in order to protect the fish and fur-bearing animals would be made, and that they would be as free to hunt and fish after the treaty as they would be if they never entered into it.*

We assured them that the treaty would not lead to any forced interference with their mode of life, that it did not open the way to the imposition of any tax, and that there was no fear of enforced military service.[58]

On the issue of education, the government negotiators stated that they told the assembled people that there was no need to make any treaty provisions for education, as it was the government's policy to educate Indian children where possible.

Once the commissioners had finished their work at Lesser Slave Lake on 20 June, "we came to the conclusion that it would be best to make one treaty covering the whole of the territory ceded, and to take adhesions thereto from the Indians to be met at the other points rather than to make several separate treaties. The treaty was therefore so drawn as to provide three ways in which assistance is to be given to the Indians, in order to accord with the conditions of the country and to meet the requirements of the Indians in the different parts of the territory."[59]

To give the treaty the flexibility that was needed to address the varied economic circumstances of Indian bands, the commissioners committed the government to annuity rates that were equal to those of Treaty 6 and to the provision of agricultural assistance to those Indians who actually took up farming. The commissioners anticipated that only Indians living around Lesser Slave Lake and in the Peace River valley would ever do so. The commissioners also granted Indians the option of holding reserve lands in common or in severalty. In either case, the parcels were to be surveyed in the future when development pressures warranted doing so.[60]

It is clear from the above discussion, which is based on the documentary record, that the federal government was motivated to obtain consent to Treaty 8 to facilitate the development of mineral and timber resources in this section of the North-West Territories. Government officials did not envisage that the realization of this objective would significantly upset the local Indian livelihoods. But, the treaty commissioners acknowledged that these people held a very contrary view. To obtain the consent of the First Nations, therefore, the commissioners had to promise that the treaty would protect their traditional livelihoods while offering them the additional benefits of supplies of ammunition, twine for net-making, annuity income, medical aid, and agricultural assistance for those who took up farming. With the assurance that they had all this to gain and nothing of significance to lose, the First Nations agreed to the treaty.

In retrospect, it is clear that Treaty 8 accomplished the federal government's major objective. It allowed for the peaceful economic development of the region at a time when federal and provincial policing powers were stretched thin.[61] It did not have the capability of handling simultaneously an insurrection (or what the province termed an "unusual" policing situation) in the very remote northeast. Furthermore, the White population in the latter region was too small to raise a militia. Aboriginal peoples, on the other hand, thought they had received the promise of protection of their traditional right to live off the land as they had since time immemorial, with the addition of annuities and other economic benefits in exchange for the pledge to live peacefully with White intruders. It is certain that the economic development of the Athabasca, Mackenzie, and Peace River districts in the late nineteenth and early twentieth centuries could not have been accomplished peacefully without Treaty 8. The Indigenous peoples had warned that they would put up armed resistance to any further encroachment on the area by Whites. They had also made it clear that in the absence of a treaty they did not recognize the authority of Canada, which was represented in the NWMP, or of the province of British Columbia, which was manifest in the mining licenses it issued to prospectors operating in the area. To bring law and order to the region the government essentially had two choices: bring in a sizable armed force at considerable expense or conclude a treaty.

Having chosen the latter option, the government proceeded with Treaty 8. In this agreement it guaranteed Indians that they "would have the right to pursue their usual vocations of hunting and trapping and fishing throughout the tract surrendered ... subject to such regulations as may from time to time be made by the Government of the country ... saving and excepting such tracts as may be required or taken up from time to time for settlement, mining, lumbering, trading, or other purposes."[62] These terms were very similar to the livelihood provisions first offered in the Robinson Treaties, except that the government reserved the option to regulate hunting, trapping, and fishing activities. The commissioners repeatedly assured the local First Nations that such regulations would be implemented largely for their own benefit, however, and that nothing would be done to interfer with their traditional way of life. The oral histories of Treaty 8 people make it clear that the descendants of those who agreed to the treaty believe that this promise was not kept.

Treaty 8 also provided for reserves, but in recognition of the different socioeconomic circumstances of northern hunters and fishers, it allowed Indians to hold their land collectively as bands or in severalty as individuals. Offering the latter option was also in keeping with the government's policy of discouraging communal economic life. The other provisions of the treaty paralleled those of the 1870s by providing cash payment at the time Indians signed the treaty, annuities thereafter, ammunition and twine for those who continued to hunt, trap, and fish, and help with the development of agriculture for those who chose to do so.

CHAPTER ELEVEN

Treaty 10

INTRODUCTION

Treaty 10, which covers the vast northern portion of the province that was not encompassed by Treaty 8, was the last of the Saskatchewan treaties (see tables A13 and A14 for details).[1] The Treaty 10 region includes areas that had been traditionally occupied and used by bands that adhered to Treaty 6. As had been the case in the Treaty 8 region, Indians pressed to establish treaty relations with the Crown for a number of years before they were successful. The agreement they finally achieved was largely modelled after Treaty 8.

PRELUDE TO TREATY 10, 1883–1906

The Department of Indian Affairs (DIA) first gave consideration to treating with Indians in northern Saskatchewan in 1883, in response to a letter officials had received from the Roman Catholic Bishop of St Albert concerning the "Montagnais Indians" of Ile à la Crosse. Although outside the treaty area (north of Treaty 6), these Indians had been "receiving assistance in ammunition and twine for the past few years."[2] Deputy Superintendent-General Lawrence Vankoughnet wrote that he

was informed from several quarters while in the North West that very much uneasiness exists among the Indians in the unceded part of the Territories at parties making explorations into their country in connection with railroads, &c., without any Treaty being made with them; and it was reported to him by persons who were well acquainted with these Indians that they are most anxious to enter into Treaty relations with the Government and that it is in the interests of humanity very desirable that the Government, should render them assistance, as their condition at many points is very wretched. The Indians in the unceded portions of the Territories are not numerous; but at the same time they could of course do great injury to any railway or other public work which might be constructed in their country, unless the Government had a previous understanding with them relative to the same.[3]

In other words, the Ile à la Crosse Indians' reasons for wanting an agreement were similar to those of other Subarctic Indians who found themselves living beyond treaty territories. They wished to have the same economic benefits that their treaty neighbours were receiving from the Crown.

Vankoughnet's response to the bishop's letter made two important points, which were somewhat at variance with those he subsequently made in 1890 with respect to the call of the Lesser Slave Lake Cree for a treaty. He pointed out that the Indians' conditions could be wretched and that a treaty should be made for humanitarian reasons. He also observed that it was in the public interest to treat with the Indians in order to have an understanding with them before railroads and other developments entered their country. Indian Commissioner Dewdney considered Vankoughnet's recommendation and requested additional information from HBC chief factor Lawrence Clarke, who also recommended entering into a treaty with the Indians of this region, but he reported that their economic circumstances were "Fairly good with but very few destitute."[4] In 1884 the DIA took the possibility of making a treaty with the Dene and Cree of Ile à la Crosse seriously enough to calculate what the costs of doing so would be, but in the end decided not to do so. Four years later the department informed the Bishop of St Albert that a treaty with the Isle à la Crosse Indians would be delayed further.[5]

The completion of Treaty 8 placed the Indians of the Ile à la Crosse region in a gap between the lands of this treaty and those of Treaties 5 and 6. McKenna discussed this problem in 1902 after he had held an interview with Bishop Pascal of Ile à la Crosse: "I have never been in the country referred to, but I do not think that it is of a nature that will lead to much inroad upon the natives. At the same time the making of treaties with the neighbouring aboriginies makes them feel that they are being treated differently. I, therefore, think that it would be good policy to round off the ceded tract by extinguishing the aboriginal title shown on the attached map."[6]

There were other reasons why the status of the Ile à la Crosse region had to be reconsidered at the turn of the century. One of these was the pressure to issue scrip to local Métis. This agitation led the DIA to consult the 1901 census to determine how many Métis and Indians would have to be dealt with by a treaty and scrip commission.[7] Using these data, officials estimated what the annuities would cost if a treaty was negotiated, in order to prepare the supplementary estimate for parliament that was an essential step in moving forward with a treaty. But once again, the government took no further action.

In 1904 Indian Commissioner David Laird offered the most detailed rationale for the government's repeated delaying in bringing the Ile à la Crosse Indians under treaty:

there was no particular necessity that the treaty should extend to that region. It was not a territory through which a railway was likely soon to run, nor was it frequented by miners, lumbermen, fishermen, or other whites making use of the resources of its soil or waters, in which case, in my opinion, the Indians and Halfbreeds are better left to their hunting and fishing as a means of making a livelihood. The conditions there are the same still, and I therefore do not approve of any immediate steps being taken to include the territory mentioned by Mr. Inspector Conroy in treaty limits. The matter, I suggest, may very well stand over for the present; and, when the autonomy question [creation of new provinces] is settled in the Northwest Territories, if it is found that any Province, or organized territory with representation, extends over a considerable tract of country in which the aboriginal title has not been relinquished, then in such case, or from the entrance of a railway, the discovery of mines, or other cause to bring an inrush of whites, a Treaty should be made without delay.[8]

Clearly, the DIA was continuing the policy that had been established during the Macdonald era of leaving Indian and Métis peoples to their hunting and fishing livelihoods unless an inrush of Whites took place or the political status of a territory changed through the introduction of local representative government. As had happened in the Treaty 8 area before 1899, Indians received some government relief through the HBC when they needed it. In 1904 Duncan Campbell Scott reported that the relief for destitute Portage La Loche and Ile à la Crosse Natives through a similar arrangement had "cost us very little," totaling only $363.64.[9] No doubt the DIA understood that this system was much less costly than the annuity and other obligations that a new treaty would create.

The creation of the province of Saskatchewan in 1905 led the government to revisit the treaty question yet again. DIA secretary, J. D. McLean, pointed out to Laird that "the boundary of one of the new provinces has been extended over this country" and that the question of a treaty might be reconsidered.[10] In 1905, Inspector of Indian Agencies William J. Chisholm recommended:

In view of the fact that the boundaries of the newly organized Province of Saskatchewan extend far beyond the present treaty limits, I would suggest that measures be taken to bring the remainder of the Indians within the said boundaries into treaty, and that then a point of payments be fixed on the Churchill, at Stanley or at Rapid River. The principal centers of Indian population outside of present treaty limits and within the Province of Saskatchewan are, I am informed, Reindeer Lake, Wollaston or Hatchett Lake, and farther west, Waterhen Lake, Ile à la Crosse, Buffalo River, Island Lake, and Portage la Loche.[11]

An adhesion that extended Treaty 8 to the Indians of northwestern Saskatchewan was one option.[12] Geographical considerations led Laird to oppose this approach, however, pointing out that "the nearest way to reach it is from Prince Albert, while the payments of Treaty 8 are made by the route of the Peace and Athabasca rivers."[13] Indian Commissioner Laird thought that the terms of Treaty 8 were more appropriate than those of Treaty 6, but he said he "would recommend that a separate or new treaty be made with the Indians of the northern portion of Saskatchewan."[14]

Chisholm's and Laird's views notwithstanding, the possibility of bringing northwestern Saskatchewan under Treaty 8 remained an option for some time. For instance, DIA inspector of reserves H. A. Conroy (who later served as commissioner for Treaty 11) proposed an adhesion to Treaty 8 in December 1905. He also reported, "I beg to state that in paying [annuity] at Fort McMurray in August last a deputation of these Indians again waited on me asking to be admitted to Treaty and would say that they have brought this question before my notice for the past five years."[15] Apparently, these Indians had some familiarity with the terms of Treaty 8. Conroy provided a map showing the areas that the adhesion of these people would include. He also pointed out that "The Indians in this territory are partially in Saskatchewan and Alberta and are the same class of Indians as those already in Treaty 8 and live by hunting and fishing. They not only follow the same means of obtaining a livelihood as the Indians of Treaty 8, but they are closely related to them by ties of marriage."[16]

Evidently, Conroy thought that a similarity in livelihood would make an adhesion to Treaty 8 more appropriate for the Indians of Ile à la Crosse than a new agreement would be. With respect to the Indians in the unceded part of Saskatchewan, he recommended against making a new treaty: "I do not consider that as the conditions of the Indians now sought to be admitted are the same as those of Treaty 8 that a new treaty should be made but should be an adhesion to that Treaty."[17] Considering that part of Saskatchewan already was covered by Treaty 8, a further expansion of it in the province certainly made sense.

In April 1906, Frank Pedley, whom Sifton had appointed as deputy superintendent general of Indian Affairs in 1902, wrote a lengthy memorandum about the northern Saskatchewan treaty issue to Frank Oliver, who had replaced Sifton in 1905. Pedley documented important features of government treaty policy. He began by reviewing the problem that the Ile à la Crosse Indians posed and the solutions that had been considered:

The Department has for sometime had under consideration the advisability of admitting to Treaty No. 8 the Indians of Portage la Loche and Ile à la Crosse. Not long after this treaty was made, the Department began to be urged to admit these Indians. The half-breed claims within the district were also brought up, but action upon these cognate matters has remained in abeyance until the present.

The Department is lately in receipt of a report from Inspector Conroy, urging that Treaty No. 8 should be extended by the admission of the Indians of Portage la Loche and Ile à la Crosse and the delimitation of a boundary for the said adhesion, which would include other Indians. The Secretary of the Department of the Interior, writing on the 1st. ultimo, requests information from this Department as to how the matter stands with particular reference to the half-breed claims, in which that Department is of course interested. In considering the Indian division of this proposition, two lines of action might be recommended: one to take as an adhesion to Treaty No. 8 a surrender of all that portion of the Province of Saskatchewan uncovered by any Indian treaty, – the other to delimit that extensive unorganized territory outside and east of the boundaries of the Province of Saskatchewan, together with such portions of that Province as are now not included within the boundaries of any treaty, and to prepare for a new treaty extending over the whole of this vast territory. The last-mentioned action would be preferable. It may be necessary in a few years to treat with the Indians of Hudson Bay at Fort Churchill and the Indians of the interior upon any line of railway that might be pushed north to that post.[18]

Having explored these options, Pedley proceeded to argue against extending Treaty 8 further into Saskatchewan, on the rationale that the land had less agricultural potential than the Athabasca–Peace River country. For this reason, he thought that Treaty 9 (1905), covering northern Ontario, provided a more appropriate model:

I have due regard for the economics of the questions as well as the policy of obtaining a cession of the Indian title, and I think we should be careful not to burden the Dominion with any extensive charges for the purchase of the Indian title to this country. We may be reasonably sure that it is not an agricultural country whatever its capacities may be, and that to give a *quid pro quo* on the same basis as for a country with great agricultural possibilities would be a mistake.

I do not favor the treatment of any of these Indians, even those of Portage la Loche and Ile à la Crosse, on the same basis as Treaty No. 8. The Indians of the whole of that territory received the benefit of the opinions formed of portions of it, viz: the Peace River Valley, and the Indians inhabiting the districts where agriculture can not be engaged in with profit have a right under the treaty to expect (subject, of course, to the discretion of the Department) issues of implements, cattle and tools. It appears to me that new treaty on the same lines as treaty No. 9 should be made to extend over the district to which I have just alluded, the boundaries of which I will shortly give in detail, and that the main stipulations be the provision of a gratuity of $10.00 per head upon signing the treaty, and a perpetual annuity of $5.00 per annum: reserves of the usual area, i.e., one square mile to every family of five or in like proportions: the provision of schools where they could be established to advantage.

Pedley's closing remarks make it clear that his proposal was, in essence, another manifestation of the government policy, which had been well established by the 1880s, that advocated undertaking new treaty obligations with Indians only when it was absolutely necessary to do so and in ways, where possible, that minimized costs:

Such a treaty would entail upon the Dominion the minimum of cost and whatever might be done in the future to promote civilization amongst the Indians would be done under the general policy of the Department, and as a matter of grace. An important part of this treaty would be a clause which would permit the Department to extend its benefits to any bands within the limits of the territory when it became necessary or advisable to do so. Under this clause, while it is advisable to now deal with the Indians of Portage la Loche and Ile à la Crosse and vicinity, it might be necessary soon to deal with the Indians of Forts Nelson and Churchill, but, until the treaty obligation should be imposed, the Department would be responsible solely for the ordinary supplies to prevent destitution which are now issued at remote posts by the Hudson's Bay Company; upon the partition of the unorganized districts between existing Provinces of the Dominion, they could be taken over with the definite understanding that the obligation, potential or otherwise, to the Indians was a certain fixed quantity under treaty. The large territory which would be covered by the new treaty would not extend farther north than the 64th. parallel of latitude; although a portion of Treaty No. 8 following the south shore of the Great Slave Lake is farther north than this parallel, I think we should have a definite policy that the aborigines north of that line should not be brought into treaty but that Indian affairs should be administered in that far northern country as the needs of the case suggest. The new treaty would cover, roughly, the following territory: – Bounded on the West by the eastern boundary of British Colombia and Treaty No. 8: on the North by the 64th parallel of latitude and Hudson Bay: on the East by Hudson Bay and James Bay: on the South by the Albany River and the northern boundaries of Treaties Nos. 6, 5 and 3. The expenditure necessary to take the adhesions now pending would not be very large. Accurate information is not at hand as to the number of Indians but they might be estimated at seven hundred:

Gratuity of $10 per head to 500 Indians	$5,000.00
Provisions for treaty negotiations	2,000.00
Cost of negotiating treaty, including half-breed commission	5,000.00
	12,000.00

In other words, Pedley proposed a new treaty that would cover much of the central subarctic, including the unceded parts of northern Saskatchewan and Keewatin (northern Manitoba and northern Ontario) – as conditions determined – by allowing individual bands to make adhesions to it. The reason for treating the entire central subarctic at this time was that provinces would know the fixed cost of treaty obligations when they acquired northern territories. Using Treaty 9 as the archetype for this proposed agreement was attractive to Pedley because it offered a less costly way of addressing Aboriginal title than Treaty 8 did, inasmuch as Treaty 9 excluded agricultural assistance provisions and provided a smaller signing bonus. In addition, Pedley favoured a flexible policy of "grace" over one that stipulated treaty rights.

On 12 July 1906 Oliver submitted a report and treaty recommendation to the Privy Council that departed substantially from what Pedley had recommended:

The undersigned has the honour to report that the aboriginal title has not been extinguished in the greater proportion of that part of the Province of Saskatchewan which lies north of the 54th parallel of latitude and in a small adjoining area in Alberta; that the Indians and Half-breeds of that territory are similarly situated to those whose country lies immediately to the south and west, whose claims have already been extinguished by, in the case of those who are Indians, a payment of a gratuity and annuity and the setting aside of lands as reserves, and in the case of those who are Half-breeds, by the issue of scrip; and they have from time to time pressed their claims for settlement on similar lines; that it is in the public interest that the whole of the territory included within the boundaries of the Province of Saskatchewan and Alberta should be relieved of the claims of the aboriginees; and that $12000.00 has been included in the estimates for expense in the making of a treaty with Indians and in settling the claims of the Half-breeds and for paying the usual gratuities to the Indians.[19]

Oliver next proposed what some of the terms of the treaty should be: reserves or land in severalty, gratuities and annuities, provision for the education of Indian children, and assistance to Indians for farming and stock-raising. (The criteria for satisfaction of scrip claims were stated, as well.) Some terms, such as the annuity and signing gratuity were to be fixed; however, other terms, such as those on schooling and agricultural assistance, were not defined.[20] The record does not explain why Oliver did not accept Pedley's suggestion that Treaty 9 be used as the model and opted, instead, to use Treaty 8.[21] In any event, on 20 July 1906 Privy Council order no. 1459 set up the Treaty 10 commission based on the terms Oliver had recommended.[22] It also again appointed J.A.J. McKenna "as Commissioner to treat with the Indians and Halfbreeds."[23] Given his involvement with making Treaty 8, it is not surprising that McKenna had wanted this agreement to serve as the template for Treaty 10. On 2 August 1906, E. L. Newcombe, deputy minister of justice, received instructions to draft a treaty along the lines of the order-in-council of 20 July 1906.[24] He was supplied with a copy of Treaty 8 to serve as his guide. Newcombe replied the same day but pointed to the problems he had encountered when trying to carry out his directions:

The instructions you give me and the provisions of the Order-in-Council are not sufficient to enable me to make a complete draft of the treaty, and as the matter is represented to be very urgent, I have simply made such changes in form in the applicable portions of Treaty No. 8, to which you refer me, as are rendered necessary by the differing conditions, and marked with an interrogation point those portions thereof, the applicability of which appears to be doubtful, having made in them also such changes as are necessary if they are to be embodied in the new treaty. I have also struck out the two clauses providing for the supplying of tools, machines, cattle, etc., on the assumption that paragraph (d) in the Order-in-Council providing generally for the affording of assistance in farming or stock raising, or other work, is intended as a substitute for these.

The copy of Treaty 8, as thus amended and otherwise dealt with, is the best I can do, with the information given me, towards furnishing the required draft, but I shall be glad to afford any further assistance in my power if you will supplement your instructions as to the points now in doubt.[25]

J.D. McLean, who had become acting deputy superintendent general in addition to his duties as department secretary, sought no further assistance from Newcombe. The same day he received Newcombe's letter and amendments, he forwarded them to McKenna and advised him, "I hope from the outline that you will be able yourself to draft the treaty, as was done by the Commissioners in the case of Treaty No. 8."[26] Given the familiarity of the Ile à la Crosse Indians with Treaty 8, the more parsimonious Treaty 9 terms undoubtedly would have been unacceptable. This may explain why Treaty 8 evidently was the model for Treaty 10.

TREATY-MAKING EVENTS

McKenna's treaty party arrived in northwestern Saskatchewan in the late summer; it included Royal North-West Mounted Police superintendent J.V. Begin, and Mr Charles Fisher and Charles Mair. Fisher and Mair acted as secretaries, and Bishop Pascal accompanied the party. Once again the government contracted the HBC to transport the treaty party and treaty goods. McKenna said of the bishop: "I had the pleasure of the company, on most of the inward trip, of His Lordship Bishop Pascal; and I desire to repeat here the acknowledgment I made and the gratitude I expressed to his lordship personally for the assistance of his influence on my first meeting the natives of the country, which is filled with reverence for his name because of his devoted labours."[27] In other words, as before, missionaries were present at the treaty talks and facilitated the making of the agreement. Commissioner McKenna also acclaimed the work of others in his party: "I desire to express also, my appreciation of the help ever readily rendered by Major Begin of the Royal Northwest-Mounted-Police, who was in command of the escort, by Dr. J.J.A. Lebrecque, the medical officer; by Mr. Charles Fisher of Duck Lake and Mr. Charles Mair of Ottawa, secretaries to the Commission, by the Hudson's Bay Company's chief factor, and by Mr. Angus McKay, the officer of the company who was especially charged with the carrying out of the transportation contract."[28]

McKenna drew particular attention to the important and arduous work the HBC's boatmen had performed: "To the men of the country on whose labour we had so much to depend I acknowledge my obligation. They worked long hours at paddling and rowing and poling, and endured great hardships in tracking and walking our canoes and flat boats over the rapids and shoals, so that I might keep my appointments. Camp was made late and broken early. Yet there was never a complaint, but always a zestful interest and cheerfulness as pleasant as the campfires that brightened the night."[29]

Clearly, the HBC transport system, which was built on the backs of Native boatmen, greatly facilitated government agents' visits to the north.

Notification had been given about the dates and places the commission would meet the Indians, but the weather disrupted the treaty party's schedule. On the 26 August, at Ile à la Crosse, McKenna met with a party of English River Chipewyan and ten families from Clear Lake. These Indians wanted to treat immediately and return to their hunting grounds. McKenna opened talks with them on 28 August and encountered some difficulty. Nonetheless, "By the end of the day, the treaty was signed and the annuity and gratuity moneys paid" (see tables A13 and A14 for details of the treaty signing).[30] Two chiefs, two headmen, and 195 other Indians received payments at this first signing of Treaty 10.

The commission moved on to Portage la Loche, where it arrived on 5 September. McKenna reported that "The people at this point were all half-breeds and were dealt with as such."[31] Several days later the treaty party reached the La Loche Lake mission, where more claims for scrip were taken. On the way back to Ile à la Crosse McKenna stopped at Buffalo Narrows, where more than 117 members of the Clear Lake band and three members of Bulls House band were paid for joining the treaty. Headmen for the Clear Lake band also were selected at that time.

At Ile à la Crosse McKenna, assisted by interpreter Archie Park, secured secured the adhesion of the Canoe Lake Cree on 19 September 1906. Chief John Iron, Baptiste Iron, and Jerome Couilloneur signed the adhesion. The chief, two headmen, and 79 other Indians were paid. The treaty party had intended to head east to Stanley Mission and take adhesions in northeastern Saskatchewan. However, very low water levels led HBC officials to advise McKenna that his group would not reach Stanley before freeze-up. They also told him that it was unlikely that the Indians would wait there. Accordingly, McKenna canceled the meeting.

Because McKenna was unable to complete Treaty 10 in 1906, the government appointed Thomas Borthwick, an Indian agent stationed at Mistawasis, Saskatchewan, to serve as a treaty commissioner and finish the task. Borthwick's treaty party included Dr H.A. Stewart, whom Borthwick described as being "a skilful physician, he was most successful in his efforts to relieve their suffering."[32] HBC trader W.J. McLean also assisted Borthwick as the senior secretary. Borthwick said that McLean "displayed special ability in the performance of the onerous duties of his position, his previous experience in treaty payments standing him good stead; while his knowledge of the French language, his long residence as a chief factor of the Hudson's Bay Company, in the part of the country traversed, and his personal acquaintance with many of the applicants, materially contributed to the success of my commission."[33] Thus, once again, a treaty commissioner drew upon the knowledge and connections of HBC personnel.

In addition to treating with Indians at Brochet (Reindeer Lake), Borthwick was directed to pay annuities at Ile à la Crosse and to try to get the Lac la Plonge band to join the treaty. Specifically, his instructions stated: "The copy of the Treaty which was enclosed in official letter of 22nd. March sets forth the terms and conditions which you are empowered to offer to the Indians. These should not be added to or curtailed and you should be careful not to make any verbal promises as varying or extending the terms of the Treaty. If any questions arise with which you are not familiar enough to give an explicit answer you should reserve them for the consideration of the Department."[34] Thus, as with other adhesions, the terms were set. Although cautioned not to make verbal promises, Borthwick received little guidance on how he was supposed to explain the nature of their future treaty relations with the Crown to the Indians.

On 14 October 1907 Commissioner Borthwick reported on the adhesions he had been able to make to Treaty 10. According to his report, in late June he discussed the treaty with the Canoe Lake, English River, and Clear Lake bands and paid them their annuities. He also took more applications for scrip. Next, he visited the La Loche mission, where he accepted additional scrip applications. In late July the treaty party departed from Ile à la Crosse for Stanley Mission, arriving there on 1 August. Here the commissioner paid annuities to some fifty families of the Lac la Ronge band. The treaty party then traveled north to the HBC post and Oblate mission located at Brochet, which was at the north end of Reindeer Lake. Again the party was late. Borthwick described the problems this caused for the Indians who were waiting for him:

they were detained for ten days awaiting my arrival ... which led to their running out of provisions, they being all assembled with their families, and finding that they were reduced to such a state, that I felt that it was proper for me to relieve their immediate necessities, and accordingly I supplied them with a limited quantity of provisions, for which they appeared to feel very thankful. I consider it proper that I should mention here that considerable help was afforded these Indians whilst waiting my arrival by Mr. A. McDermot, the Hudson's Bay Company's agent at this place, by giving them some light work to do and paying them for it in provisions, and likewise by the agent of the Revillon Bros.[35]

Borthwick next held a council with the Barren Land (Brochet) and Lac la Hache (Wollaston Lake) bands on 19 August 1907. The Reverend Father Turquetil, OMI (Oblates of Mary Immaculate), acted as Dene language interpreter. Borthwick reported: "I explained to them why I was sent to meet them, and after various thoughtful questions put by the Indians bearing upon the treaty and answered by me to their satisfaction, they asked for a short recess to discuss the terms of the treaty more fully among themselves; which was granted them."[36] That afternoon, the Barren Lands band signed the treaty (see table A13 for details). One Chief, two headmen and 229 Indians were paid.[37] On 22 August, the Lac La Hache band signed the treaty after Borthwick had read its terms and "thoroughly explained [it to them] in their own language."[38] One chief, two headmen and 94 Indians from this band received payments.[39] Several months after Borthwick's party completed its work, cabinet approved Treaty 10 with Privy Council Order No. 2490.[40]

The use of Treaty 8 as the template for Treaty 10 is reflected in the wording of the agreement. It states that the object was to fulfill "His Majesty's desire to open up for settlement, immigration, trade, travel, mining, lumbering and such other purposes as to His Majesty may seem meet" and "to obtain the consent thereto of his Indian subjects inhabiting the said tract and to make a treaty with them so that there may be peace and good will between them and His Majesty's other subjects" and that "His Indian people may know and be assured of what allowances they are to count upon and receive from His Majesty's *bounty and benevolence*."[41] Treaty 10 provided for hunting, fishing, and trapping rights, the right of Indians to have reserves or hold land in severalty, cash presents for signing, annuities, medals, flags, suits for chiefs and headmen, education for children, and assistance for agriculture, stock raising, or twine and ammunition (see tables A14 and A15 for details).

TREATY 10 ISSUES

Despite the absence of detailed written accounts of what was said at the Treaty 10 talks, it is possible to identify many of the issues that were of concern to Indians and the Crown. McKenna's report on 18 January 1907 summarized in a general way some of the issues the First Nations had raised and recorded his responses. At Ile à la Crosse, McKenna recalled,

It appeared for a time as if there would be some considerable difficulty in effecting a settlement on the lines of the treaty, for it was evident from the trend of the talk of the leaders among the Indians that there had been at work an influence which tended to make them regard the treaty as a means of enslaving them. I was able to disabuse their minds of this absurd notion and to make it clear that the Government's object was simply to do for them what had been done for neighboring Indians when the progress of trade or settlement began to interfere with the untrammelled exercise of their aboriginal privileges as hunters.[42]

In short, the commissioner had argued that the treaty was designed to protect and provide for Indians when their livelihood was threatened by development.

According to McKenna, Indians pressed for a variety of economic concessions:

There was a marked absence of the old Indian style of oratory, the Indians confining themselves to asking questions and making brief arguments. They all demanded even more liberal terms than were granted to Indians treated with in past years, the Chief of the English River Band going so far as to claim payment of "arrears" from the year when the first

Treaty was made; some expected to be entirely fed by the Government, after the making of the treaty; all asked for assistance in seasons of distress; and it was strongly urged that the old and indigent who were no longer able to hunt and trap and were consequently often in destitute circumstances, should be cared for by the Government.[43]

McKenna responded as follows:

I convinced them that such a claim as they put forward for what they called "arrears" had never before been heard of, and that I could not for a moment recognize any obligation on the Government's part except such as would be put upon it in virtue of the execution of the treaty. I pointed out to them that the Government could not undertake to maintain Indians in idleness; that the same means of earning a livelihood would continue after the treaty was made as existed before it; and that Indians would be expected to make as good use of them in the future as in the past. I stated that the Government was always ready to assist Indians in actual destitution; that in times of distress they would, without any special stipulation in the treaty, receive such assistance as it was usual to give in order to prevent starvation among them, and that the attention of the Government would be called to the necessity of some special provision being made for assisting the old and indigent who were unable to work and dependent on charity for subsistence.[44]

Thus, in McKenna's view the treaty was designed to secure the traditional livelihood, and furthermore, those Indians who were too old or indigent would obtain assistance from the government.

Apparently, at the initial talks Indians raised the problem of maintaining a livelihood without access to resources. According to McKenna, "There was a general expression of fear that the making of the treaty would be followed by the curtailment of their hunting and fishing privileges, and the necessity of not allowing the lakes and the rivers to be monopolized or depleted by commercial fishing was emphasized."[45] McKenna's reassurance about the first of these two interrelated concerns regarding the future of traditional livelihood pursuits was very clear:

I guaranteed that the treaty would not lead to any forced interference with their mode of life. I explained to them that whether treaty was made or not, they were subject to the law, bound to obey it and liable to punishment for any infringement thereof; that it was designed for the protection of all and must be respected by all the inhabitants of the country, irrespective of colour or origin; and that, in requiring them to abide by it, they were only being required to do the duty imposed upon all the people throughout the Dominion of Canada I dwelt upon the importance, in their own interest, of the observance of the laws respecting the protection of fish and game.[46]

Significantly, McKenna presented fish and game laws as ones that Indians would have to obey, regardless of the treaty. Yet he minimized the negative aspect of this type of legislation by saying that respecting it would not interfere with the pursuit of a livelihood and that it would serve Indian interests. Notably, McKenna did not address the problem of outsiders encroaching upon traditional resources. Regarding another issue of livelihood, McKenna explained that "the assistance in farming and ranching mentioned in the Treaty, is only to be given when the Indians are actually prepared to go into those industries."[47]

At the 1906 talks, the Indians had pressed for education rights that were compatible with the instruction schemes missionaries already had introduced: "There was evidenced a marked desire to secure educational privileges for their children. In this connection and speaking for the Indians generally, the Chief of the English River Band insisted that in the carrying out of the Government's Indian educational policy among them, there should be no interference with the system of religious schools now conducted by the mission, but that public aid should be given for improvement and extension along the lines already followed."[48] McKenna said he responded as follows: "As to education, the Indians were assured that there was no need for special stipulation over and above the general provision in the Treaty, as it was the policy of the Government to provide in every part of the country, as far as circumstances would permit, for the education of the Indian children, and that the law provided for schools for Indians maintained and assisted by the Government, being conducted, as to religious auspices, in accordance with the wishes of the Indians."[49] In other words, Commissioner McKenna gave verbal assurances that the government would provide education for Indian children and that the mission schools operating in their territory would continue.

The Indians also raised concerns about health care with McKenna: "they … requested that medicines be furnished and made an earnest appeal for the appointment of a resident medical man."[50] The commissioner explained in practical terms how the government would fulfill its commitment to Indian health:

I promised that medicines would be placed at different points in the charge of persons to be selected by the Government, and would be distributed to those of the Indians who might require them. I showed them that it would be practically impossible for the Government to arrange for a resident doctor owing to the Indians being so widely scattered over such an extensive territory; but I assured them that the Government would always be ready to avail itself of any opportunity of affording medical service just as it provided that the physician attached to the Commission should give free attendance to all Indians whom he might find in need of treatment.[51]

Shortly after the conclusion of the treaty, McLean noted that "Under the terms … Treaty 10, medicines were promised to be placed at certain points," and he took action to fulfill that obligation.[52] Given that a doctor traveled with each of the commissions and attended to the sick they encountered, Indians had evidence that the government was sincere about its commitment to their health.

It seems that the discussions between the English River, Clear Lake, and Canoe Lake bands and Commissioner McKenna did not lead to any alterations in the written terms of the treaty. McKenna apparently avoided having to do so by telling the Indians that it was not necessary to stipulate the government's intentions in the written text of the treaty. Instead, he made promises and assurances with respect to their general livelihood and well-being.

Commissioner Borthwick's 1907 report on his Treaty adhesions provided even fewer details than McKenna's report of the previous year. But a lengthy memorandum on his commission's activities was drafted, that discusses the adhesion talks in northeastern Saskatchewan and, additionally, records some of the concerns the English River, Clear Lake, and Canoe Lake bands raised the year after they agreed to the treaty.

The memorandum indicates that at the meeting with Borthwick on 20 June 1907, Chief William Apisis of the English River Band stated that his people "were afraid that they would be prevented from fishing and hunting in their country as usual, and that they would starve if such should be the case."[53] According to the memo, "the Commissioner answered them that they would not at any time be prevented from hunting and fishing for their own use as heretofore, which answer seemed to give general satisfaction." Plainly, hunting and fishing remained in the forefront of Indian concerns. Chief Apisis also asked for a resident doctor, but "the Commissioner answered that the Government would not be able to get a Doctor to reside among them for sometime to come yet, as it would not pay him to do so, but later on when the white settlers would come nearer to them, a Doctor might reside within reach of them." Borthwick did, however, indicate that a doctor might continue to make annual visits.[54]

Chief Apisis also provided information on the destitute among the band: "The Chief stated that there are thirty-two old and destitute people in his Band and [he] would be pleased if the Government would be so kind as to help them with some food and clothing. The Commissioner said that he would present their condition and request to the Government, and would try to have some blankets, cotton and some warm wearing clothing sent to the destitute and old men and women of his Band."[55]

At the same meeting, the Canoe Lake band asked for a reserve, a school, more provisions, tools, and seeds. The chief informed the commissioner that there were seven old and feeble people in the band. Illustrating the Indians' belief that the dominion government was assuming the kind of relationship with them that the Hudson's Bay Company previously had had, the Canoe Lake bands also "submitted to the Commissioner that heretofore they were in the habit of receiving a regale from the Hudson's Bay Company at New Years and Easter time and they would like the Government to do similar to that given by the H.B.Co. The Commissioner answered them and said that he could not promise them anything in that way."[56] Formerly, the traditional New Year's regale, an inclusive event in which no one was excluded for social or racial reasons was the high point in the social life of a fur trade post.

The Chief of the Clear Lake band wanted a canoe, buggy, and lumber wagon. He also indicated that there were sixteen destitute people in his band. The commissioner responded by saying "that he felt sure that the Government would be willing to help his poor people with some food and useful clothing."[57] And consistent with the idea of the spirit of the treaty, "The Commissioner assured the Chiefs that the Government would treat them kindly, and with consideration for their circumstances."[58]

Thus, the discussions with these two bands, which took place shortly after the signing of the treaty, show that although the government's representatives did not agree to all of the two chiefs' specific requests, many of the commissioners' assurances, especially those respecting assistance for the destitute, reinforced the general commitments that the Crown had made during the treaty negotiations.

The memorandum indicates that similar issues arose at the Brochet treaty talks in 1907:

In his opening remarks the Commissioner explained to them why he was sent to meet them, and also tell them what His Majesty the King was willing to do for them and help themselves and their children in the future provided they entered into such an agreement with him as he had come to offer them on behalf of the King ... The Commissioner also told them that the Government would render assistance to their old and indigent people when they cease to be able to gain a livelihood for themselves ... provided they accepted the terms of the agreement which he had to offer them as well as some other useful articles such as fishing twine, gunpowder, shot and gun caps, etc. to help them to make a living for themselves, but more especially for the old and feeble people among them; provided always that they continue to live peaceably honestly and law-biding people. At this stage one of their elderly men, Petit Casimir, by name, representing the Barren Lands' Band, spoke and said that this was the first time that they were told of the value of money ... they however, he said were anxious to know to what extent the Treaty if they accepted it would affect their present system of hunting and fishing in their country. This query was satisfactorily answered and explained by the Commissioner.[59]

The promise that the "present system of hunting and fishing" would not be interfered with essentially repeated similar ones made at other locations, as did the pledge that the government would help the old and indigent. Significantly, Borthwick invoked the name of the King and indicated that the treaty was designed to help "their children in the future."

At Brochet, Commissioner Borthwick told the Indians "that the Chief and his Headmen would be expected to look after the interest of their Band, and therefore it would be well for them to select for office the best self-governing men among them. The Commissioner then told them that in order to distinguish their Chief and Headmen among themselves, and also to make their standing known to strangers, he had a silver medal for the Chiefs and bronze medals for the Headmen."[60] Treaty medals served as symbols of the position of chief in the era following treaty-signing.

It is particularly interesting that the Barren Lands band also wanted to know if the treaty could be changed later: "the Chief said that on behalf of his people he would like to know if in the event of another person coming to deal with them from time to time, he would or could change the agreement, which they were now entering into. The Commissioner answered them in the negative."[61]

After questioning the commissioner, the Barren Lands band discussed the treaty among themselves. After reassembling,

Chief, Petit Casimir, addressing the Commissioner said that his people after they left the meeting at noon, complained to him that the money which he (the Commr) was giving them, viz: $12.00 each this year and $5.00 for every year hereafter, was not enough to support them. The Commissioner explained to them that the money which the Government was giving them was a gift, and did not expect them to be [de]pendent or live upon it, as they were not depriving them of any of the means of which they have been in the habit of living upon heretofore, and added that they had the privilege of hunting and fishing as before, and that with the money and some other useful articles which the Government proposed to give them yearly, they would be in a better position to live than they were at the present time.[62]

What is striking here is that, even though they were unsure of the value of money, the band quickly realized that the annuities alone would not secure a livelihood. To counter this concern, the treaty commissioner gave the traditional government reply, which stressed that hunting and fishing would continue as before. But, their lives would be richer thanks to the addition of the "gifts" of annuities and goods that the treaties would provide them year after year.

Chief Casimir made a very specific request of the government for the destitute in his band. He indicated that there were eighteen such individuals, and he requested ammunition, twine or nets, and warm clothing and blankets to help them. Since this band lived eight or nine days from the post, Chief Casimir did not want to receive heavy goods, such as flour and bacon. Rather, he wanted a large Peterborough canoe to help him deal with the destitute. Chief Benaouni of Lac Hache band had fourteen destitute. For them he requested flour, nets, and warm clothing.[63] In effect, Casimir and Benaouni asked the government to offer the destitute the kind of help the Hudson's Bay Company traditionally provided. Apparently the government did not respond to their request.

The Ile à la Crosse Indians' request for a settlement was consistent with the general pattern of attempts by other northern bands living in the unsurrendered parts of the Subarctic to establish treaty relations with the Canadian government. Canada's reluctance to do so stemmed from its continuing unwillingness to shoulder the kinds of social and economic responsibilities toward Indians that the HBC had formerly undertaken. Indians expected treaties to provide those kinds of benefits. It was the creation of the province of Saskatchewan, however, that acted as a catalyst in persuading federal government officials to change their minds and move forward with a new treaty. After considering various approaches, they decided to use Treaty 8 as the template for the new agreement and chose McKenna, who had severed as a commissioner for this accord, to head up the new treaty party. In the course of their talks with him and Borthwick, who continued the work McKenna began, Indians raised the kinds of concerns that had arisen during the negotiation of the previous Saskatchewan treaties. These were the maintenance of traditional livelihoods, access to land, and the provision of health and education.

CHAPTER TWELVE

Problems of Treaty Implementation

The First Nations encountered a series of problems with the implementation of the terms of the agreements in the decades following their negotiation. Post-treaty incidents arising from these implementation difficulties often led the First Nations to articulate their understanding of what they had agreed to when they had made treaty. From the complex history of relations between the Crown and the First Nations in the five treaty areas, several such incidents have been selected to illustrate a small sample of the problems that were encountered in treaty implementation, as well as First Nations' understanding of some of the key terms of the treaties.

TREATY 4: LIVELIHOOD AND SOVEREIGNTY

Of the many treaty issues that were illuminated by post-treaty incidents that occurred in relation to Treaty 4 in the quarter century following the negotiations at Fort Qu'Appelle, those that demonstrate First Nations' understanding of the relationship of livelihood and sovereignty to the treaty are discussed in this section.

Complaints that the government of Canada was not honouring Treaty 4 by providing the means of subsistence that First Nations negotiators believed they had secured were voiced early, frequently, and with increasing vehemence. At the payment of annuities at Fort Qu'Appelle in August 1878, for example, Kawkeeshiway (Loud Voice) and O'Soup took advantage of the presence of James Trow, a member of the Canadian parliament in the treaty party, to express their unhappiness. (James Trow was chairman of the Commons Immigration and Colonization Committee.)[1] Kahkeewishay said that the treaty commissioner "told us to keep our ears open. I saw then what our Great Mother gave us, and promised us. Our Great Mother told us to try hard and sustain her. We have done so. Now we ask for our Great Mother to be charitable." O'Soup insisted that "all he had said [be] put on paper and given to our Great Mother, and if what they wanted was not granted the paymaster need not come back next year."[2] The clear implication of such statements was that if the Crown was not willing to honour the underlying promise of subsistence by increasing the level of material assistance, then the First Nations took the position that the treaty was repudiated and null.

The argument that Treaty 4 was meant to ensure that First Nations continued to have the means of livelihood, in return for their agreeing to share the use of the territory with Euro-Canadian newcomers, was made again three years later, during the visit of Governor General Lorne to Western Canada. Lord Lorne's visit was particularly important because the governor general had a direct, personal link to Queen Victoria, being married to her daughter, the Princess Louise. A number of Native speakers, including Day Bird, who began by saying "I am sorry I did not see your lady," remarked on the governor general's marital connection with the Crown. Another, Cannosis [Kanasis?], or Strong Grass, asked for "a gold medal for each chief ... also a flag."[3] However, the main burden of the message that several speakers at Fort Qu'Appelle in 1881 delivered to Lorne was that the terms of Treaty 4 had to be improved to make it possible for the First Nations who had signed it to live. If this meant alteration of the individual terms of the Qu'Appelle Treaty, so be it. Even though Lorne said explicitly that "I am come here to hear what you have to say but not to make any change in treaties," Kanasis said plainly, "We want a Reformation of the Treaty."

Several speakers made it clear to Lord Lorne that "reformation" was necessary because the existing terms did not provide the means to live. Day Bird listed the concessions he wanted to see, and then concluded, "If you do this it is the only way I see that I can live." Pahsung, after saying "If the Princess was here I would like to see her too and shake hands and The Queen – the Mistress of Everything," explained the problem:

All those here wish to live. Today is a fine day. Let His Excellency show it a fine day by his kindness. Give us an answer. We do not do it on purpose if we do wrong, or say anything wrong. We know no better. All these here say they can't live by the Treaty made by the first Governor. Those Chiefs told me in Council two days ago. We can't live by the First Treaty. I can't say that those sent here manage things badly because you don't give them power to act as they wish. If you don't give them power they can't help us. I am telling you our complaints. This is what they are afraid of these chiefs. I see some things by which we can't live.

Kanasis tried, "We can't make our living by what was given to us by The Treaty. The Chiefs want a different arrangement so that the things we get may be our own and not on loan." Yellow Quill continued the refrain: "I do not understand the Treaty. Now I see what has been done to us. Our property has been taken from us. I cannot live by what I was then told ... We think that because His Excellency has the powers he can do what we ask. The reason is we cannot live by the first

Treaty; we shall die off. Provisions are the only thing that will make us live long. They cannot hold to the Treaty that was made before." More pointedly, Yellow Quill concluded, "we all say if what we want is not done we will not take the treaty. We were first told we should be helped and given long life and again it was promised a Doctor should be sent. This we have not seen. Many of us would live if we had a Doctor. If you comply with this we will take all the Treaty. If not we cannot do it."

If there was any doubt that these spokesmen thought that Treaty 4 justified their demand for improved terms, it was removed by Louis O'Soup: "I think we don't understand each other thoroughly. I wish to make it plain when they say let us break the Treaty. The first person Governor Morris came here and made this Treaty. You will receive help for 20 years and again he promised the Indian should never starve. Now they have told you a little of their starvation. Of course when a person breaks their promises that person is first to break the treaty ... Why they ask to break the Treaty is because since treaty was made they have found they have not enough to keep them alive." [4]

Although Lord Lorne's response to these statements showed that he had not understood what the First Nations' position was, in fact it can reasonably and accurately be inferred from the statements of these leaders. They saw the underlying obligation that the government incurred in Treaty 4 as one of ensuring they would continue to have the means of livelihood as immigration occurred and the traditional economy was undermined. The specific terms guaranteeing assistance, which had proven in less than a decade to be inadequate, were not the main issue. Rather, the issue was that the precise wording of Treaty 4 was no longer adequate to guarantee the underlying objective – to repeat, livelihood. Therefore, those specific terms should be modified; there should be a "reformation" of the terms of Treaty 4 that concerned material assistance to ensure that subsistence was what resulted. [5]

One alternative to "reformation" of the treaty terms if conditions became severe enough was forcible action by First Nations to seize the means of subsistence from a recalcitrant federal government. Given the severity of conditions in the prairies after the making of Treaty 4 it is amazing that there was so little violence. (One historian of the North-West Mounted Police, Rod Macleod, writes that the police did not fire a shot in anger against any First Nation or Métis person until 1885.)[6] Around Fort Ellice, for example, in the early spring of 1877 the Hudson's Bay Company officer in charge hired local men "to save them from starvation as they were without food and being in daily expectation of receiving their seed they did not go to the hunt."[7] If conditions were serious by the later 1870s, in the 1880s they became horrific, as lack of game, harsh winters, poor crop yields, and widespread disease combined to make Plains Cree, Saulteaux, and Assiniboine desperate. Matters were made worse by the policies of the newly formed Department of Indian Affairs, or at least its commissioner, Edgar

Dewdney. Dewdney used the desperation of the Plains First Nations to force the last of them into treaty and to compel them to adjust swiftly to a sedentary, agricultural economy. "No work, no rations" and "sheer compulsion" became the watchwords of the harshly coercive regime that Dewdney and the superintendent general of Indian Affairs, Sir John A. Macdonald, fastened on the prairies.[8] To complete the alarming picture, in 1883 the department decided to reduce Indian Affairs funding as part of an overall retrenchment of government expenditure, while diverting a larger part of the departmental budget to an expensive experiment in Indian education – industrial (or residential) schools.[9]

In this setting, the only thing that is surprising about the Yellow Calf incident of 1884 is that it took so long to occur, was an exception to the rule, and passed without loss of life.[10] In the latter part of February 1884 some two-dozen armed men on the Sakimay reserve demanded bacon and flour from Agent Hilton Keith. When the agent, following the "work for rations" rule that Dewdney had put in place, refused food to men who would not labour for it, the party stormed the warehouse, took provisions, and then barricaded themselves in a building. Dewdney's assistant commissioner, Hayter Reed, and a party of Mounted Police under Inspector R.B. Deane proceeded a few days later to the reserve. During the confrontation Louis O'Soup acted as principal spokesman for the men who had taken the provisions. According to a report filed by Inspector Deane, O'Soup told Reed and the mounties that the young men reasoned that "If he were allowed to starve he would die, and if he were doomed to die he might as well die one way as another." O'Soup also told the government that "their women and children were starving and that the men [the police] wanted would not allow themselves to be arrested – that they would fight to the death – that they were well-armed and might just as well die than be starved by the government." He also told the government officers that the Plains peoples regarded food in on-reserve warehouses as belonging to them, justifying their helping themselves to it under the dire conditions they found themselves in. O'Soup said "that in helping themselves they were taking nothing but that was their own. 'If,' he asked, 'the provisions were not intended to be eaten by the Indians why were they stored on their reserve?'" Eventually the crisis was resolved when four of the armed men, including Yellow Calf, surrendered to the police. This confrontation and its peaceful resolution illustrated both that the First Nation group considered they had a treaty right to subsistence, even if force was required to secure it, and that they wished to abide by Treaty 4's requirement that both First Nations and the Crown coexist peacefully.

Although the incident on the Sakimay reserve was perhaps the most spectacular assertion of a guaranteed means of livelihood, it was by no means the only one. In 1888, for example, the Gambler, who had been present at Fort Qu'Appelle in 1874, found himself explaining his view of the treaty to Major Charles Alexander, a British army officer, who forwarded it to Governor General Stanley with a request that measures be taken to conserve animal resources for First Nations of the western plains:

They state that they have not obtained fulfilment of Treaty, especially of late years. Their widows and orphans are not provided for in any way, that their complaints remain unattended to; that they have no way of making themselves heard by the Department every complaint having to bear the signature of the Agent. They consider themselves wronged in every particular by their Agent ... That at treaty time or subsequently there was nothing given out with the exception of thirty pounds of tea to three hundred and thirty individuals, some snare wire and three dozen balls of fishing twine. The Agent then told them he would supply them with as much ammunition as they wanted, and they were to go and make a living for themselves in the woods. They are now in great want. The game will not last another Season. Many of them are supporting widows and orphans on their slender means ... That under the present state of affairs the game will disappear in another year and they will then be reduced to starvation and will be depending on the charity of the surrounding settlers, Chief Gambler being of opinion that much trouble will then arise. The timber is also being stolen off their reserves by the Whites and nothing is done about it. The Reserves also being made common grazing land for all the neighbouring settlers. The Government stock bulls also being made use of. The Agent urged them to leave and hunt last spring when they should have been sowing their crop. The Gambler is certain that if they got assistance they would return to the Reserves and start farming again. They hate this Agent bitterly. Everything having gone to ruin since he came. Some of these abuses I was a witness to myself. [11]

The memorial that Major Alexander prepared on behalf of the aggrieved Saulteaux was referred by the deputy minister in Ottawa to Commissioner Hayter Reed in Regina, who in turn referred it to the Indian Agent. No more was heard of the matter.[12]

Finally, in 1893 the head men at Pasqua and Muscowpetung petitioned the House of Commons about a series of specific grievances, underlying all of which was their frustration that they were being denied the means of subsistence by their Agent:

The Petition of the undersigned Head-men of the Indian Reserves of Pasqua and Muscowpetung in the North West Territories begs to draw the attention of the Government to the following grievances:

1 The Government promised to support all old people unable to work, but the Agent refuses to give any food for such people, and if it was not for help given by others who have hearts these old people would starve.
2 We are at present supporting ourselves by selling wood, but that will be all gone in three (3) years or less, and we will then be unable to live; at present the [Farming] Instructor pays us with beef-heads (minus the tongue) and liver, for wood sold to white settlers.

3 Whenever we have a chance to sell anything and make some money the Agent or Instructor steps in between us and the party who wants to buy, and says we have no power
to sell; If this is to continue how will we be able to make a living and support ourselves?
We are not even allowed to sell cattle that we raise ourselves ...

7 The Agent drives us to work, and promises that we will be well paid, but all the payment
we get is the grub and clothes rightfully belonging to us by Treaty.

8 We understood at the Transfer that we would be paid for any timber or hay taken off the
Reserve, but we have not got a cent for the hay fed to the Government herd of cattle or
the timber used in the buildings. When we want good beef or bacon for the hauling of
the hay to the herd the Agent gives us poor starved beef, which is not good food for ourselves or our families. When we work for a whiteman we always get good pay, what we
ask for.

9 We will starve this summer unless rations are issued as we have to go in debt for our
grub, and our annuities are eaten up long before payment.[13]

The contents of this petition, like the views of the Gambler, the young men on
Sakimay in 1884, O'Soup, Yellow Quill, and others testify consistently and elo-
quently that the First Nations signatories of Treaty 4 understood that their pact
with the Crown included a guarantee of government assistance sufficient to enable them to maintain themselves when the arrival of large numbers of newcomers affected their ability to subsist by traditional methods.

TREATY 4: WHITE BEAR AND AUTONOMY

The experience of Wahpeemakwa (White Bear) in southeastern Saskatchewan in
the two decades after his 1875 adherence to Treaty 4 represents a different strategy for pursuing self-sufficiency, a strategy that involved the chief and his followers in a clear, repeated, and sustained assertion of their right to control their own
affairs.

Wahpeemakwa led a mixed Saulteaux-Cree community in the Moose Mountain
region. Although this territory technically fell within Treaty 2, as noted earlier White
Bear adhered instead to Treaty 4. White Bear chose his reserve in a region of lightly
wooded hills and a large lake, land not well suited to agriculture, but obviously appropriate for a hunting-gathering economy that relied on fish, game, some gardening,
sale of hand-produced goods, medicinal plants, and firewood to local settlers, and ca-
sual employment. Obviously related to Wahpeemakwa's subsistence strategy was
the desire that he, his sons, and their followers manifested throughout the 1880s of
rebuffing the ministrations of Christian missionaries, both Presbyterian and Roman
Catholic, and withholding their children from Euro-Canadian schools, especially the
far-off residential schools that occupied a prominent place in Ottawa's educational
program from 1883 onward. While there was not unanimity within the White Bear
community about this approach – there was a faction that the agent reported as being

more amenable to farming, residential schooling, and Christianity – it dominated the band's behaviour through the 1880s and 1890s. Perhaps surprisingly, this strategy enabled White Bear and his followers to fare better in a material sense than neighbouring bands, such as those of Ocean Man and Pheasant Rump, who cooperated more with the DIA "policy of the Bible and the plough." What is not surprising at all is that this independent course – the determined maintenance of autonomy – brought White Bear and his like-minded followers into direct conflict with the DIA.[14]

Although Wahpeemakwa was already an elderly man when he adhered to Treaty 4, he continued to exercise leadership for years afterwards. In 1878 he was reported to have requested at treaty time that his triennial chief's suit be passed on to his son, because "he was getting feeble, and it was his desire and the wish of the whole tribe that his son should put on his mantle."[15] However, in 1885 he was the official spokesman for a movement to remove Waywinshehappo as headman, in favour of Kapapahmanaykoitem, on the grounds that the former was not pulling his weight, a request that the federal government acted upon by order in council.[16] All the same, within a couple of years White Bear and his strategy for pursuing a livelihood brought him into conflict with the agent, J.J. Campbell, whose 1887 report charged that

White Bear's Band, on the other hand [i.e., in contrast to neighbouring Assiniboine bands], have steadily resisted every effort to make them work properly; a large lake on their reserve providing them with sufficient fish in addition to the game and fur which they obtain, to render them more independent of the Department's wishes, than are the Assiniboine bands. This spring, while my interpreter was rationing the workers liberally, and assisting them to prepare their land and sow their grain, they left their reserve; and, consequently, have only a few acres under crop ...

There is at present no school in operation on these reserves, the attempt to establish one in 1885 under the auspices of the Church of England, not having succeeded owing to the prejudice of the Indians.[17]

By late 1888 Agent Campbell sought to have White Bear deposed as chief, in accordance with the provisions of the Indian Act that permitted such action. Claiming to speak for a majority of band members who desired the action, the agent outlined the case against Wahpeemakwa:

White Bear is law abiding in his intercourse with the Settlers, and is an industrious fisherman, but he is very obstinate and prejudiced, and resents anyone but himself controlling his band. He refused his consent to building on his reserve, a house for the storing of provisions, and the use of the Instructor and myself when visiting the band, and when the band asked for a resident Instructor, he strongly opposed it, and only yielded, when the Indians were about to ask for his deposition. He then concurred in the request of which I informed you when in Regina last summer.

For some time he opposed the cutting of the deadwood on the Reserve, and claimed that when he signed the treaty, 6 miles by 8 [?] miles of the reserve were given to him and his family, and that an additional half mile was added to both the length and breadth of the reserve, which portion was to be for the other members of the band.

This opposition in 1886 rendered it impossible for Dr. Beamish, who was accompanied by Mr. Lawford to vaccinate more than a few of his band, and this autumn I had some difficulty in gaining this point, and he only yielded when I had induced the Indians to obey me without his consent.[18]

The result was that by order-in-council (4 January 1889) Wahpeemakwa was deposed.

If the DIA thought its coercion meant that Wahpeemakwa and his insistence on pursuing a different way of governing and earning a living were at an end, it was mistaken. Throughout the 1890s, apparently, a group headed by White Bear's son, Tom, led an opposition to the agent and official Indian Affairs policy. Matters came to a head when the department noticed in 1897, while turning down its official's request that Tom, one of the head men on White Bear, be deposed, that none of the bands in the Moose Mountain agency appeared to have a chief. In responding to the department's query about this matter, the farmer in charge, H.R. Halpin, laid bare the situation: "This man [headman Tom], with his father, the deposed Chief White Bear does everything in his power to hinder work on the reserve, will not farm or keep cattle himself, and uses all his influence to prevent other Indians from doing so. Will not allow his children to be sent to school, says he would sooner see them dead, and on every chance he gets speaks against education and the Industrial Schools provided by the Government. His children are bright, healthy lads, but have been brought up to think that anything in the way of work at farming[,] cattle keeping or schools is not good for Indians."[19] If the department, added Halpin, wanted a chief to be appointed, "I would respectfully recommend that Kakakeway, chief headman of White Bear's band, be appointed to the position as he is a good hard-working man, has the best farm and buildings in the agency, has had five of his children sent to school (three have died there) and does all in his power to help on the work on the reserve, and has a large following."[20]

Tom was deposed on 16 October 1897 by the federal government, but his deposition apparently provoked a strong reaction. Precisely a month later, Halpin wrote to request the restoration of Wahpeemakwa as chief. The official had attended a meeting of the council at which White Bear's followers made their wishes clear:

You will see that the Indians want the old Chief reinstated. They also want a day school placed on the Reserve ...

White Bear is a very old man, and has been blind for many years. He has a great deal of influence with more than half of the working Indians (or those fit to work) of the Band. He has six sons all grown up living on the reserve. None of these work on the reserve for themselves but can make from $1.50 to $2.00 per diem working for settlers. Before White Bear was deposed these men were the best workers on the reserve, but since they have let their farms go and refuse to keep cattle or send children to school. Old White Bear cannot live, in my opinion, more than two or three years and should the request of himself and his sons and others be granted I am of opinion it would be a good thing for the reserve. I mean I should have a hold upon them in the way of getting work done on the reserve.[21]

The DIA acted upon the band's request and restored Wahpeemakwa, who lived until 1900, as chief. A day school was arranged for the reserve, diminishing the long-running struggle over sending children to distant – and unhealthy – residential schools. It seemed as though the strategy that White Bear, his sons, and supporters had developed of insisting on managing their affairs as they, rather than the department, wished was succeeding. However, the DIA soon wreaked havoc by arranging for a so-called surrender of all of the Ocean Man and Pheasant Rump reserves and moving the population of those reserves onto the White Bear reserve. The resulting problems of overcrowding and interband tension caused the community serious problems throughout most of the remainder of the twentieth century, although conditions have begun to improve since the 1980s, when litigation won the White Bear band compensation and Ocean Man and Pheasant Rump new reserves. The tradition of autonomous pursuit of their own version of economic development that Wahpeemakwa pioneered in the late nineteenth century was continued in the 1990s, when the band opened the Bear Claw Casino – to familiar Crown opposition, this time in the form of police raids and criminal prosecutions by the provincial Crown.

These post-treaty incidents, stretching from the late 1870s to the 1890s, illustrate very clearly and consistently how a number of the bands in Treaty 4 interpreted the agreement they had fashioned with the Crown as guaranteeing them assistance while maintaining their rights to the resources of the land and control of their own affairs. Louis O'Soup, who had attended the negotiations at Fort Qu'Appelle in 1874, expressed it simply and clearly during a meeting of Western First Nations representatives with the minister and officials of the department in Ottawa in 1911: "I was very young when the Treaty [4] was made but I was with the crowd that he [Morris] made the bargain with. When I heard what was said I thought to myself 'Oh, we will make a living by the promises that were made to us.'"[22] In other words, these incidents illustrate that in the case of Treaty 4 subsistence and sovereignty were seen as treaty rights by the First Nations.

TREATY 6: LIVELIHOOD AND SOVEREIGNTY

Many of the issues and incidents that became historically noticeable in Treaty 6 in the first two decades after 1876 were similar in character to the matters that have been discussed in relation to Treaty 4. For example, when some of the Treaty 6 chiefs, including Mistawasis and Ahtakakup, who had been so prominent in the 1876 negotiations, met with Governor-General Lorne at Fort Carlton in 1881, they emphasized the need for more help in providing subsistence in terms that echoed what had been said by Treaty 4 chiefs not long before. Mistawasis told Lorne, "Many a time I was very sad when I saw my poor people [illegible] starving, and I could do nothing for them." Ahtakakup said, "The first thing is some strength, i.e., farm implements & cattle. These are necessary if we are to progress faster than in the past years ... I remember right at the treaty it was said that if any famine or trouble came the Government would see to us and help."[23]

As in Treaty 4, chiefs in Treaty 6 also on occasion asserted rights that were consistent with their view that they should continue to control their own affairs in treaty. In his meeting with Lord Lorne in 1881, Chief James Smith demanded speedier action both on the treaty commitment to lay out a reserve and its implementation in a manner that the Cree could control: "I want that my Band and reserve may receive assistance. Then that a survey be made to mark out my reserve as soon as possible, and what I desire is that it should be left to me where the survey runs to satisfy my people. I want good land not sand hills."[24] In 1890, the farming instructor assigned to the John Smith reserve forwarded to the Indian agent a memorial from the leadership of both John Smith and James Smith. One of the complaints from John Smith was "that members of this Band have been transferred to other Reserves without the consent of all parties. I believe it to be justly grounded as in one or two instances transfers have been made of men from this Band without the Band's consent." Although the Indian commissioner was dismissive of some of the complaints, feeling that the instructor should have squelched the expression of them, he did concede ground on the complaint from John Smith about transfers: "As to the transference of members of their Bands to other points, as you yourself are aware, instructions have been issued that this shall not in the future be permitted, unless with the consent of both Bands concerned, having been first formally obtained."[25]

Another instance of efforts by leaders in Treaty 6 to maintain control over their communities' affairs came a few years later from Kapetekoos, or Thunderchild, chief of the reserve that bore his English name:

I must say things are not going the way I would wish them on account of the Instructor Mr. McConnell. I consider that I am here for the purpose of when anything is not right, to put it right as far as I am able. I am unable to do anything more as the instructor is not doing right. You told me to try and agree with the instructor, but I am very much afraid something will go wrong as the instructor Mr. McConnell has threatened to use the gun four times as he wants to scare my people and he has struck two of the young men for nothing. The people are talking so much now of his dealings with women that it's going so far I am compelled to believe the report. Any of the people can verify what I say as he goes round with the women he has in his house. Why I believe it is that one family has plenty while we are short of provisions and why I am writing to you. I want the present instructor Mr. McConnell to leave my reserve, and I have been telling the Agent what he is doing but he does not seem to pay any heed to my telling.[26]

These assertions from Thunderchild share with the complaints from James Smith and John Smith an underlying belief that the leadership of these communities continued to control their political affairs.

If Treaty 6 chiefs gave evidence of their pursuit of livelihood and sovereignty, they also manifested a concern about another of the terms of Treaty 6. During their meeting with the governor general at Fort Carlton in 1881 several of them expressed annoyance that the treaty promise concerning education was not being honoured. Mistawasis, for example, said, "We want teachers for schools" (as well as complaining about not having enough ammunition for hunting). Chief John Smith listed assistance with adjustment to Euro-Canadian ways as his top priorities: "The first thing," he said, "is a school teacher to teach my children. Why I want a teacher is to learn the English language and to teach it [to] my children. 2nd I want a Native missionary to preach to them and supported by Government."[27]

TREATY 6: SCHOOLING AND CO-EXISTENCE

Many of these concerns, as well as explicit reference to the treaty relationship and to the First Nations' commitment to peaceful coexistence under treaty, were articulated forcefully by Treaty 6 chiefs at Fort Carlton in August 1884. This meeting, which chiefs from Battleford and Carlton agencies attended, came as leaders such as Piapot and Mistahimusqua (Big Bear) were trying to fashion a diplomatic coalition of chiefs to put pressure on Ottawa for a revision of the treaties.[28] The conclave included both leaders who had advocated making treaty in 1876, such as Mistawasis and Ahtakakup, and some, like Mistahimusqua, who had remained aloof from treaty until forced by starvation to sign, as the latter had done in December 1882. The meeting at Carlton also came on the heels of Louis Riel's return to the South Saskatchewan at the request of Métis who wanted him to lead a peaceful movement for redress of their grievances. Most recently of all, in mid-June, during a Thirst Dance near Battleford, a confrontation known as the Craig Incident, which in some respects resembled the Yellow Calf set-to of the same year, had frightened authorities that violence might erupt. All these factors – increasing hardship, growing diplomatic unity and militancy of Cree leaders, and the eruption of Métis discontent – were well known to Indian Commissioner Edgar Dewdney, who, it will be recalled, had adopted, in response to these forces and in anticipation of trouble, a policy that he described as "sheer compulsion."[29] In this atmosphere of hardship and restiveness, Mistahimusqua, Chief James

Smith from Fort à la Corne, and Plains Cree chiefs from the Battleford and Carlton regions proceeded from Duck Lake, where they had been holding a council of their own, to Fort Carlton to meet with a representative of the DIA. Agent J. Ansdell Macrae reported to Dewdney on his meeting of 28 August 1884 with Treaty 6 chiefs under a series of headings concerning agricultural assistance, aid, education, and the unresponsiveness of the DIA:

1 *Work* The cattle given them are insufficient for them to gain their livelihood with. That wild oxen have been given to them, and in some instances have died, or been killed, because they were so intractable that they could not be cared for. These should be replaced.

2 *Cows* Many of the cows supplied were wild, and as they could not be stabled, died of cold and exposure. These should also be replaced.

3 *Horses* Some of the horses given them were too wild for them to use. This was bad faith on the part of the government, as the Commissioners who made the treaty promised them well broken beasts. These therefore should be replaced.

4 *Waggons* The waggons supplied were of poor make, and now the Chief had to travel on foot, as they [*sic*] are old men, means of conveyance should be given them.

5 *Conveyance for Chiefs* For the same reason (just quoted) horses as well as vehicles should be given to all the Chiefs, not excepting those who got good gifts under the treaty.

The chiefs also sought more aid for their followers:

6 *Eleemosynary* [Charitable] *Aid* The promise made to them at the time of their treaty was that when they were destitute, liberal assistance would be given to them. That the crops are now poor, rats are scarce and other game likely to be so, and they look forward with the greatest fear to the approaching winter. In view of the above mentioned promise they claim that the Government should give them liberal treatment during that season, for having disposed of all the property that they owned before the treaty in order to tide over times of distress since, they are now reduced to absolute and complete dependence upon what relief is extended to them. With the present amount of assistance they cannot work effectively on their reserves, and it should be increased.

7 *Clothing* It was promised by Mr. Commissioner Morris that they should not be short of clothing, yet they never received any, and it is feared that this winter some of them will be unable to leave their houses without freezing to death.

They were also concerned about the government's failure to help them adjust in the educational as well as the agricultural area:

8 *Schools* That schools were promised to them, but have not been established on all the reserves. They want these and desire the government to fulfil its promise entirely by putting up school houses and maintaining them in repair.

9 *Machinery* That they were told that they would see how the white man lived, and would be taught to live like him. It is seen that he has threshing mills, mowers, reapers, and rakes. As the Government pledged itself to put them in the same position as the white man, it should give them these things.

Above all, they objected to the unresponsiveness of the government when they informed it of their problems:

10 *Request* That requests for redress of these grievances have been again & again made without effect. They are glad that the young men have not resorted to violent measures to gain it. That it is almost too hard for them to bear the treatment received at the hands of the Government after its "sweet promises," made in order to get their country from them. They now fear that they are going to be cheated. They will wait until next summer to see if this council has the desired effect, failing which they will take measures to get what they desire. (The proposed "measures" could not be elicited, but a suggestion of the idea of war was repudiated.)

11 *Renewals* That all bad things, implements and tools, as well as stock etc. should be replaced by gifts of better articles.

12 *Insufficiency of government assistance* That many are forced to wander from the reserves, who desires [*sic*] to settle, as there is not enough of any thing supplied to them to enable all to farm. Although a living by agriculture was promised to them.

13 *Lack of confidence in the Government* That at the time of making the treaty they were comparatively well off, they were deceived by the sweet promises of the Commissioners, and now are "full of fear" for they believe that the government which pretended to be friendly is going to cheat them. They blame not the Queen, but the government at Ottawa.

14 *Medicines* That they were promised medicine chests for each reserve, but have never received them. Many live among them, or near them who could administer drugs beneficially but as they have not them, they suffer from complaints that might be cured.

15 *Beef* That they want to have beef at all payments.

16 *Effect of not fulfilling promises* That had the Treaty promises been carried out "all would have been well," instead of the present feeling existing.

17 *Maps of Reserves* That every Chief should be given a map of his reserve in order he may not be robbed of it.

18 *Harness* That harness should be given them for all their cattle, and that when oxen are given to them, the harness should be on them.

Joseph Badger, an Indian of the South Branch, spoke very plainly on the alleged grievances, and warns the Government that it must redress them, to escape the Measures that may be taken.

A familiar adversary indicated how First Nations' opinions were turning against the government:

Big Bear, asked permission to address me, and received it. He said that the Chiefs should
be given what they asked for, that all treaty promises should be fulfilled. A year ago, he
stood alone, in making these demands; now the whole of the Indians are with him. That
the Mounted Police treated him very well after a disturbance was created at B'ford. That
he averted any serious results at that place, by his efforts as a peacemaker.

After hearing the above, which is submitted to you under headings suggested by the
subjects of their complaints, I broke up the Council and gave them some food with which
to reach home.

Agent Macrae concluded by emphasizing the seriousness of the chiefs' protest:
"An answer in detail is expected by the Council, which declared itself to be a representative one of the Battleford as well as Carlton Crees. No doubt need be enter-
tained that the Indians regard it as such."[30]

In Treaty 6, in other words, there is considerable evidence in post-treaty events
of an emphasis on the First Nations' understanding of treaty obligations such as
education, sovereignty, and livelihood, not to mention their strenuous efforts to
have the treaty commitments implemented as they understood them. By means
of repeated complaints and petitions – but stopping short of threatening violence
against the government – a large number of chiefs and councillors made it clear
that they believed they had received promises of livelihood and schooling while
maintaining their authority by treaty.

The environment in which the first three Saskatchewan treaties were implemented in the 1870s and 1880s and that in which the two northern treaties were
later negotiated and implemented were dramatically different. Many of the problems in the south that have been discussed to this point stemmed from a changed
attitude and approach on the part of the DIA. While the government of Canada
had had a healthy respect for and need to conciliate western First Nations as
treaty-making began in the first part of the 1870s, conditions and government attitudes had shifted dramatically by the 1880s. The collapse of the buffalo economy and continuing problems with loss of life to disease, not to mention the
hardships created by Dewdney's "sheer compulsion" policy, had reduced the
Plains Nations to a shadow of their former strength. In addition, the aftermath of
the Northwest Rebellion in 1885, during which the government of Canada took
advantage of the panicky climate of public opinion to crush Plains Cree diplo-
mats like Mistahimusqua and Poundmaker judicially and to disperse some
bands, intimidated many reserve communities in the south.

The temporary emergency decree of May 1885 that ordered First Nations to
remain on their reserves evolved into an enduring, extralegal policy that has
come to be known as the pass system. An awareness of the pass system had
spread to northern Nations by the 1890s, when what became Treaty 10 was contemplated. Later in the 1880s the DIA had mounted an attack on reserve farming
by means of the "peasant farming" system and on the reserve land base by the

adoption in 1888 of the severalty policy.[31] All these retrograde policy developments help to explain both the serious problems with treaty implementation that southern First Nations experienced in the 1880s and 1890s and the heightened suspicions with which northern Nations approached treaty-making in the 1890s and first decade of the twentieth century.

TREATY 10: CONTINUED RIGHT TO HUNT

It is hardly surprising, then, that northern First Nations were assertive in gaining recognition and respect for their continuing rights to hunt and fish. In the Saskatchewan portion of Treaty 10, as was the case in Treaty 8, the treaty commitment to continuation of the Aboriginal right to hunt, fish, and gather was extremely prominent. A particularly telling incident occurred just a few days after the Clear Lake band entered Treaty 10. According to testimony provided during a 1996 court case by Elmer Harry Campbell, Chief of Buffalo River, recognition of the continued right to hunt and fish was extremely important to the Dene band to which his grandfather had belonged. Indeed, during treaty adhesion talks "the people decided to leave Ile-à-la-Crosse because they couldn't get any – any commitments from the government of that their treaty – their hunting – their traditional way of life would not be affected but they were eventually convinced that there would be no effect on the way – the way they continued their livelihood and therefore they signed." In response to a question for clarification from counsel, Chief Campbell reiterated that his grandfather's party had signed on to Treaty 10 "because they were told that there was – there was a guarantee that they wouldn't lose their traditional way of life. They could continue living the way they – they lived." Another clarifying question: "And the traditional way of life is what you've been describing up until now?" Chief Campbell: "Yes, living off the land."[32]

A second incident that occurred during the same group's trip from Ile à la Crosse back to Buffalo River reinforced the importance of continuing rights of hunting and gathering in Treaty 10: "When they left Ile-à-la-Crosse the Chief at that time with the party headed back to Buffalo River were – were stopped at one – at one of their camps on their way back there where they were supposedly going to be charged for shooting some ducks. At that time their chief decided that they should all go back there and rescind the treaty there but were convinced right there I guess at that spot by the then conservation officers that it was an error on our part there. We'll continue on. You guys can continue on, we won't bother you." In answer to a further question, Chief Campbell testified that it was "the conservation officer [who] had erred." The Dene "were convinced that they weren't going to be bothered with the way they do their – the way they do their livelihood so they continued on to Dillon."[33] In other words, not only did the Dene decline to sign Treaty 10 until they were reassured that it would not infringe on their hunting rights, but when events shortly afterwards seemed to suggest that the provincial Crown might be acting contrary to this reassurance, they were prepared to "rescind" their adhesion to Treaty 10.

The problems encountered by First Nations in the implementation of the Saskatchewan treaties illustrate the themes of continuity and change. To an impressive degree, First Nations, especially in the southern portions of the province, persisted with support of what they understood to be the treaties' guarantee of their way of life and autonomy in combination with an optional program of schooling and economic adjustment. When they complained that they "could not live" by the treaties as Canada was implementing them and demanded an increase in supplies and aid, they were not seeking to alter the treaties. They understood treaties as guaranteeing a relationship within which specific terms could be modified from time to time to accomplish the overriding objective of maintaining their livelihood and maintaining control of their own affairs. When one of their leaders spoke of a desire for a "reformation" of the treaty, what was meant was the proper fulfillment of the treaty relationship and guarantees. The concept embraced what later would become recognized as the insistence by western First Nations that Canada honour "the spirit of the treaties," and not just the individual terms in the government version of the treaties. Northern Nations observed and learned from the unhappy experience of their southern colleagues, which led them to be more assertive about hunting and fishing rights, in particular, during the negotiations leading to Treaty 8 and Treaty 10. As noted in the case of Treaty 10, in particular, some of them were also vigilant and determined in protecting those rights, too.

If First Nations demonstrated continuity of purpose and objective throughout treaty-making and treaty implementation, the government of Canada manifested a drastically changed attitude and drastically changed tactics in the decades after 1876. It is a striking coincidence that Parliament codified legislation affecting First Nations in the Indian Act of 1876, the same year in which Plains Nations won major advances in the Treaty of Fort Carlton and Fort Pitt, Treaty 6. The latter document embodied a relationship between nations that contemplated a future based on dialogue and accommodation. The former, the Indian Act, treated First Nations throughout Canada as legal minors and approached them as a problem to be administered. In consequence of the collapse of the Plains buffalo economy by 1879, and more particularly in the harsh atmosphere that prevailed after the Northwest Rebellion, the DIA carried out a series of policies that aimed at political control, enforced economic transition, and cultural subjugation and assimilation. Department policy in the south after 1886 bore almost no resemblance to the attitudes that treaty commissioners such as Archibald and Morris had displayed during the 1870s. The DIA was reluctant to make treaties in the

north until forced to do so in response to southerners coveting northern resources. For their part, northern First Nations became determined to protect their
lands and riches because of the negative attitudes towards them as manifested in
the residential schools, "peasant farming," and severalty and other measures of
the 1880s. It is in the clash between the continuity of First Nations' objectives
and strategy on the one hand, and the changed attitude and tactics of Canada on
the other that the primary cause of the difficulties experienced in implementing
the Saskatchewan treaties is to be found.

CHAPTER THIRTEEN

Reflections

To appreciate the context in which this study fits, as well as the contribution that it makes to the research on treaty-making, it is necessary to review the evolution of the historiography of treaty-making in western Canada. Writing about the treaties began with advocates posing as commentators and then proceeded to an uncritical survey of the topic that dominated academic understanding for half a century. Only during the past two decades, stimulated in part by claims research commissioned by organizations such as the (then) Federation of Saskatchewan Indians, has close examination and reinterpretation been occurring. This study belongs in the unfolding process of reinterpreting the genesis, contents, and impact of the treaties that is still going on. Readers should view our findings within that context: that the prior Hudson's Bay Company relationship with First Nations was a powerful influence on treaty-making, that First Nations negotiators did much more to bring about treaty negotiations and to influence the parleys than the older historiography acknowledged, that the government's written account of both the process and the text of the numbered treaties is incomplete and sometimes inaccurate, and that the implementation of the treaties was fraught with difficulties for First Nations communities.

TREATY HISTORIOGRAPHY

A major part of the explanation for the poverty of the older written account of the Saskatchewan treaties is to be found in the fact that individuals deeply involved on behalf of the government of Canada in negotiating treaties shaped the semiprocessed materials on which academic historians would for many decades depend. It is impossible to exaggerate the long-term impact of scholars' uncritical readings of Alexander Morris' 1880 publication, *The Treaties of Canada with the Indians*, on the understanding of treaty-making that dominated in Canadian universities until the 1980s.[1] The treaty commissioner's attitude of complacent self-satisfaction with what he and other government negotiators had done oozes from the volume's dedication to Governor-General Lord Dufferin, in which Morris alluded to "the work of obtaining the alliance and promoting the welfare of the Indian tribes in the North-West of Canada, and in opening up the Territories for settlement, by obtaining the relinquishment of the natural title of the Indians to the lands of the Fertile Belt on fair and just terms."[2] Morris then proceeded to deliver close to four hundred pages of narrative and interpretation that depicted Canada's motives as high-minded and wise and its treaty negotiators as paragons of patience, reasonableness, and good humour. First Nations negotiators, on the other hand, come through as high-flying orators with unreasonable "demands" in negotiations, unless, like a Sweet Grass of the Cree or Crowfoot of the Blackfoot Confederacy, they were portrayed as amenable and eager to sign treaties. From Morris' seminal work emerged an interpretation that emphasized government generosity, First Nations passivity, and treaties as contracts that extinguished the property rights of the original occupiers. Taken at face value, Morris' account seemed to show the "bounty and benevolence" of the Crown.

If Morris' contribution to shaping Canadians' understanding of the treaties is reasonably obvious and well known, the same is not true of two other treaty negotiators who reinforced the view that Canada was far-sighted, compassionate, and honourable. David Laird, who participated in the negotiation of Treaty 4, began his account of 1905, *Our Indian Treaties*, with the observation that the "British Crown, in acquiring territories beyond the seas, has in general been conceded the high honor of dealing kindly with aboriginal races."[3] He went on to emphasize the honourable quality of the Crown's behaviour in western Canada as it "extinguished" Aboriginal title to a vast patrimony in the first eight numbered treaties. For example, on page 4 of his essay he used "extinguished" or another form of the same word ("extinguish," "extinguishing") no fewer than four times. The role of First Nations participants was to deliver "Grandiloquent speeches" and "extravagant demands" before a wise government provided for their future.[4] It "was foreseen that owing to the rapid disappearance of the buffalo, the only resource of the plain [*sic*] Indians, large expenditure would soon have to be incurred by the Dominion Government to keep them from starvation."[5] However, these "large expenditure[s]" were to be understood as an investment, not a true expenditure: "The Treaties saved us from Indian wars, for the Indians were not the instigators of the Saskatchewan rebellion in 1885. They have helped to make way for the peaceful march of the settler all over the prairies of the West, and to enable him to cultivate his broad acres in safety."

Duncan Campbell Scott, the other government negotiator who helped to solidify this impression of an all-wise and generous federal government busily "extinguishing" title, certainly agreed with Laird and Morris about Ottawa's foresight, honour, and generosity. Scott, who began employment in the Department of Indian Affairs in 1880 and rose to its highest office in 1913, was a negotiator of Treaty 9 in northern Ontario in 1905. Scott strengthened the favourable depiction of the Department of Indian Affairs in general and of the government's behaviour in treaty-making in particular, with three lengthy articles he contributed during the Great War to the multivolume *Canada and Its Provinces*. Like Laird, Scott portrayed pre-Confederation policy towards First Nations as manifesting "a spirit of generosity" and "an increasing desire to deal effectively with the Indian problem."[6] Scott's description of the treaties was seemingly matter of fact, with the usual wise government negotiators dominating the account. And afterwards, he noted, "As may be surmised from the record of past Indian administration, the government was always anxious to fulfil the obligations which were laid upon it by these treaties."[7]

Laird's and Scott's contributions were, in fact, part of a deliberate and systematic campaign by high-ranking officials in the Department of Indian Affairs to propagandize in favour of the government's handling of relations with First Nations. Since the 1880s, when Edgar Dewdney and Hayter Reed had manipulated the public's perception of First Nations behaviour in the Northwest Rebellion to further their campaign for the "subjugation of the Plains Cree," Indian Affairs had regularly devoted considerable efforts to ensuring that journalists and other opinion-makers saw their policies through the same rose-coloured glasses that the bureaucrats in Ottawa did. As early as the first decade of the twentieth century the Department of Indian Affairs became involved in manipulating its image by such devices as a model colony for graduates of residential schools, which it used to persuade journalists and others that department policies in education and agricultural development were succeeding.[8] Another tactic was to control the information that investigators received. So, for example, when American Bureau of Indian Affairs official F.H. Abbott came to Canada to look into Canadian policy, he was subjected to six days' briefing in the department before spending six weeks visiting reserves. The result was *The Administration of Indian Affairs in Canada*, an influential volume that lauded Canadian practice.[9] A later parallel involved A.G. Harper, who came north in 1935 to investigate conditions in Canada and published three highly positive articles about Canadian policy in *America Indigena*.[10] By the interwar period an idealized picture of Indian Affairs that bore little resemblance to reality on reserves was well entrenched in academic and bureaucratic circles.

In light of this background, the manner in which the first extended academic examination of Western Canadian developments after Confederation portrayed the treaties and Canadian government policy is more understandable. In 1936 George F.G. Stanley produced *The Birth of Western Canada* (his revised doctoral dissertation) and thereby established the interpretation that would dominate the teaching of this part of Canadian history for almost fifty years.[11] Stanley's interpretation is also explained by two additional factors. First, he was a military historian who was interested primarily in martial conflict, in this case the "Riel Rebellions" that figured in the subtitle to his book. Second, he was a disciple of the American school of history known as Frontierism, or the Turner School, which sought the dynamic and meaning of a nation's history in the impact of the frontier, "the hither edge of free land," on its peoples. The clashes that he examined, he explained, were but "the manifestation in Western Canada of the problem of the frontier, namely the clash between primitive and civilized peoples."[12] These confrontations consequently must have had First Nations and Métis on one side, and Canada, representing "civilized peoples," on the other.

From that starting point it followed that the numbered treaties were the work of a beneficent government working out the logic of its greater sophistication and foresight. Of the history of policy in general, *The Birth of Western Canada* observed:

The European, conscious of his material superiority, is only too contemptuous of the savage, intolerant of his helplessness, ignorant of his mental processes and impatient at his slow assimilation of civilization. The savage, centuries behind in mental and economic development, cannot readily adapt himself to meet the new conditions. He is incapable of bridging the gap of centuries alone and unassisted. Although white penetration into native territories may be inspired by motives of self-interest, such as trade and settlement, once there, the responsibility of "the white man's burden" is inevitable.[13]

Of western treaties in particular, Stanley wrote in terms reminiscent of D.C. Scott two decades earlier: "The policy followed by Canada in the North-West was a continuation of that which had governed the relations between the whites and the Indians since the days of Sir William Johnson. Western Indian history was merely the application of these well-founded principles to a new problem, the acknowledgment of the Indian title, and the formal negotiation for the surrender of the same."[14] In the thirteen endnotes in *The Birth of Western Canada* covering Treaties 1 through 6, there were seven citations of Morris, five of Parliament's *Sessional Papers*, and one of Mounted Police records as found in Colonial Office papers. There were no citations of the records of the Department of Indian Affairs, missionaries, or First Nations sources. Needless to say, *The Birth of Western Canada* contained general, but very influential, statements on Indian policy, based on very little investigation of archival sources and an uncritical reliance on Morris.

The tragedy of the interpretation pioneered by *The Birth of Western Canada* was that it monopolized academic historians' coverage of the treaties until the late 1970s and early 1980s. Stanley's work was so massive in scope and detailed in description that few challenged it or saw the need to explore his topics further. Moreover, until the 1970s Canadian historians were preoccupied with national and/or "nation-building" history that spared little thought or concern for minority groups that were not involved with high politics and economic expansion.

It was only slowly in the 1970s that the forces of criticism and revision began to gather. Certainly Harold Cardinal's *The Unjust Society: The Tragedy of Canada's Indians* challenged widespread assumptions. It is important to acknowledge that the government of Canada, especially the Department of Indian Affairs, contributed substantially to that process by making DIA records (RG 10) more accessible on microfilm, and by providing basic reference works such as *The Historical Development of the Indian Act*.[15] For example, these materials made possible a study such as John L. Taylor's examination of policy for a doctoral dissertation at Queen's University, a work that in part was made accessible by his 1977 publication, "Canada's North-West Indian Policy in the 1970s: Traditional Premises and Necessary Innovations."[16] However, more important to the process of drawing attention to policy and treaties was the claims research that First Nations have conducted since the 1970s. In this respect, *Aski-Puko – The Land Alone* documented a treaty history for the territorial adhesion to Treaty 6.[17] With respect to the reserve provisions of treaties, Stewart Raby's "Indian Land Surrenders in Southern Saskatchewan" demonstrated the importance of archival sources to substantiate specific claims.[18]

In particular, John Tobias, a researcher for the Federation of Saskatchewan Indians demonstrated by detailed research in RG 10 and other official sources that Canadian policy, both during treaty-making and afterwards, was anything but far-sighted, provident, generous, or even honourable. Tobias' article "The Subjugation of the Plains Cree" (1983) had a powerful influence on academic historians.[19] Among its many contributions, Tobias' work made it impossible for researchers to take the self-serving professions of government treaty negotiators and other officials at face value. The interpretation pioneered by Tobias was reinforced by Gerald Friesen's *The Canadian Prairies: A History*[20] and then by E. Brian Titley's study of Duncan Campbell Scott and Indian Affairs policy, *A Narrow Vision*. Jean Friesen explored First Nations' motivation, stressing economic concerns, in two important articles shortly afterwards.[21] During the latter half of the 1980s the revisionist interpretation of policy and treaty-making crafted initially by Tobias was becoming widely accepted in academic historical writing and was beginning to spread beyond the groves of academe to more general outlets. By the late 1990s, this viewpoint could legitimately be described as the new, more critical orthodoxy.[22]

THE FINDINGS OF "BOUNTY AND BENEVOLENCE" IN HISTORIOGRAPHICAL CONTEXT

The influence flowing from the interpretive innovations described above were reinforced by several other scholarly viewpoints that have also informed this study. During the 1970s and 1980s anthropologists such as Bruce G. Trigger were revising Canadian historians' understanding of the early decades of contact between

Europeans and First Nations in eastern Canada.[23] Also important was work by historical geographers such as Conrad Heidenreich and Arthur J. Ray that was throwing new light on relations in the fur trade at the same time.[24] Finally, first from the United States and then from Canadian sources there flowed a rich current of historical work that focused upon the diplomatic activities of First Nations in eastern North America from the sixteenth century to the aftermath of the War of 1812.[25] All these studies, and other similar treatments on similar themes, combined to put forward a portrait of First Nations leaders as shrewd in business, adept in diplomacy, and ingenious in coping with threatening social, economic, and political change.

Our findings are consistent with this more recent interpretation that emphasizes the activism and prescience of First Nations in their dealings with Europeans and Euro-Canadians. The complex business of the western fur trade brought First Nations of Saskatchewan and other regions into sustained contact with Europeans and shaped the diplomatic, economic, and political practices and protocols that would carry over into the relations that culminated in the making of treaties in the 1870s and beyond. Specifically, we have found that the commercial relationship in the western fur trade provided a context and tradition in which the negotiation of the numbered treaties took place. From the earliest days, London officials of the HBC recognized the authority of Indian nations and sought permission to build posts and to enter into trade relations. The trade ceremony conducted at the company's posts on Hudson Bay was an elaborate ritual involving a series of important Indian symbols, most notably the pipe ceremony, and it recognized the importance of First Nations leaders through the ceremonial giving of "captains and lieutenants" uniforms. The annual trade ceremony served to renew the social/economic alliance. The various practices, most notably giving credit, gift giving, and the provision of relief for the sick and destitute, recognized that the livelihood and well-being of Indians and fur traders were interrelated.

We have also found that government-to-government relations in the eastern part of North America in the period from the 1760s to the 1850s were important, particularly to the government of Canada. The Royal Proclamation of 1763 established the basic principle that First Nations lands could only be dealt with by the Crown at a public gathering arranged specifically for that purpose. Between 1763 and 1849 a succession of treaties dealt with Aboriginal territories and established relationships in present-day southern Ontario, while the Robinson Treaties of 1850 constituted one of the models for the numbered treaties of western Canada. Among the key points that Robinson established were annuities, reserves, protection of livelihood through recognition of First Nations' continuing right to hunt and fish on undeveloped lands, and the fact that resistance by First Nations to Euro-Canadian economic incursions – not the Royal Proclamation – had sparked treaty-making in Ontario's near North. Mining development, not agriculture, on Indian lands was the catalyst for the Robinson Treaties. Because mining was less extensive than agriculture, the Crown recognized a right to a livelihood (subsistence and commercial) on undeveloped Crown lands in antici- pation that lands away from mining sites would not be disrupted. Commissioner Robinson implied that settlers and miners would provide new markets for Ojibwa producers.

The surrender of the HBC's old charter rights allowed the Dominion of Canada to expand, and a financial take-over of the HBC by concerns interested in promot- ing colonization of Rupertsland initiated a process that led eventually to the ab- sorption of the Hudson's Bay Company Territory into the Canadian nation state. In this process, Indian interests received very little attention, because the broad possessory claims made by the HBC conflicted with the idea of Indian title and because the HBC claim was accorded a higher priority. Recognition of Indian in- terests occurred so that the HBC could be relieved of their traditional responsibil- ities. However, the transfer of Rupertsland, effected by the Rupertsland Order, an Imperial Order in Council, entailed more than a change in political geography: the HBC secured long-term and lucrative compensation for its "rights," and Canada acquired responsibility, independent of a treaty-making process, for the well-being of the Indigenous inhabitants of the "Northwest." With respect to northern treaties, Canada's policies were not informed by the responsibilities ex- pressed and implied by the Rupertsland Order.

The first three numbered treaties in the West expanded on the provisions of the Robinson Treaties and laid the background for the Saskatchewan treaties. The Crown was interested in obtaining land for agriculture, infrastructure rights of way, and timber. With the completion of the transfer of Rupertsland, Indian lead- ers and others campaigned for the establishment of a treaty relationship. The Crown's framework for a treaty relationship was not completed prior to the start of treaty negotiations and proved to be adaptive to local circumstances. Concern about the future livelihood needs of Indian nations figured prominently in the written documentation on the treaty negotiations. Indian leaders were well aware of pending changes, and they sought a relationship with the Crown that was future-oriented. (First Nations' negotiators would pursue a similar strategy in treaties that followed.) The Crown agreed to provide a number of social/ economic provisions to ensure First Nations well-being. Provision by the Crown of schools and support for agriculture, and the recognition of continuing hunting and fishing rights were designed to compensate for loss of land and to ensure a sustainable livelihood. The Crown justified the provision of small reserves by promising to secure future livelihoods for First Nations. Revisions to Treaties 1 and 2 demonstrate that the written versions of these treaties were an inadequate summary of the agreement reached at treaty talks.

Next we attempted to describe Saskatchewan on the eve of the treaties. Tradi- tionally, Saskatchewan Indian nations had two basic economic relations: one was oriented to the woodlands of central and northern Saskatchewan, emphasizing fishing, hunting, and trapping; the other was parkland-grassland oriented and was focused on hunting bison. On the eve of treaty-making the bison hunting economies were facing collapse, and leaders sought through treaties a way of dealing with a very uncertain future. Compounding their problems was the recent experience of the horrific impact of smallpox. The government of Canada and the HBC officials feared a general uprising of the militarily powerful Plains nations if satisfactory treaty arrangements were not made expeditiously. The Council of the Northwest Territories feared a general uprising that could involve the Prairie nations and the Sioux.

In the past, much treaty research has focused on a particular numbered treaty, but that approach has a tendency towards myopia. Identification of common historical patterns in all treaty-making encounters between the Crown and First Nations generates a deeper appreciation of the treaty relationship. Lieutenant-Governor Morris stated that Treaties 4 to 7 were modeled on the Robinson treaties and Treaty 1, 2, and 3. After laying the historical context for the Saskatchewan treaties, we examined each treaty in turn. In our investigation, though we often relied on Morris' account, we read that version in the new critical manner that has become the standard in academic research over the last fifteen years.

Treaty 4, the Qu'Appelle Treaty, initiated the Saskatchewan treaties. Again, representatives of the Crown promised the Queen's support in dealing with future needs, but it was understood that acceptance of change on the part of Indian nations would be voluntary. It was also understood by the First Nations that the treaty would establish an ongoing relationship with the Crown. The beneficial terms acquired by the HBC with the Rupertsland transfer caused great difficulty for the Crown's representatives during the negotiations. Indians rejected the premise that the HBC had any rights to sell or otherwise obtain benefits from First Nations lands. The response to this issue by Canada was to suggest that the Crown wanted to share the land with First Nations and settlers. First Nations negotiators also expressed concerns about land surveys associated with various interests in lands. The Crown promised to teach Indians "the cunning of the white man" so that they could sustain their livelihoods in changing circumstances.

Treaty 5, the Lake Winnipeg Treaty, involved three Saskatchewan bands. The lack of third-party written records severely limits documentary-based historical analysis of Treaty 5 events. Because of steamboat navigation and bountiful fisheries, the Crown interest in the Treaty 5 territory was as much about water as it was about land. Livelihood issues arose in Treaty 5, but not because of the demise of the bison economy or because of an onset of a large number of agricultural settlers. Following the transfer of Rupertsland and the concomitant restructuring of the Hudson's Bay Company's transport system, incomes to sustain Indian livelihood were affected negatively. Indian bands sought a solution to these problems through a treaty relationship with the Crown. A complex of territorial motives justified the Crown's decision to pursue a treaty with the Swampy Cree and the Ojibwa of this region. The Crown agreed to assist a portion of the Norway House bands with fur trade restructuring, even though there were no development pressures on the Norway House region. The Crown's strategy in Treaty 5 negotiations involved splitting the issue of Aboriginal title from the question of reserve sizes and locations.

Treaty 6, the Treaty of Fort Carlton and Fort Pitt, continued the process begun with the Plains Cree/Saulteaux/Assiniboine in Treaty 4 territory. Many of the primary First Nation concerns voiced during the Treaty 4 talks were expressed again in Treaty 6 negotiations. First Nation chiefs once again stated their anger about the sale of Rupertsland to Canada. Apart from this festering issue, Indian nations were extremely worried about the prospects of starvation that loomed as the bison herds continued their full retreat, and the recent ravages of smallpox were uppermost on their minds. Morris, on the other hand, expounded a negotiation strategy he had developed in Treaty 4, which involved stressing that treaties provided "gifts" from a beneficial queen mother that took away "nothing" from Indian nations' "ways of living," but, rather, added to them. Treaty 6 had had many symbolic parallels to the unwritten accords with the company. Treaty coats were similar to captain's coats, annuities and other recurring allowances recalled the annual gifts of the fur trader, and government commitments to provide relief and medical aid served the same ends as the HBC custom of providing necessary credit to the able-bodied and aid to the elderly, sick, and destitute. Treaty 6 granted the same written provisions as Treaty 4, with the significant promise to provide assistance in times of famine and medical help in times of pestilence. The government promised to take steps to help preserve the buffalo. Morris promised that Canada, acting on behalf of the Queen, would look after Indian welfare better than the HBC had. Morris held that the Crown would not feed Indians daily but that it would help them settle down and would not interfere with their means of living.

The Klondike goldrush was the catalyst for Treaty 8. A large portion of northern Saskatchewan is covered by Treaty 8, and one band signed an adhesion. The risk of conflict between First Nations and miners/prospectors forced the government to address the concerns of First Nations people. The Indian nations sought protection of their livelihood in the forests of the Athabasca and Mackenzie River basins, and they refused to let Canada extend its authority over the region without first addressing the issue of Aboriginal title. Negotiators for the Crown recognized that the cultural/economic traditions of First Nations in the Treaty 8 area were very different from those of the Indian nations that had signed the prairie treaties in the 1870s. Officials doubted that the reserve system would work in the north. Moreover, government negotiators did not anticipate that mining development would interfere with traditional Aboriginal economic activities. First Nations leaders feared the imposition of reserves because of the abuse of that system by Canada through the practice of issuing passes after the 1885 Rebellion to restrict the free movement of First Nations people. Government negotiators addressed Aboriginal concerns by promising that Canada would not infringe on their usual vocations, that any conservation legislation would be enacted for their benefit, and that they would not be restricted to reserves.

Treaty 10 was the last of the Saskatchewan treaties. Canada did not offer the Queen's "bounty and benevolence" to northern bands, unless and until the government wanted to promote and secure development on First Nations' lands. Treaty 10 followed on Treaty 8 and was closely related. Years after the transfer of Rupertsland, senior officials from the Department of Indian Affairs held the view that in the north the Hudson's Bay Company was still responsible for the well-being of Indians. Long-standing agitation from Indians of the Ile à la Crosse region for an adhesion to Treaty 8 and the creation of the province of Saskatchewan in 1905 prompted consideration by Ottawa officials to enter into treaty talks. Traditional livelihood concerns were foremost in the minds of First Nation participants. Treaty 10 was drafted directly from a copy of Treaty 8. Negotiators for the Crown made promises to provide for the sick and indigent. Indians were concerned that their hunting and fishing rights would be curtailed, and the Crown promised that there would be no forced interference with the Indian mode of life, although Indians would be subject to Canadian law. The treaty commissioner gave verbal assurances that the government would provide education for children. First Nations requested medicines and a resident doctor.

Our investigation of treaties also involved a few, but illustrative, post-treaty implementation issues. Following the conclusion of treaties, problems of implementation arose immediately. Part of the reason was that Canada was shifting from a mode of negotiating to one of administering its relations with western First Nations as the latter's economic and political strength declined rapidly with the demise of the buffalo. This calamity happened in the midst of a severe global economic depression, which delayed economic development and taxed the financial resources of the dominion government. The ensuing difficulties in implementing the treaties highlighted the fact that First Nations' understandings of the accords differed fundamentally from those of Canadian officials who subsequently interpreted and implemented the documents. A key area of disagreement arose because of the First Nations' belief that the Queen Mother's largesse would be sufficient to assure them a sustainable livelihood. Government officials, on the other hand, increasingly determined the level and type of support they would authorize in terms of budgetary considerations and short-term policy objectives of the Department of Indian Affairs. A related problem arose because the general promise that the Queen would protect First Nations livelihoods if they shared the land through treaties with new settlers clashed with the specific written provisions

of the treaties, which reflected the prevailing economic conditions at the time negotiations took place. First Nations had been promised that they would be free to
make their own choices about future economic options, but the increasingly paternalistic and coercive practices of officials of the Department of Indian Affairs in
the late nineteenth century contravened that promise. First Nations had been
promised that their usual ways would not be interfered with, but post-treaty conservation legislation often was very disruptive of traditional livelihood practices.

The documentary record permits a detailed discussion of the history of treaty-
making. That record cannot provide a complete and finished historical version of
the meanings of a treaty relationship between First Nations and the Crown. Nevertheless, the documentary record connected to treaty-making events strongly indicates that the written version of any treaty text is an incomplete and inadequate
representation of the understandings and agreements made at treaty talks. Several important historical findings would seem to be relevant to current interests
in the treaty relationship between Saskatchewan First Nations and the Crown.
The relationship between First Nations and the HBC predates the treaty-making
era by two hundred years, and both substantive and symbolic elements were retained or were associated in treaties with the Dominion of Canada. While each
treaty has unique and local qualities with respect to livelihood and the benevolence of the Queen, the Crown maintained a consistent position throughout the
treaty-making era that the Queen's representatives would assure the sustained
livelihood of the First Nations. Indian livelihood was to be secured or enhanced
by a treaty relationship, rather than diminished or encroached upon by it. In the
immediate treaty-signing era, problems arose that reflect on the different understandings of the treaties and/or the failure to implement the treaties in good faith.
"The Queen's bounty and benevolence" was a powerful and persuasive expression to capture the treaty relationship.

Data on Treaties

Table A1
Key Participants in Robinson Treaty Negotiations

Participant	Position	Interests	Activities
Anderson, T. Gummersall	Visiting superintendent of Indian Affairs, 1848–49	Survey area in 1846 and obtain information about terms of a treaty that would be acceptable to Native people.	Encourage Native people to sell their title as cheaply as possible.
Macdonnell, Allan	Indian negotiator/mining development promoter	Represent Indian interests and his own.	Press for high annuities in return for land concessions and protect his own interests on Michipicoten Island and at Sault Ste Marie.
Nebenaigoching	Indian negotiator	Represent Indian and Métis interests in Sault Ste Marie/Batchewana Bay area.	Press for high annuities in return for land concessions and seek land concessions for Métis.
Peau de Chat, Joseph	Indian negotiator	Represent Indian interests in the western Lake Superior area.	Press for high annuities in return for land concessions.
Robinson, William B.	Government (chief) negotiator	Negotiate terms of a treaty.	Encourage Native people to sell their title as cheaply as possible.
Shinguakouse (spelled variously)	Indian negotiator	Represent Indian and Métis interests in Garden River/Sault Ste Marie area.	Press for high annuities in return for land concessions and seek land concessions for Métis.
Swanston, John	Chief trader, HBC, Michipicoten	Represent Métis of Lake Superior.	Secure Métis interests. (He had a personal interest as a Métis.)
Vidal, Alexander	Government commissioner, 1846	Survey area in 1846 and obtain information about terms of a treaty that would be acceptable to Native people.	Encourage native people to sell their title as cost effectively as possible.

Table A2
Basic Data for Treaties 1, 2, and 3

	Date	Signatories	Witnesses
Treaty 1	3 August 1871	Wemyss M. Simpson, Indian commissioner Miskookenew (or Red Eagle) Kakekapenais (or Bird Forever) Nashakepenais (or Flying Down Bird) Nanawananan (or Centre of Bird's Tail) Kewetayash (or Flying Round) Wakowush (or Whip-Poor-Will) Oizawekwun (or Yellow Quill)	Adams G. Archibald, lieutenant-governor of Manitoba and North-West Territories James McKay, P.L.C. A.G. Irvine, Major Abraham Cowley Donald Gunn, M.L.C. Thomas Howard Henry Cochrane James McArrister Hugh McArrister E. Alice Archibald Henry Bouthillier
Treaty 2	21 August 1871	Wemyss M. Simpson, Indian commissioner Mekis Sonsense Masahkeeyash François Richard Woodhouse	Adams G. Archibald, lieutenant-governor of Manitoba and North-West Territories James McKay, P.C.C. E. A. Archibald Lily Archibald Henri Bouthillier Paul De Laronde Donald McDonald Eliza McDonald Alexander Muir, Sr.
Treaty 3	3 October 1873	Alexander Morris, lieutenant-governor of North-West Territories J.A.N. Provencher, Indian commissioner S.J. Dawson, Indian commissioner	James McKay Molyneux St John Robert Pither

Source: Morris, Treaties of Canada, 316, 320, 325–6.

Table A2 (*continued*)

Date	Signatories	Witnesses
	Keetakaypinais	Christine V.K. Morris
	Kithigaykake	Charles Nolin
	Notenaquahung	A. McDonald
	Mawedopenais	James F. Graham
	Powwasang	Joseph Nolin
	Cadacomigowininie	A. McLeod
	Papasskagin	George McPherson, Sen.
	Maynowahtauwayskung	Sedley Blanchard
	Kitchinekabehan	W. Fred Buchanan
	Sahkatcheway	Frank G. Becher
	Mukadaywahsin	Alfred Codd, M.D.
	Mekiesies	Gordon S. Corbault
	Oosconnageist	Pierre LeVieller
	Wahshiskince	Nicholas Chatelaine
	Rahkieyash	
	Gobay	
	Kametiash	
	Neeshotal	
	Keejeegokay	
	Shashagance	
	Shahwahnabinais	
	Ayashawash	
	Payahbeewash	
	Rahtaytaypaocutch	

Table A3
Summary of Terms of Treaties 1, 2, and 3: Government and Indian obligations (Written Version)

Treaty 1	Treaty 2	Treaty 3	Revisions of Treaties 1 and 2
They [chiefs] "do hereby cede, release, surrender, and yield up to Her Majesty the Queen and her successors for ever, all the lands included within the following limits."	Same land surrender wording as Treaty 1.	They "do hereby cede, release, surrender, and yield up to the Government of the Dominion of Canada, for Her Majesty the Queen and her successor for-ever, all their rights, titles and privileges whatsoever to the lands included within the following limits."	They "abandon all claim whatever against the government in connection with the so-called outside 'promises' other than those contained in the mem-orandum attached to the treaty."
They pledge "strictly to observe this treaty, and to maintain perpetual peace between themselves and Her Majesty's white or other subjects."	They "solemnly promise and engage to strictly observe this treaty, and also to conduct and behave them-selves as good and loyal subjects of Her Majesty the Queen."	Same wording as Treaty 2.	
	"They promise and engage that they will, in all respects obey and abide by the law; that they will maintain peace and good order."	Same wording as Treaty 2.	
They will "not interfere with the property or in any way molest the persons of her Majesty's white or other subjects."	They "will not molest the person or property of any inhabitants of such ceded tract; or the property of Her Majesty the Queen, or interfere with or trouble any person passing or trav-eling through the said tract."	Same wording as Treaty 2.	
	They "will aid and assist the officers of Her Majesty in bringing to justice and punishment any Indian offend-ing against the stipulations of this treaty."	Same wording as Treaty 2.	

Source: Morris, *Treaties of Canada*, 313–29, 338–9.

Table A3 (continued)

Treaty 1	Treaty 2	Treaty 3	Revisions of Treaties 1 and 2
		"Indians, shall have right to pursue their avocations of hunting and fishing throughout the tract surrendered ... subject to such regulations as may from time to time be made or taken up for settlement, mining, lumbering or other purposes."	
		Government will "lay aside reserves for farming lands, due respect being had to lands at present cultivated by the said Indians, and also to lay aside and reserve for the benefit of the said Indians."	
Location of reserves was specified.	Location of reserves was specified.	"Reserves shall be selected and set where it shall be deemed most convenient and advantageous for each band or bands of Indians, by the officers of the said Government appointed for that purpose, and such selection shall be so made after conference with Indians."	
Reserves land allocations of 160 acres per family of five.	Same as Treaty 1.	Reserve land allocations of one square mile per family of five.	
Present of 3 dollars per person.	Same as Treaty 1.	Present of 12 dollars per person. Same as Treaty 1.	
School on each reserve "whenever the Indians of the reserve should desire it."	Same as Treaty 1.	Same as Treaty 2.	
No intoxicating beverages allowed on reserves.	Same as Treaty 1.	Same as Treaties 1 and 2.	

Table A3 (continued)

Treaty 1	Treaty 2	Treaty 3	Revisions of Treaties 1 and 2
		"Sections of the reserves … as may at any time be required for public works or buildings, of what nature soever, may be appropriated for that purpose by Her Majesty's Government."	
Accurate census of Indians to be taken each year.	Same as Treaty 1.	Same as Treaties 1 and 2.	
Annuity for each family of five persons of 15 dollars to be paid in goods based on current Montreal prices.	Same as Treaty 1.	Annuity of 5 dollars per person.	Annuity for each Indian raised from 3 dollars to 5 dollars.
		1500 dollars per annum for ammunition and twine.	
		The following articles will be supplied: "two hoes for every family actually cultivating; also one spade per family as aforesaid; one plough for every ten families, as a foresaid; five harrows for every twenty families as aforesaid; one scythe for every family as aforesaid; and also one axe and one cross-cut saw, one hand saw, one pit saw, the necessary files, one grindstone, one auger for each band … also for each band, enough wheat, barley, potatoes and oats to plant the land … also for each band, one yoke of oxen, one bull and four cows: all the aforesaid articles to be given once for all for the encouragement of the practice of agriculture among the Indians."	
		Chief's salary of 25 dollars per year, and 15 dollars per year for subordinate's salary; once every three years a suit of clothing for chiefs and subordinates, and for each chief a flag and medal.	For each chief 25 dollars per year, a suit of clothes every three years for each chief and headman.

Table A4
Basic Data for Treaty 4 and Adhesions, from Original Documents

Document	Date Signed	Place	Aboriginal Peoples Involved	Aboriginal Signatories	Queen's Representatives	Interpreter
Treaty 4	15 September 1874	Qu'Appelle Lakes	Cree, Saulteaux, and other Indians (including bands from Qu'Appelle River, Leech Lake, Upper Qu'Appelle Lakes, Cypress Hills, Little Touchwood Hills, the south side of the south branch of the Saskatchewan, and Fort Pelly	Kakiishiway (Loud Voice), Pisqua (the Plain) and Kawezauce (the Little Boy), Kakeenawup (One That Sits Like an Eagle), Kuskeetewmuscoomusqua (Little Black Bear), Kaneonuskatew (One That Walks on Four Claws), Cauahhachapew (Making Ready the Bow), Kiisicawahchuck (Day-Star), Kawacatoose (the Poor Man), Kakiwistahaw (Him That Flies Around), Chacachas, Wapiimoosetoosiis (the White Calf, or Puscoos), Gabriel Cote (Meemay, the Pigeon)	Alexander Morris (lt-governor), David Laird (minister of the interior), William J. Christie (Indian commissioner)	Charles Pratt[1]
Adhesion[2]	21 September 1874	Fort Ellice	Saulteaux	Waywasecapow (the Man Proud of Standing Upright), Otamakooewin (Shapousetung's first son, or the Man Who Stands on the Earth)	Alexander Morris (lt-governor), David Laird (minister of the interior), William J. Christie (Indian commissioner)	Joseph Robillard

Note: Wherever possible, spellings of names have been copied from original documents; however, where the writing was not legible, spellings were taken from texts in *Indian Treaties and Surrenders* (3 vols.), first published by the Queen's Printer in 1891 and 1912, and Morris, *Treaties of Canada*.

1 Although it is Charles Pratt's name that appears on the treaty document, in his description of treaty negotiations at Fort Qu'Appelle Morris, *Treaties of Canada* (87), identifies William Daniel as the acting interpreter.

2 This adhesion was attached to the original treaty document.

Table A4 (continued)

Document	Date Signed	Place	Aboriginal Peoples Involved	Aboriginal Signatories	Queen's Representatives	Interpreter
Adhesion	8 September 1875	Qu'Appelle Lakes	Cree, Saulteaux, and Stonie	Cheecuck (chief of band at Qu'Appelle Lakes)	William J. Christie (Indian commissioner), M.G. Dickieson (acting commissioner), W.J. Wright	William the second McKay
Adhesion	9 September 1875	Qu'Appelle Lakes	Cree, Saulteaux, and Stonie	Wahpeemakwa (the White Bear), Okanes, Payepot, Le croup de pheaseant, Kitchikahmewin	William J. Christie (Indian commissioner), M.G. Dickieson (acting commissioner), W.J. Wright	Charles Pratt
Adhesion	24 September 1875	Swan Lake	Cree and Saulteaux (bands at Shoal River)	Owtahpeekakaw, KiishiKouse	W.J. Christie (Indian commissioner), M.G. Dickieson (acting commissioner)	George Brass
Adhesion	24 August 1876	Fort Pelly	Members of the Saulteaux tribe of Indians	Oozawaskooquinape (Yellow Quill), Kenistin (Cree), and Nepinawa (Summer Fur)	A. McKay, W.H. Nagle	A. McKay
Adhesion	25 September 1877	Fort Walsh	Assiniboine	Long Lodge (Teepee Hoska), the One That Fetched the Coat, the Poor Man (Wichawostaka)	J.M. Walsh (inspector of NWNP, in command at Fort Walsh)	Constant Provost

Table A5
Summary of Terms of Treaty 4, from the Original Document

Date signed	15 September 1874 (Qu'Appelle Lakes)
Terms of treaty	"The Cree and Saulteaux tribes of Indians, and all other, the Indians, inhabiting the district hereinafter described and defined, do hereby cede, release, surrender, and yield up to the Government of the Dominion of Canada, for Her Majesty the Queen, and Her successors forever, all their rights, titles and privileges whatsoever to the lands included within the following limits."
Land Involved	Document contains a description of treaty boundaries, but the area (i.e., in square miles) is not given.
Reserves	"And her Majesty the Queen hereby agrees … to assign reserves … to be selected by officers of Her Majesty's Government of the Dominion of Canada … after conference with each Band of the Indians, and to be of sufficient area to allow one square mile for each family of five, or in that proportion for larger or smaller families."
Presents	To show her satisfaction with the good conduct and behaviour of the Indians, Her Majesty the Queen will give "a present, for each Chief of twenty-five dollars in Cash, a coat, and a Queen's silver medal; for each headman, not exceeding four in each Band, fifteen dollars, in Cash, and a coat; and for every other man, woman, and child twelve dollars, in Cash, and for those here assembled some powder, shot, blankets, calicoes, strouds [?] and other articles."
Annuities	"[Her Majesty will] next year, and annually afterwards forever, cause to be paid, in cash, at some suitable season to be duly notified to the Indians, and at a place, or places, to be appointed for that purpose, within the territory ceded, − each Chief twenty-five dollars; each headman, not exceeding four to a band fifteen dollars, and to every other Indian, man, woman, and child five dollars per head; such payment to be made to the heads of families for those belonging thereto, unless for some special reason it be found objectionable."
Clothing, medals, etc.	"Her Majesty also agrees that each chief, and each headman, not to exceed four in each Band, once in every three years during the term of their offices, shall receive a suitable suit of clothing, and that yearly and every year she will cause to be distributed … powder, shot, ball and twine in all to the value of seven hundred and fifty dollars, and each chief shall receive, hereafter, in recognition of the closing of the Treaty, a suitable flag."
Articles for cultivation	"the following articles shall be supplied to any Band thereof, who are now actually cultivating the soil, or who shall hereafter settle on their Reserves, and commence to break up the land, that is to say: − two hoes, one spade, one scythe, and one axe for every family so actually cultivating, and enough seed wheat, barley, oats and potatoes, to plant such land as they have broken up, also one plough, and two harrows for every ten families so cultivating as aforesaid, and also to each chief for the use of his Band, as aforesaid, one yoke of oxen, one bull, four cows, a chest of ordinary carpenter's tools, five handsaws, five augers, one cross-cut saw, one pit Saw, the necessary files and one grindstone, all the aforesaid articles to be given once for all, for the encouragement of the practice of agriculture among the Indians."

Table A5 (continued)

Education	"Further, Her Majesty agrees to maintain a school in the Reserves allotted to each Band, as soon as they settle on said Reserve and are prepared for a teacher."
Alcohol	"within the Boundary of the Indian Reserves, until otherwise determined by the Government of the Dominion of Canada, no intoxicating liquor shall be allowed to be introduced or sold."
Hunting, trapping, and fishing	"And further, Her Majesty agrees that Her said Indians, shall have right to pursue their avocations of hunting, trapping, and fishing throughout the tract surrendered, subject to such regulations as may from time to time be made by the Government of the country acting under the authority of Her Majesty and saving and excepting such tracts as may be required or taken up from time to time for settlement, mining, or other purposes under grant or other right given by Her Majesty's said Government."
Adherence to treaty and policing	"And the undersigned chiefs and Headmen [and those they represent] … do hereby solemnly promise and engage to strictly observe this Treaty … They promise and engage that they will, in all respects, obey and abide by the law, that they will maintain peace and good order … and that they will assist the officers of Her Majesty in bringing to justice and punishment any Indian offending against the stipulations of this Treaty, or infringing the laws in force in the country so ceded."

Table A6
Basic Data for Treaty 5 and Adhesions, from Original Documents

Document	Date Signed	Place	Aboriginal Peoples Involved	Aboriginal Signatories	Crown Representatives Witnesses	Interpreter
Treaty No. 5	20 September 1875	Berens River	Saulteaux and Swampy Cree tribes of Indians, bands in the Berens River and Norway House regions.	For Berens River: Chief Nah-weekeesickquahyash (Jacob Berens) and Councillors Kah-nahwahkeeweenin (Antoine Gouin), Nahkeequanmayyash, and Peewahrooweenin (of Poplar River)	Alexander Morris (lieutenant-governor), James McKay (Indian commissioner). Witnesses: Thomas Howard, A.G. Jackes, MD, Christine Morris, E.C. Morris, Elizabeth Young, Egerton Ryerson Young, William McKay, John McKay	
	24 September 1875	Norway House		For Norway House: Chief David Rundle, and Councillors James Cochrane, Harry Constatag, and Charles Pisequinip; and Chief Tapastanum (Donald William Ross Sinclair) and Councillors George (or James) Garriock and Proud McKay	Alexander Morris (lt-governor), James McKay (Indian commissioner). Witnesses: Roderick Ross (HBC), John H. Ruttan (Methodist missionary), D.C. McTavish, Alexander Sinclair, L.C. McTavish, Christine V.K. Morris, E.C. Morris, A.G. Jackes, MD, and Thomas Howard.	James McKay
Adhesion[1]	27 September 1875	Grand Rapids	The band of the Saulteaux tribe of Indians residing at the mouth of the Saskatchewan River on both sides thereof.	Chief Peter Beardy and Councillors Joseph Atkinson and Robert Sanderson.	Alexander Morris (lt-governor), James McKay (Indian commissioner). Witnesses: Thomas Howard, Roderick Ross, E.C. Morris, A.G. Jackes, MD, Alexander	James McKay

1 This adhesion was included with the original treaty document, beginning on the last page of signatures from the treaty at Norway House. The docket title for the original treaty document states, "Treaty No. 5 and Supplementary Treaties with Indians at Berens River, Norway House, Grand Rapids and Wapang."

Table A6 (continued)

Document	Date Signed	Place	Aboriginal Peoples Involved	Aboriginal Signatories	Crown Representatives Witnesses	Interpreter
					Matheson (HBC Grand Rapids), Joseph Houston, and Christine Morris	
Memorandum[2]	28 September 1875	Wapang, or Dog Head Island	Thickfoot and a portion of the Islands band of Indians.	Thickfoot (a principal Indian)	Alexander Morris (lt-governor), James McKay (Indian commissioner). Witnesses: Thomas Howard, Roderick Ross	Not stated
Adhesion	26 July 1876	Wapang, or Dog Head Island (Lake Winnipeg)	The Saulteaux Indians residing at or near Big Island or other islands in Lake Winnipeg (including the Blood Vein River band, Big Island band, Dog head band and Jack Head band)	Chief Sakachewayas (of Blood Vein River) and Councillors Katukepinais (or Hardisty, of Big Island), Thickfoot (of Dog Head), and Sanggwawakapow (or James Sinclair, of Jack Head)	Thomas Howard and John Lestock Reid Esquire	Rev. Henry Cochrane
Adhesion	4 August 1876	Berens River	The band of Saulteaux residing in the vicinity of the Grand Rapids of the Berens River	Chief Nahweekeesickquahyash (Jacob Berens) and Councillor Nunakowahnukwape.	Thomas Howard and John Lestock Reid, Esquire	Rev. Henry Cochrane
Adhesion	7 September 1876	Winnipeg	The band of the Saulteaux tribe residing at the mouth of Black River on the East shore of Lake Winnipeg	James Bird, Sayer Joseph, and Sayer John	Acting Indian superintendent (no name given)	Not stated

2 This document is called a "Memorandum" in the original. In it, Thickfoot agrees to accept the terms of Treaty No. 5 and to notify the Island band of Indians to meet at Wapang the following summer to receive payment for the treaty in which they are included. Morris, *Treaties of Canada*, notes that the official adhesion was obtained 26 July 1876 by Thomas Howard and John Lestock Reid. This adhesion was also signed by Thickfoot.

Table A6 (continued)

Document	Date Signed	Place	Aboriginal Peoples Involved	Aboriginal Signatories	Crown Representatives Witnesses	Interpreter
Adhesion	7 September 1876	The Pas on the Saskatchewan River	Saulteaux and Swampy Cree including the Pas band, the Cumberland band, and the Moose Lake band	For the Pas band: Chief John Constant and Councillors James Cook Sr, John Bell Jr, Peter Bell, and Donald Cook Sr For the Cumberland band: Chief John Cochrane and Councillors Peter Chapman and Albert Flett For the Moose Lake Band: Chief Otinikimaw and Councillors Maikwuhekapow, Wamekwuwuhop, and Kachachuckoos	Thomas Howard (acting for Her Majesty the Queen, under special authority)	Rev. Henry Cochrane
Adhesion	26 June 1908	Split Lake	Split Lake and Nelson House bands	For Split Lake: Wm Keche-Kesik, Charles Morris and Albert Spence (names are also given in syllabics)	John Semmens (Indian commissioner)	Possibly John Semmens
	13 July 1908	Nelson House		For Nelson House: Chief Peter Moose and Councillors Murdock Hart and James Spence (names are also given in syllabics)		
Adhesion	8 July 1908	Norway House	Non-treaty Indians resident at these places	At Norway House: Sandy Sanders, Peter Maham, and Thomas Grieve (224 others present)	John Semmens (Indian commissioner)	Possibly John Semmens

Table A6 (continued)

Document	Date Signed	Place	Aboriginal Peoples Involved	Aboriginal Signatories	Crown Representatives Witnesses	Interpreter
	15 July 1908	Cross Lake		At Cross Lake: Daniel Meswakun, David Moneas, and Simon Moneas (70 others present)		
	24 August 1908	Fisher River		At Fisher River: Peter Mundo, and James Kirkness (17 others present)		
Adhesion	29 July 1909	Oxford House	Oxford House, God's Lake, and Island Lake bands	For Oxford House: Chief Jeremiah Chubb and Councillors Kahist Chubb and James natawayo	John Semmens (Indian commissioner)	Possibly H.S. Stead (secretary)
	6 August 1909	God's Lake		For God's Lake: Chief Peter Watt and Councillors Big Simon and Peter Chubb (names also given in syllabics)		
	13 August 1909	Island Lake		For Island Lake: Chief George Nott and Councillors Joseph Lenklolis [?] and John Mason		
Adhesion	9 June 1910	Deer's Lake East	Deer's Lake, Fort York, and Fort Churchill bands of Indians	For Deer's Lake East: chief Robert Fiddler	John Semmens (Indian commissioner)	Possibly John Semmens

Table A6 (*continued*)

Document	Date Signed	Place	Aboriginal Peoples Involved	Aboriginal Signatories	Crown Representatives Witnesses	Interpreter
	1 August 1910	Fort Churchull		For Fort Churchill: Chief French John and Councillors Sam Chinashagun and Thomas Crazy		
	10 August 1910	York Factory		For York Factory: Chief Charles Wastasekoot and Councillors Robert Beardy and Sandy Beardy (names at York Factory are also given in syllabics)		

Table A7
Summary of Terms of Treaty 5, from the Original Document

Date signed	20 September 1875 (Berens River) and 24 September 1875 (Norway House)
Terms of treaty	"The 'Saulteaux and Swampy Cree Tribes of Indians' and all other the Indians inhabiting the district hereinafter described and defined, do hereby cede, release, surrender, and yield up to the Government of the Dominion of Canada, for Her Majesty The Queen and Her Successors forever, all their rights, titles and privileges whatsoever to the lands included within the following limits."
Land involved	Document contains a description of treaty boundaries, with an area of 100,000 square miles bounded in part by Treaties 1, 3, and 4, "it being understood that in all Cases where Lakes form the Treaty limits ten miles from the shore of the Lake shall be included in the Treaty."
Reserves	"And her Majesty the Queen hereby agrees and undertakes to lay aside Reserves for farming lands … and other Reserves for the benefit of the said Indians … provided all such Reserves shall not exceed in all one hundred and sixty acres for each family of five or in that proportion for larger or smaller families, in manner following." Following this, the boundaries of Reserves are described for each band. The Saulteaux band in the Berens River region were allotted a reserve commencing at the outlet of Berens River into Lake Winnipeg and extending along the shores of the Lake and inland, to the amount of 160 acres per family of five or in that proportion. The Indians residing at Poplar River (falling into Lake Winnipeg north of Berens River) also received a reserve of 160 acres per family of five. The Indians represented by Chief David Rundle residing around Norway House were allotted only 100 acres per family of five for a reserve on the west side of Lake Winnipeg in the vicinity of Fisher River. The band of Wood Indians represented by Ta-pas-pa-num was allotted a reserve at Otter Island on the west side of Cross Lake in the amount of 160 acres per family of five. In all cases, emphasis is placed on retaining rights of free navigation on all lakes and rivers for Her Majesty's subjects.
Presents	To show her satisfaction with the good conduct and behaviour of the Indians, Her Majesty the Queen will give "a present of Five dollars for each man, woman and child belonging to the Bands here represented, in extinguishment of all claims heretofore preferred."
Annuities	"[Her Majesty will] in every year ensuing the date hereof at some period in each year, to be duly notified to the Indians, and at a place or places to be appointed for that purpose within the Territory ceded, pay to each Indian person the sum of Five dollars per head yearly. – It is further agreed between Her Majesty and the said Indians that the sum of five hundred dollars per annum shall be yearly and every year expended by Her Majesty in the purchase of Ammunition, and twine for nets for the use of the said Indians," "to be distributed among the Indians in the several reserves at the discretion of "Her Majesty's Indian Agent having the supervision of this Treaty."
Clothing, medals, etc.	"each Chief duly recognized as such, shall receive an annual salary of twenty five dollars per annum, and each subordinate officer, not exceeding three for each Band, shall receive fifteen dollars per annum; and each such Chief and subordinate officer as aforesaid shall also receive, once every three years a suitable suit of clothing; and each Chief shall receive in recognition of the closing of the Treaty, a suitable Flag and medal."

Table A7 (continued)

Articles for cultivation	"the following articles shall be supplied to any Band of the said Indians who are now cultivating the soil, or who shall hereafter commence to cultivate the land, that is to say: – two hoes for every family actually Cultivating: also one spade per family as aforesaid: one plow for every ten families as aforesaid: five harrows for every twenty families as aforesaid: one Scythe for every family as aforesaid, and also one Cross Cut saw, one hand saw, one pit saw, the necessary files, one grindstone, and one auger for each Band: and also for each Chief for the use of his Band, one chest of ordinary carpenter's tools: also for each Band enough of Wheat, Barley, Potatoes, and Oats to plant the land actually broken up for cultivation by such Band: also for each Band, one yoke of oxen, one bull, and four cows: all the aforesaid articles to be given once for all for the encouragement of the practice of agriculture among the Indians."
Education	"And further, Her Majesty agrees to maintain Schools for instruction in such Reserves hereby made as to Her Government of the Dominion of Canada may seem advisable, whenever the Indians of the Reserve shall desire it."
Alcohol	"within the boundary of Indian Reserves, until otherwise determined by Her Government of the Dominion of Canada, no intoxicating liquor shall be allowed to be introduced or sold."
Hunting, trapping, and fishing	"Her Majesty further agrees with Her Said Indians, that they, the said Indians, shall have right to pursue their avocations of hunting and fishing throughout the tract surrendered as hereinbefore described, subject to such regulations as may from time to time be made by Her Government of Her Dominion of Canada, and saving and excepting such tracts as may from time to time be required or taken up for settlement, mining, lumbering or other purposes by Her said Government of the Dominion of Canada, or by any of the subjects thereof duly authorized therefor by the said Government."
Adherence to treaty and policing	"And the undersigned Chiefs [and those they represent] … do hereby solemnly promise and engage to strictly observe this Treaty … They promise and engage that they will, in all respects, obey and abide by the law, and they will maintain peace and good order … and that they will aid and assist the officers of Her Majesty in bringing to justice and punishment any Indian offending against the stipulations of this Treaty, or infringing the laws in force in the Country so ceded."

Table A8
Basic Data for Treaty 6 and Adhesions, from Original Documents

Document	Date Signed	Place	Aboriginal Peoples Involved	Aboriginal Signatories	Crown Representatives	Interpreter
Treaty No. 6	23 August 1876 28 August 1876	Fort Carlton	The Plain and Wood Cree and other tribes of Indians, including the Willow Indians (who signed on 28 August)	At Carlton: Mistowasis and Ahtukukkoop (head chiefs); Peeyahnkahmihkoosit, Ahyahtaskumikimun, Keetoowahaw, Chakastapaysin, John Smith, James Smith, and Chipeewayan (chiefs); Massan, Pierrie Cadien, Ooyahtikwahpahn, and Mahskeetetimun (councillors of Mistowasis); Sahsahkoomoos, Benjamin, Meenowahchahkway, and Keesikowasis (councillors of Ahtukukkoop); Peetookahhanupeeginew, Peeaychew, Tahwahpiskeekahppow, and Ahskoos (councillors of Peeyahnkahmihkoosit); Petequacay, Jean Baptiste, Isidore Wolfe, and Keekoohoos (councillors of Keetoowahaw); Oosahnuskoonukik, Yahyahtooway, Soosowaimeekuahn, and Nuswahyakeenahkoos (councillors of Ahyahtaskumikimum); Kahtipiskowaht,	Alexander Morris (Lt Governor) James McKay (Indian commissioner) W.J. Christie (Indian commissioner)	At Fort Carlton: Peter Erasmus, Peter Ballendine, and the Rev. John McKay Willow Indians: James McKay and Peter Erasmus

Table A8 (continued)

Document	Date Signed	Place	Aboriginal Peoples Involved	Aboriginal Signatories	Crown Representatives	Interpreter
				Kahkuneeknahnahsum, Nahpach, and Musinahwekimahn (councillors of Chakastapaysin); William Badger, Benjamin Joyful, John Badger, and James Bear (councillors of John Smith); Bernard Constant, Henry Smith, Matwaahstinoowegin, and Jacob McLean (councillors of James Smith); Nahpoocheechees, Wahwis, Kahpahpahmahchatiknay, and Keeyewahkahpimwaht (councillors of Chipeewayan); Wahweekahnickkahootahmahhote (chief) For the Willow Indians: Kahmee-yis-too-way-sit, Kahpayyukwahskoonum, and Seeseekwahnis (joint chiefs of Willow Indians); Kahnahkahskowwaht, Kahahteekoowew, Kahnahmahchew, Moonedyahs, Oowinahkaw, and Ootukkoopahkahmaytowwayyit (councillors of Willow Indians)		

Table A8 (continued)

Document	Date Signed	Place	Aboriginal Peoples Involved	Aboriginal Signatories	Crown Representatives	Interpreter
Treay No. 6	9 September 1876	Fort Pitt	The Plain and Wood Cree and other tribes of Indians, including the Willow Indians (who signed on 28 August)	At Fort Pitt: Weekaskookeesayyin, Peeyaseewakkahwechakoot, James Seenum, Oomahtakmeenahhoos, Seekahskootch, Tustukeeshwais, Peewaysis, and Keeyewin (Cree chiefs); Kinoosayoo (Chipewyan chief); Seewuskwan and Wahwaysuhooweyin (councillors to Weekaskookeesayyin); Tipeeskowahchak and Paypayseeseemoo (councillors to Peeyaseewakkahwechakoot); Oowowakeepakchas, and Myoowaysus (councillors to Seekahskootch); Oosperahkhanis and Neeyeputayaseekayse (councillors to Tustukeeshwais); Mahchahmeenis and Isaac Cardinal (councillors to Peewaysis); Antoine Xavier (councillor to Kinoosayoo); William Bull (councillor to James Seenum); Wahkegseekoot (councillor to Seekahskootch); Charles Cardinal and Pierre Wahbiskaw (councillors to Keeyewin); Kiyaseekun and Kahkeeoopahtow (councillors to Weekaskookeesayyin); Cakecake (councillor to	Alexander Morris (lt-governor) James McKay (Indian commissioner) W.J. Christie (Indian commissioner)	James McKay and Peter Erasmus.

Table A8 (continued)

Document	Date Signed	Place	Aboriginal Peoples Involved	Aboriginal Signatories	Crown Representatives	Interpreter
				Oomahtakmeenahhoos); Kamoowin (councillor to James Seenum); and Ahsiss (councillor to Seekahskootch)		
Adhesion	9 August 1877	Fort Pitt	Cree and other bands of Indians	At Fort Pitt: Paymotayahsoo, Kahseemutapoo, and Nahpaysis (Kehiwin's headman)	M.G. Dickieson (commissioner for the Queen)	Peter Erasmus
	21 August 1877	Edmonton		At Edmonton: Alexis Keeskeecheechi (chief), Oomusinahsoowawsinee (headman), Catchistahwayskum (chief), Koosahwanaskayo (headman), Pahspahschase, and Tahkootch		
Adhesion	25 September 1877	The Blackfoot Crossing of the Bow River	Members of the Cree tribe of Indians	Kiskayein (or Bob Tail, chief, Meminowataw (or Sometimes Glad, councillor, and Tchowek (or Passing Sound, councillor)	David Laird (lt-governor and Indian superintendent)	Rev. J. McDougall
Adhesion	19 August 1878	Not stated	Cree Nation	Puskeeyahkayweeyin, Mahkayo, Paypahmuskumickinum, and Isidore	David Laird (superintendent of Indian Affairs for the NWT)	Peter Erasmus

Table A8 (continued)

Document	Date Signed	Place	Aboriginal Peoples Involved	Aboriginal Signatories	Crown Representatives	Interpreter
Adhesion	29 August 1878	Battleford	Plain Stony tribe of Indians	Sukemaw (or Misketo), Etamepeton (or Uses Both Arms), Nesoauasis (or Two Child), and Kawasaskotropahik (or Lightning)	David Laird (superintendent of Indian Affairs for the NWT)	Peter Ballendine
Adhesion	3 September 1878	Carlton	Wood Cree tribe of Indians	Kopahawakenum (chief), Banjiel Maristye (councillor), James (chief's son, councillor), Sasewahum, Kenemotay, and Masenaschase	David Laird (superintendent of Indian Affairs for the NWT)	Peter Ballendine
Adhesion	18 September 1878	Not Stated	Not stated (docket title is "Adhesion of Edmonton Chief")	Michel Calishois, Louis Pay pahmahmayo, and Acoosee	Not stated	Peter Erasmus
Adhesion	2 July 1878	Fort Walsh	Cree bands represented by Little Pine (Minahequosis) and Lucky Man (Papaway)	Little Pine (Minahequosis) and Lucky man (Papaway)	Edward Dewdney (Indian commissioner for the NWT)	Edward McKay and P. Leveilly
Adhesion	8 December 1882	Fort Walsh	Cree band represented by Chief Big Bear	Big Bear (chief)	Allan Macdonald (Indian agent)	Peter Hourie and Louis Leveillee

Table A8 (continued)

Document	Date Signed	Place	Aboriginal Peoples Involved	Aboriginal Signatories	Crown Representatives	Interpreter
Adhesion	11 February 1889	Montreal Lake	Wood Cree Tribe of Indians	James Roberts and William Charles (chiefs); Amos Charles, Joseph Charles, Elias Roberts and John Cook (councillors of James Roberts' band); Benjamin Bird, Isaac Bird, Patrick Bird, and Moses Bird (councillors of William Charles's Band)	A.G. Irvine (lt-colonel, commissionner) R. Goulet (commissioner)	The Venerable Archdeacon MacKay
Adhesion	25 June 1913	Waterhen Lake	Non-treaty Indians resident at Water Hen Lake and Big Island Lake	Joseph Big Head, Atimosis, Peeweyenese, Kanoasosko-wat, Nahpaysis, Kah-peepunapew, and Nahpays.	D.J. Chishalew [Chisholm?] (special commissioner for His Majesty the King)	Alex Campbell
Adhesion	25 May 1944	Rocky Mountain House	Cree Indians residing at Baptiste River (Alberta)	L. Sun Child, J. Yellow Eyes, and possibly one other (name unintelligible)	Malcolm McCrimmon (commissioner) John Lothrop Grew (commissioner)	Not stated
Adhesion	13 May 1950	Rocky Mountain House	Chippewa Indians located at Rocky Mountain House	James Daychief, Thomas Daychief, Simon Strawberry, James Beaverbones, Alex Whitford, Frank Strawberry, Andrew Strawberry, Joseph Bremnes, Wawakachin, Thomas Bremnes, Jimmie Strawberry, chakasee, John Muskeg, Nocass Muskeg, Susie Strawberry, Josie Strawberry, John Muskeg	M. McCrimmon (commissioner), for His Majesty King George VI	Not stated

Table A8 (continued)

Document	Date Signed	Place	Aboriginal Peoples Involved	Aboriginal Signatories	Crown Representatives	Interpreter
Adhesion	21 November 1950	Witchekan Lake	Cree Indiens located on the Witchekan Lake Indian Reserve (SK)	Louie Thomas (chief), Jack Bear, Peter Bear, Shorty Jim, George Thomas, John Thomas, Joe Thomas, and Paddy Bear	James Pember Brookbank Ostrander (commissioner), for King George	Not stated
Adhesion	18 August 1954	Cochin	Saulteaux Band located on the Saulteaux Indian Reserve (SK)	Alex Kacheech, George Dahpance, John Night, Jim Night, Job Night, Harry Thomas, Richard Gopher, Joe Katcheech, Bill Gopher, Clara Gopher, Helen Katcheech, Bill Night, Joseph Ironbon, Alex Gopher, Alex Mocassin, Annie Gopher, Margaret Ironbon, Mary Kacheech, Francis Katchich, Jim Gopher, Annie Wiapanuse	M. McCrimmon (commissioner), for Queen Elizabeth	Not stated
Adhesion[1]	15 May 1956	Cochin	Members of the Saulteaux Indian band in the province of Saskatchewan	John Swimmer, Johnnie Swimmer, George Katcheech, Bonnie Swimmer, Francis Moccasin, and Atlas [?] Moccasin	Not stated	Not stated

1 The signature sheet of this adhesion was attached to the previous adhesion at Cochin and did not have a separate text or cover page.

Table A9
Summary of Terms of Treaty 6, from the Original Document

Date signed	23 August 1876 (Fort Carlton), 28 August 1876 (Fort Carlton), and 9 September 1876 (Fort Pitt)
Terms of treaty	"The Plain and Wood Cree Tribes of Indians, and all other the Indians inhabiting the district hereinafter described and defined, do hereby cede, release, surrender, and yield up to the Government of the Dominion of Canada, for Her Majesty the Queen and Her successors forever, all their rights, titles and privileges whatsoever to the lands included within the following limits."
Amount of land involved	Document contains a description of treaty boundaries, with an area of approximately 121,000 square miles bounded in part by Treaties 4 and 5. Note that in the Montreal Lake adhesion of 11 February 1889, an additional tract of land with an area of 11,066 square miles is added to Treaty 6. This additional tract of land is "the North part of the Land District of Prince Albert ... being North of the Northerly limit of Treaty No. 6 North West Territory."
Reserves	"And her Majesty the Queen hereby agrees and undertakes to lay aside Reserves for farming lands ... and other Reserves for the benefit of the said Indians ... provided all such Reserves shall not exceed in all one square mile for each family of five, or in that proportion for larger or smaller families ... the Chief Superintendent of Indian Affairs shall depute and send a suitable person to determine and set apart the reserves for each band after consulting with the Indians thereof as to the locality which may be found to be most suitable for them."
Presents	To show her satisfaction with the good conduct and behaviour of the Indians, Her Majesty the Queen will give "a present of 12 dollars for each man, woman and child belonging to the Bands here represented, in extinguishment of all claims heretofore preferred."
Annuities	"[Her Majesty will] in every year ensuing the date hereof, at some period in each year, to be duly notified to the Indians, and at a place or places to be appointed for that purpose within the Territory ceded, pay to each Indian person the sum of five dollars per head yearly. It is further agreed ... that the sum of $1500 per annum shall be yearly and every year expended by Her Majesty in the purchase of ammunition, and twine for nets for the use of the said Indians" to be distributed among the Indians in the several reserves at the discretion of "Her Majesty's Indian Agent having the supervision of this treaty."
Salary, clothing, medals, etc.	"each Chief duly recognized as such, shall receive an annual salary of twenty-five dollars per annum; and each subordinate officer, not exceeding four for each band, shall receive fifteen dollars per annum, and each such Chief and subordinate officer as aforesaid shall also receive, once every three years, a suitable suit of clothing; and each Chief shall receive, in recognition of the closing of the treaty, a suitable flag and medal and also as soon as convenient one horse, harness and wagon."

Table A9 (continued)

Articles for cultivation	"the following articles shall be supplied to any Band of the said Indians who are now actually cultivating the soil, or who shall hereafter commence to cultivate the land, that is to say: – four hoes for every family actually cultivating; also two spades per family as aforesaid; one plough for every three families as aforesaid; one harrow for every three families as aforesaid; two scythes and one whetstone for every family as aforesaid and two hay forks and two reaping forks for every family as aforesaid, and also two axes, and also one cross-cut saw, one hand-saw, one pit saw, the necessary files, one grindstone and one auger for each Band; also for each Chief for the use of his band, one chest of ordinary carpenter's tools; also for each Band, enough of wheat, barley, potatoes and oats to plant the land actually broken up for cultivation by such Band; also for each Band, four oxen, one bull, and six cows; also one boar and two sows, and one hand mill when any band shall raise sufficient grain therefor; all the aforesaid articles once for all, for the encouragement of the practice of agriculture among the Indians." Later in the treaty, it is stated that chiefs that sign at Fort Pitt, or those signing in subsequent adhesions, may choose to receive (instead of a wagon) "two carts with iron bushings and tires."
Education	"And further, Her Majesty agrees to maintain schools for instruction in such Reserves hereby made, as to Her Government of the Dominion of Canada may seem advisable, whenever the Indians of the Reserve shall desire it."
Alcohol	"within the boundary of Indian Reserves, until otherwise determined by her Government of the Dominion of Canada, no intoxicating liquor shall be allowed to be introduced or sold."
Hunting, trapping, and fishing	"Her Majesty further agrees with her said Indians, that they, the said Indians, shall have right to pursue their avocations of hunting and fishing throughout the tract surrendered as hereinbefore described, subject to such regulations as may from time to time be made by Her Government of Her Dominion of Canada, and saving and excepting such tracts as may from time to time be required or taken up for settlement, mining, lumbering or other purposes by her said Government of the Dominion of Canada, or by any of the subjects thereof duly authorized therefor by the said Government."
Medical and other provisions	"That a medicine chest shall be kept at the house of each Indian agent for the use and benefit of the Indians at the discretion of such agent." "That in the event hereafter of the Indians … being overtaken by any pestilence or by a general famine, the Queen … will grant to the Indians assistance of such character and to such extent as her chief superintendent of Indian affairs shall deem necessary and sufficient to relieve the Indians from the calamity that shall have befallen them. That during the next three years … there shall be granted to the Indians included under the Chiefs adhering to the treaty at Carlton; each Spring the sum of one thousand dollars to be expended for them by Her Majesty's Indian agent in the purchase of provisions for the care of such of the band as are actually settled on the reserve and are engaged in cultivating the soil, to assist them in such cultivation." The provision is added for those that signed at Fort Pitt, or subsequent adhesion that in the next three years, the Indian Agent will distribute each spring "in his discretion a sum not exceeding one thousand dollars in the purchase of provisions."
Adherence to treaty and policing	"And the undersigned Chiefs [and those they represent] … do hereby solemnly promise and engage to strictly observe this Treaty … They promise and engage that they will, in all respects, obey and abide by the law, and they will maintain peace and good order … and that they will aid and assist the Officers of Her Majesty in bringing to justice and punishment any Indian offending against the stipulations of this treaty, or infringing the laws in force in the country so ceded."

Table A10
Summary of Oral History of Treaty 6

Name	Comments
Rev. Phillip Charles, Lac La Ronge	"The first treaty promise to the Indians was just like he was promised the lakes and the rivers also because the fish are in the water and these were for food for the people and children, to make a living from. And the same with animals. They were promised they could hunt and fish without restriction, to make a living. They did not want to sell their land but they were asked to sell it. No, they did not give up any rights to anything else only the land. The government who was representing the Queen at that time, said I am buying your land nothing else. Not your way of making a living such as hunting, etc."
Daniel McKenzie, Lac La Ronge	"In the Treaties there was no mention of water being sold, because that is where the people make their living, mostly from the water, and of course, also from the land. But in the Treaties, no mention of water."
Martha Roberts, Lac La Ronge	"Only the land was sold. The people made a living from the land and the waters. They did not get any ration or help, at that time."
George Halkett, Lac La Ronge	"No, they did not sell the lakes and the rivers. Only the land was bought at that time. When they were asked to sell their land, [the commissioner said] 'your way of life will not be taken away, such as hunting, fishing and trapping. It's only the land that you are asked to sell.' That's what they were told."
Philip McDonald, Peter Ballantyne Reserve	"the only symbol that's been used as long as the waters flow that these treaty rights were to last, that was the only thing that was talked about as far as water is concerned. They didn't actually talk about water, or rivers, or lakes, but they did talk about fish that live in the water, also muskrats and beavers, those animals that live on the water."
Angus Merasty, Peter Ballantyne Reserve	"In the signing of the treaties the Indians just gave up their land, land exclusively. Only land. Not their natural resources."
Nancy McCallum, Peter Ballantyne Reserve	"It was just the land that the Queen bought from the people. They said it was just the land they wanted to buy and nothing else."

Source: Ballantyne, et al., *Aski-Puko: The Land Alone,* 63–4.

Table A11
Basic Data for Treaty 8 and Adhesions, from Original Documents

Document	Date Signed	Place	Aboriginal Peoples Involved	Aboriginal Signatories	Crown Representatives	Interpreter
Treaty No. 8	21 June 1899	Lesser Slave Lake	Cree, Beaver, Chipewyan and other Indians	At Lesser Slave Lake: Keenooshayoo (chief), Moostoos (headman), Felix Giroux, Weecheewaysis, Charles Neesuetasis, and Captain (headman from Strugeon Lake)	At Lesser Slave Lake: David Laird (Indian commissioner), James Andrew Joseph McKenna (Indian commissioner), and James Hamilton Ross (Indian commissioner)	At Lesser Slave Lake: Albert Tate and Samuel Cunningham
	1 July 1899	Peace River Landing		At Peace River Landing: Duncan Tastaoots (headman of Crees)	At Peace River Landing and Vermillion: David Laird (chairman of Indian Treaty commissioners)	At Peace River Landing and Vermillion: Father A. Lacombe and John Boucher
	8 July 1899	Vermillion		At Vermillion: Ambrose Tete Noir (chief of Beaver Indians), Pierrot Fournier (headman of Beaver Indians), and Kuiskuiskowcapoohoo (headman of Cree Indians)		
Adhesion	25 July 1899 27 July 1899	Fond du Lac	Chipewyan Indans at Fond du Lac (Lake Athabaska)	Laurent Dzieddin (headman), Toussaint (headman), and Maurice Piche (chief of band)	David Laird (chairman of Indian treaty commissioners)	Pierre des Chambeault, Father Douceur, and Louis Robillard
Adhesion	6 July 1899	Dunvegan	Beaver Indians of Dunvegan	Natooses (headman)	Commissioners James Hamilton Ross and James Andrew Joseph McKenna	Rev. Joseph Le Treste and Peter Gunn

Table A11 (*continued*)

Document	Date Signed	Place	Aboriginal Peoples Involved	Aboriginal Signatories	Crown Representatives	Interpreter
Adhesion	13 July 1899	Fort Chipewyan	Chipewyan Indians of Athabaska River, Birch River, Peace River, Slave River and Gull River, and the Cree Indians of Gull River and Deep Lake	Alex Laviolette (Chipewyan chief), Julien Ratfat, and Sept. Heezeli (Chipewyan headmen); Justin Martin (Cree chief), Ant. Taccarroo, and Thomas Gibbot (Cree headmen).	Commissioners James Hamilton Ross and James Andrew Joseph McKenna	Peter Mercredi (Chipewyan) and George Drever (Cree interpreter)
Adhesion	17 July 1899	Smith's Landing	Chipewyan Indians of Slave River and thereabouts	Pierre Squirrel (chief), Michael Mamdrili, and William Kiscorray (headmen).	Commissioners James Hamilton Ross and James Andrew Joseph McKenna	John Trindle
Adhesion	4 August 1899	Fort McMurray	Chipewyan and Cree Indians of Fort McMurray	Adam Boucher (Chipewyan headman) and Seapotakinum Cree (Cree headman).	James Andrew Joseph McKenna (treaty commissioner)	Rev. Father Lacombe and T.M. Clarke
Adhesion	14 August 1899	Wapiscow Lake	Indians of Wapiscow	Joseph Kapasikonew (chief), Joseph Ansey (headman), Wapoose (headman), Michael Ansey (headman), and Louisa Beaver (headman)	James Hamilton Ross (treaty commissioner)	Alexander Kennedy
Adhesion	8 June 1900	Lesser Slave Lake	Cree Indians of Sturgeon Lake and country thereabouts	Meesookaminookapow, William Pakyutagweetum, Mukcoo Mooseos, Alexis Papasschay, and the Captain.	James Ansdell Macrae	Peter Gunn and Albert Tate
Adhesion	30 May 1900	Fort St John	Beaver Indians of the Upper Peace River	Muckithay, Aginaa, Dislisici, Tachea, Appan, Attachie, Allalie, and Yatsoose	James Ansdell Macrae (commissioner)	John Shaw

Table A11 (continued)

Document	Date Signed	Place	Aboriginal Peoples Involved	Aboriginal Signatories	Crown Representatives	Interpreter
Adhesion	23 June 1900	Vermillion	Slave Indians of Hay River	Alexis Tatatechay, Francois Tehatee, Giroux Nahdayyah, Koka, and Kachweesala	James Ansdell Macrae (commissioner)	Louis Cardinal
Adhesion	25 July 1900	Fort Resolution	Indians inhabiting the south shore of Great Slave Lake, between the mouth of Hay River and old Fort Reliance, and near the mouth of Lockheart's River (Dog Ribs, Yellow Knives, Chipewyans, and Slaves of Hay River)	For the Dog Ribs: Dried Geese (chief), Waymiah (headman), and Crapwatee (headman) For the Yellow Knives: Snuff (chief), Tzintu (headman), and Ateeten (headman) For Chipewyans: Louison Ah Thay (chief) and Oliver Ajericon For Slaves of Hay River: Sunrise (headman) and Lamelise (headman) For the Chipewyan: Vital [syllabics] Lamoëlle and Paulette [syllabics] Chandelle	James Ansdell Macrae (commissioner)	Rev. Father Dupirer, W.R. Norn, and A. Mercredi
Adhesion	15 August 1910	Fort Nelson	Slaves and Sicanees of Fort Nelson (BC)	Jimmie Badnie (chief) and Tommy Whitehead (headman)	Henry Anthony Conroy (commissioner), for His Majesty	Joseph Villeneuve

Table A12
Summary of Terms of Treaty 8, from the Original Document

Date signed	21 June 1899 (at Lesser Slave Lake), 1 July 1899 (at Peace River), and 8 July (at Vermillion)
Terms of treaty	"the said [Cree, Beaver, Chipewyan, and other] Indians DO HEREBY CEDE, RELEASE, SURRENDER, AND YIELD UP to the Government of the Dominion of Canada, for Her Majesty the Queen and Her successors forever all their rights, titles and privileges whatsoever, to the lands included within the following limits."
Amount of land involved	Document contains a description of treaty boundaries, but no area (in square miles) is given.
Reserves	"And her Majesty the Queen hereby agrees and undertakes to lay aside reserves for such bands as desire reserves, the same not to exceed in all one square mile for each family of five for such number of families as may elect to reside on reserves, or in that proportion for larger or smaller families; and for such families or individuals Indians as may prefer to live apart from band reserves, Her Majesty undertakes to provide land in severalty to the extent of 160 acres to each Indian … the Superintendent General of Indian Affairs shall depute and send a suitable person to determine and set apart such reserves and lands, after consulting with the Indians concerned as to the locality which may be found suitable and open for selection."
Presents	To show her satisfaction with the good conduct and behaviour of the Indians, and in extinguishment of all past claims, Her Majesty the Queen will give "each Chief a present of thirty-two dollars in cash, to each Headman twenty-two dollars, and to every other Indian of whatever age, of the families represented at the time and place of payment, twelve dollars."
Annuities	"Her Majesty also agrees that next year, and annually afterwards forever, she will cause to be paid to the said Indians in cash, at suitable places and dates, of which the Indians shall be duly notified, to each Chief twenty-five dollars, each Headman, not to exceed four to a large Band, and two to a small Band, fifteen dollars, and to every other Indian of whatever age five dollars, the same, unless there be some exceptional reason, to be paid only to heads of families for those belonging thereto."
Salary, clothing, medals, etc.	"each Chief, after signing the treaty, shall receive a silver medal and a suitable flag, and next year, and every third year thereafter, each Chief and Headman shall receive a suitable suit of clothing."

Table A12 (continued)

Articles for cultivation	"FURTHER, Her Majesty agrees to supply each Chief of a Band that selects a reserve, for the use of that Band, ten axes, five hand-saws, five augers, one grindstone, and the necessary files and whetstones. FURTHER, Her Majesty agrees that each Band that elects to take a reserve and cultivate the soil, shall ... receive two hoes, one spade, one scythe, and two hay forks for every family so settled, and for every three families one plough and one harrow, and to the Chief for the use of his Band two horses or a yoke of oxen, and for each Band, potatoes, barley, oats and wheat (if such seed be suited to the locality of the reserve), to plant the land actually broken up, and provisions for one month in the spring for several years while planting such seeds; and to every family one cow, and every Chief one bull, and one mowing machine and one reaper for the use of his Band when it is ready for them; for such families as prefer to raise stock instead of cultivating the soil, every family of five persons two cows, and every Chief two bulls and two mowing machines when ready for their use ... The aforesaid articles, machines and cattle to be given once for all for the encouragement of agriculture and stock raising; and for such bands as prefer to continue hunting and fishing, as much ammunition and twine for making nets annually, as will amount in value to one dollar per head of the families so engaged in hunting and fishing."
Education	"FURTHER, Her Majesty agrees to pay the salaries of such teachers to instruct the children of said Indians as to Her Majesty's Government of Canada may seem advisable"
Alcohol	NA
Hunting, trapping, and fishing	"And Her Majesty the QEEN HEREBY AGREES with the said Indians that they shall have right to pursue their usual vocations of hunting, trapping and fishing throughout the tract surrendered as hereintofore described, subject to such regulations as may from time to time be made by the Government of the country, acting under the authority of Her Majesty, and saving and excepting such tracts as may be required or taken up from time to time for settlement, mining, lumbering, trading or other purposes."
Medical provisions	NA
Adherence to treaty and policing	"And the undersigned Cree, Beaver, Chipewyan and other Indian Chiefs and Headmen [and those they represent] ... DO HEREBY SOLEMNLY PROMISE and engage to strictly observe this Treaty ... THEY PROMISE AND ENGAGE that they will, in all respects, obey and abide by the law: that they will maintain peace ... and that they will assist the officers of Her Majesty in bringing to justice and punishment any Indian offending against the stipulations of this Treaty, or infringing the laws in force in the country so ceded."

Table A13
Basic Data for Treaty 10, from Original Documents

Document	Date Signed	Place	Aboriginal Peoples Involved	Aboriginal Signatories	Crown Representatives	Interpreter
Treaty No. 10	28 August 1906	Ile à la Crosse	Chipweyan, Cree, and other Indians (English River band, Clear Lake band, and Canoe Lake band).	At Ile à la Crosse: William Apisis (chief of English River band), Joseph Gun (headman), and Jean Baptiste Estralsheen (headman); and Rapheal Bedshidekkge (chief of Clear Lake Band)	J.A.J. McKenna (Indian commissioner)	At Ile à la Crosse: Magloire Maurice
	19 September 1906	Canoe Lake		At Canoe Lake: John Iron (chief of Canoe Lake band), Baptiste Iron (headman), and Jerome Couilloneur (headman)		At Canoe Lake: Archie Park
Treaty No. 10[1]	19 August 1907	Lac du Brochet	Chipewyan, Cree, and other Indians (Barren land band and Hatchet Lake band)	19 August 1907: Peter Casimir (chief of Barren Land band), Jean Baptiste (headman of Barren Land band), and Andre Antsasen (Indian of Barren Land band)	Thomas Alexander Borthwick (Indian commissioner)	August 19: A. Turquetil and Charles La Violette
	22 August 1907			22 August 1907: Thomas Benaouni (chief of Hatchet Lake band), and Pierre Aze (headman of Hatchet Lake band).		August 22: E.S. Turquetil[2]

1 This document had its own treaty text and was not listed as an adhesion.
2 The names of interpreters were very difficult to decipher from the original document. These spellings are from the DIAND publication of Treaty 10.

Table A14
Summary of Terms of Treaty 10 (1906), from the Original Document

Date signed	28 August 1906 (Ile à la Crosse), 19 September 1906 (Canoe Lake)
Terms of treaty	"Now therefore the said [Chipewyan, Crees and other] Indians do hereby cede, release, surrender and yield up to the Government of the Dominion of Canada for His Majesty the King and His successors for ever all their rights, titles and privileges whatsoever to the lands included within the following limits."
Amount of land involved	85,800 square miles lying east of Treaty No. 8 and north of Treaties No. 5 and 6 (and the addition to Treaty no. 6) and contained within Saskatchewan and Alberta.
Reserves	"And His Majesty the King hereby agrees and undertakes to lay aside reserves of land for such bands as desire the same, such reserves not to exceed in all one square mile for each family of five for such number of families as may elect to reside upon reserves or in that proportion for larger or smaller families; and for such Indian families or individual Indians as prefer to live apart from band reserves His Majesty undertakes to provide land in severalty to the extent of one hundred and sixty (160) acres for each Indian … the Superintendent General of Indian Affairs shall depute and send a suitable person to determine and set apart such reserves and lands, after consulting with the Indians concerned as to the locality which may be found suitable and open for selection."
Presents	To show his satisfaction with the good conduct and behaviour of the Indians, and in extinguishment of all past claims, His Majesty the King will give "each chief a present of thirty-two (32) dollars in cash, to each Headman twenty-two (22) dollars and to every other Indian of whatever age of the families represented at the time and place of payment twelve (12) dollars."
Annuities	"His Majesty also agrees that next year and annually thereafter for ever He will cause to be paid to the Indians in cash, at suitable places and dates of which the said Indians shall be duly notified, to each chief twenty-five (25) dollars, each Headman fifteen (15) dollars and to every other Indian of whatever age five (5) dollars."
Salary, clothing, medals, etc.	"each Chief, after signing the Treaty shall receive a silver medal and a suitable flag, and next year, and every third year thereafter each Chief shall receive a suitable suit of clothing, and that after signing the Treaty each Headman shall receive a bronze medal and next year and every third year thereafter a suitable suit of clothing."
Articles for cultivation	"Further, His Majesty agrees to furnish such assistance as may be found necessary or advisable to aid and assist the Indians in agriculture or stock raising or other work and to make such a distribution of twine and ammunition to them annually as is usually made to Indians similarly situated."
Education	"Further, His Majesty agrees to make such provisions as may from time to time be deemed advisable for the education of the Indian children."
Alcohol	NA

Table A14 (continued)

Hunting, trapping, and fishing	"And His Majesty the King hereby agrees with the said Indians that they shall have the right to pursue their usual vocations of hunting, trapping and fishing throughout the territory surrendered as heretofore described, subject to such regulations as may from time to time be made by the Government of the country acting under the authority of His Majesty and saving and excepting such tracts as may be required or as may be taken up from time to time for settlement, mining, lumbering, trading or other purposes."
Medical and other provisions	NA
Adherence to treaty and policing	"And the undersigned Chipewyan, Cree and other Indian Chiefs and Headmen [and those they represent] … do hereby solemnly promise and engage to strictly observe this treaty in all and every respect … They promise and engage that they will in all respects obey and abide by the law; that they will maintain peace … and that they will assist the officers of His Majesty in bringing to justice and punishment any Indian offending against the stipulations of this treaty or infringing the law in force in the country so ceded."

Table A15
Summary of Terms of Treaty 10 (1907), from the Original Document

Date signed	19 August 1907 (Barren Land band), 22 August 1907 (Hatchet Lake Band) at Lac du Brochet
Terms of treaty	"NOW THEREFORE the said [Chipewyan, Crees and other] Indians do hereby cede, release, surrender and yield up to the Government of the Dominion of Canada, for His Majesty the King and His successors for ever all their rights, titles and privileges whatsoever to the lands included within the following limits."
Amount of land involved	85,800 square miles lying east of Treaty No. 8 and north of Treaties No. 5 and 6 (and the addition to Treaty no. 6) and contained within Saskatchewan and Alberta.
Reserves	"AND His Majesty the King hereby agrees and undertakes to lay aside reserves of land for such bands as desire the same, such reserves not to exceed in all one square mile for each family of five for such number of families as may elect to reside upon reserves or in that proportion for larger or smaller families; and for such Indian families or individual Indians as prefer to live apart from band reserves His Majesty undertakes to provide land in severalty to the extent of one hundred and sixty (160) acres for each Indian … the Superintendent General of Indian Affairs shall depute and send a suitable person to determine and set apart such reserves and lands, after consulting with the Indians concerned as to the locality which may be found suitable and open for selection."
Presents	To show his satisfaction with the good conduct and behaviour of the Indians, and in extinguishment of all past claims, His Majesty the King will give "each Chief a present of thirty-two (32) dollars in cash, to each Headman twenty-two (22) dollars and to every other Indian of whatever age of the families represented at the time and place of payment twelve (12) dollars."
Annuities	"His Majesty also agrees that next year and annually thereafter for ever He will cause to be paid to the Indians in cash, at suitable places and dates of which the said Indians shall be duly notified, to each Chief Twenty-five (25) dollars, each Headman fifteen (15) dollars and to every other Indian of whatever age Five (5) dollars."
Salary, clothing, medals, etc.	"each Chief, after signing the Treaty shall receive a silver medal and a suitable flag, and next year and every third year thereafter each Chief shall receive a suitable suit of clothing, and that after signing the Treaty each Headman shall receive a bronze medal and next year and every third year thereafter a suitable suit of clothing."
Articles for cultivation	"Further, His Majesty agrees to furnish such assistance as may be found necessary or advisable to aid and assist the Indians in agriculture or stock raising or other work and to make such a distribution of twine and ammunition to them annually as is usually made to Indians similarly situated."
Education	"Further His Majesty agrees to make such provision as may from time to time be deemed advisable for the education of the Indian children."
Alcohol	NA

Table A15 (*continued*)

Hunting, trapping, and fishing	"AND His Majesty the King hereby agrees with the said Indians that they shall have the right to pursue their usual vocations of hunting, trapping and fishing throughout the territory surrendered as heretofore described, subject to such regulations as may from time to time be made by the Government of the country acting under the authority of His Majesty and saving and excepting such tracts as may be required or as may be taken up from time to time for settlement, mining, lumbering, trading or other purposes."
Medical and other provisions	NA
Adherence to treaty and policing	"And the undersigned Chipewyan, Cree and other Indian Chiefs and Headmen [and those they represent] … do hereby solemnly promise and engage to strictly observe this Treaty in all and every respect … They promise and engage that they will in all respects obey and abide by the law: that they will maintain peace … and that they will assist the officers of His Majesty in bringing to justice and punishment any Indian offending against the stipulations of this treaty or infringing the law in force in the country so ceded."

NOTES

INTRODUCTION

1 Tobias, "Canada's Subjugation of the Plains Cree"; Stonechild, "The Indian View of the 1885 Uprising"; Stonechild and Waiser, *Loyal Till Death*.
2 Friesen, "Magnificent Gifts"; "Give Me Wherewith to Make My Living."
3 Price et al., *Spirit of the Alberta Treaties*; Treaty 7 Tribal Elders, et al., *Treaty 7*.

CHAPTER ONE

1 This chapter draws heavily on Ray, "Economic Background to Treaty 6."
2 Rich, *Copy-Book of Letters*, 9 (emphasis added).
3 Ibid., 13 (emphasis added). "Forreign" in this instance referred to the French.
4 Ibid., 36 (emphasis added).
5 Ibid., 46. When Henry Sergeant replaced Nixon in the spring of 1683, he too received these orders.
6 Rich, *Isham's Observations*; Williams, *Graham's Observations*.
7 Williams, *Graham's Observations*, 316.
8 Ibid.
9 Ibid., 317.
10 Ibid.
11 Ibid., 370.
12 Ray, "The Factor and the Trading Captain."
13 Williams, *Graham's Observations*, 317–18.
14 Ibid., 318.
15 Ibid., 319.
16 Ibid., 320.
17 Ibid., 321.
18 Ibid., 321–2.
19 Cited in Stevenson, "Red River Mission," 189.
20 Francis and Morantz, *Partners in Furs*, 50–3.
21 There were, of course, instances when officers refused to provide aid. This issue was discussed during a 1749 investigation of HBC trading practices by a select committee of

Parliament. Witnesses who appeared, mostly former company servants (some of whom were disgruntled with their former employer), reported that governors occasionally physically abused their clients and sometimes refused food to those in need. Aboriginal people so offended often did not return.

22 This attitude prevailed into the twentieth century. See Ray, *Canadian Fur Trade*, 105–6.

23 Ray, "Periodic Shortages."

24 Ray, *Indians in the Fur Trade*, 141.

25 For an extended discussion of this subject see, Ray, "The Factor and the Trading Captain."

26 Provincial Archives of Manitoba, Hudson's Bay Company Archives, D.4/85, Correspondence Outward, fol. 16 (hereafter referred to as HBCA).

27 Ray, *Indians in the Fur Trade*, 197.

28 The negative impact of the fur trade during this era has received a great deal of attention. See, for example, Ray, *Indians in the Fur Trade*, 124–81; Morton, *History of the Canadian West*, 421–622.

29 These inquiries were related to the renewal of the company's license in 1838 and the renewal that was due in 1859. See Parliamentary Select Committee on Hudson's Bay Company, 1837, Minutes of Evidence E.18/3–5.

30 HBCA, E.18/4, fols. 30–1.

31 Cowie, *Company of Adventurers*, 272.

32 HBCA, E.18/4, fol. 129. Simpson's replies, of course, were intended to present the company, and his management, in the best possible light.

33 Ibid., fol. 131.

34 Ibid.

35 The administration of justice and the alcohol trade received a lot of attention.

36 HBCA, E.18/5, fol. 145.

37 Ray, *Canadian Fur Trade*, 199–221.

38 HBCA, E.18/5, fol. 20–1.

39 In fact, beads had always been an article of trade and still were. Traders did include them among gifts also.

40 HBCA, E.18/5, fol. 21.

41 The chairman was referring to a barter fur trading territory beyond the area of colonial settlement.

42 HBCA, E.18/5, fol. 24.

43 Concerned as the committee was about the welfare of Aboriginal people, it was not prepared to have the fur trade block the expansion of the agricultural and other development frontiers.

44 HBCA, A.11/100, Graham, Cyril (Sir), "Untitled Report to Sir Stafford Northcote," 15 March 1871, fols. 68–91.

45 Cowie, *Company of Adventurers*, 42–3.

CHAPTER TWO

1 Roy C. Dalton, "William Bacheler Coltman," *Dictionary of Canadian biography (DCB)*, vol. 6, 166–8.

2 PAM, MG2 A1, Selkirk Papers, M Series, vol. 11 (reel M174), Selkirk to Coltman, 12 July 1817, 3738.

3 Ibid., Selkirk to Coltman, 14 July 1817, 3777–8.

4 Ibid., Coltman to Selkirk, 16 July 1817, 3803.

5 Ibid., Selkirk to Coltman, 16 or 17 July 1817, 3807.

6 Ibid., Selkirk to Coltman, 17 July 1817, 3809–10.

7 Ibid., 3810.

8 Ibid.

9 Ibid., 3810–11.

10 Ibid., Coltman to Selkirk (17 July 1817), 3812–13. He added, "I shall take care & get the sentiments of the Indians on this & all other subjects faithfully recorded, but have some doubts of the propriety of my taking part in any deed of Sale; on this point I will reflect and will at all events send to your Lordship before the Indians leave me & communicate to any Agent you may send what they say & my own ideas."

11 Ibid., 3814.

12 Ibid.

13 Ibid., Coltman to Selkirk (18 July 1817), 3818.

14 Ibid., 3818–19.

15 Confidential report of W.B. Coltman to Lieutenant-General Sir John C. Sherbrooke, Quebec, 20 May 1818, dispatched to Earl Bathurst by Sherbrooke, 1 July 1818, as "A General Statement and Report Relative to the Disturbances in the Indian Territories of British North America, by W.B. Coltman, Special Commissioner for Inquiring into the Offences Committed in the Said Indian Territories, and the Circumstances Attending the Same," Great Britain, *Papers Relating to the Red River Settlement* (1819). A manuscript copy of Coltman's report can be found in NA, MG11, Colonial Office records, Governor Sir J.C. Sherbrooke, 1818, Q Series, vol. 148, part 2, 551–66.

16 The original copy is located in NA, RG10, vol. 1846, IT 257, Selkirk Treaty (18 July 1817) (hereafter Selkirk Treaty). Morris also published the Selkirk Treaty, Morris, *Treaties of Canada*, 298–300. A copy can be found in PAM, MG2 A1, Lord Selkirk Papers, M Series, vol. 11 (Reel M 174), 3824–5.

17 Morris, *Treaties of Canada*, 15.

18 "Selkirk Treaty," in Morris, *Treaties of Canada*, 299. It should be noted that the copy of the original treaty in the National Archives of Canada omits the phrase "to have and to hold forever the said tract of land."

19 Ibid.

20 Peguis (Begouais, Begwais, Pegeois, Pegouisse, Pegowis, Peggas, Pigewis, Pigwys, also know as the Destroyer and Little Chip, baptized William King), ca. 1774–1864, was a Saulteaux Indian chief. In "1817 he was one of five Saulteaux and Cree chiefs who signed a treaty with Lord Selkirk to provide land for settlement purposes." Following the transfer of Rupertsland, his son Miskookeenew (Red Eagle, or Henry Prince) negotiated Treaty 1 in 1871. See Hugh A. Dempsey, "Peguis," in *DCB*, vol. 9.

21 PAM, MG2 A1, Selkirk papers, M series, vol. 14 (reel M175), Matthay to Selkirk, 12 September 1818, 5371. Similarly, Alexander MacDonell wrote, "Dalcour with Six Roll of Tobacco arrived four days ago at Pembina from point meuron [*sic*] and I shall be able to pay his quit Rent Tobacco to Peguish [Chief Peguis] and the Robnou also." Ibid., vol. 13 (reel M175), MacDonell to Selkirk (27 December 1817), 4274.

22 Ibid., vol. 14 (Reel M175), Graham to Selkirk, 13 September 1818, 5382.

23 Ibid., vol. 13 (Reel M175), MacDonell to Selkirk, 27 December 1817, 4275.

24 HBCA, B.22/e/1, Brandon House District Report, 1819.

25 It seems that the medal and chieftainship were associated. Morris reported: "The original Chief of the Portage band was Peequahkeequah, who was a party to the treaty with Lord Selkirk. On his death he was succeeded by his son, who died some years ago, leaving a boy, who has now grown up … Another rose and produced Pee-quah-pee-quah's King George medal, and said the chief had placed it in his keeping and charged him to deliver it to his sons, when he was old enough to be chief, and then placed it round the neck of Kee-kee-maquah, or the Short bear. They then asked that I should receive him as chief, in place of Yellow Quill." Morris to the minister of the Interior, 2 August 1875, in Morris, *Treaties*, 135.

26 Morton, *Manitoba*, 105.

27 Ibid., 116. Apparently this included land east of Rat River and between Lake Manitoba and the Assiniboine River.

28 PAM, MG12 A1, Box 1, Sir Adams George Archibald Papers, reel 1, no. 155, Archibald to Howe, 20 December 1870. When it came time for the Treaty 1 negotiations, Archibald made sure that the talks began with a formal recognition of chiefs. Archibald reported in 1871, "At the time of the treaty with the Earl of Selkirk, certain Indians signed as Chiefs and representatives of their people. Some of the Indians now deny that these men ever were Chiefs or had the authority to sign the treaty." Archibald's report to Howe (29 July 1871), in Morris, *Treaties*, 33.

29 At the Treaty 1 talks, Chief Henry Prince stated, "Whatever I do, I do it for all the Indians. I have done it always for all the Indians ever since my father [Chief Peguis] spoke for them (at Lord Selkirk's treaty)." *Manitoban*, 12 August 1871.

30 PAM, MG12 A1, Archibald Papers, reel 1, no. 155, Archibald to Howe, 20 December 1870.

31 Ibid., reel 1, no. 176, Molyneux St John to Archibald, 17 January 1871.

32 On the question of reserves during the Treaty 1 talks, Kamatwakanasnin pointed out that "The Indians wish to hold the Selkirk Reserve [St Peters] as one of the number." *Manitoban*, 12 August 1871.

CHAPTER THREE

1 A secondary source regarding the early eastern treaties is Allen's *Indian Allies*.

2 Morse, *Aboriginal Peoples*, 52, 56. See also Canada, Royal Commission on Aboriginal Peoples, *Report*, vol. 1, 111–19. (Hereafter RCAP, *Report 1*.)

3 For the background of the proclamation see Barck and Lefler, *Colonial America*, 470–5. For Pontiac's War, see Schmalz, *Ojibwa of Southern Ontario*, chap. 4, "The Beaver War," 63–84.

4 Borrows, "Wampum at Niagara," 155–72, 256–67, especially 161–5.

5 Ibid., 155. A similar interpretation is found in "From the Anishnabek, the Ojibway, Ottawa, Potowatomi and Algonquin Nations to the Parliament of the Dominion of Canada," *Ontario Indian* 3 (12), December, 1980: 18–27. We are indebted to Bill Waiser who produced a copy of this item for us.

6 Morse, *Aboriginal Peoples*, 52–4.

7 The standard source is Surtees, "Indian Land Cessions in Ontario." See also Canada, *Indian Treaties and Surrenders*.

8 Morse, *Aboriginal Peoples and the Law*, 56; Hamilton and Sinclair, *Report of the Aboriginal Justice Inquiry of Manitoba* vol. 1, 120–1.

9 Substantial portions of this section are abstracted from Ray, "Economic History of the Robinson Treaties Area."

10 This phase of the local economic history is discussed by Newell, *Technology on the Frontier*, 59–69.

11 This issue arose when Canada sent Alexander Vidal to the region in 1849 to survey the area in preparation for a possible treaty. While he was at Sault Ste Marie the issue of the HBC's post arose. William Mactavish, who was in charge of the post, described Vidal's talks with local Natives. See the second paragraph of the extract of Mactavish's description of the meeting with the Lake Superior Ojibwa (page 40) for his observations. HBCA, D.5/26, Simpson Correspondence Inward, fol. 299.

12 Government agents T. G. Anderson and Alexander Vidal reported that Macdonnell had obtained leases to nine tracts already granted by the government. See Archives of Ontario, F 1027–1–2, T. G. Anderson and Alexander Vidal, "Report to His Excellency, the Governor-General in Council, Toronto, 5 December 1849," 8 (hereafter referred to as OA, F 1027–1–2, Anderson and Vidal Report).

13 Hansen, "'Half-breed' Rolls," 161–70.

14 Newell, *Technology on the Frontier*, 63.

15 The standard reference on the treaty is Surtees, *Robinson Treaties*. This work does not explore the economic motives for making the treaty, apart from the issue of compensation for title, nor does it take into account the HBC records pertaining to this accord. See also Chute, *Legacy of Shigwaukonse*, 108–45.

16 Surtees, *Robinson Treaties*, 6.

17 HBCA, D.5/26, Simpson Correspondence Inward, fol. 444.

18 Ibid., fol. 547.

19 Ibid., fol. 692.

20 MacTavish expressed his doubt to Simpson on 14 February 1850: "they talk here [Sault Ste Marie] of 2000 Indians coming down in Spring from up the Country, some of them from Saskatchewan. I fancy they will also have an auxiliary of Esquimaux." HBCA, D.5/27, Simpson Correspondence Inward (14 February 1850), fol. 283.

21 Ibid. (29 January 1850), fol. 171 (emphasis in the original).

22 William Benjamin Robinson, 1797–1873, was known as "'one of the chief Indian traders throughout northern Ontario, a most intelligent and well-informed gentleman,' and his reputation for fair dealing gave him a position of influence among the Indians." In 1844 he negotiated the first of the Robinson Treaties in which several hundred acres of the district of Simcoe were "set aside to be held in trust for the use of the Chippewa Tribe of Lake Simcoe." Their chief, William Yellowhead, was a signatory. In 1850 Robinson was commissioned to negotiate for lands in the vicinity of Lakes Superior and Huron. The Robinson Treaties were used as models and contained an "escalator clause" to increase annuity payments when the value of the land increased. See Julia Jarvis, "William Benjamin Robinson," *DCB*, vol. 10, 622–3.

23 Surtees, *Robinson Treaties*.

24 OA, F 1027–1–2, Anderson and Vidal Report, 7.

25 Ibid., 12.

26 Vidal, *Mission to the Indians*, 1 (emphasis in original).

27 Ibid., 25.

28 Ibid., 7.

29 HBCA, D.5/26, Simpson Correspondence Inward, fol. 76.

30 Ibid., fol. 288.

31 Ibid.

32 Ibid. (17 October 1849), fol. 299.

33 OA, F 1027–1–2, Anderson and Vidal Report, 7.

34 Ibid., 8.

35 Ibid., 9.

36 Report by Robinson (24 September 1850), in Morris, *Treaties of Canada*, 17 (emphasis added).

37 Ibid., 19.

38 The Robinson Huron Treaty, copy in Morris, *Treaties of Canada*, 306.

CHAPTER FOUR

1 For a more detailed analysis of this topic see Tough, "Aboriginal Rights." See also Narvey, "The Royal Proclamation"; McNeil, "Native Rights"; "Native Claims."

2 Indian opposition to the terms of the transfer was expressed during Treaty 3 and Treaty 4 talks. See Morris, *Treaties of Canada*, 73, 99–106.

3 The Royal Charter, Oliver, *Canadian North-West*, 137. The charter made several references to the Company's proprietary rights to the lands in the Hudson's Bay basin and was repetitious on this point, stating, "WE HAVE given ... together with all the lands and territories upon" the basin and made the company "the true and absolute lords and proprietors of the same territory" and, again, "TO HAVE, HOLD, possess and enjoy the said territory." It granted resource rights, such as "the fishing of all sorts of fish, whales, sturgeons, and all the other royal fishes in the seas, bays, inlets and rivers within the premises, and the fish therein taken, together with the royalty of the sea upon the coasts within the limits aforesaid, and all mines royal, as well discovered as not discovered, of gold, silver, gems and precious stones." Furthermore, the Charter granted to the HBC "all lands, islands, territories, plantations, forts, fortifications, factories or colonies, where the said Company's factories and trade are or shall be." The Royal Charter, Oliver, *Canadian North-West*, 143–44, 149.

4 Specifically, the charter stated that the shareholders and the successors had "the sole trade and commerce of all those seas, straits, bays, rivers, lakes, creeks and sounds, in whatsoever latitude they shall be, that lie within the entrance of the straits, commonly called Hudson's Straits, together with all the lands, countries and territories upon the coasts and confines of the seas, straits, bays, lakes, rivers, creeks and sounds aforesaid, which are not now actually possessed by any of our subjects, or by the subjects of any other Christian Prince or State." The Royal Charter, in Oliver, *Canadian North-West*, 136.

5 This was a prairie/parkland belt that was deemed to have adequate moisture for agriculture. The area south of the fertile belt was thought to be too arid.

6 Rich, *Hudson's Bay Company*, 826.

7 Galbraith, "The HBC under Fire," 333.

8 Rich, *Hudson's Bay Company*, 832.

9 For details, see Mitchell, "Edward Watkin"; Rich, *Hudson's Bay Company*, 816–49.

10 "Report of Delegates Appointed to Negotiate for the Acquisition of Rupert's Land and the North-West Territory" (hereafter, Delegate's Report) (Cartier and MacDougall to Rogers, 8 February 1869), 19.

11 Ibid.

12 Rich, *Hudson's Bay Company*, 841; for details concerning implications of the failure to realize quick profits on colonization schemes, see Ray, *Canadian Fur Trade*, 3–17.

13 Rich, *Hudson's Bay Company*, 848.

14 Hargrave, *Red River*, 299.

15 For details of the negotiations, see Rich, *Hudson's Bay Company*, passim.

16 Section 146, British North America Act, 1867, copy in Oliver, *Canadian North-West*, 871.

17 "Address to Her Majesty the Queen from the Senate and House of Commons of the Dominion of Canada," 16 and 17 December 1867, Oliver, *Canadian North-West*, 945.

18 Ibid.

19 Rupert's Land Act, 1868, (U.K.) c. 105; copy in Oliver, *Canadian North-West*, 937.

20 Delegate's Report (Cartier and MacDougall to Rogers, 8 February 1869), 23–5.

21 Ibid., 26. This calculation was based on the difference between the purchase price of the old HBC stock and inventory, carried out at the time of the sale of the company assets (other than the territorial claim).

22 Delegate's Report (Granville to Northcote, 9 March 1869), 32. The terms also defined the fertile belt and disposed of some of the telegraph material the company had purchased. This memorandum also provided that the HBC would retain posts in the North Western Territory; it made a number of provisions for the company's land around its posts; it allowed the company to defer selected land in townships; and it allowed Canada to charge for surveying company land.

23 Term 8 of the agreement stated, "It is understood that any claims of Indians to compensation for lands required for purposes of settlement shall be disposed of by the Canadian Government, in communication with the Imperial Government, and that the Company shall be relieved of all responsibility in respect of them." Memorandum, "Details of Agreement between the Delegates of the Government of the Dominion, and the Directors of the HBC," 22 March 1869, copy in Oliver, *Canadian North-West*, 950.

24 HBCA, A.13/16/4, Rogers to Northcote (17 April 1869), fol. 292. The memorandum of March 29 allowed the company to select lots in townships adjacent to the north bank of the North Saskatchewan River and made it possible for the Canadian government to expropriate for public purposes land allocated to the company.

25 Rupertsland Order, copy in Oliver, *Canadian North-West*, 941–4.

26 HBCA, A.13/16/4, Northcote to Rogers, 10 April 1869, fol. 207. There was considerable opposition from shareholders, who had invested £2,000,000, to a deal that returned only £300,000 and some vague prospects about potential returns from future land sales. Ray, "Adventures at the Crossroads."

27 Rupertsland Order, Oliver, *Canadian North-West*, 959.

28 Important documents are scheduled with the Rupertsland Order: "Address to Her Majesty the Queen from the Senate and House of Commons of the Dominion of Canada," 16 and 17 December 1867 (hereafter Address of 1867), the "Address from the Senate and House of Commons," 29 and 31 May 1869 (hereafter Address of 1869), term 14 of the draft of

surrender, which is synonymous with the HBC's Deed of Surrender, and term 8 of the "Memorandum of the Details of Agreement between the Delegates of the Government of the Dominion and the Directors of the HBC," 22 March 1869 (hereafter Memorandum of 22 March 1869). The "Order of Her Majesty in Council admitting Rupert's Land and the North-Western Territory into the Union," 23 June 1870, is printed in Oliver, *Canadian North-West*, 939–63. A handwritten manuscript of the Rupertsland Order can be found in the HBCA, A.13/16/5; a galley proof of this address can also be found in A.13/16/5. A printed copy of this address can be found in HBCA, A.12/L 121/1. See also Canada, Sessional Papers, 1869, no. 25, Delegate's Report, i–ii, 1–39.

29 Address of 1867, Oliver, *Canadian North-West*, 946.

30 Delegate's Report (Cartier and MacDougall to Rogers, 8 February 1869), 17.

31 Ibid. (Granville to Governor General of Canada, Sir John Young, 10 April 1869), 38.

32 Ibid.

33 Ibid.

34 Address of 1869, Oliver, *Canadian North-West*, 954.

35 HBCA, RG2/2/109, fol. 14.

36 For copies of these drafts see HBCA, A.13/16/3, fols. 206–7.

37 See the Company's position in NA, RG10, vol. 3708, file 19,502, pt. 1. The shift in responsibility from the HBC to the Canadian government is discussed in Tough, "Buying Out the Bay," 398–408.

38 The *Manitoba Act*, 1870, S.C., c. 3, s. 4. Reprinted in Revised Statutes of Canada, 1985, App. 8. Since 1982 the *Manitoba Act* has been known as the *Constitution Act*, 1870.

39 NA, Records of the Department of Public Works, RG11, vol. 265, S.J. Dawson, report to government, 1864; quoted in RCAP, Report 1, 165. Dawson (1818–1902) was a negotiator preliminary to Treaty 3 concluded with the Saulteaux of Lake of the Woods. He supported Indian fishing rights and his support of Aboriginal peoples was apparent through his interventions on their behalf. He was a surveyor, engineer, office holder, and politician. See Elizabeth Arthur, "Dawson, Simon James," DCB, vol. 13, 261–2.

40 NA, RG11, vol. 265, report to government 1869; quoted in RCAP, Report 1, 165.

41 Friesen, *Canadian Prairies*, 137–8.

42 The *Manitoba Act*, 1870, S.C., c. 3, s. 31.

43 Ibid.

44 Parl. Deb., 3d session, 1st Parl. (1870), vol. 1 (House of Commons, 2 May 1870), 1292–3. Later in the process, but prior to third reading of the bill, the Métis allotment was increased to 1.4 million acres (see 1354). Macdonald's allusion to two miles on each side of the Red River and the Assinboine was a reference to the Selkirk Treaty (1817).

45 Parl. Deb. (4 May 1870), 1353. Macdonald, like some later historians, was confused about the identity of the First Nation dwelling east of "96 degrees." The First Nation in the region at this time was part of the Ojibwa, an Anicinabe people. "Sioux Indians," to return to Macdonald's words, did not negotiate treaties with Canada in the nineteenth century because of the federal government's opposition. Morton, *Birth of a Province*, 201.

46 MacKay, *Honourable Company*, 349.

47 HBCA, A.12/L 77; A.86/1–11; and RG1, series 1. This figure is derived from annual data between 1891/92 and 1930/31. It is based on balance statements showing net revenue, deposits to the capital reserves, and net profits.

1 Secondary sources on Treaties 1, 2, and 3 include Friesen, "Magnificent Gifts"; "Grant Me Wherewith to Make My Living"; Hall "Treaty 1 Revisited"; Daugherty, *Treaty 3*; McNab, Administration of Treaty 3.

2 Morris, *Treaties of Canada*, 45. In fact, Treaty 3 was significant to Treaties 1 and 2, since the three-dollar annuity for these treaties was raised to five dollars, the same basis as Treaty 3.

3 Official Dispatch, Simpson (3 November 1871), in Morris, *Treaties of Canada*, 41.

4 Ibid., 42.

5 Morris, *Treaties of Canada*: Treaty 1, 313–14; Treaty 2, 316–20; Treaty 3, 320–29.

6 Sir Adams George Archibald (1814–92) had a successful career as a lawyer and politician who favoured Confederation, prior to being appointed first lieutenant-governor of Manitoba in 1870. He was involved in the negotiation of Treaties 1 and 2 and attempted to deal with Indian complaints about the provision of farm supplies. See K.G. Pryke, "Sir Adams George Archibald," *DCB*, vol. 12, 30–6.

7 Alexander Morris (1826–89) was a lawyer, judge, businessman, politician, and public servant. As lieutenant-governor of the NWT and Manitoba, 1872–76, he negotiated and signed Treaty 3 in 1873, Treaty 4 in 1874, Treaty 5 in 1875, and Treaty 6 in 1876. He was also responsible for revisions to Treaty 1 and Treaty 2. After he had successfully negotiated Treaty 3, it became "the prototype for those that followed." See Jean Friesen, "Alexander Morris," *DCB*, vol. 11, 608–14. Joseph Albert Provencher (Villebrun, Provencher) (1843–87) was a lawyer, journalist, and public servant. In 1869 he acted as secretary to William McDougall, who had been named lieutenant-governor of the NWT. In 1871 he became immigration commissioner in Manitoba, and in 1873 he became a commissioner of the Department of Indian Affairs. He served on the Treaty Commission that negotiated Treaty 3. See Kenneth Landry, "Joseph Albert Provencher," *DCB*, vol. 11, 716–17.

8 James McKay (1828–79), a fur trader, guide, and politician, had facility in Indian and Métis languages. He served both as a negotiator and interpreter at the negotiations of Treaties 1, 2, 3, 5, and 6. Alexander Morris stated that McKay "possessed large influence over the Indian tribes, which he always used for the benefit and the advantage of the government." In Treaty 6, McKay along with other commissioners accorded "additional benefits to the Indians including... medical supplies and for assistance in times of epidemic and general famine." See Allan R. Turner, "James McKay,"*DCB*, vol. 10, 473–4. Charles Nolin (1837–1907), Métis farmer, fur trader, and politician, acted as interpreter for Lieutenant Governor Morris during the Treaty 3 negotiations with the Ojibwa in 1873. See Diane Payment, "Charles Nolin," *DCB*, vol. 13, 807.

9 Morris, *Treaties of Canada*, 322. For the original manuscript copy of Treaty 3, see RG10, vol. 13, IT 266.

10 Morris, *Treaties of Canada*, 323.

11 Ibid.

12 Ibid., 339.

13 For an account of the transition in 1870, see Ray, *Canadian Fur Trade*, 1–29.

14 HBCA, A.2/18, London Minutes Books–General Courts and Proprietors, 1821, fol. 16.

15 Ibid.

16 Morris, *Treaties of Canada*, 16.

17 Canada, *Sessional Papers*, 1874, Annual Report of Indian Affairs, Paper no. 17, 5 (hereafter all annual reports on Indian Affairs published in the Sessional Papers, will be CSP, Indian Affairs).

18 CSP, 1872, Indian Affairs, no. 22, 6.

19 Ibid., 17.

20 Instructions issued to Hon. Wm McDougall, as lieutenant-governor of the North-West Territories, September 28, 1869. Copy in Oliver, *Canadian North-West*, 879. The actions of Louis Riel precluded McDougall from fulfilling his duties as lieutenant-governor.

21 Commission issued to Donald A. Smith, appointing him special commissioner, 17 December 1869, ibid., 908.

22 Instructions issued to Lieutenant-Governor Archibald, 4 August 1879. Oliver, *Canadian North-West*, 974.

23 CSP, 1872, Indian Affairs, no. 22, 4.

24 PAM MG12 A1, Archibald Papers, reel 1, no. 153, Dawson Memorandum (19 December 1870).

25 CSP, 1872, Indian Affairs, no. 22, 6.

26 Ibid. On the treaty, Pether's name is spelled Pither.

27 Morris, *Treaties of Canada*, 25.

28 Morris to the Minister of the Interior, 2 August 1875, in Morris, *Treaties of Canada*, 138.

29 Hall, "Treaty 1 Revisited," 337.

30 CSP, 1872, Indian Affairs, no. 22, 11.

31 Ibid.

32 Ibid., 6.

33 Morris, *Treaties of Canada*, 46.

34 CSP, 1876, Indian Affairs, no. 9, xxxiv.

35 PAM, MG12 B1, Alexander Morris Papers, Reel 2, no. 1003, D. Laird to Morris (7 July 1875).

36 Ibid., no. 668, Reverend E.R. Young to Morris, 18 March 1874.

37 CSP, 1872, Indian Affairs, no. 22, 12.

38 Ibid., 13.

39 Ibid., 4. Simpson obtained a uniform with his commission as lieutenant-colonel of the Regimental Division of Algoma.

40 Offical Dispatch, Morris, 14 October 1873, in Morris, *Treaties of Canada*, 47.

41 *Manitoban*, 12 August 1871.

42 CSP, 1872, Indian Affairs, no. 22, 14.

43 Ibid., 16.

44 Ibid., 16–17.

45 Ibid., 17.

46 Ibid., 16.

47 Ibid., 31.

48 Ibid., 15.

49 Ibid., 28.

50 *Manitoban*, 11 October 1873.

51 Ibid.

52 Even before the talks had commenced, he observed: "The principal cause of the delay was divisions and jealousies among themselves. The nation had not met for many years, and some of them had never before been assembled together. They were very jealous of each other, and dreaded any of the Chiefs having individual communication with me, to prevent which they had guards on the approaches to my house and Mr. Dawson's tent." Official Dispatch, 14 October 1873, in Morris, *Treaties of Canada*, 47–8.

53 There is some variation in the account of Métis participation in the Indian council. The account of the *Manitoban* (18 October 1873) indicates that the Métis were invited to the council in the evening. However, Morris reported that the Métis had gone to the council the next morning.

54 Report by the *Manitoban*, 2 October, 1873, in Morris, *Treaties of Canada*, 74.

55 Official dispatch, Morris, 14 October 1873, in Morris, *Treaties of Canada*, 51.

56 Ibid.

57 NA, Church Missionary Society, reel A-99 (24 November 1871).

58 PAM, MG 12 A1, Archibald Papers, reel 1, no. 15, Schultz to Archibald, 6 September 1870; reel 1, no. 22, Notes of an Interview with Henry Prince, 13 September 1870.

59 Ibid., no. 114, Archibald to J.W. Wright, 27 November 1870.

60 PAM, MG12 A1, Archibald Papers, reel 1, no. 164, Notice from Fairford Indians, (ca. January 1870).

61 Ibid.

62 Daniel, "Native Claims Processes," 3.

63 PAM, MG12 A1, Archibald Papers, reel 2, no. 332, Resolutions Made by Portage Indians (30 May 1871).

64 *Manitoban*, 1 July 1871. This notice was signed by Yellow Quill and others and was addressed to John Garrioch and the public.

65 Ibid.

66 Morris to the Minister of the Interior, 2 August 1875, in Morris, *Treaties of Canada*, 136–7.

67 CSP, 1872, Indian Affairs, no. 22, 10.

68 HBCA, E.9/1, Red River and North West Rebellions, Red River Rebellion, 1869–70, fols. 11a–12.

69 Great Britain, *Report from the Select Committee, 1857*, 445. A letter from Peguis, Chief of the Saulteaux Tribe at Red River Settlement, to the Aborigines Protection Society, London.

70 Chute, *The Legacy of Shingwakonse*, 108–9, 138–43.

71 *Report from the Select Committee, 1857*, 445. A letter from Peguis to the Aborigines Protection Society, London, 445–6.

72 Rich, *Hudson's Bay Company*, 814.

73 CSP, 1872, Indian Affairs, no. 22, 27.

74 Report on Treaty 1 and 2 (3 November 1871), in Morris, *Treaties of Canada*, 37.

75 *Manitoban*, 11 October 1873.

76 Ibid.

77 Ibid.

78 *Manitoban*, 11 October 1873; Morris, *Treaties of Canada*, 59–62. The wording in the newspaper was slightly different from Morris' account.

79 Ibid. (emphasis found in Morris, but not the original).

80 Ibid.

81 Tribal concepts about Aboriginal title are also apparent in the records. The Cree had occupied the Red River valley, but were replaced by the Ojibwa when the Cree had migrated further west. The Ojibwa had entered the Red River area some seventy to eighty years prior to Treaty 1. The reaction to Treaty 1 by the Saskatchewan Cree was recorded by Archibald: "The Cree consider the Red River Country theirs, and could not understand what right the Indians here, had except such of them as were Crees, had to treat with for it." PAM, MG12 A1, Archibald Papers, reel 3, no. 2, Interview with Kasisheway (5 January 1872).

82 *Manitoban*, 11 October 1873.

83 Ibid.

84 CSP, 1872, Indian Affairs, no. 22, 31.

85 *Manitoban*, 11 October 1873.

86 Ibid. (emphasis in original).

87 CSP, 1872, Indian Affairs, no. 22, 28.

88 Ibid., 14.

89 CSP, 1875, Indian Affairs, no. 8, 18.

90 *Manitoban*, 18 October 1873.

91 See Hall, "Treaty 1 Revisited," for copies of the coverage of the treaty talks by the *Manitoban* and an analysis. Although the correspondent for this weekly was ethnocentric at times, and treated some issues in a jocular manner, the observations are from a different perspective than government records. Moreover, the *Manitoban* had called for a permanent treaty and considered the treaty to be a serious issue.

92 *Manitoban*, 5 August 1871.

93 Ibid.

94 *Manitoban*, 12 August 1871.

95 Ibid.

96 CSP, 1872, Indian Affairs, no. 22, 14–15. Archibald identified the four jailed Indians as "Swampies."

97 *Manitoban*, 5 August 1871.

98 Ibid.

99 The underlying reasoning for the process offered by the Crown was a fair land policy; it did not once admit that Indians had a special or unique interest in the land. Homesteads were 160 acres, but settlers had the right of pre-empting another 160 acres. Homestead settlers had the means to expand their acreage. Moreover, Canada had agreed already to a huge land grant for the HBC. (Later, millions of acres would be given to railway companies.) While claiming to be equitable in practice, the allocation of reserve lands and the subsequent allocation of Dominion lands was uneven and unfair.

100 *Manitoban*, 5 August 1871.

101 Ibid., 28 July 1871.

102 Ibid.

103 Ibid., 12 August 1871.

104 Ibid., 28 July 1871.

105 Ibid., 12 August 1871.

106 Ibid.

107 Ibid.
108 Ibid.
109 Ibid.
110 Ibid.
111 Ibid.
112 Ibid.
113 Ibid.
114 Ibid.
115 Ibid.
116 CSP, 1872, Indian Affairs, no. 22, 16.
117 *Manitoban*, 12 August 1871.
118 Ibid., 5 August 1871.
119 CSP, 1872, Indian Affairs, no. 22, 28.
120 Official Dispatch, Simpson (3 November 1871), in Morris, *Treaties of Canada*, 40.
121 Simpson does refer to the assistance to agriculture as a "supplement to the treaty." Official Dispatch, Simpson (3 November 1871) in Morris, *Treaties of Canada*, 40.
122 "The Manitoba Indian Treaty," *Canadian Illustrated News*, 9 September 1871, 162.
123 For example: $700.00 was paid to Jos. Hall Manufacturing for 50 iron beam ploughs and $554.00 was paid to Rice, Lewis and Son for 50 sets of iron harrows. See "The Statement of Special Payments," 1873, CSP, 1873, Indian Affairs, no. 17, 21.
124 NA, RG10, vol. 3598, file 1447.
125 CSP, 1875, Indian Affairs, no. 8, 53.
126 Ibid., 61.
127 NA, RG10, vol. 3604, file 2553, Petition, St Peters (15 October 1873).
128 Ibid.
129 NA, RG10, vol. 3555, file 7 (4 January 1873 and 23 September 1872).
130 Morris, *Treaties of Canada*, 128.
131 Ibid., 137.
132 Order-in-Council (30 April 1875), in Morris, *Treaties of Canada*, 338–39.
133 The revisions of Treaties 1 and 2 are found in Morris, *Treaties of Canada*, 338–42. The memorandum of 3 August 1871 can be found in Simpson's report of 3 November 1871 and is printed in CSP, 1872, Indian Affairs, no. 22, 28. Morris also discussed the outside promises in his book; see Morris, *Treaties of Canada*, 126–7. Morris met with the Indian commissioners in March 1874, see NA, RG10, vol. 3608, file 3117 (13 March 1874). A report to the Privy Council on 30 April 1875 is printed in Canada, *Indian Treaties*, vol. 1, 286.
134 Morris, *Treaties of Canada*, 128.
135 Treaty 1, in Morris, *Treaties of Canada*, 315.
136 Morris to the Minister of the Interior (2 August 1875), in Morris, *Treaties of Canada*, 135.
137 *Manitoban*, 11 October 1873, and Morris, *Treaties of Canada*, 62.
138 Ibid., 61.

CHAPTER SIX

1 This section is generalized from Ray, *Indians in the Fur Trade*; Ray, *I Have Lived Here*; Harris, *Historical Atlas of Canada*, vol. 1.; and Royal Commission on Aboriginal Peoples, *Report*, vol. 1.

2 Among some groups, such as the Plains Cree, chieftainship tended to be hereditary, provided that a chief's son was competent. See Mandelbaum, *The Plains Cree*, 106–10.

3 Ibid., 172.

4 Ibid., 173.

5 Ibid.

6 Taylor, "Treaties Six and Seven."

7 For a discussion of this movement, see Ray, *Indians in the Fur Trade*, 18–23, 101–3.

8 Ibid., 90.

9 PAM, MG12 A1, Archibald Papers, reel 1, no. 20 (12 September 1870).

10 Ibid., no. 207 (28 February 1871).

11 Ibid., Christie to the Secretary of the Board of Health, Red River Settlement, 28 February 1871.

12 Ibid.

13 Milloy, *The Plains Cree*, 103–18.

14 Cowie, *Company of Adventurers*, 205.

15 Erasmus, *Buffalo Days*, 205.

16 His account says 1857, but editor I. Spry says other evidence points to 1858. Ibid., 312.

17 Ibid., 50–1.

18 Hind, *Narrative* vol. 1, 168.

19 Ibid., vol. 2, 168.

20 The Sioux represented a multiple threat to Canada. There was a risk that United States military forces would chase them across the boundary. There was the possibility they would ally with Canadian groups, as noted here. Alternatively, Canadian groups might attack them as invaders of their traditional homelands.

21 Ibid., 169–70.

22 Ahenakew, *Voices of the Plains Cree*, 72–3.

23 The district included most of the area later included under Treaties 4 and 6.

24 HBCA, D.12/1, HBC Commissioners Correspondence Inward (28 December 1870). Hardisty had sent a copy of the letter to Commissioner Donald A. Smith.

25 Official Dispatch, Christie (13 April, 1871), in Morris, *Treaties of Canada*, 170 (Emphasis added).

26 PAM, MG12 B2, Morris Papers, reel 7, no. 35, Morris to A. Campbell, 2 August 1873 (emphasis added).

27 Ibid., no. 39, Campbell to Morris, 6 August 1873.

28 Ibid., no. 69, Morris to Campbell, 23 October 1873. Morris had sent a letter to Campbell on 18 October 1873 saying he was disappointed the treaties had been delayed because the "Lac Qu'Appelle tribes" were "very excited" and "wishing to resist settlers." Ibid., no. 67, 18 October 1873.

29 Ibid., no. 103, Morris to Laird, 6 March 1874.

30 HBCA, D.20/2, Comissioners Correspondence Inward, 1875–76, fol. 587.

31 "Minutes of the Council of the North West Territories" (4 September 1873), copy in Oliver, *Canadian North-West*, vol. 2, 1000.

32 Ibid., "Minutes of the Council" (16 March 1874), 1021–2.

33 Ibid., "Minutes of the Council" (1 June 1874), 1026.

34 Morris, *Treaties of Canada*, 171–2.

35 "Minutes of the Council" (1 June 1874), copy in Oliver, *Canadian North-West* 1025.

36 Official dispatch, McDougall to Morris, 22 October 1875, in Morris, *Treaties of Canada*, 173–4.

37 Ibid., 174.

38 HBCA, D.20/2, Commissioners Correspondence Inward, 1875–76, fol. 349–50.

39 Treaty 7 Elders et al., *Treaty 7*, 226.

CHAPTER SEVEN

1 Morris, *Treaties of Canada*, 285.

2 Ibid., 285–8.

3 The authors wish to acknowledge the help of Walter Hildebrandt with research on Treaty 4. Other relevant literature includes RCAP, *Report 1*; Stanley, *Birth of Western Canada*, chapter 10, "The Indian Problem"; Friesen, *Canadian Prairies*, 136–49.

4 Treaty 4, copy in Morris, *Treaties of Canada*, 337–8. In fact, bands residing in the Moose Mountain region, which was embraced by Treaty 2, presumably were too distant from the 1871 treaty-making site to be party to the early talks. Indeed, some of them were not present at the making of Treaty 4 in 1874 and adhered a year later at Qu'Appelle. The 1875 adherents who were located in territory covered by Treaty 2 were Wahpeemakwa (White Bear), Le croup de Pheasant (Pheasant Rump), and Kitchikahmewin (Ocean Man). See also table A5.

5 Charles Pratt (ca. 1816–88) was born into a "Cree-Assiniboine band known as the Young Dogs." He was taken to Red River, where he was educated and served as a school teacher, HBC fur trader, and Church of England catechist. In 1874 he acted as one of the interpreters at the Treaty 4 negotiation at Fort Qu'Appelle. See Frits Pannakoek, "Pratt, Charles," DCB, vol. 11, 711–12.

6 PAM, MG12 B 2, Alexander Morris Papers, Ketcheson Collection, letter 67, Morris to Campbell, 18 Oct. 1973, "Confidential."

7 Ibid., Letter 79, Morris to Minister of the Interior, 19 November 1873.

8 Ibid., Letter 116, Morris to Dorion, 29 May 1874, "Confidential."

9 Mimiy Gagriel Coté, Meemay, Pigeon, who died in 1884 was chief of a band of Saulteaux who were woodland hunters. Government commissioners regarded Coté as the principal leader of the Saulteaux, but Saulteaux from Qu'Appelle and Quill lakes did not, because of his relationship with the HBC and easy cooperation with government officials. At council they confined him to his tent during the treaty negotiations to send a clear message to the government that they were annoyed with the sale of Rupertsland by the HBC. They regarded the lands as theirs, and Paskwaw wanted the money paid to the Indians. Coté signed Treaty 4 and took a reserve in the Swan River area. Tobias noted, "Oral tradition among some Saulteaux bands to this day names Coté a 'company chief,' or one who owed his position to the HBC." See John Tobias, "Mimiy," *DCB*, vol. 11, 589–97.

10 Paskwaw, Pasquah, Pisqua, The Plain, Les Prairies (ca. 1828–89) was a Plains Cree and yet chief of a band of Plains Saulteaux. He attended the negotiations for Treaty 4 and argued that the money from the sale of Rupertsland belonged to the Indians. He signed the treaty, and in 1875 his band was the only one "ready to receive its cattle and oxen." His reserve was about five miles west of Fort Qu'Appelle. Initially, when surveyor Wagner was ready to survey a reserve for him near Leech Lake, Paskwaw refused and tried to get other chiefs to do the same. He believed that if he agreed to a survey of the land it was tantamount to submitting to the domination of the white man. In 1878 he complained to Lieu-

tenant-Governor G. Cauchon that the "food and building materials that had been promised had not been delivered." In 1882 he rejected the payment of annuities at each reserve, preferring payment at a large gathering at Fort Qu'Appelle. See Kenneth J. Tyler, "Paskwaw," *DCB*, vol. 11, 674–5.

11 Treaty 4, Morris, *Treaties of Canada* , 334. Wawasecapow (the Man Proud of Standing Upright) and Otamakoowin (the Man Who Stands on the Earth) adhered at Fort Ellice. Ibid., 337.

12 In Treaty 6 negotiations at Fort Carlton and Fort Pitt, for example, there were both pipe ceremonies and impressive displays of horsemanship. Ibid., 182–3, 190; Erasmus, *Buffalo Days*, 240, 259. Peter Erasmus was the mixed-blood interpreter hired by Chiefs Mistawasis and Ahtakakoop for the Fort Carlton parleys. That displays of horsemanship were offered at the Qu'Appelle talks is documented in PAM, MGI A7, "Memories of the Treaty of 1874," undated and unsigned. Caution is required on this point: the documentary record of Treaty 4 negotiations has no evidence of ritual or ceremony, but, as noted earlier, that record is not necessarily complete.

Kakiwistahaw, Kahkewistahaw, He Who Flies Around (ca. 1810–1906), was a Plains Cree chief, son of Le Sonnant, a warrior and medicine man of the Rabbit Skin people who signed the Selkirk Treaty in 1817. Kakiwistahaw signed Treaty 4 in 1874, along with his nephews Okanese and Paskwaw. His reserve, located on the south side of the Qu'Appelle valley between Round and Crooked Lakes, was a traditional wintering place and had good farm hay land bordering the Canadian Pacific railway to the south. During the 1880s, he, along with others, called for better agricultural assistance. Members of his band were all concientious farmers. Covetous neighbors wanted to acquire his reserve lands next to the railway through surrender, but Kahkewistahaw resisted, although a year following his death, 70 percent of the reserve had been surrendered. See Sarah Carter, "Kakiwistahaw," *DCB*, vol. 13, 536–7.

Keeseekoowenin, Kesekoinin, Kitchikahmewin, Sky Man, or Sky Chief, baptized Moses Burns (ca. 1818–1906) was a Saulteaux Chief. His band made their living through hunting and trapping and trading at the HBC posts of Fort Ellice and Riding Mountain House. He signed an adhesion to Treaty 4 in 1875. See Peter Lorenz Neufeld, "Keeseekoowenin," *DCB*, vol. 13, 537–8.

Necanete, Nekahnea, Nekahnew, Foremost Man, Front Man, who died in 1897, was a Plains Indian chief. He was raised in the Forts Qu'Appelle and Pelly area, but later went to Cypress Hills. He signed Treaty 4, but collected his annuities as a member of Kahkewistahaw's band. In 1881, as a headman of over 400 Crees, he was promised a reserve in the Cypress Hills area, as part of the Indian territory strategy, but the government coerced the dispersal of bands to the north the following year. In destitution, many of his followers left, but he did not take a reserve and remained aloof. He remained neutral in 1885 and his group of "stragglers" managed to survive without help. Following his death, his successor Crooked Legs was given a reserve near Maple Creek in 1913, but treaty benefits were restored to the band only in 1975. See David Lee, "Necanete," *DCB*, vol. 12, 779–80.

Kiwisance, Cowesessess, Kawezance, Little Child, who died in 1886, had been chief of a mixed band of Plains Cree and Saulteaux. He signed Treaty 4 in 1874. When the buffalo were gone his "band was reduced to selling its horses, eating its dogs, and begging for food from the NWMP." In 1879 he selected a reserve site near Maple Creek next to Piapot, but it was never surveyed. In 1881–82, as the government coerced bands to move north and east, away from the Cypress Hills area, Agent McDonald persuaded O'Soup to resign as headman and welcome Kiwisance at Crooked lake. His people progressed in agriculture, and in 1884 he was awarded a yoke of oxen in recognition of their achievement. See Kenneth J. Tyler "Kiwisance," *DCB*, vol. 11, 477–8.

13 "Report of Proceedings" (8 September 1874), in Morris, *Treaties of Canada*, 97.

14 See, for example, remarks by the Gambler: "I know what I have to tell you. Who surveyed this land? Was it done by the Company? This is the reason I speak of the Company, why are you staying in the Company's house?" "Report of Proceedings" (12 September 1874), in Morris, *Treaties of Canada*, 99. As these comments make clear, Saulteaux concerns about the location of the militia and the talks, about where the commissioners slept, and other such matters were tied to their opposition to the HBC's behaviour concerning their lands. "Who surveyed this land? Was it done by the Company?"

15 "Report of Proceedings," 8 September 1874, in Morris, *Treaties of Canada*, 97.

16 Government surveyors had begun surveying these lands as early as 1872, albeit cautiously, to avoid confrontations with local Native people. See HBCA D.25/19, Correspondence of Inspecting Chief Factor W.J. Christie, Christie to R. Hardisty, 1 September 1872.

17 "Report of Proceedings," in the *Manitoban*, 21 October 1873, in Morris, *Treaties of Canada*, 73.

18 Ibid., 99, 101, 102, 8 September 1874.

19 Ibid., 103, 12 September 1874. F.L. Hunt was probably the author of two newspaper articles, "The Indian Treaty! Scenes en Route" and "Qu'Appelle Treaty," that appearred in the *Manitoban*, 26 September 1874 and 3 October 1874, respectively. The first was an idiosyncratic description of his trip to Qu'Appelle; the latter a straightforward description of the terms of the government version of Treaty 4.

20 Ibid., 104, 12 September 1874.

21 Ibid., 106.

22 Hunt, "Qu'Appelle Treaty," 179.

23 *Manitoban*, 12 September 1874, 100.

24 Ibid., 106, 12 September 1874. (Emphasis added).

25 Rich, *Hudson's Bay Company*, 200–4.

26 "Report of Proceedings" (14 September 1874), in Morris, *Treaties of Canada*, 110, 111.

27 Ibid., 112.

28 Ibid., 113.

29 Ibid., 118.

30 Ibid.

31 11 September 1874, ibid., 91.

32 12 September 1874, ibid., 102.

33 Ibid., 105.

34 8 September 1874, ibid., 88.

35 Ibid., 108, 14 September 1874.

36 Treaty 4, ibid., 331.

37 "Report of Proceedings," ibid., 119–20, 15 September 1874.

38 Ibid., 120. For a summary of the terms, see table A5.

39 Ibid., 121.

40 Treaty 4, ibid., 332.

41 "Report of Proceedings," ibid., 122, 15 September 1874.

42 Treaty 4, ibid., 332.

43 Ibid.

44 "Report of Proceedings," ibid., 121–2, 15 September 1874.

45 Treaty 4, ibid., 331.

46 "Report of Proceedings," ibid., 92–3, 11 September 1874 (emphasis added).

47 Ibid., 95, 97.

48 Ibid., 122, 15 September 1874.

49 Treaty 4, ibid., 332–3.

50 Ibid., 291.

51 Ibid., 92, 11 September 1874.

52 Ibid., 93.

53 Treaty 4, ibid., 333.

54 Ibid., 96, 11 September 1874.

55 Treaty 4, ibid., 333.

56 "Report of Proceedings," ibid., 120–21, 14 September 1874. See also the government text, 332.

57 Ibid., 115, 15 September 1874.

58 Ibid., 117–18, 15 September 1874.

59 Ibid., 88, 8 September 1874.

60 Ibid., 90, 9 September 1874.

61 Ibid., 92, 11 September 1874.

62 Ibid., 96, 12 September, 1874.

63 Ibid., 95, 11 September 1874.

64 Ibid., 109, 14 September 1874.

65 Ibid., 121, 15 September 1874.

66 Treaty 4, ibid., 330.

67 Ibid., 98, 99, 8 September 1874.

68 Ibid., 123, 15 September 1874.

69 Hunt, "Qu'Appelle Treaty," 176, remarked that the Métis who were present were disappointed at not being included in Treaty 4.

70 Petition of "The half-breeds of Lake Qu'Appelle" to Morris, 11 September 1874. CSP 1871, no. 8, Indian Affairs, 31 (translation).

71 Morris' reply, 16 September. 1875, ibid., 32. See also Morris' covering letter to Ottawa, 30–1.

72 "Report of Proceedings," Morris, *Treaties of Canada*, 107, 14 September 1874.

73 Ibid., 114–15, 15 September 1874.

74 Ibid., 122–3, 15 September 1874. See also table A4.

75 Report of Interview at Fort Ellice, 14 September 1874, ibid., 124–5; and the Fort Ellice Adhesion, ibid., 335–6.

76 "Adhesion of Fort Ellice Saulteaux Indans," ibid., 336–8.

77 "Report of Proceedings," ibid., 97, 8 September 1874.

78 Ibid., 137, Morris' despatch of 2 August 1875.

CHAPTER EIGHT

1 For the literature on Treaty 5, see S. Raby, "Indian Treaty No. 5"; Coates and Morrison, *Treaty Research Report*; Tough, "*As Their Natural Resources Fail*"; and "Economic Aspects of Aboriginal Title."

2 PAM, MG12 B1, Morris Papers, reel 2, no. 783. Petition, Rossville, 25 June 1874. Several changes in spelling and capitalization have been made to the original.

3 Ibid., reel 5, no. 53, Fort Garry, 22 August 1873.

4 Ibid., reel 2, no. 874, James Settee to Morris, 27 November 1874.

5 Morris, *Treaties of Canada*, 143.

6 PAM, MG12 B2, Morris Papers, reel 7, no. 108, Morris to the Minister of the Interior, 16 April 1874.

7 CSP, 1876, Indian Affairs, no. 9, xxxiii, Lieutenant-Governor Morris Report on Treaty 5 to Minister of the Interior, 11 October 1875.

8 Morris, *Treaties of Canada*, 143.

9 CSP, 1876, Indian Affairs, no. 9, xxxiv, 11 October 1875.

10 PAM, MG12 B2, Morris Papers, reel 5, no. 258, Morris to the Minister of the Interior, 31 May 1875.

11 The *Colville*, an HBC steamer, was put at service of the treaty commissioners. Later the London office of the HBC decided not to charge for this service.

12 CSP, 1876, Indian Affairs, no. 9, xxxi, 11 October 1875.

13 Ibid.

14 Ibid., xxxii.

15 Ibid.

16 Ibid.

17 Ibid.

18 Ibid., xxxiii.

19 NA RG6, Public Records of the Secretary of State, vol. 23, file 1251.

20 CSP, 1877, Indian Affairs, no. 11, xiv, Howard to Lieutenant-Governor Morris, 10 October 1876.

21 Henry Cochrane (ca. 1834–98) was a son of Cree Indians who became a schoolmaster, Church of England minister, and Cree interpreter and translator. Along with his second wife, he "translated the Bible, the Book of Common Prayer, and many hymns into Cree." Cochrane was a witness at the signing of Treaties 1 and 5. He served as an interpreter at East Doghead, Berens River, Grand Rapids, and The Pas in the negotiation of Treaty 5. Because of his good reputation with the Indians, he was critical in securing a treaty relationship. See Frits Pannekoek, "Henry Cochrane," *DCB*, vol. 12, 200–1.

22 The desire for each of these bands to have a separate chief and the request for a reserve at Big Island were the main problems that arose at this adhesion.

23 CSP, 1877, Indian Affairs, no. 11, xlvi, Report of Thomas Howard to Lieutenant-Governor Morris, 10 October 1876.

24 Ibid., xlvii, 10 October 1876.

25 Ibid.

26 Ibid.

27 Ibid., xlviii.

28 CSP, 1877, Indian Affairs, no. 11, xlii, 10 October 1876.

29 Morris, *Treaties of Canada*, 143 (emphasis added).

30 PAM, MG12 E3, Papers of John Christian Schultz, box 19, Notes of an Indian Council at Treaty Rock, Berens River, July 12, 1890. For a published version of this document see "Notes on Indian Council at Treaty Rock, Beren's River, Lake Winnipeg, Man. 12th July 1890," *Native Studies Review*, 3, no. 1 (1987): 117–27.

31 CSP, 1877, Indian Affairs, no. 11, li, 14 October 1876.

CHAPTER NINE

1 Secondary literature relating to Treaty 6 includes Sliwa, "Treaty Day"; Price, *Alberta Indian Treaties*; Kerr, "Indian Treaties of 1876"; Saskatchewan Indian Cultural Centre, *Treaty 6*; Venne, "Understanding Treaty 6."

2 Report of Proceedings by Jackes, 18 August 1876, in Morris, *Treaties of Canada*, 211.

3 Erasmus, *Buffalo Days*, 246–7.

4 Ibid., 248–9.

5 Ibid., 249–50.

6 Report of Proceedings by Jackes, 18 August 1876, in Morris, *Treaties of Canada*, 197–8.

7 Ibid., 183–98.

8 Taylor, "Two Views on Treaties", 18.

9 Erasmus, *Buffalo Days*, 240–1.

10 Ibid.

11 Ibid., 241.

12 Ibid., 242–3.

13 The *Edmonton Post Journal* for that date indicates that the Cree were very agitated and used very strong language to indicate their displeasure with the government for not negotiating with them.

14 Official Dispatch, Christie, 13 April 1871, in Morris, *Treaties of Canada*, 169 (emphasis in original).

15 Ibid., 170–1.

16 Mc Dougall to Morris, 23 October 1875, ibid., 174–5.

17 Ibid.

18 Pitikwahanapiwiyn (Poundmaker, ca. 1842–86), was a Plains Cree chief who signed Treaty 6 in 1876. In 1879 he "accepted a reserve and settled at the confluence of Battle River and Cutknife Creek, about forty miles west of Battleford." Hugh A. Dempsey, "Pitikwahanapiwiyn," *DCB*, vol. 11, 695–7.

19 Morris, *Treaties of Canada*, 184–5, Official Dispatch, Morris, 4 December 1876.

20 Ibid., 186.

21 Report of Proceedings by Jackes, 22 August 1876, in Morris, *Treaties of Canada*, 211.

22 Official Dispatch, Morris, 4 December 1876, ibid., 185.

23 Report of Proceedings by Jackes, 22 August 1876, ibid., 213.

24 Official Dispatch, Morris, 4 December 1876, ibid., 186.

25 Ibid.

26 Report of Proceedings by Jackes, 22 August 1876, ibid., 216–17.

27 Ibid., 217.

28 Ibid.

29 Kamiyistowesit (Beardy, literally, Little Mustache, in French, Barbu), ca. 1828–89 was chief of the Willow band of the Plains Cree. Despite refusing to attend council during the negotiations for Treaty 6, he signed five days later at a special meeting near Duck Lake. Because the buffalo were gone, he believed that the assistance offered was inadequate. He also wanted a plan for managing the remaining buffalo. He continued to try to modify the treaty and insist on the treaty promises, first protesting to David Laird, Lieutenant-Governor of the NWT in 1877, and later in writing to the governor-general of Canada, Lord

Dufferin, in 1878. He indicated that the destitution of his people would require them to take what was needed from local merchants. This stance assured prompt payment of the treaty money. When the government tried to exclude certain sections of his reserve, he complained that treaty promises were not being honoured. He complained to Governor-General Lorne and attended the 1884 meeting to discuss treaty grievances. Because of hunger, his people left their reserve during the 1885 troubles, were suspended from treaty, and Beardy was no longer recognized as leader. He continually sought to have the terms of the treaty fulfilled and modified. See John Tobias, "Kamiyistowesit,"*DCB*, vol. 11, 458–9.

30 Official Dispatch, Morris, 4 December 1876, in Morris, *Treaties of Canada*, 189.

31 Report of Proceedings by Jackes, 26 August 1876, ibid., 226–8.

32 Ibid.

33 Ibid., 228.

34 Minutes of the Council, 23 November 1875, in Oliver, *Canadian North-West*, 1046–7.

35 Report of Proceedings by Jackes, 27 August 1876, in Morris, *Treaties of Canada*, 233.

36 Ibid.

37 Correspondence Inward, Clarke to Graham, 19 April 1875, HBCA, D.20/2, fol. 448.

38 3 May 1875, ibid., fol. 485.

39 Saskatchewan District Report, 1875, HBCA, B.27/e/8, fol. 5.

40 Report of Proceedings by Jackes, 27 August 1876, in Morris, *Treaties of Canada*, 229–39; Dempsey, *Big Bear*, 71–3. Talks at Fort Pitt were delayed by Morris for two days until Sweet Grass could come in from the plains.

41 Glenbow Archives, M 477, Richard Hardisty papers, fol. 96, no. 549, McKay to Hardisty, 28 August 1874.

42 Ibid.

43 Report of Proceedings by Jackes, 13 September 1876, in Morris, *Treaties of Canada*, 239.

44 Ibid., 240.

45 Tobias, "Canada's Subjugation of the Plains Cree," 215.

46 Report of Proceedings by Jackes, 13 September 1876, in Morris, *Treaties of Canada*, 240.

47 Ibid., 237.

48 Ibid., 241.

49 Ibid., 242.

50 Dempsey, *Big Bear*, 73–111; Miller, *Big Bear*, 78–91.

51 Treaty 6, Morris, *Treaties of Canada*, 354.

52 Ibid., 355.

53 *Aski-Puko: The Land Alone*, 19–40.

54 During the talks for the 1889 adhesion, Chief James Roberts "said they had heard of other treaties having been made and they were anxious to join in a similar one: but they had already represented their case and no attention was given to them." CSP, 1890, "Indian Affairs," no. 12, xliv. For more details on the adhesion see NA RG10, vol. 3815, file 56,662.

55 CSP, 1890, "Indian Affairs," no. 12, xiii.

56 PC 2675, 14 December 1889, dealt with the scrip claims associated with the "negotiations with the Green Lake Indians."

57 CSP, 1890, "Indian Affairs," no. 12, xliii, Irvine's Report, 6 April 1889.

58 Ibid.

59 In the 1876 Treaty 6 documents Reverend McKay's surname was spelt "McKay" whereas in the Treaty 6 adhesion of 1889, in the original signature and published documentation, his surname is "Mackay" or "MacKay."

60 CSP, 1890, "Indian Affairs," no. 12, xliii, Irvine's Report, 6 April 1889.

61 Ibid.

62 Ibid., xlvlii, McNeill's Notes of Adhesion.

63 Ibid.

64 Ibid., xlix.

65 Ibid.

66 Ibid.

67 Ibid.

68 Ibid., xlv, Irvine's Report, 6 April 1889.

69 Ibid., xlv–xlvi.

70 Ibid., xlvi.

71 Ibid., 3, Copy of Treaty, Special Appendix on the Treaty 6 adhesion.

72 See Morrison, "Treaties 8 and 11."

73 CSP, 1890, "Indian Affairs," no. 12, 3, Copy of Treaty, Special Appendix on the Treaty 6 adhesion. An Order-in-Council of 20 April 1889 accepted the adhesion.

74 *Aski-Puko: The Land Alone*, 57–61.

75 Ibid., 57.

CHAPTER TEN

1 For examples of requests for treaties, see Tough, "*As Their Natural Resources Fail*," 101–4.

2 NA, RG10, vol. 4009, file 241,209–1 (19 January 1887).

3 Ibid.

4 For information on fur prices following the transfer, see Ray, *Canadian Fur Trade*, 14, 56–63, 65; Tough, "*As Their Natural Resources Fail*," 310–17.

5 Ray, *Canadian Fur Trade*, 211–18.

6 The Treaty 8 discussion is abstracted from Ray, "Historical Background to Treaty 8," Ray, "Treaty 8: An Enigma."

7 Ray, *Canadian Fur Trade*, 201.

8 Ibid., 198–228; Madill, Treaty Research Report, 3–5.

9 Dieudonne Desjarlais to Dewdney, 4 February 1890, NA RG10, vol. 3708, file 19,502.

10 NA RG10, vol. 3708, file 19,502, Vankoughnet to Dewdney (22 February 1890).

11 Ibid.

12 HBC, Inspection Report, Hudson's Hope, Peace River District, 1897, HBCA B.293/e/2: 9, and Inspection Reports, St Johns Post (1891, 1897) HBCA, B.189/e/2–3.

13 *Annual Report of Commissioner of the NWNP, 1900*, SP no. 15, 12. Cited in Fumoleau, *As Long As This Land Shall Last*, 55.

14 Ibid.

15 Ibid.

16 Draft Memo Opposing a Treaty, 7 January 1891, NA, RG 10, vol. 3848, file 75,236–1.

17 Report of the Privy Council, Ibid., 26 January 1891.

18 The value of the Peace River corridor as a railway route to the West was recognized by the early 1870s and promoted thereafter. See Horetzky, "First Railway Survey," 81–5.

19 In fact, the Omineca strike drew prospectors into the Peace River and Liard River area by the early 1870s. See ibid., 82–3.

20 It continued this role when the Klondike gold rush drew prospectors into the Peace River country once again. See HBCA, B171/b/6 Correspondence Book, Quesnel, 1897–1900.

21 For a more extended discussion of developments in British Columbia, see Ray, "Treaty 8: An Anomaly."

22 "Annual Report of the North-West Mounted Police," Canada, *Sessional Papers*, 1899, no. 15, 20.

23 Ibid., 12.

24 Ibid., 13.

25 F. White, "Extract from a Report of the N.W.M. Police Stationed at Fort Smith" (31 October 1898), NA RG10, vol. 3848, file 75,236–1.

26 Ibid., Walker, J. (Officer, NWMP) to Sifton, 30 November 1897.

27 Ibid., L.W. Herchmer to Comptroller of NWMP, 2 December 1897.

28 Privy Council, 2 March 1899 and 3 May 1899. Subsequently Forget became lieutenant-governor of the North-West Territories and the Privy Council appointed Indian Commissioner David Laird. It also named J. H. Ross of Regina and Father Albert Lacombe as members of the treaty commission.

29 Privy Council clerk to Superintendent-General of Indian Affairs (27 June 1898) NA RG10, vol. 3848, file 75,236–1.

30 Ibid., Reed to Superintendent-General, 2 April 1891.

31 Ibid.

32 Order in Council no. 1703, Privy Council, 27 June 1898.

33 HBCA, B.189/e/3, Fort St John Inspection Report (1897) fols. 4, 8.

34 HBCA, A.12/FT243/2, London Inward Correspondence from Commissioners (19 April 1897).

35 Macgregor, *Klondike Rush*, 202.

36 Indeed, other North-West Mounted Police reports about law enforcement problems in the area received press coverage. See *Winnipeg Free Press*, 25 April 1898, copy found in HBCA, A.12, FT243, 1, London Inward Correspondence; similarly, McKenna transmitted a *Winnipeg Free Press* story about five hundred Fort St John Indians blocking miners and asked Forget to call it to the attention of the minister. NA RG10, vol. 3848, file 75,236–1, McKenna to Forget (28 June 1898).

37 HBCA, A.12/FT243/2, Correspondence Inward, 25 March 1899, fols. 14–17.

38 Ibid. In 1858 Governor James Douglas instituted the policy of issuing mining licenses as a way of asserting Crown authority. See Public Records Office, Kew, UK, Colonial Office Papers, 12177, CO 60/1, Correspondence by Governor James Douglas on the Fraser River Gold Rush (27 August 1858; 9 September 1858; 11 October 1858; and 29 November 1858).

39 On 12 May 1899 Chipman also sent copies of all these letters to the company's London secretary, William Ware.

40 NA, RG10, vol. 3848, file 75,236–1, McKenna to Laird, 5 December 1898.

41 Ibid.

42 Ibid., McKenna to Clifford Sifton 17 April 1899.

43 Ibid.

44 Ibid., Sifton to Laird, McKenna, and Ross, 12 May 1899. See also Fumoleau, *Treaty 8 and 11*, 65.

45 NA, RG10, vol. 3848, file 75,236–1, McKenna to Sifton, 17 April. Cited in Fumoleau, *Treaty 8 and 11*, 61–2.

46 Carter, *Lost Harvests*, 195–6.

47 NA RG10, vol. 3848, file 75, 236–1, McKenna to Sifton, 17 April 1899.

48 Indian title could be alienated only to the Crown, regardless of the nature of the reserve.

49 The company's copy of its estimate is located in the fur trade correspondence files of C. C. Chipman, HBCA A.12/FT/1.

50 NARG10, vol. 3848, file 75, 236–1, W. H. Routledge to the commanding officer of G Division, 31 December 1898.

51 Commissioners for Treaty 8, *Treaty No. 8 Made June 21 1899*, 7.

52 This time period is evident from the diary of the HBC supplier who accompanied Laird. "Diary of a Tour (Peace River, Athabasca) for Indian Treaty No. 8, 1899," HBCA, E.26/1.

53 Ibid., 7.

54 Ibid., 7–8.

55 Macrae, "Report of Commissioner for Treaty 8," 21.

56 Fumoleau, *As Long As This Land Shall Last*, 65–8; and Madill, *Treaty Eight, 36.*

57 Commissioners for Treaty 8, *Treaty No. 8* (1889), 5.

58 Ibid., 5–6 (emphasis added).

59 Ibid., 6–7.

60 Ibid., 7.

61 Ray, "Treaty 8: An Anomaly."

62 Commissioners for Treaty 8, *Treaty No. 8* (1899), 12.

CHAPTER ELEVEN

1 The literature concerning Treaty 10 includes Coates and Morrison, *Treaty 10.* One of the main points established by Coates and Morrison is that the northern and southern treaties reflected significantly different processes. See also Gulig, "In Whose Interests?"

2 The main Treaty 10 file is NA, RG10, vol. 4009, file 241,209–1, "General Housekeeping Records and Correspondence Regarding Ile-à-la-Crosse Treaty (maps and charts), 1883 – 1905." Vankoughnet to Macdonald (5 November 1883). This file on Treaty 10 actually ends 21 May 1908.

3 Ibid.

4 Ibid., Information from Chief Factor Clarke, 28 December 1883.

5 Ibid., DIA to Bishop of St Albert, 29 May 1883.

6 Ibid., McKenna to Sifton, 18 March 1803.

7 For example, T.O. Davis, MP, wrote to the department about this problem. See ibid., 21 October 1902 and Correspondence from the Department of the Interior. Ibid., 6 April 1906.

8 Ibid., Laird to McLean, 29 April 1904.

9 Ibid., Memorandum, Scott, 5 May 1904.

10 Ibid., McLean to Laird, 29 March 1905.

11 Chisholm's Report, quoted ibid., Laird to MacLean, 7 October 1905.

12 Ibid., McLean to Laird, 8 August 1905.

13 Ibid., Laird to McLean, 7 October 1905.

14 Ibid.

15 Ibid., Conroy to Pedley, 5 December 1905.

16 Ibid.

17 Ibid.

18 Ibid., Pedley to Oliver, 7 April 1906.

19 Ibid., Oliver to Governor General in Council, 20 July 1906.

20 Ibid.

21 In northern Manitoba, for instance, adhesions to Treaty 5 were used to deal with Indian ti-
    tle, and the part of northern Ontario that had not been included in Treaty 9 in 1905 was
    brought in with an adhesion in 1929.

22 PC no. 1459, 20 July 1906, copy in Canada, *Treaty No. 10*, 3–4.

23 Ibid. For McKenna's appointment as treaty commissioner see NA, RG 6, vol. 124, file 2186.

24 NA, RG 10, vol. 4009, file 241,209–1 (2 August 1906).

25 Ibid.

26 Ibid.

27 Ibid., McKenna's Report, 18 January 1907; see also Canada, *Treaty No. 10, Report of First
    Commissionner.*

28 NA, RG 10, vol. 4009, file 241, 209–1, McKenna's Report, 18 January 1907.

29 Ibid.

30 Ibid.

31 Ibid.

32 Canada, *Treaty No. 10, Report of Second Commission*, 14 October 1907.

33 Ibid.

34 NA, RG 10, vol. 4009, file 241, 209–1. 29 April 1907.

35 Canada, *Treaty No. 10, Report of Second Commission*, 14 October 1907.

36 Ibid.

37 Ibid.

38 Ibid.

39 Ibid.

40 The ratification of the treaty was based on a submission from the Superintendent General
    of Indian Affairs. See NA, RG 10, vol. 4009, file 241, 209–1, 7 November 1907.

41 The original of Treaty 10 is found in NA, RG10, vol. 1852, item 443 (hereafter *Treaty 10.*)
    Treaty 10 has been published in *Treaty No. 10 and Reports of Commissioners* 1966, origi-
    nal 1907).

42 NA, RG10, vol. 4009, file 241,209–1, McKenna's Report, 18 January 1907. This concern
    was not absurd, in light of the restrictions on southern Treaty Indians for traveling off-re-
    serve, after 1885.

43 Ibid.

44 Ibid.

45 Ibid.

46 Ibid.

47 Ibid.

48 Ibid.

49 Ibid.
50 Ibid.
51 Ibid.
52 NA, RG 10, vol. 4009, file 241, 209–19, McLean to Laird, 9 March 1907.
53 Ibid., "Memorandum, Re: Indians of Treaty No. 10" (ca December 1907).
54 Ibid.
55 Ibid.
56 Ibid.
57 Ibid.
58 Ibid.
59 Ibid.
60 Ibid.
61 Ibid.
62 Ibid.
63 Ibid.

CHAPTER TWELVE

1 Trow, *Manitoba*, title page.
2 Trow, *Manitoba*, 53.
3 NA, RG10, vol. 3768, file 33642. Unless otherwise noted, all other quotations from the 1881 meeting at Qu'Appelle are from this source.
4 Ibid.
5 It is worth noting that Louis O'Soup also informed Lorne that Morris's promises of Crown protection from wrongdoers had also not been properly honoured in the years since the talks at Fort Qu'Appelle and Fort Ellice.
6 Macleod, *North West Mounted Police*, 8.
7 NA, RG10, vol. 3642, file 7581, Angus McKay to Indian Affairs, 2 March 1877.
8 John L. Tobias, "Plains Cree," 216–22.
9 Stonechild and Waiser, *Loyal till Death*, 101–4.
10 This account is based on NA RG10, vol. 3666, file 10,181, especially Report of R. Burton Deane of NWMP and Hayter Reed to Superintendent General (27 February 1884), and Andrews, "Indian Protest against Starvation," 41–51.
11 NA, MG29 E 106, Hayter Reed Papers, vol. 19, file July-December 1888, notes "taken verbatim from Chief Gambler and others of the Saulteaux" by Major Charles Alexander, and enclosed with letter from Alexander to Lord Stanley (10 November 1888). Informants listed were Chief Gambler, Chief Waysacapow, and councillors.
12 NA, MG29 E106, Reed Papers, vol. 19, file July-December 1888, L. Vankoughnet to Reed, 23 November 1888, (draft) Reed to Agent Markle, 12 December 1888, and Markle to Commissioner Reed, 31 December 1888.
13 Ibid., vol. 20, file March 1893, W.M. McGirr to Hayter Reed, 8 March 1893, enclosing typed copy of petition (To the Honourable the House of Commons, Ottawa) of 24 February 1893 from four Pasqua headmen (Charles Asham, Kahkakeesick, Howinacasa, and Johnny Asham), and three from Muscowpetung (Muscocaffa, A. Pisteenow, and Keesick). The petition elicited a legalistic, hair-splitting refutation from Reed, who be-

came deputy minister of the DIA about this time. Ibid. (copy), Reed to Hon. T. Mayne Daly, 12 March 1893.

14 This complex tale has been reconstructed from a large body of primary information: the annual reports of the Department of Indian Affairs, 1881–1900; and RG10, vol. 3940, file 121,698–13 A, "Moose Mountain Elections, 1888–1911." Individual documents from this body of data will be cited only as is absolutely necessary for clarity or to provide the source of a direct quotation.

15 Trow, *Manitoba,* 46.

16 NA, RG10, vol. 3725, file 24,382, William McGirr to Superintendent General of Indian Affairs, 31 October 1885, and Order-in-Council, 17 November 1885.

17 CSP, 1888, Indian Affairs, no. 15, 82–3.

18 NA, RG10, vol. 3940, file 121,698–13, Campbell to Indian Commissioner, 10 December 1888.

19 NA, RG10, vol. 3940, file 121,698–13, O, H.R. Halpin to Indian Affairs, 28 August 1897.

20 Ibid., Halpin to Indian Affairs, 28 August 1897.

21 Ibid., RG10, vol. 3940, file 121,698–13, Halpin to Indian Affairs, 16 November 1897.

22 NA, RG10, vol. 4053, file 379, 203–2, Notes of Representation Made by Delegation of Indians from the West, A. Gadie Intrepreter, 24–26 January 1911.

23 NA, RG10, vol. 3768, file 33642, Notes of Lord Lorne's Meeting at Fort Carlton, 1881.

24 Ibid.

25 NA, MG29 E106, Reed Papers, vol. 19, file April 1890, Justin Wilson to R.S. McKenzie (25 April 1890); and ibid., file May 1890 (copy), Indian Commissioner to Indian Agent, Duck Lake [R.S. McKenzie] (30 May 1890).

26 Ibid., vol. 20, file July 1893, Kapetekoos (Thunderchild) to Reed, 15 July 1893. Marked "confidential" and signed with an X. Later, Chief Thunderchild addressed Reed as "my master, as I can well call you my master." For Thunderchild's account of his 1879 adhesion to Treaty 6, see Ahenakew, *Plains Cree,* 26.

27 Notes of Lorne Meeting at Fort Carlton, 1881, NA, RG 10, vol. 3768, file 33, 642.

28 Tobias, "Subjugation," 222. Payipwat (Piapot, "Hole in the Sioux," Kisikawasan, Flash in the Sky), ca. 1816–1908, was one of five major leaders of the Plains Cree. He was taken prisoner as a child by the Sioux and "learned their medicine." On his return to his own people he was given the name Payipwat (The One Who Knows the Secrets of the Sioux). In 1875 he took adhesion to Treaty 4, but only after making it very clear that he regarded it as a "preliminary negotiation" and that a final treaty must contain provisions for "farm instructors, mills, forges, mechanics, more tools, machinery and medical assistance." Although the government did not alter Treaty 4, many of Payipwat's conditions were written into Treaty 6 in 1876. With other Cree leaders he continued to press for changes to the treaties. He was independent-minded and believed that an Indian territory was desirable. He urged other chiefs to present a united front to the government, but the plans were thwarted by the government, which could coerce the Indians to do its bidding because of the destitute conditions following the demise of the buffalo. Plans for a council to achieve the coalition strategy were destroyed when the government took advantage of the Métis rebellion to quash it. Troops near his reserve and surveillance by the NWMP prevented him from achieving his goal of an Indian territory. An order in

council deposing him as chief was passed the day he died. See John Tobias, "Payip-wat,"*DCB*, vol. 13, 807.

Mistahimusqwa (Big Bear, Gros Ours), ca. 1825–88, a prominent Cree leader, did not adhere to Treaty 6 until 1882. He was continually associated with complaints about treaty and the necessity for better treatment, and consequently he was considered recal-citrant and independent. A wise chief, aware of the deleterious effects on Indian civiliza-tion, he could not be controlled by government. He understood the wisdom of an Indian confederacy and sought to promote it with all bands, but the government took advantage of the 1885 situation to assure that Native political solidarity could not be maintained. Big Bear and Poundmaker were convicted of treason-felony and imprisoned. See Rudy Wiebe, "Mistahimaskwa,"*DCB*, vol. 11, 597–601.

29 Tobias, "Subjugation," 222.

30 NA, RG10, vol. 3697, file 15,423, J.A. Macrae to Dewdney, 25 August 1884. For the department's unsympathetic response (draft), Lawrence Vankoughnet to Dewdney, 4 Feb-ruary 1885. Other chiefs and influential leaders included Mosomin, Papewes, Kapeyak-waskonam, and Minahikosis. Mosomin (Moosomin, Low Bush Cranberry, or Squash Berry), who died in 1902, was chief of a Cree and Saulteaux band that generally wintered in the Jackfish and Turtle Lakes area. During winter they trapped, hunted, and fished, and in summer they hunted the buffalo, thereby combining a woodland and a plains economy. In 1876 their chief, Yellowsky, refused to take treaty, but in 1879 Mosomin and 124 mostly Cree followers did take treaty, and a reserve was surveyed for them in 1881. After treaty, Mosomin and his people continually expressed dissatisfaction with the implementation of the treaty promises, although they enjoyed reasonable success as farmers and ranchers, de-spite government policies to restrict competition with surrounding settlers. See Sarah Carter, "Mosomin," *DCB*, vol. 13, 721–2.

Papewes (Papaway, Lucky Man), ca. late 1830s–1901, was chief of the River people, a Plains Cree group, and initially a headman in Big Bear's band. After 1879, hunger coerced many into treaty, including Papewes and 409 followers. He, along with other chiefs was trying to establish an Indian territory of contiguous reserves near Fort Walsh, but in 1882 government assistance was cut off, forcing them to move north. When Big Bear took treaty in 1882, many of Lucky Man's people returned to Big Bear. He continued to work with other Cree chiefs to bring about treaty revision. After 1885, he and 26 followers fled to the United States. Returning to Canada in 1896, he was arrested for murder but was not con-victed. Upon his release he returned to the United States, where he died. See John Tobias, "Papewes," *DCB*, vol. 13, 807.

Kapeyakwaskonam (Kahpahyakastocum, One Arrow, Une Flèche), ca. 1815–86, was a chief of a band of Willow Crees who settled in 1879 on a reserve near Batoche after sign-ing Treaty 6 with Beardy five days after it was concluded. In 1880 he was charged with in-citing his followers to butcher government cattle but was not convicted. In 1884 his people still had not received the livestock, implements, or instruction promised. He attended a large council of chiefs dealing with grievances the same year. After 1885 he was arrested and charged with treason-felony and sentenced to three years in Stony Mountain peniten-tiary, but he was released because of deteriorating health after serving seven months. See Kenneth J. Tyler, "Kapeyakwaskonam," *DCB*, vol. 11, 461–2.

Minahikosis (Little Pine, Petit Pine), ca. 1830–85, a Plains Cree chief, refused to take treaty in 1876 because the treaty contained no protection "against the imposition of an alien culture" – particularly white men's laws. He was also one of the chiefs seeking to establish an Indian confederacy. However, in 1879 starvation forced adhesion to Treaty 6, and hunger assured compliance with the government plans for dispersal. In June of 1884, Little Pine helped to organize the council of chiefs. His band settled down next to Poundmaker. At the council of August 1884 plans were being made for a meeting in the summer of 1885 of all Plains Cree, but events of 1885 ended that. Little Pine's band was involved in the looting of Battleford and at Cut Knife Hill, leading them to be "regarded as rebels." Little Pine had sought to "maintain their political and cultural integrity against the threat from alien values." See John L. Tobias, "Minahikosis," *DCB*, vol. 11, 596–7.

31 The literature on this oppressive regime is large and growing. A sample includes Miller, *Skyscrapers Hide the Heavens*, 189–207; Tobias, "Plains Cree"; Carter, "Two Acres and a Cow," and *Lost Harvests*, 159–236; and Titley, *Duncan Campbell Scott*, chaps. 3–5.

32 Chief Elmer Harry Campbell, 31 July 1996, in *R. v. Harry Catarat and James Sylvestre*, Prov. Ct. Sask., Buffalo Narrows (unreported), Transcript of Testimony, vol. 2, 264–5.

33 Ibid., 265–7.

CHAPTER THIRTEEN

1 Morris, *Treaties of Canada*.

2 Ibid., dedication page.

3 Laird, *Our Indian Treaties*, 3.

4 Ibid., 6–7.

5 Ibid., 10.

6 Scott, "Indian Affairs," 593.

7 Ibid., 600.

8 Carter, "Demonstrating Success," 157–83.

9 Abbott, *Administration of Indian Affairs*. For an account of how Canada's Indian Affairs Department influenced Abbott, see Samek, *Blackfoot Confederacy*, 9–10.

10 Harper, "Basic Concepts"; "The Indian Act"; and "The Treaty System." See Samek, *Blackfoot Confederacy*, 188n38.

11 Stanley, *Birth of Western Canada*, 208–12, 431nn35–48.

12 Ibid., xiv.

13 Ibid., 194.

14 Ibid., 206.

15 Leslie and Maguire, *Historical Development of the Indian Act*.

16 Taylor's revisionist picture is in Muise, J.R. Miller, *Approaches to Native History* 207–11.

17 Ballantyne, et. al. *Aski-Puko: The Land Alone*.

18 Raby, "Indian Land Surrenders."

19 The article had first appeared in *Canadian Historical Review* 64, no. 4 (1983): 519–48.

20 Friesen, *Canadian Prairies*.

21 Friesen, "Grant Me Wherewith to Make My Living"; "Magnificent Gifts."

22 An exemplar of this interpretation, J.R. Miller, was chosen to write the booklet *Canada and the Aboriginal Peoples 1867–1927* for the Canadian Historical Association.

23 Of Bruce G. Trigger's many works, the most accessible to and influential for historians was *Natives and Newcomers: Canada's "Heroic Age" Reconsidered*. Also significant, though somewhat overlooked, was Trigger's booklet for the Canadian Historical Association, *The Indians and the Heroic Age of New France*.

24 Heidenreich, *Huronia*; Ray, *Indians in the Fur Trade*.

25 The dominant force in American historiography was Francis Jennings, whose Covenant Chain trilogy was a major influence as it appeared between 1975 and 1988. A prominent Canadian example was Robert S. Allen, *His Majesty's Indian Allies*.

BIBLIOGRAPHY

MANUSCRIPT SOURCES

NATIONAL ARCHIVES OF CANADA
Church Missionary Society, microfilm
Colonial Office Records, MG11
Hayter Reed Papers, MG29 E106
Sir John A. Macdonald Papers, MG26 A
Records of the Secretary of State, RG6
Records of the Department of Indian Affairs, RG10

PROVINCIAL ARCHIVES OF MANITOBA (PAM)
Sir Adams George Archibald Papers, MG12 A1
Hudson's Bay Company Archives (HBCA)
  Canadian Committee Records, 1917, RG2/2/109
  Correspondence Inward from Commissioners: Fur Trade Subject Files, Northern Treaties, A.12/FT243/1–2
  Correspondence Inward, Donald Smith D.12/1
  Correspondence Inward, London 1875–76 D.20/2–4
  Correspondence Outward, London 1874–75, D.13/1
  Christie, W. J., Inspecting Chief Factor, Inspection Reports , 1872–73, D.25/19
  Fort Carlton District Report, 1875, B.27/e/8
  George Simpson, Correspondence, Inward Letters, 1849–51, D.5/24–32
  Fort Edmonton Post Journals, 1861–76, B.60/a/33–40
  Graham, Cyril (Sir). "Untitled Report to Sir Stafford Northcote," Fort Garry, 15 March 1871. Official Correspondence Inward, A.11/100, 1871: 68–91
  Inspection Report, St John's Post, Peace River District, 1891 and 1897, B.189/e/2 and 3
  Inspection Report, Hudson's Hope, Peace River District, 1897, B.293/e/2
  Land Department Accounts, 1912–26, RG1/1/1, 6, 9, 12, 13, 15
  Land Department Accounts, 1927–31, A.86/1–11
  London Correspondence with Her Majesty's Government, A13/16/3–5
  London Minute Books, General Courts and Proprietors, 1871, A2/18
  Miscellaneous Papers [Correspondence, Re: Yukon Gold Rush], 1857–1913, D.26/34–36
  Parliamentary Select Committee on Hudson's Bay Company, 1837: Minutes of Evidence, E.18/3

Parliamentary Select Committee on Hudson's Bay Company, 1857: Minutes of Evidence, E.18/4

Red River and North West Rebellions E.911, 2868–70

Rupertsland Order, London Correspondence Inward from Commissioners, A.12/l 121/1 and A.13/16/5

York Factory, Returns for Districts of the Northern Department, B.239/h

Alexander Morris Papers, MG12, B1 and B2

John Christian Schultz Papers, MG12, E3

Lord Selkirk Papers, MG2, A1

PROVINCIAL ARCHIVES OF ONTARIO (AO)

Anderson, T. G. "Diary of [Captain.] Thomas Gummersell Anderson, a Visiting Superintendent of Indian Affairs at This time, 1849, at Cobourg."

Vidal, Alexander, and T. G. Anderson, "Report to His Excellency, the Governor-General in Council, Toronto, 5 December 1849." 1027–1–2 Robinson Treaties, appendix B

PUBLISHED PRIMARY SOURCES

Ahenakew, Edward. *Voices of the Plains Cree*. Ruth M. Buck, ed. Toronto: McClelland and Stewart, 1973.

Ahenakew, Freda, and H. C. Wolfart, eds. *Ana kâ-pimwêwêhahk okakêskihkêmowina*: The *Counselling Speeches of Jim Kâ-Nîpitêhtêw*. Winnipeg, MB: University of Manitoba, 1998.

Bowes, G.E. *Peace River Chronicles*. Vancouver, BC: Prescott Publishing, 1963.

British Columbia, Legislative Assembly. *Journals of the Legislative Assembly of the Province of British Columbia from 10th February to the 20th May, 1989, Both Days Inclusive*. Victoria, BC: Queen's Printer, 1897.

Canada. *British Columbia: An Official Handbook of Information Relating to the Dominion of Canada, 1897*. Ottawa: Queen's Printer, 1897.

– *Indian Treaties and Surrenders*. 3 vols. Ottawa: C.H. Parmelee, 1891 and 1912.

– *Parliamentary Debates*. 3d. session, 1st Parliament, vol. 1 (1870).

– *Sessional Papers. Annual Reports for the Department of Indian Affairs*. 1869–1910.

– *Sessional Papers*. No. 8. "Annual Report of the Department of the Interior, 1875."

– *Sessional Papers*. No. 15. "Annual Report of the North-West Mounted Police, 1898."

– *Sessional Papers*. No. 25. "Report of Delegates Appointed to Negotiate for the Acquisition of Rupert's Land and the North-West Territory."

Cowie, Isaac. *The Company of Adventurers: A Narrative of Seven Years in the Service of the Hudson's Bay Company during 1867–1874 on the Great Buffalo Plains, with Historical and Biographical Notes and Comments*. Toronto: William Briggs, 1913.

Erasmus, Peter. *Buffalo Days and Nights*. Irene Spry, ed. Calgary, AB: Glenbow, Alberta Institute, 1976.

"From the Anishnabek, the Objbway, Ottawa, Potowatomi, and Algonquin Nations to the Parliament of the Dominion of Canada." *Ontario Indian* 3, no. 12 (1980): 18–27.

Gauvreau, N. B. *Exploration Survey of New Caledonia*. Pt 2. *Crown Land Surveys*. Victoria, BC: Surveyor General, 1891.

Graham, William M. *Treaty Days: Reflections of an Indian Commissioner*. Calgary, AB: Glenbow, Alberta Institute, 1991.

Great Britain. Papers Relating to the Red River Settlement. London, 1819.

Horetzky, Charles. "The First Railway Survey." 1872. Reprinted in G. E. Bowes, *Peace River Chronicles*, Vancouver, BC: Prescott Publishing, 1963, 81–5.

Hunt, F.L. "Notes of the Qu'Appelle Treaty." *Canadian Monthly and National Review* 9, no. 3 (1876) 179.

Macrae, J.A. "Report of Commissioner for Treaty 8." Department of Indian, *Affairs Annual Report, 1900*. Canada, *Sessional Papers*, no 27. Ottawa: Queen's Printer, 1901.

Morris, Alexander. *The Treaties of Canada with the Indians of Manitoba and the North-West Territories, Including the Negotiations on Which They Were Based*. 1880. Reprint Saskatoon, SK: Fifth House Publishers, 1991.

Oliver, E.H. *The Canadian North-West: Its Early Development and Legislative Records: Minutes of the Councils of the Red River Colony and the Northern Department of Rupert's Land*. 2 vols. Ottawa: Government Printing Bureau, 1914 and 1915.

Poudrier, A.L. *Exploration Survey of New Caledonia, Part 3*. Crown Land Surveys. Victoria, BC: Surveyor General, 1891.

– *Exploration Survey of New Caledonia, Minerals, Part 3*. Crown Land Surveys. Victoria, BC: Surveyor General, 1891.

Rich, E.E. *Copy-Book of Letters Outward &c: Begins 29th May, 1680 Ends 5 July, 1687*. London: The Hudson's Bay Record Society, 1948.

Treaty No. 8 Made June 21 1899, and Adhesions, Reports, Etc. 1899. Ottawa: Queen's Printer, 1966 [1899].

Treaty No. 10 and Reports of Commissioners. 1907. Ottawa: Roger Duhamel, Queen's Printer and Controller of Stationery, 1966.

Trow, James. *Manitoba and North West Territories: Letters by James Trow*. Ottawa: Department of Agriculture, 1878.

Vidal, Alexander. *A Journal of Proceedings on My Mission to the Indians [of] Lake Superior and Huron, 1849*. Transcribed by George Smith, with historical notes by M. E. Arthur. Brightens Grove: George Smith, 1974.

Williams, Glyndwr, ed. *Andrew Graham's Observations on Hudson's Bay 1767–91*. London: The Hudson's Bay Record Society, 1969.

SECONDARY SOURCES

Abbott, F.H. *The Administration of Indian Affairs in Canada*. Washington, DC: Government Printing Office, 1915.

Allen, Robert S. *His Majesty's Indian Allies: British Indian Policy in the Defense of Canada, 1774–1815*. Toronto: Dundurn Press, 1992.

Asch, Michael, ed. *Aboriginal and Treaty Rights in Canada: Essays on Law, Equity, and Respect for Difference*. Vancouver, BC: University of British Columbia Press, 1997.

Aski-Puko: The Land Alone. A Report of the Expected Effects of the Proposed Hydroelectric Installation et Wintego Rapids. Mimeograph, 1976.

Ballantyne, Philip, et. al. *Aski-Puko: The Land Alone: A Report on the Expected Effects of the Proposed Hydro-electric Installation at Wintego Rapids upon the Cree of the Peter Ballantyne and Lac La Ronge Bands*. Prince Albert, SK: Federation of Saskatchewan Indians, 1976.

Barron, F. Laurie, and James B. Waldram, eds. *1885 and After: Native Society in Transition*. Regina, SK: Canadian Plains Research Centre, University of Regina, 1986.

Barck, Oscar T., and Hugh T. Lefler. *Colonial America*. 2d ed. New York: Macmillan, 1968.

Borrows, John. "Wampum at Niagara: The Royal Proclamation, Canadian Legal History, and Self-Government." In *Aboriginal and Treaty Rights in Canada: Essays on Law, Equity, and Respect for Difference*, ed. Michael Asch. Vancouver: University of British Columbia Press, 1997, 155–72.

Brown, Jennifer. *Strangers In Blood: Fur Trade Company Families in Indian Country.*
Vancouver, BC: University of British Columbia Press, 1980.

Brown, Jennifer, W.J. Eccles, and Donald P. Heldman, eds. *The Fur Trade Revisited: Selected Papers of the Sixth North American Fur Trade Conference, Mackinac Island,
Michigan, 1991.* East Lansing, MI: Michigan State University Press, 1994.

Burrell, Gordon, Robert Young, and Richard Price, eds. *Indian Treaties and the Law: An
Interpretation for Laymen.* Edmonton, AB: Indian Association of Alberta, 1975.

Calloway, Colin G. *Crown and Calumet: British Indian Relations, 1783–1815.* Norman,
OK: University of Oklahoma Press, 1987.

Campbell, Marjorie Wilkins. *The North-West Company.* Toronto: University of Toronto
Press, 1957.

Canada. Royal Commission on Aboriginal Peoples. *Report of the Royal Commission on
Aboriginal Peoples.* Vol. 1, *Looking Forward, Looking Back.* Ottawa: Canada Communication Group, 1996.

– *Report of the Royal Commission on Aboriginal Peoples.* Vol. 2, *Restructuring the Relationship, Part 1.* Ottawa: Canada Communication Group, 1996.

Cardinal, Harold. *The Unjust Society: The Tragedy of Canada's Indians.* Edmonton, AB:
Hurtig, 1969.

Carter, Sarah. "Demonstrating Success: The File Hills Farm Colony." *Prairie Forum* 16,
no. 2 (1991): 157–83.

– *Lost Harvests: Prairie Indian Reserve Farmers and Government Policy.* Montreal:
McGill-Queen's University Press, 1990.

– "Two Acres and a Cow: Peasant Farming for the Indians of the Northwest, 1889–1897."
In *Sweet Promises: A Reader on Indian-White Relations in Canada,* ed. J. R. Miller.
Toronto: University of Toronto Press, 1991: 353–77.

Chute, Janet E. *The Legacy of Shingwaukonse: A Century of Native Leadership.* Toronto:
University of Toronto Press, 1998.

Cleland, Charles E. "Indian Treaties and American Myths: Roots of Social Conflict Over
Treaty Rights." *Native Studies Review* 6, no. 2 (1990): 81–8.

Coates, Kenneth S., and William R. Morrison. *Treaty Research Report: Treaty Ten.* Ottawa:
Treaties and Historical Research Centre, Indian and Northern Affairs Canada, 1986.

Daniel, Richard C. "A History of Native Claims Processes in Canada: 1867–1979." Prepared by Tyler, Wright, and Daniel Limited, Research consultants, Research Branch,
Department of Indian Affairs, 1980.

– "The Spirit and Terms of Treaty Eight." In *The Spirit of the Alberta Indian Treaties.* ed.
Richard Price. Edmonton, AB: Pica Pica Press, 1987, 46–96.

Daugherty, Wayne E. *Treaty Research Report: Treaty One and Treaty Two.* Treaties and
Historical Research Centre, Indian and Northern Affairs Canada, 1983.

– *Treaty Research Report: Treaty Three.* Treaties and Historical Research Centre, Indian
and Northern Affairs Canada, 1986.

Dempsey, Hugh A. *Big Bear: The End of Freedom.* Vancouver, BC: Douglas and McIn-
tyre, 1984.

– *Treaty Research Report: Treaty Seven.* Ottawa: Treaties and Historical Research Centre,
Indian and Northern Affairs Canada, 1987.

Dickason, Olive Patricia. *Canada's First Nations: A History of Founding Peoples from
Earliest Times.* Toronto: McClelland and Stewart, 1992.

Dyck, Noel. *What is the Indian Problem? Tutelage and Resistance in the Canadian Indian
Administration.* St. John's, Institute of Social and Economic Research, Memorial University of Newfoundland, 1991.

Ellwood, Elizabeth. "The Robinson Treaties of 1850." BA honours thesis, Wilfrid Laurier University, 1977.

Foster, J.E. "The Saulteaux and the Numbered Treaties: An Aboriginal Rights Position?" In *The Spirit of the Alberta Indian Treaties*, ed. Richard Price. Edmonton, Alberta: Pica Pica Press, 1987.

Francis, Daniel, and Toby Morantz. *Partners in Furs: A History of the Fur Trade in Eastern James Bay 1600–1870*. Montreal and Kingston: McGill-Queen's University Press, 1983.

Friesen, Gerald. *The Canadian Prairies: A History*. Toronto: University of Toronto Press, 1984.

Friesen, Jean. "Grant Me Wherewith to Make My Living." In *Aboriginal Resource Use in Canada*, ed. Kerry Abel and Jean Friesen. Winnipeg, University of Manitoba Press, 1991: 141–56.

– "Magnificent Gifts: The Treaties of Canada with the Indians of the Northwest, 1869–76." *Transactions of the Royal Society of Canada*. Series 5, vol. 1 (1986), 41–51.

Fumoleau, Rene. *As Long as This Land Shall Last: A History of Treaty 8 and 11 1870–1939*. Toronto: McClelland and Stewart, 1973.

Galbraith, John S. "The HBC under Fire, 1847–62." *Canadian Historical Review* 30, no. 4 (1949): 322–35.

Goldstick, Miles. *Wollaston: Peoples Resisting Genocide*. Montreal: Black Rose Books, 1987.

Gosse, Richard, James Youngblood Henderson, and Roger Carter, eds. *Continuing Poundmaker and Riel's Quest: Presentations Made at a Conference on Aboriginal Peoples and Justice*. Saskatoon, SK: Purich Publishing, 1994.

Goulet, Keith N. "Oral History as an Authentic and Credible Research Base for Curriculum: The Cree of Sandy Bay and Hydroelectric Power Development 1927–67." MEd. thesis, University of Regina, 1986.

Gulig, Anthony Gerard. "In Whose Interest? Government-Indian relations in Northern Saskatchewan and Wisconsin, 1900–1940," PHD diss., University of Saskatchewan, 1997.

Hall, D.J. "'A Serene Atmosphere'? Treaty 1 Revisited." *Canadian Journal of Native Studies* 4, no. 2 (1984): 321–58.

Hamilton, A.C., and C.N. Sinclair. *Report of the Aboriginal Justice Inquiry of Manitoba*. Vol. 1, *The Justice System and Aboriginal People*. Winnipeg, MB: Province of Manitoba, 1991.

Hansen, James L. "'Half-breed Roles' and Fur Trade Families in the Great Lakes Region: An Introduction and Bibliography." In *The Fur Trade Revisited*, ed. J. Brown, W.J. Eccles, and Donald P. Heldman. East Lansing, MI: Michigan State University Press, 1994, 161–70.

Hargrave, Joseph James. *Red River*. Montreal: J. Lovell, 1871 (reprinted 1877 edition).

Harper, Allen G., "Canada's Indian Administration System: Basic Concepts and Objectives." *America Indigena* 5 (1945): 119–32.

– "Canada's Indian Administration: The Indian Act." *America Indigena* 6 (1946): 297–314.

– "Canada's Indian Administration: The Treaty System." *America Indigena* 7 (1947): 129–48.

Harris, R.C. ed. *Historical Atlas of Canada*. Vol. 1. Toronto: University of Toronto Press, 1987.

Heidenreich, Conrad. *Huronia: A History and Geography of the Huron Indians, 1600–1650*. Toronto: McLelland and Stewart, 1971.

Hind, Henry Youle. *Narrative of the Canadian Red River Exploring Expedition of 1857 and of the Assiniboine and Saskatchewan Exploring Expedition of 1858.* 1860. M.G. Hurtig, 1971.

Innis, Harold Adams. *The Fur Trade in Canada: An Introduction to Canadian Economic History.* Toronto: University of Toronto Press, 1999.

Jenness, Diamond, ed. *The American Aboriginies: Their Origin and Antiquity: A Collection of Papers by Ten Authors Assembled and Edited by Diamond Jenness.* Toronto: University of Toronto Press, 1933.

– *The Indians of Canada.* Ottawa: Queen's Printer, 1932.

Jennings, Francis. *The Invasion of America: Indians, Colonialism, and the Cant of Conquest.* Chapel Hill, University of North Carolina Press, 1975.

– *The Ambiguous Iroquois Empire.* New York: Norton, 1984.

– *Empire of Fortune: Crowns, Colonies and Tribes in the Seven Years' War in America.* New York: W.W. Norton, 1988.

Kerr, John Andrew. "The Indian Treaties of 1876." *Dalhousie Review* 17 (1937): 186–95.

Krech, Shepard III, ed. *The Subarctic Fur Trade: Native Social and Economic Adaptations.* Vancouver, BC: University of British Columbia Press, 1984.

Laird, David. "Our Indian Treaties." *The Historical and Scientific Society of Manitoba.* Winnipeg, The Manitoba Free Press, 1905.

Macgregor, J.G. *The Klondike Gold, Rush through Edmonton: 1897–1898.* Toronto: McClelland and Stewart, 1970.

MacKay, Douglas. *The Honourable Company.* 2d ed. Toronto: McClelland and Stewart, 1949.

Macleod, R.C. *The North West Mounted Police.* Ottawa: Canadian Historical Association, 1978.

– *The North West Mounted Police and Law Enforcement, 1873–1905.* Toronto: University of Toronto Press, 1976.

McNab, David T. *The Administration of Treaty 3: The Location of the Boundaries of Treaty No. 3 Indian Reserves in Ontario, 1873–1915.* Ottawa: Indian and Northern Affairs Canada, n.d.

McNeil, Kent. "Native Claims in Rupert's Land and the North-Western Territory: Canada's Constitutional Obligations." *Studies in Aboriginal Rights.* No. 5. Saskatoon, SK: University of Saskatchewan Native Law Centre, 1982.

– "Native Rights and the Boundaries of Rupert's Land and the North-Western Territory." *Studies in Aboriginal Rights.* No. 4. Saskatoon, SK: University of Saskatchewan Native Law Centre, 1982.

Madill, Dennis F.K. Treaty Research Report: Treaty Eight. Ottawa: Treaties and Historical Research Centre, Indian and Northern Affairs Canada, 1986.

Maguire, John Leslie, and Ron Maguire. The Historical Development of the Indian Act. Ottawa: Department of Indian Affairs, 1975.

Mandelbaum, David G. *The Plains Cree: An Ethnological, Historical and Comparative Study.* Regina, SK: Canadian Plains Research Centre, 1979.

Miller, J.R. *Big Bear (Mistahimusqua) A Biography.* Toronto: ECW Press, 1996.

– *Canada and the Aboriginal Peoples, 1867–1927.* Ottawa: Canadian Historical Association 1997.

– *Shingwauk's Vision: A History of Native Residential Schools.* Toronto: University of Toronto Press, 1996.

– *Skyscrapers Hide the Heavens: A History of Indian-White Relations in Canada.* 2d ed. Toronto: University of Toronto Press, 1991.

– ed. *Sweet Promises: A Reader on Indian-White Relations in Canada.* Toronto: University of Toronto Press, 1991.

Milloy, John S. *The Plains Cree: Trade, Diplomacy and War, 1790 to 1870.* Winnipeg, University of Manitoba Press, 1988.

Mitchell, Elaine Allan. "Edward Watkin and Buying Out the Hudson's Bay Company." *Canadian Historical Review,* 34, no. 3 (1953): 219–44.

Morrison, James. "Research Report: Historical Context of the Blanket Extinguishment Clause and Negotiations, Treaties 8 and 11." Prepared for Federation of Saskatchewan Indian Nations, 30 June 1990. Mimeograph.

Morse, Bradford, ed. *Aboriginal Peoples and the Law: Indian, Metis, and Inuit Rights in Canada.* Ottawa: Carleton University Press, 1985.

Morton, Arthur S. *A History of the Canadian West to 1870–71, Being a History of Rupert's Land (The Hudson's Bay Company's Territory) and of the North-West Territory (Including the Pacific Slope).* Toronto: University of Toronto Press, in co-operation with the University of Saskatchewan, 1973.

Morton, W.L. *Manitoba: A History.* Toronto: University of Toronto Press, 1957.

– ed. *Manitoba: Birth of a Province.* Altona, MB: Manitoba Record Society, 1965.

Muise, D.A., ed. *Approaches to Native History in Canada.* Ottawa: National Museum of Man, 1977.

Narvey, Kenneth M., "The Royal Proclamation of 7 October 1873, the Common Law and Native Rights to Land within the Territory Granted to the HBC." *Saskatchewan Law Review* 38, no. 1 (1973–74): 123–233.

Newell, Dianne. *Technology on the Frontier: Mining in Old Ontario.* Vancouver, University of British Columbia Press, 1986.

Oscar, Theodore Barck Jr., and Hugh Talmage Lefler. *Colonial America.* New York: Macmillam Company, 1968.

Price, Richard, ed. *The Spirit of Alberta Indian Treaties.* Edmonton: Pica Pica Press, 1987.

Price, Richard T., and Shirleen Smith. "Treaty 8 and Traditional Livelihoods: Historical and Contemporary Perspectives." *Native Studies Review* 9, no. 1 (1993–94): 51–92.

Raby, S. "Indian Land Surrenders in Southern Saskatchewan." *Canadian Geographer* 17, no. 1 (1973): 36–52.

– "Indian Treaty No. 5 and The Pas Agency, Saskatchewan, N.W.T." *Saskatchewan History* 25, no. 3 (1972): 92–114.

Ray, Arthur J. "Adventures at the Crossroads." *The Beaver* 62, no. 2 (1986): 4–12.

– *The Canadian Fur Trade in the Industrial Age.* Toronto: University of Toronto Press, 1990.

– "Commentary on the Economic History of the Treaty 8 Area." *Native Studies Review* 10 no. 2 (1995): 169–95.

– "The Economic Background to Treaty 6." Unpublished expert report filed in the Federal Court of Canada, Trial Division (Edmonton), between *Chief Victor Buffalo and the Samson Cree Indian Nation v. Regina,* Court file nos. T-2022–89, June 1997.

– "An Economic History of the Robinson Treaties Area before 1860." Unpublished Expert Report for *Regina v. Powley,* Ontario Court of Justice (Provincial Division), Sault Ste Marie, Ontario, May 1998.

– "The Factor and the Trading Captain in the Hudson's Bay Company Fur Trade before 1763." Mercury Series, National Museum of Man, Ethnology Service. Paper 28 (1975): 586–602.

– "Historical Background to Treaty 8." Unpublished report prepared for Litigation Support Directorate, Indian and Northern Affairs Canada, Vancouver, June 1997.

– *I Have Lived Here Since the World Began: An Illustrated History of Canada's Native People.* Toronto: Lester Publishing, 1996.

- "Indians as Consumers in the Eighteenth Century." In *Out of the Background: Readings on Canadian Native History,* ed. Robin Fisher and Ken Coates. Toronto: Copp Clark Pitman, 1988: 255–71.
- *Indians in the Fur Trade: Their Role as Trappers, Hunters, and Middlemen in the Lands Southwest of Hudson Bay, 1660–1870.* 2d ed. Toronto: University of Toronto Press, 1998 (1974).
- "Periodic Shortages, Native Welfare and the Hudson's Bay Company 1670–1930." In *The Subarctic Fur Trade: Native Social and Economic Adaptations, ed. Shepard Krech III.* Vancouver, BC: University of British Columbia Press, 1984, 1–20.
- "Treaty 8: An Anomaly of British Columbia's History." *BC Studies,* no. 123 (autumn 1999): 5–58.
Ray, Arthur, and Donald B. Freeman. *"Give us Good Measure": An Economic Analysis of Relations between the Indians and the Hudson's Bay Company before 1763.* Toronto: University of Toronto Press, 1978.
Rich, E.E. *The History of the Hudson's Bay Company 1670–1870.* 3 vols. Toronto: McClelland and Stewart, 1960.
Rich, E.E., ed. *James Isham's Observations on Hudson's Bay, 1743, and Notes and Observations on a Book Entitled A Voyage to Hudson's Bay in the Dobbs Galley, 1749.* Toronto: Champlain Society, 1949.
Samek, Hana. *The Blackfoot Confederacy, 1880–1920: A Comparative Study of Canadian and U.S. Indian Policy.* Albuquerque, NM: University of New Mexico Press, 1987.
Saskatchewan Indian Cultural College. *Treaty Six, "... for as long as the sun shines, the grass grows, and the rivers flow ..." Saskatchewan and Alberta 100 Years, 1876/1976.* Saskatchewan Indian Cultural College, Curriculum Studies and Research, Federation of Saskatchewan Indians, 1976.
Schmalz, Peter S. *The Ojibwa of Southern Ontario.* Toronto: University of Toronto Press, 1991.
Scott, D.C. "Indian Affairs, 1867–1912." In *Canada and Its Provinces,* ed. A. Shortt and A.G. Doughty. Toronto: Glasgow Brook and Company, 1914.
Sliwa, Stephen. "Treaty Day for the Willow Cree." *Saskatchewan History* 47 no. 1 (1995): 3–12.
Stanley, G.F.G. *The Birth of Western Canada.* 1936. Toronto: University of Toronto Press, 1961.
Stevenson, Winona. "The Church Missionary Society Red River Mission and the Emergence of a Native Ministry, 1820–1860, with a Case Study of Charles Pratt of Touchwood Hills." MA thesis, University of British Columbia, 1988.
Stonechild, Blair. "The Indian View of the 1885 Uprising." In *Sweet Promises: A Reader on Indian-White Relations in Canada,* ed. J.R. Miller. Toronto: University of Toronto Press, 1991, 259–76.
Stonechild, Blair, and Bill Waiser. *Loyal till Death: Indians and the North-West Rebellion.* Saskatoon, SK: Fifth House Publishers, 1997.
Stonier-Newman, Lynne. *Policing A Pioneer Province: The BC Provincial Police 1858–1950.* Vancouver, BC: Harbour Publishing, 1991.
Sturtevant, William C., ed. *Handbook of North American Indians.* Vols. 4–7, 15. Washington, DC: Smithsonian Institution Press, 1978–90.
Surtees, Robert J. "Indian Land Cessions in Ontario, 1763–1862: The Evolution of a System." PHD diss., Ottawa, Carleton University, 1982.
- "Indian Land Cessions in Upper Canada, 1815–1830." In *As Long As the Sun Shines and Water Flows,* ed. A. Getty and I. Lussier. Vancouver, BC: University of British Columbia Press, 1983, 65–84.

– Treaty Research Report: The Robinson Treaties. Ottawa: Treaties and Historical Research Centre: Indian and Northern Affairs Canada, 1986.
– Treaty Research Report: Treaty Four (1874). Ottawa: Treaties and Historical Research Centre, Indian and Northern Affairs Canada, 1985.
– Treaty Research Report: Treaty Six (1876). Ottawa: Treaties and Historical Research Centre, Indian and Northern Affairs Canada, 1985.
– "Two Views on the Meaning of Treaties Six and Seven." In *The Spirit of the Alberta Indian Treaties,* Richard Price. ed. Edmonton, AB: Pica Pica Press, 1987.
Taylor, John L. "Canada's North-West Indian Policy in the 1970s: Traditional Premises and Necessary Innovations." In *Sweet Promises: A Reader on Indian-White Relations in Canada*, ed. J.R. Miller. Toronto: University of Toronto Press, 1991, 207–11.
– "The Development of an Indian Policy for the Canadian North-West, 1869–79." PHD diss., Queen's University, 1975.
Titley, Brian. *A Narrow Vision: Duncan Campbell Scott and the Administration of Indian Affairs in Canada.* Vancouver, BC: University of British Columbia Press, 1986.
Tobias, John L. "Canada's Subjugation of the Plains Cree, 1879–1885." In *Sweet Promises: A Reader on Indian-White Relations,* ed. J. R. Miller. Toronto: University of Toronto Press, 1991, 212–40.
Tough, Frank. "Aboriginal Rights Versus the Deed of Surrender: The Legal Rights of Native Peoples and Canada's Acquisition of the Hudson's Bay Company Territory." *Prairie Forum* 17, no. 2, 1992: 225–50.
– *"As Their Natural Resources Fail": Native Peoples and the Economic History of Northern Manitoba, 1870–1930.* Vancouver, BC, University of British Columbia Press, 1996.
– "Buying Out The Bay: Aboriginal Rights and the Economic Policies of the Department of Indian Affairs after 1870." In *The First Ones: Readings in Indian/Native Studies,* ed. D. Miller, C. Beal, J. Dempsey, and R.W. Heber. Piapot Reserve No. 75: Saskatchewan Indian Federated College Press, 1992.
– "Economic Aspects of Aboriginal Title in Northern Manitoba: Treaty Five Adhesions and Metis Scrip." *Manitoba History*, no. 15, 1988: 3–16.
Treaty 7 Elders and Tribal Council, with Walter Hildebrandt, Dorothy First Rider, and Sarah Carter. *The True Spirit and Original Intent of Treaty 7.* Montreal: McGill-Queen's University Press, 1996.
Trigger, Bruce G. *The Indians and the Heroic Age of New France.* Ottawa: Canadian Historical Association, 1977.
– *Natives and Newcomers: Canada's Heroic Age Reconsidered.* Montreal: McGill-Queen's University Press, 1985.
Usher, Peter. *Fur Trade Posts of the North-West Territories 1870–1970.* Ottawa: Department of Indian Affairs and Northern Development, 1971.
Usher, Peter, Frank Tough, and Robert M. Galois. "Reclaiming the Land: Aboriginal Title, Treaty Rights and Land Claims in Canada." *Applied Geography*, no. 12 (1992).
Van Kirk, Sylvia. *Many Tender Ties: Women In Fur Trade Society in Western Canada, 1670–1870.* Winnipeg, MB: Watson and Dwyer, 1980.
Venne, Sharon. "Understanding Treaty 6: An Indigenous Perspective." In *Aboriginal and Treaty Rights in Canada: Essays on Law, Equity, and Respect for Difference*, ed. Michael Asch. Vancouver, BC: University of British Columbia Press, 1997, 173–207.

INDEX